ASIAN AMERICA RISING

Asian America Rising

New Directions for Political Activism

Edited by Diane Wong and Mark Tseng-Putterman

NEW YORK UNIVERSITY PRESS
New York

NEW YORK UNIVERSITY PRESS
New York
www.nyupress.org

© 2025 by New York University
All rights reserved

Please contact the Library of Congress for Cataloging-in-Publication data.

ISBN: 9781479834006 (hardback)
ISBN: 9781479834020 (paperback)
ISBN: 9781479834051 (library ebook)
ISBN: 9781479834037 (consumer ebook)

This book is printed on acid-free paper, and its binding materials are chosen for strength and durability. We strive to use environmentally responsible suppliers and materials to the greatest extent possible in publishing our books.

The manufacturer's authorized representative in the EU for product safety is
Mare Nostrum Group B.V., Mauritskade 21D, 1091 GC Amsterdam, The Netherlands.
Email: gpsr@mare-nostrum.co.uk.

Manufactured in the United States of America

10 9 8 7 6 5 4 3 2 1

Also available as an ebook

CONTENTS

Introduction   1
Diane Wong and Mark Tseng-Putterman

Revisiting the Legacy of the Asian American Movement   10
Diane C. Fujino

PART I: REFUGE AND REFUSALS: CONFRONTING MIGRANT DETENTION AND DEPORTATION   37

1. The Politics of Transnational Activism in Southeast Asian Deportation   39
Loan Thi Dao

2. From Accessing Power to Generating Power: SAALT's Decade of Transformation (2014–2024)   63
Lakshmi Sridaran

3. Organizing Inside and Out: The ReleaseMN8 Campaign   83
Vichet Chhuon, Ched Nin, and Jenny Srey

PART II: ABOLITION AND DECOLONIZATION: MILITARISM, INCARCERATION, AND TRANSNATIONAL ACTIVISM   107

4. Asian Settlers in a Decolonial and Abolitionist Movement: Honoring Mauna a Wākea and the Laws of the Elements   109
Candace Fujikane

5. Internationalizing Abolition: Toward Transformative Justice for Women Living (and Dying) along the Fence Line   136
Kim Compoc

6. How Death and Crisis Are Co-Opted into Carceral Reform: Abolitionist Perspectives from No New Jails NYC and Red Canary Song 153
Shaun X. Lin and Yves Tong Nguyen

PART III: RADICAL REPRESENTATIONS: MOVEMENT ART, NARRATIVE, AND CULTURAL PRODUCTION 173

7. Asian American Feminist Roundtable on Media for World-Building: Documenting, Archiving, Amplifying 175
Asian American Feminist Collective (Salonee Bhaman, Julie Ae Kim, Rachel Kuo, Senti Sojwal, and Tiffany Diane Tso)

8. The Party Is Not Just a Party: Reflections on Basement Bhangra 196
Rekha Malhotra

9. Sounding the Alarm and Reclaiming an Asian American Politics for Racial Equity 205
Sally Chen, Douglas H. Lee, OiYan A. Poon, and Janelle Wong

PART IV: ROOTING RESISTANCE: PERSPECTIVES ON ENVIRONMENTAL JUSTICE AND ECOLOGICAL POLITICS 231

10. Messy Solidarities: Asian American, Native Hawaiian, and Pacific Islander Environmental Justice in the Pandemic and Beyond 233
Vivian Shaw, Jacqueline Leung, and Julie Sze

11. Resist Recycle Regenerate: A Conversation around Sustainable Leadership and Regenerative Art Practices 255
Ja Bulsombut and Kristin Chang

12. Creating and Sustaining Chinatown: Gardens and the Right to Los Angeles 272
Frances Huynh

PART V: LOOKING BACK, MOVING FORWARD:
COMMUNITY MEMORY, ARCHIVES, AND
INSTITUTIONS   299

13. A Movement to Stay: The Grassroots Archive of CAAAV
    Organizing Asian Communities   301
    Vivian Truong and Minju Bae

14. Movement Joy, Seriously: Learning from AIDS
    Activism   322
    Eric C. Wat

15. An Insurgent Manual on Organizing for Asian
    American Studies   339
    *Amber Lee, Linda Luu, Kevin Park, Mimi Khúc,
    and Lawrence-Minh Bùi Davis*

    Acknowledgments   365
    About the Contributors   367
    About the Editors   377
    Index   379

Introduction

DIANE WONG AND MARK TSENG-PUTTERMAN

Gathered at Jackson Heights' Diversity Plaza on Valentine's Day, 2019, hundreds came together to celebrate the defeat of a proposed Amazon headquarters in Queens, New York. The scene reflected the resilience and spirit of New York City's most diverse borough: Filipino youth held up signs that read, "Dear Jeff Bezos, It's Not Us, It's You," Bangladeshi restaurant workers stood beside a piñata decorated with a picture of Amazon CEO Jeff Bezos's face, and a mariachi band played music that lit up the chill February night with the sound of horns and raucous singing.[1] Two years prior, Amazon had announced a plan to build a second corporate headquarters—dubbed "HQ2"—in North America, spurring a competitive multi-city bid for the campus. Fears that Amazon would come to New York City became reality when Jeff Bezos announced that HQ2 would be split into two locations: Crystal City, Virginia, and Long Island City in Queens, New York, with 25,000 workers at each site. To the dismay of local residents, labor organizers, and housing activists in Queens, the proposed HQ2 campus would be built along the East River waterfront, directly next to Queensbridge Houses, also known as "The Bridge," one of the borough's largest public housing developments, which provides housing to 7,000 residents.

Bypassing the public review process and receiving $3 billion in subsidies, Bezos was poised to transform Long Island City into Silicon Valley's most competitive rival.[2] Immediately, grassroots groups dedicated to building the political power of working-class Asian immigrant communities came together to organize against the proposed HQ2, including Desis Rising Up and Moving, Queens Neighborhoods United, Chhaya CDC, and CAAAV Organizing Asian Communities. Forming the Neighbors Beyond Amazon coalition, they collectively argued that Amazon would price out immigrant residents and workers and increase real estate speculation in already gentrifying parts of Queens like Astoria, Sunnyside, Woodside, Jackson Heights, Elmhurst, and Corona.[3] In the months that followed, dozens of rapid response rallies, community forums, and tense city council hearings brought out a diverse group of activists from across the borough, mounting pressure that led to the ultimate withdrawal of the proposed headquarters. The defeat of Amazon and the richest man in the world was not only a victory for working-class communities in Queens, but it also demonstrated the power of cross-racial coalition building and issue-based Asian American activism in shaping alternative futures.

These days, we hear mainstream media repeating the platitude that Asian Americans—as consumers, voters, and a demographic bloc—are poised to shape the future of the United States. As Pew Research Center declared in a 2012 report titled "The Rise of Asian Americans," Asian Americans have become the "highest-income, best-educated and fastest-growing racial group" in the nation.[4] Yet, it has never been clear what we are rising toward. Perpetually depicted as the sleeping giant in American politics, this "rise" of Asian Americans is figured in naturalistic and passive terms, as the crest of a wave promising abstract racial progress in future projections of the United States as a "majority minority" nation. The title of this anthology, *Asian America Rising*, playfully tweaks this formulation by bestowing on it a sense of political agency and intentionality. As the chapters herein demonstrate through the diversity and power of Asian American political organizing, Asian Americans are rising not in terms of simple demography, but through coordinated organization and movement action.

These grassroots political engagements can only be partly understood as the legacy of the Asian American movement of the late 1960s and 1970s. More than fifty years since the movement that birthed Asian American identity and the field of Asian American studies, the Asian American community has grown and transformed in ways that movement activists could never have imagined. The material conditions of Asian American communities and the political issues at stake have also become more multifaceted. Today, refugees of U.S. wars in Southeast Asia face detention and deportation under resurgent nativist policies; a conservative Chinese American faction has emerged in vocal opposition to affirmative action in higher education; an undocumented Asian underclass coexists with upwardly mobile Asian professionals in urban hubs like New York, San Francisco, and Los Angeles; and Korean, Okinawan, Filipino, and other diasporas continue to grapple with U.S. economic and military dominance in their homelands. In the face of new forms of racialized state violence, we have also seen Japanese Americans build in solidarity with Muslim Americans to dismantle systemic Islamophobia, the families of those victimized by police violence speak out in support of one another, deported refugees doubly displaced by U.S. wars in Asia and the U.S. immigration regime demand their right to return, and other moments of contemporary resistance that have created new pathways for understanding Asian American politics.[5]

Amazon's defeat by a coalition of working-class immigrant communities is just one of many such critical moments of community resistance that require us to expand how we think, write, and teach about Asian American politics. These movement stories challenge us to recenter social movements as incubators of Asian American political theory that must inform and reframe academic perspectives. Through a series of contemporary case studies that represent the diversity of Asian American political activism, cultural work, community building, mutual aid, and issue-based organizing, our volume aims to confront and contextualize these new directions in Asian American community politics. We are guided by what we see as urgent questions facing the theory and practice of Asian American activism in our current moment: What are the uses and limits of Asian American identity in the context of an increasingly diverse Asian American community? How do local and transnational movements around the issues of prison abolition, deportation, gentrification, decolonization, and militarization decenter the U.S. nation-state as the sole arbiter of political rights? What kinds of cross-pollination are possible between the academic discipline of Asian American studies and the social movements that represent the field's origin and continuing object of aspirational solidarity? And how do we grapple with our own complicity in colonial structures of power within the academy and other institutions that we occupy? We invite our readers to interact with these questions as we do ourselves, to draw lessons from each chapter that inform ongoing campaigns and grassroots movements that are currently unfolding as we write.

This book builds on two strands of existing scholarship on Asian American politics: (1) studies of Asian American social movements that are primarily historical and focus on the "long sixties," and (2) social science approaches to Asian American communities in the 1980s and beyond that have focused on electoral politics and demographic trends.[6] While the former body of work provides a rich theorization of revolutionary Asian American politics, the massive changes to Asian American demographics, racial politics, and the erosion of the Third World movement mandate new paradigms of social change, rooted as they may be in the legacy of the Asian American movement. The latter body of work has grown in the past decades, particularly as social scientists have made use of newly available methods in data collection and analysis to document Asian American voting behavior and policy preferences.[7] Yet this focus on the formal political sphere and activities that can be measured through survey questionnaires and statistical models can at times obscure the radical registers of Asian American political engagement. In conversation with Diane Fujino, Dylan Rodriguez, and others who have called to theorize Asian American politics beyond a liberal framework of electoral politics, hate crimes legislation, and modes of action that seek representation and recognition by the state, our volume centers critiques of the limitations of rights-based approach to political activism and explores tactics that challenge the state as the ultimate arbiter of rights.[8] From abolitionist campaigns to decriminalize sex work in New York City to transnational anti-deportation activism in Cambodia that troubles "good immigrant" narratives of belonging, we offer case studies that help to envision new practices of safety, sanctuary, and self-determination that grapple with the contradictions of what Naomi Paik identifies as "looking to the state to address the problems the state itself creates" and the process of building anew.[9]

This book is organized around five key themes: (1) Refuge and Refusals: Confronting Migrant Detention and Deportation; (2) Abolition and Decolonization: Militarism, Incarceration, and Transnational Activism; (3) Radical Representations: Movement Art, Narrative, and Cultural Production; (4) Rooting Resistance: Perspectives of Environmental Justice and Ecological Politics; and (5) Looking Back, Moving Forward: Community Memory, Archives, and Institutions. In an introductory chapter, Diane Fujino builds on her groundbreaking scholarship on Asian American movement studies by tracing both the legacies of and disjunctures from the Asian American movement of the 1960s and 1970s. In centering "Asian American" as a rubric for political action, we recognize the demographic and political divergences that can be occluded under a pan-ethnic framework. Our anthology thus takes seriously Aihwa Ong's inquiry into the institutionalization of pan-ethnic Asian American identity in the form of nonprofit funding, social services, and census enumeration to ask not only who claims pan-ethnic Asian American identity, but "who benefits the most from it—and at whose expense?"[10] At the same time, the deconstructionist approach proposed by cultural studies scholars such as Kandice Chuh provides a framework to attend to the contested boundaries of Asian American identity not only through centering previously overlooked communities, but also through critical attention to the "various configurations of power and knowledge" through which bodies come to be read, racialized, and acted upon as Asian American.[11] In this sense, while we have been conscious to ensure a diversity of perspectives from Asian American, Native Hawaiian, and Pacific Islander scholars and organizers within this volume, we approach the plurality of Asian American activism not through the simple addition of "diverse" or "underrepresented" voices, but by centering those communities at the front lines of opposing the *systems* of empire, racial capitalism, incarceration, environmental injustice, and so on. Similarly, our choice of thematic and topical coverage does not intend to comprehensively document the multiplicities of Asian American political struggle. Instead, we selected themes that we believe offer points of theoretical and practical departure for scholars and practitioners of Asian American activism, and that center practices of community care and grounded solidarity that we believe are critical to sustainable movement building amid the crises of our times.

As scholars that traverse disciplines, we weave together scholarship in Asian American studies, political science, sociology, history, cultural studies, environmental studies, and feminist and gender studies to develop an expanded view of contemporary Asian American political life. We conceive of Asian American politics as not only reactive to existing systems of power but fugitive, interstitial, and visionary in the sense that ordinary people are forging new spaces for activation and contesting the terrain of the political itself. Beyond the elite and electoral sphere, we are interested in uncovering the realm of possibility that exists between the clandestine and formal expressions of politics. We find Monisha Das Gupta's call to excavate moments of "space-making" politics instructive as a way to reconceive dominant notions of citizenship, belonging, and engagement that "transforms daily life into an arena of political contest."[12] Beyond conventional modes of participation, we look to the ordinary spaces that provoke political engagement, from curio shops and backyard gardens to detention centers and military bases. We remain committed to uplifting the politics of emergent grassroots formations that have supported a new generation of Asian American activists who are challenging the status quo and developing new tactics to sustain bottom-up movements for justice.

This volume follows in the footsteps of foundational collections such as *Roots: An Asian American Reader* (1971) and *Counterpoint: Perspectives on Asian America* (1976) in which students, community historians, and organizers built the foundations for Asian Americanist inquiry rooted in a praxis of knowledge production that centered the grassroots—a praxis at the core of the founding commitments of Asian American studies.[13] In that same spirit, this volume brings together a range of contributors: established and emerging scholars of Asian American activism, community organizers, archivists, cultural workers, formerly incarcerated writers, and student activists. Our volume introduces cutting-edge research and debates across a diverse range of methodologies and disciplines. We put extra care into soliciting a multigenerational range of voices that speak to this moment, in hopes of channeling the spirit of previous community publications like *Gidra*, *Bridge*, *Yellow Seeds*, and *East Wind* to promote intercommunity and cross-disciplinary dialogue. In contrast to the bulk of Asian American movement studies that is anchored on the West Coast, our volume draws from our own experiences of being rooted in the New York metropolitan area, emphasizing case studies of East Coast, Midwest, and transnational activism. In light of our shared vision for an anthology that breaks down binaries between academic scholarship and community praxis, we asked that all contributors in this volume think creatively about academic and nonacademic collaboration—to push the boundaries and to explore new possibilities for writing about Asian American politics that honors the expertise of directly impacted people.

As coeditors, we approach this anthology in the spirit of the context in which we met: as emerging scholars and organizers trying to connect what we learned in the classroom to the Asian American political movements we were seeing—and participating in—on the streets of New York. We first met while working at 18 Million Rising (18MR) together, a media-based grassroots Asian American organization. While at 18MR we offered skills-building workshops and coordinated rapid-response campaigns related to civic engagement, youth criminalization, media disinformation, deportation and detention, and police violence. Our digital organizing work coincided with the politics of the city we were living in on November 20, 2014, when Brooklyn resident Akai Gurley was shot and killed by Chinese American police officer Peter Liang. Inspired by the community interventions in the Bay Area after the police murders of Mario Woods and Alex Nieto, we were part of the initial formation of #Asians4BlackLives-NYC, a group of Asian Americans who self-mobilized after the light sentencing of Liang by Korean American judge Danny Chun.[14] We later became involved in other grassroots interventions, including efforts to stop the expansion of the city's prison infrastructure and construction of new borough-based jails. Our ongoing collaborative work is informed by these points of origin and our journey to uncover the subtleties, messiness, capaciousness, and transformations in Asian American politics in the twenty-first century.

It is a strange exercise to write this introduction on the future of Asian American activism during a moment of rupture and uncertainty. By design, collections such as this one are meant to index a particular juncture, but such demarcation is always surpassed by the shifting terms of oppression that births new grounds of resistance. From the time we began meeting in summer of 2019 to conceptualize the proposal, to the time this book reaches you, we have lived through too many flashpoints and crises to name. We solicited contributors amid the resurgent Black-led movement against police violence, as millions took to the streets in the wake of the murders of George Floyd, Breonna Taylor, Ahmaud Arbery, and so many others. We held co-writing sessions and peer feedback meetings by Zoom while caught in the throes of a global pandemic that continues to wreak disproportionate havoc on Black, Indigenous, poor, and disabled communities. We workshopped chapter drafts in the aftermath of the electoral defeat of Donald Trump and the triumphant return of racial liberalism, which promised a return to a "normal" that always masked systemic violence. We reviewed citation styles as calls to "Stop Asian Hate," spurred by the persistent racialization of COVID-19 and the murder of Asian migrant massage workers in Atlanta, have been channeled into calls for police expansion. And we submitted the final manuscript as Palestinian resistance to occupation and global calls for Palestinian liberation inspire a new generation of freedom fighters on campuses around the world. The juxtaposition of the procedural mundanities of compiling an academic book with the dire turbulence of the world around us is not lost on us, and it is our aspiration that this volume may contribute in some small way to the revolutionary work to be done to meet the challenges of our times.

Notes

1. Meghan Sackman, "Community Activists Come to Jackson Heights to Celebrate Victory after Amazon Abandons HQ2 Plans," *Jackson Heights Post*, February 16, 2019, https://jacksonheightspost.com.
2. Josh Barro, "Here's Why New York Is Resorting to Paying Amazon $3 Billion for What Google Will Do for Free," *New York Magazine*, November 13, 2018.
3. Organizers from the coalition described their analysis of the campaign in an interview with the New Economy Project podcast: "Neighbors Beyond Amazon," Let's Be Real (podcast), May 6, 2019. www.neweconomynyc.org.
4. Pew Research Center, "The Rise of Asian Americans," June 19, 2012, www.pewresearch.org.
5. In referencing these examples, we were inspired by the work of Vigilant Love, Coast to Coast Chinatowns Against Displacement Network, CAAAV Organizing Asian Communities, Southeast Asian Freedom Network, and ReleaseMN8.
6. Key scholarship on the Asian American Movement of the 1960s and 1970s includes Daryl Maeda, *Chains of Babylon: The Rise of Asian America* (Minneapolis: University of Minnesota, 2009); Laura Pulido, *Black, Brown, Yellow and Left: Radical Activism in Los Angeles* (Berkeley: University of California Press, 2006); Karen Ishizuka, *Serve the People: Making Asian America in the Long Sixties* (New York: Verso Books, 2016); and Michael Liu, Kim Geron, and Tracy Lai, *The Snake Dance of Asian American Activism: Community, Vision, and Power* (Lanham, MD: Lexington Books, 2008).
7. Key texts in the field include Janelle Wong, Karthick Ramakrishnan, Taeku Lee, and Jane Junn, *Asian American Political Participation: Emerging Constituents and Their Political Identities* (New York: Russel Sage Foundation, 2011); Pei-te Lien, *The Making of Asian America through Political Participation* (Philadelphia: Temple University Press, 2001); Don T. Nakanishi and James Lai, *Asian American Politics:*

Law, Participation and Policy (Washington, DC: Rowman & Littlefield, 2003); Pei-te Lin, Margaret Conway, and Janelle Wong, *The Politics of Asian Americans: Diversity and Community* (Abingdon, UK: Routledge, 2004); Andrew Aoki and Okiyoshi Takeda, *Asian American Politics* (Hoboken, NJ: Wiley, 2009); and Gordon H. Chang, *Asian Americans and Politics: Perspectives, Experiences, Prospects* (Redwood City, CA: Stanford University Press, 2002).

8   Diane Fujino, "Who Studies the Asian American Movement?: A Historiographical Analysis," *Journal of Asian American Studies*, no. 11 (2008): 127–169; Dylan Rodriguez, "The 'Asian Exception' and the Scramble for Legibility: Toward an Abolitionist Approach to Anti-Asian Violence," *Society & Space*, April 8, 2021, www.societyandspace.org.

9   Naomi Paik, "Abolitionist Futures and the US Sanctuary Movement," *Race & Class* 59, no. 2 (2017): 19.

10 Yen Le Espiritu, *Asian American Panethnicity* (Chicago: Temple University Press, 1992), 14.

11 Kandice Chuh, *Imagine Otherwise: On Asian American Critique* (Durham, NC: Duke University Press, 2003), 11.

12 Monisha Das Gupta, *Unruly Immigrants: Rights, Activism, and Transnational South Asian Politics in the United States* (Durham, NC: Duke University Press, 2006), 11.

13 We are also in conversation with more recent works in this tradition of community knowledge, such as Diane Fujino and Robyn Rodriguez's *Contemporary Asian American Activism: Building Movements for Liberation* (Seattle: University of Washington Press, 2022).

14 For a survey of #Asians4BlackLives efforts across the country, see May Fu, Simmy Makhijiani, Anh-Thu Pham, Meejin Richart, Joanne Tien, and & Diane Wong, "#Asians4BlackLives: Notes from the Ground," *Amerasia Journal* 45, no. 2 (2019): 253–270.

Revisiting the Legacy of the Asian American Movement

DIANE C. FUJINO

What does it matter that the Asian American movement (AAM) of the 1960s–1970s, as arguably the single most significant Asian American social movement to date, is barely legible in dominant discourses? What can we learn from the study of Asian American activism? I contend that how we analyze and narrate Asian American activism will shape how we come to understand not only Asian America, but the U.S. nation-state itself. Asian Americans, racialized as the model minority since the early Cold War, have been widely used to popularize a success narrative that depends on avoiding activism, especially radical critiques of power and disruptive forms of resistance. The five principles defining the AAM, as offered in this chapter, call forth an interpretation that rejects the model minority positioning and instead reveals the actuality of a radical and unruly history of Asian America. This radical knowing has significant implications for the strategies, tactics, and ideologies shaping liberation movements today, especially in the wake of the pandemic and resurgent anti-Asian violence.

Asian American activism and its narration does particular work that differs from the recitation of Black or Chicano/a activism. This is, in part, because Black, Latinx, and Indigenous communities are already understood to be impacted by structural racism. Though all racism involves disavowal and denial, the racialization of Asian Americans as model minorities has made anti-Asian racism particularly illegible in the dominant culture. This is evident from the Atlanta sheriff spokesperson's statement after the March 2021 massage parlor shootings that the killer was just having a "bad day," even though he targeted one Asian American establishment after another. This statement represents a larger national narrative that obfuscates anti-Asian racism and further fails to discern the intersectional nature of sexism, racism, and empire in the attacks on Asian women.[1] I ask: what does it mean to recognize the need for antiracist resistance by a community assumed to not be affected by racism? What is revealed by demonstrating Asian American organizing against white supremacy, imperialism, gendered racial capitalism, and state violence?

The tropes and mechanisms that enable anti-Asian racism are specific and require a discussion beyond the scope of this chapter. It is important, however, to locate our analysis in two contexts. First, we cannot understand today's anti-Asian racism without understanding the longer history of violence, oppression, and legal exclusion against Asian American communities. Second, we cannot understand today's anti-Asian racism without locating it within U.S. militarism, state violence, and imperialism. When seen through the lens of war and colonialism, the latest wave of anti-Asian racism appears less like individual attacks that suddenly emerged during the pandemic and more patterned, systemic, and deeply rooted in U.S. institutions. Activism by the group deemed the model minority disrupts the national narrative of U.S. exceptionalism and challenges its professed commitments to democracy and equality. This shifts the analysis away from blaming individuals and communities for their own impoverishment and subordination to a systemic analysis of oppression that finds culpability with the nation-building project itself. Asian American activism and Asian American studies critique reveals the structural racism embedded in the very formation of the nation in opposition to what the model minority logic is supposed to bury—and provides a logic for its erasure.[2]

The COVID-19 pandemic and the uprisings against racist violence, and the watershed moment for Asian America—the March 16, 2021, killings of six Asian women in Atlanta, Georgia—has created an unprecedented opening for public dialogue about Asian American issues. How scholars, activists, and artists interpret and narrate the past and present of Asian American activism is critical to the kinds of futures we collectively create.

The Asian American Movement: An Overview

The AAM emerged in the late 1960s through the collective action of ordinary people in a sustained and widely distributed struggle to effect social change. The AAM was largely student based and urban but also included multiple generations of activists from diverse socioeconomic backgrounds and took place in rural areas such as Delano, California. The major sites of organizing were in the San Francisco Bay Area, Los Angeles, and New York City, and also in Honolulu, Seattle, Stockton (CA), Denver, Boston, and elsewhere. The AAM is distinguished from earlier spheres of activism (notably, labor strikes, resistance to exclusion and racist legislation, and support for homeland issues) by its pan-Asian focus, bringing together mainly Chinese, Japanese, and Filipinos, and also Koreans, South Asians, and Southeast Asians in a joint struggle against racism. Influenced by Black Power and Third World revolutions, the AAM drew heavily from an anti-imperialist, antiracist politic that emphasized solidarity with U.S. and international Third World struggles. The AAM emerged through its opposition to the Vietnam War, which extended to critiques of U.S. militarism and imperialism in Japan, Okinawa, Hawai'i, the Philippines, and Southeast Asian broadly, as well as struggles for Third World Studies, starting at San Francisco State College and UC Berkeley and spreading to colleges across the nation. The AAM created numerous community service programs, many of which exist to this day; inspired a rich outpouring of music, visual art, poetry, theater, and other creative works; generated a radical vision for a transformed society; raised the political consciousness and practice of an entire generation; and inspired future generations to struggle for justice.

The Significance of the Asian American Movement: Five Defining Characteristics

The Asian American movement of the 1960s and 1970s can be interpreted through five defining features: (1) radicalism, anti-imperialism, and internationalism; (2) collective leadership and feminist challenges to patriarchy; (3) Third World solidarity; (4) community organizing and service; and (5) movement building across the long haul. This is not intended to standardize or constrict a heterogeneous and wide-ranging social movement, but rather to provide an analytic framework for its major ideologies and practices. While a special issue of *Amerasia Journal* argues for the growing legitimacy of "Asian American activism studies," the still understudied state of the scholarship on the AAM makes it relevant to characterize its crucial features.[3] As we expand the studies of the AAM, this framework will be developed in more nuanced and complex ways, but it will still, I anticipate, retain its analytic core. In this section, I discuss each characteristic and then show the enduring significance of the AAM on later generations of struggle.

1. Radicalism, Anti-Imperialism, and Internationalism

While the AAM of the 1960s–1970s was heterogeneous, scholars and activists have argued that radicalism, anti-imperialism, and internationalism provided the core ideology for the movement as a whole. Many joined their indictments of structural racism with anticapitalist and/or anti-imperialist critiques and in particular framed the Vietnam War within histories of U.S. imperial aggression. Many read Marx, Lenin, and Mao to develop analyses of capitalism as a system designed to create wealth for the few owners of production and impoverishment and misery for the masses of workers. They thus embraced an analysis of class struggle—and not simply economic stratification—that pointed to a fundamental contradiction between the ruling class and the common people. They were developing racial ideologies that viewed racism not as aberrant or reformable per se, but as embedded in the very formation of the nation through land theft and genocide of Native peoples, enslavement of Africans, and labor exploitation of Asians and Mexicans; and institutionalized in U.S. law, capitalist property relations, control of media representations, and so forth. They viewed U.S. conquest, land acquisition, genocide, imprisonment, exclusion, and subordination operating through systems of racial capitalism and imperialistic expansionism. They read V. I. Lenin and Kwame Nkrumah to frame imperialism developing in the late 1800s as "the highest stage of capitalism" and to recognize that "the seeds of neocolonialism" are planted at the moment nations gain formal independence from colonial rule. Many AAM activists also struggled for Asian American women's liberation as intertwined with opposition to racism, class exploitation, and U.S. militarism in Asia. By contrast, their understanding of heteropatriarchy and queer liberation was only beginning to emerge and too often obliged activists to hide their nonnormative sexuality and gender. Moreover, within this grouping of radical AAM activists was a range of political ideologies as well as sharp, sometimes hostile, sectarian ideological differences within the Left formations.

While it took time, study, and struggle to develop political analysis and ideologies, even from the earliest days of the AAM, there was a tendency toward radical critique. One of the earliest AAM organizations, the Asian American Political Alliance (AAPA), had an unambiguous politic in support of anticolonial, national liberation struggles in Asia and the Third World. The alliance's newspaper included articles on the famous Asian-African conference in Bandung, Indonesia, in 1955; the Hemispheric Conference to End the Vietnam War in Montreal, attended by four AAPA-Berkeley members; and a message from Zhou Enlai, premier of the People's Republic of China.[4] In New York City, Asian Americans for Action (AAA), in their first three newsletters, stated their positions on the Vietnam War as U.S. imperialist aggression, U.S. foreign policy as economically motivated, strong support for Black struggle, and criticism of assimilationism. From their position as Japanese Americans, they held Hiroshima Day programs, demanded the U.S. military get out of Okinawa and Japan, opposed the continuation of "emergency detention" in Title II of the McCarran Act of 1950, and condemned the new Eastland bill, which they interpreted as creating the legal foundation for a police state.[5] In Los Angeles, *Gidra*, launched by UCLA students as an AAM publication, had more diverse views than AAPA or AAA publications, while also asserting radical and internationalist politics. *Gidra* covered stories on U.S. militarism and the sexualization of Asian women, radical Asian American organizations such as the Red Guard and I Wor Kuen, and Pat Sumi and Alex Hing's travels to North Korea, North Vietnam, and China with a Black Panther Party (BPP) delegation.[6]

In the 1980s, a concern that "the movements gradually have been reinterpreted in narrower ways" motivated Glenn Omatsu to write his widely read "Four Prisons" article in *Amerasia Journal* (1989). Responding to a professor who had interpreted the Asian American movement through the politics of representation and legitimization within mainstream institutions, Omatsu argued that the AAM originated "not with the initial campaign for civil rights but with the later demand for black liberation"; it was focused "not on asserting racial pride but reclaiming a tradition of struggle by earlier generations; that the movement was not centered on the aura of racial identity but embraced fundamental questions of oppression and power."[7]

By contrast to the period in which Omatsu wrote, much of the writings since 2000 have framed the AAM through radical critique. Fred Ho edited the first anthology on revolutionary Asian American activism, *Legacy to Liberation* (2000), that features radical activists and organizations, many embracing Marxism-Leninism-Maoism, including I Wor Kuen, Wei Min She, and Katipunan ng mga Demokratikong Pilipino (KDP). Using the writings, activities, and archive of the AAM as evidence, I wrote the first historiography of AAM studies published in 2008 that states that the movement largely embraced "the ideology of Black Power, with its radical analysis of US racism, capitalism, and imperialism and its call for self-determination." Michael Liu, Kim Geron, and Tracy Lai, in *Snake Dance of Asian American Activism* (2008), also note, "The AAM was grounded in a vision for structural change and was not primarily an assertion for identity." Daryl J. Maeda, in *Chains of Babylon* (2009), articulates the twin themes of the AAM as American racism and imperialism, borrowing from a poem of Pat Sumi's.[8]

The Asian American movement has left a legacy of theoretical frameworks rooted in radical critiques of imperialism, settler colonialism, and gendered racial capitalism and grounded in internationalist analysis. I offer three examples of contemporary Asian American activism building on the AAM. First, Asian American activists have been struggling to dismantle U.S. militarism in Okinawa; working in solidarity with the anticolonial liberation struggles in Hawai'i, Guåhan (Guam), and Puerto Rico; and linking violence against Asian American women, including in Atlanta in 2021, with sexual camp towns around U.S. military bases in Korea and the violence of so-called comfort women forced into sexual slavery by Japan's military during World War II. Today's struggles inherit the longer durée of Asian American resistance to U.S. and Japanese militarism and imperialism in the Philippines, Okinawa, Japan, Korea, Vietnam, Cambodia, and Laos.[9] Second, portions of the Asian American immigration movement have propelled a shift from seeking formal state recognition and inclusion ("immigration rights") toward self-determination and radical critiques of the state to erect borders and define people as undeserving of citizenship ("immigration liberation" in Elizabeth Rubio's formulation).[10] Third, Asian Americans working in today's policing and prison abolition movements work in the legacy of Black Power and Black feminism and also of Asian American prison and political prisoner activism and opposition to militarism and imperialism.[11] In short, critiques of imperialism, racial capitalism, and racialized patriarchy provided a central analytic for Asian American activism in the 1960s–1970s and continue to the present.

2. Collective Leadership and Racialized Feminist Challenges to Patriarchy

The Asian American movement was distinctive in its emphasis on collective leadership, an approach to organizing informed by feminism and impacting the development of women's participation and leadership. Unlike most other movements, the AAM tended not to cultivate charismatic leaders, and in doing so, sought to avert the problems of individualism and celebrity. Still, the AAM is one of the most invisible social movements, a dynamic impacted by this ethos of collectivism in a society rooted in individualism. I make the argument that for the AAM, collectivity was a primary leadership model in theory and was put into practice in significant, though uneven, ways. I stake the claim that women in the AAM were particularly effective at challenging sexism, more so than in other movements at the time, with important caveats (see below). The AAM's collective approach shapes how Asian American activism has been written about and remembered, and also contributes to why women such as Yuri Kochiyama, Kazu Iijima, Emma Gee, Victoria Wong, Cynthia Maglaya, and Melinda Paras were among its foremost leaders.

Earlier models influenced the AAM's promotion of participatory democracy and horizontal leadership, including the Student Nonviolent Coordinating Committee (SNCC), the Students for a Democratic Society, and the collective ethos in many Asian cultures. Ella Baker, in particular, offered incisive criticism of the charismatic leadership approach for promoting the notion that change occurs because of powerful individuals, mostly men, and undermining the confidence of ordinary people in their capacities to transform society.[12] AAM activists often made deliberate efforts to rotate leadership and to develop the skills of ordinary people and articulated their awareness of how gender, class, and race shape access to power. I offer here but two examples. First, the Asian American Political Alliance, despite its overrepresentation of male leadership, consciously developed a model of collaborative, nonhierarchical leadership. AAPA stated that "non-structure is highly emphasized" and worked through "US groups" without a "chair" and with "complete autonomy," but that functioned in a coordinated manner to create the whole. They defined leadership as "effective action" and "*not* making good speeches, rallying people, or having charisma per se," thus rejecting the charismatic leadership model. AAPA grew to have groups nationwide, and its outsized influence shaped ideas in the larger Asian American movement. Second, throughout his self-reflective memoir, Philip Vera Cruz, the highest-ranking Pilipino leader in the United Farm Workers (UFW), promoted participatory democracy and critiqued the hierarchal leadership of the UFW and his own failings as a Filipino leader to effectively challenge that structure.[13]

I further contend their collective leadership model, central to the AAM, created space for women to participate and hone their organizing skills. In her racial comparative study of radical organizing in Los Angeles, Laura Pulido found that the Asian American group East Wind "was arguably the most effective organization at challenging sexism and traditional gender relations."[14] As one example, East Wind, along with I Wor Kuen (IWK) and KDP, implemented collective childcare so that parents, particularly women, could attend meetings, events, and do the work of organizing. In reflecting on her time in IWK, Sadie Lum noted that "doing the political work was much more difficult for women than for men," especially for women like Lum who were raising children. But her ideological commitment as an activist and a self-identified communist transformed her ideas about parenting and family life. She wrote: "Whether we had children or not, we paid a lot of attention to trying, where possible, to collectivize home responsibilities." Such collectivized households made it easier for activist mothers to participate in political organizing. Women like Lum and many others helped to develop I Wor Kuen into one of the few organizations at the time that made antisexism an explicit component of their program. Point four of IWK's 12-Point Platform and Program stated, "We want an End to Male Chauvinism and Sexual Exploitation."[15]

In addition, the AAM's focus on collectivity helped transform the meanings of leadership. The renowned activist Yuri Kochiyama, for example, embodied what I call "centerperson leadership" that promotes political networks, nurtures social relations and collective care, and encourages mutual aid. This work is often invisible within conventional notions of governance, but, as Karen Brodkin Sacks made clear, is a form of leadership essential to the success of political movements.[16]

I add two caveats to nuance these interpretations and an endnote on the use of the term *feminism*.[17] First, it is hardly surprising that social movements reflect the patriarchal ideas and organizational structures of the broader society, and the Asian American movement was no exception. Asian American women were too often relegated to taking minutes or making coffee, and male leaders predominated in the Red Guards, Yellow Seed, Hardcore, and Yellow Brotherhood. However, women founded or cofounded Asian Americans for Action in New York and AAPA at Berkeley and San Francisco State and rose to leadership positions in KDP and I Wor Kuen. Moreover, Asian American women and some men struggled for egalitarian relations and critiqued sexism as a structural problem, rather than individualized, and as a problem in its own right, rather than being reduced to "a byproduct of capitalism." This framing opened the ideological space to confront sexism.[18] Second, if the AAM was relatively effective at challenging sexism, this does not imply that greater sexism existed in other organizations and movements. Within CASA (Center for Autonomous Social Action), for example, Chicana women comprised at least half of the membership. And the Black Panther Party offered unprecedented opportunities for Black women's participation and leadership, especially in running its numerous community survival programs, even as the organization is known for its top male leadership and masculinist representations.[19]

The internationalism and inspiration of revolutionary Asia was another crucial factor shaping antisexism in the AAM. The widely circulating images of Vietnamese women, often holding a baby and a gun, created powerful symbols that expanded the subjectivities and capacities of women. Such images were reproduced in AAM publications by artists like Tomie Arai and by Black Panther artist Emory Douglas as well. When AAM activists actually met Vietnamese women revolutionaries at two international conferences in Vancouver and Montreal, it only reinforced their repetition of Mao's famous statement, "Women hold up half the sky." My point is that the AAM's promotion of collectivity was crucial to the development of stronger democratic practices and the greater leadership and influence of women in the movement.

The legacy of the AAM's collective leadership can be seen in the work of later generations to develop egalitarian models of organizing.[20] As one noteworthy example, Asian Immigrant Women Advocates (AIWA) has created a leadership model that promotes and develops the leadership of working-class Asian immigrant women. It did so at a remarkable time, shortly after winning a prominent garment worker campaign—one that had garnered national media and positioned its members to prioritize high-visibility organizing. But AIWA reflected on its strategies for change. Even as the workers spoke at rallies, testified at hearings, and actively participated, their intensive focus on the public campaign left little space to develop the organizing capacities of people to advocate for themselves. AIWA turned to create the Community Transformational Organizing Strategy (CTOS) as a seven-step approach to (a) challenge the gendered, racialized devaluation of immigrant women workers in the workplace and in the family (levels 1–3); (b) participate in social movement activity (levels 4–5); and (c) create themselves as leaders and reevaluating the meanings of leadership (levels 6–7). In short, AIWA's CTOS shifted the concept of leadership away from a naturalized possession residing in a few gifted people to a distributive approach to power where leadership is a capacity and skill to be developed and where bilingual/bicultural abilities and working-class experiences are viewed as strengths, not deficits. This paradigm has resulted in AIWA emphasizing its focus on self-determination and the participating women growing to see themselves as people who hold valuable knowledge and skills.[21]

3. Third World Solidarity

One of the most outstanding characteristics of the Asian American movement as a whole was its insistence on Third World solidarity as a strategy for fighting white supremacy, colonialism, and patriarchal racial capitalism. AAM activists recognized that forging solidarities with other organizations and communities was crucial to winning campaigns and building political movements, especially given the small size of the Asian American population and the model minority trope's erasure of anti-Asian racism.[22] But more than a pragmatic strategy, the

AAM's coalitional focus was an ideological commitment to forging liberation movements not only for their community, but for all oppressed communities. This ethos rested on the principles set at the Bandung conference to create joint struggle among newly independent Asian and African nations in the movement against racism and colonialism. It built on the ideas of Martin Luther King Jr. that we are all connected in an "inescapable network of mutuality" such that "whatever affects one directly affects all indirectly." Dr. King's expression of "brotherhood" with the people of Vietnam and Malcolm X's solidarity with anticolonial movements in Asia required the rejection of the model minority at a time when it was fast becoming the dominant racialization of Asian Americans. Such solidarities further built on the mutuality, necessitated by anti-Asian racism, that led earlier generations to create rotating credit associations, interethnic and interracial labor organizing, the Chinese Workers Mutual Aid Association in the 1930s, and the Nisei Progressives in the early 1950s—histories that the AAM activists gradually learned through their study and struggle. These examples show that the collaborative orientation of the AAM was an extension of earlier modes of organizing, rather than a departure from it.[23]

What was most visible to the early AAM was the influence of Black Power and Third World anticolonial struggles. The formidable example of Black Power and the central role of Black activism in building movements for democracy fashioned Black-Asian solidarity as primary. This was further propelled by the close proximity of Black and particularly Japanese American neighborhoods in Los Angeles, San Francisco, and Seattle arising from residential segregation policies and practices.[24] Some of the most prominent Asian American activists and organizations, notably Grace Lee Boggs, Yuri Kochiyama, Nobuko Miyamoto, Shoshana Arai, the Storefront, and the Red Guards, exemplified practices of Afro-Asian solidarity making.

While AAM activists exhibited strong commitments to solidarity, these efforts were less often reciprocated by Chicana/o and Black activists. For many activists in Los Angeles, anti-Asian racism was unrecognizable, and thus there was little basis for forming coalitions with Asian Americans.[25] This necessitates the work of educating about structural oppression facing Asian Americans, and also contesting anti-Asian sentiment in Black and Brown communities, which can raise uncomfortable questions. When, for example, the Okinawa Women Act Against Military Violence campaigned to hold U.S. servicemen accountable for the rape of a twelve-year-old Okinawan girl, some civil rights groups complained that the marines were being unfairly targeted because they were Black. While holding in tension the long history of Black men being lynched based on accusations of sexualized violence, a race-only analysis fails to also see the servicemen as agents of empire or men whose predation is a threat to Black and all women.[26] Anti-Asian racism remains largely invisible in the national narrative to the present, though with unprecedented shifts during the COVID-19 pandemic and especially since the Atlanta shootings. But, at the time of this writing, it remains to be seen how this national awakening to anti-Asian racism will impact the dominant racialization of Asian America.

While Pulido found that Asian Americans in Los Angeles forged solidarity with Black and Chicano/a groups more than the reverse, geographic variability impacted nuanced understandings of anti-Asian racism. In the 1960s–1970s, in San Francisco, Oakland, and Berkeley, for example, Black activists extended Afro-Asian solidarities in the fight against white supremacy. At San Francisco State College, the Black Student Union reached out to Asian American students to join the Third World Liberation Front's strike for Third World Studies. In its early days, the Black Panther Party accepted Asian Americans Richard Aoki, Mike Tagawa, and Guy Kurose as members. Through political study with BPP leaders, San Francisco Chinatown youth formed the Red Guard Party. In May 1967, when the BPP confronted the Mulford bill aiming to undercut their armed police patrols, Bobby Seale famously linked Black oppression with U.S. concentration camps, Hiroshima/Nagasaki, and the Vietnam War. The Black Panther Party's selling of Mao's Red Book, travels to revolutionary Asia, and Huey Newton's promotion of China, North Korea, and Vietnam as models of liberation indicated a respect for Asian struggle against imperialism as part of the Black struggle. Many U.S. Black radicals viewed world revolutions, notably in China, Korea, and Vietnam, as inspiration for their own struggles. In these ways, Black activists regarded Asian Americans as comrades.[27]

While Black struggle and Black knowledge making have had the strongest impact on the AAM, Asian Americans also formed solidarities with Indigenous, Chicano/a, Puerto Rican, and other communities. This includes, most famously, Filipino and Chicano/a farmworkers united in the now famous five-year grape strike in Delano, California—a strike started by Filipino laborers; Asian American support for the Native American occupation of Alcatraz; and Japanese Americans Michael Yasutake in Chicago and Yuri Kochiyama in New York working closely with the Puerto Rican anticolonial movement. Far from romanticizing these struggles, I want to acknowledge that solidarity work is often difficult, as Philip Vera Cruz has discussed.[28]

Cross-racial solidarity making remains an important component of Asian American activism. In the 1980s and 1990s, Asian Americans worked alongside Black, Chicana, and Indigenous activists to build the U.S. Third World feminist movement, and Japanese Americans forged solidarities with Kanaka Maoli struggles for Native Hawaiian sovereignty.[29] In the twenty-first century, a sizeable number of Asian American activists are standing in solidarity with Black communities, including the formation of multiple Asians for Black Lives chapters, addressing anti-Blackness in Asian American communities, and calling for defunding the police and building noncarceral alternatives for community safety and health. Based on their thirty-five years of grassroots organizing, CAAAV in New York mobilized support for Akai Gurley's family and critiqued the Chinese American Right's narrow promotion of equal treatment for Peter Liang, the Chinese American police officer who killed Gurley in Brooklyn. In Madison, Wisconsin, Freedom, Inc. focuses on community organizing and service provision, especially targeting state and domestic violence in Southeast Asian and Black communities.[30] Its executive directors are the Black queer and Lao-born women team of M Adams and Kabzuag Vaj. The presence of online organizing has grown remarkably, as seen in the formation of 18 Million Rising in 2012 and its e-zine, "Call On Me, Not the Cops," and the creation and postings of public intellectual writings on Black-Asian solidarity, including on Afro-Asian history, feminism, and internationalism. Like the AAM activists before them, today's Asian American activists view their opposition to police violence and their growing support for abolitionist futures as necessary for the safety and liberation of Black communities and Asian Americans as well.[31]

4. Serve the People with the People and Praxis-Based Knowledge Making

AAM activists created models of community service that were about service provision to improve the material conditions in Asian American communities, but also much more. With few resources and in an era before the launch of the nonprofit sector (and its critique), activists had to rely on ingenuity, collective work, and an approach of going directly to the people to understand their needs and to develop collaborative solutions.[32] They criticized charity models of service and instead promoted principles of self-determination in ways that re-articulated the production of knowledge itself. Harvey Dong urged students to connect with broader communities because "the only real source of power and strength has to be the community itself." As he wrestled with the question of where knowledge comes from, Mao's "On Practice" influenced him to value the unity of theory and practice and to prioritize practice, including dialogue with and organizing for people's everyday needs. Mo Nishida, in a 1970 *Gidra* article, drew on Mao's slogan "Serve the People!"—and its overlooked second part, "With the People!"—and the BPP's "All Power to the People" to promote the collective authority of the people. He rejected notions of charity in favor of the "structural development of new community institutions to serve the people."[33]

For many AAM activists, personal transformation was also an essential part of the collective struggle. For Glenn Omatsu, political growth came from world events, political study, and especially from social relations and those close to him who challenged his thinking. By working with ordinary people and hearing from older activists about the history of Asian American resistance, many AAM activists learned about how to work with people from where they are at and to mobilize and educate, not from a place of righteousness or arrogance, but by working alongside people in mutuality and reciprocal learning. These experiences profoundly shaped their thinking, social relations, and models of organizing.[34]

I offer three examples that illustrate this deep work with communities and that augment the many examples already provided in this chapter and anthology. First, in 1995, the Asian Pacific Environmental Network

(APEN) established the Laotian Organizing Project (LOP) as an intergenerational, community-led formation that worked with the Laotian community in Richmond, California, to understand their most pressing needs. In a community experiencing severe poverty (a quarter of the Bay Area Laotian community lived under the federal poverty level) and pollution (350 industrial sites and toxic hazards surrounded their neighborhood), the LOP waged a successful campaign to gain a multilingual warning system designed to alert non-English-speaking residents when there was an explosion, oil spill, or other environmental hazards at the nearby Chevron oil refinery.[35]

Second, in New Orleans, Louisiana, after Hurricane Katrina in 2005 and again after Hurricane Zeta in 2020, Vietnamese fisherfolk, together with community activists, struggled to rebuild their businesses. As Simi Kang shows, theirs is a form of mutual aid that involves nurturing networks of reciprocal care and planting community gardens as, in Dean Spade's words, "a form of political participation in which people take responsibility for caring for one another and changing political conditions, not just through symbolic acts or putting pressure on their representatives in government but by actually building new social relations that are more survivable."[36]

Third, the New York Taxi Workers Alliance (NYTWA), started in the 1990s, promotes an extraordinary model of labor organizing among its widely multilingual and primarily South Asian drivers. When Uber and Lyft drivers flooded the market, rather than treating them as competition under neoliberalism, the NYTWA organized with them to gain important victories, including recognition of app-based drivers as employees rather than independent contractors, and, most recently, a 5.3 percent pay increase for all Uber and Lyft drivers in New York City. Moreover, after a number of taxi workers died by suicide due to conditions of severe indebtedness, a fifteen-day hunger strike, and three years of direct action organizing, the NYTWA won a debt forgiveness program for taxis drivers forced to purchase medallion licenses at the extractive cost of close to a $1 million. Finally, during the pandemic, taxi drivers as frontline workers were at particular risk, with a reported sixty-two drivers dying of COVID-19 in the first couple of months. NYTWA organizers turned their attention to organizing tirelessly to supply information, get full unemployment benefits, and provide other crucial resources to drivers, fielding ten thousand calls or emails from member-drivers in the first three to four months alone.[37]

While conditions have changed since the 1960s, and there is now a sizeable Asian American nonprofit infrastructure, the priorities placed on models that "serve the people with the people" remain important today. The idea of learning from the community by working with the community is tremendously important—more so than ever at a time when social media visibility gets mistaken for political organizing and when people imagine themselves to proclaim ideas not vetted by the people who are eyewitnesses to the worst atrocities of racial capitalism and to speak for communities with whom they do not work on a daily basis.

5. Building Movements for Liberation

Alongside creating serve-the-people programs, attending seemingly never-ending meetings, studying together, and organizing protest activities, AAM activists also worked to build political movements. They recognized that no single action no matter how exhilarating, no single demonstration no matter how large, and no single campaign no matter how successful would create the transformative changes they were seeking. Those seeking *institutional change* came to recognize the necessity of persisting through multiple wins and losses. Those seeking *systems change* to capitalist, imperialist, and racial regimes understood that this would require perpetual strategizing and struggle. This acknowledgement of long-term struggle was not automatic. Many 1960s activists have expressed believing the revolution was around the corner. Only later would they talk about movement building extending beyond their lifetime.

Systems and institutional change depend on the deep sustaining work and strategic thinking necessary to collectively create a more equitable distribution of power and resources. It is important to distinguish between activism and organizing, even though both are valuable and necessary. *Activism* activates or mobilizes for change through supporting, short-term, and/or one-off activities such as attending rallies, meetings, and webinars, signing petitions, and posting or otherwise sharing information. *Organizing,* by contrast, works to build campaigns to gain material changes, wrestles with how to create effective and democratic organizational structures and processes, and cultivates a vision of long-term transformation and a midrange plan for getting there. Ultimately, organizing deepens the collective capacity for democratic deliberation and decision making by developing the capacity for leadership in others. It is work done in particular places and through relationships built over time. It is, as Alex Tom discusses, "less about the 'perfect' vision and more about having a grounded assessment of time, place, and conditions."[38] Organizing further embodies the learning gained from study, struggle, and reflection; from multilateral transfers of intergenerational knowledge; and the training and mentorship needed to develop new organizers. These networks of instruction, apprenticeship, and accompaniment are underestimated in analyses of activism.

The movement continues to influence today's Asian American grassroots struggles through ideas and organizing methods arising from the early AAM, social relationships created with former AAM activists, and sometimes through organizations sustained across fifty years. While some may lament that few AAM organizations still exist, what is remarkable is how many do, given the substantial challenges of maintaining organizations, funding, and human resources. Some of the 1960s–1970s AAM organizations that continue to the present are the Asian Law Caucus or Advancing Justice-ALC, Asian Pacific Islander Legal Outreach (formerly Nihonmachi Legal Outreach), Chinese for Affirmative Action, and the Kearny Street Workshop in San Francisco; Filipino Advocates for Justice (formerly Filipinos for Affirmative Action) in Oakland and Union City, California; Asian Law Alliance in San Jose, California; Visual Communications in Los Angeles; Chinese Progressive Association in San Francisco and Boston; and Asian Americans for Equality and the Asian American Legal Defense and Education Fund in New York City.[39] In addition, a sizeable number of AAM activist/organizers are working intergenerationally in groups such as the Asian American Resource Workshop in Boston; Great Leap and Nikkei for Civil Rights and Redress (formerly National Coalition for Redress and Reparations) in Los Angeles; the Asian Immigrant Women Advocates (AIWA) and the Asian Prisoners Support Committee in Oakland, and the Progressive Asian Network for Action in Los Angeles. A great many more activists—too many to name—had their start in the Asian American movement of the 1960s–1970s, and they continue to shape ideas and analysis in colleges and universities, labor organizing, the legal arena, community spaces, writings and publications, and broad movements for fair housing, educational equity, environmental justice, and feminism.

I offer two significant examples of movement building today: First, Grassroots Asians Rising (GAR) is a new national alliance comprised of seven long-standing organizations to advance the grassroots organizing knowledge and long-term movement building capacities of Asian American working-class communities. In 2017, GAR convened more than fifty organizations in Oakland to discuss this vision and to build power across a range of issues. They also created the "Asian American Racial Justice Toolkit" as a teaching tool for addressing structural racism, history, and systemic and intersectional oppression. Ultimately, they seek to learn from the knowledge already existing in working-class communities to develop organizing strategies that reimagine liberation and build a new Asian American movement.[40] Second, the Southeast Asian Freedom Network (SEAFN) formed in 2001 to fight the wave of deportations of Southeast Asians. For years, they have been on the cutting edge of intertwining queer and trans identity and restorative justice practices within working-class Southeast Asian refugee communities. In open letters to the Southeast Asians community on Black solidarity, they invoke their own experiences with war and genocide to call for solidarity with Black communities in the face of racist state violence. They are clear on the interconnectedness of struggles but reject easy parallelisms. They write: "Let us see that the struggle of Black communities against police and state violence directly impacts our community's survival as we face that violence as well. Let us be clear through this understanding that while our oppressions are connected, our oppression is not the same."[41] SEAFN is comprised of seven organizational members working with specificity on Southeast Asian and refugee issues, while also working through pan-Asian and cross-racial solidarities.[42] These two formations reflect the changing demographics within Asian America over the period since the mid-1970s, with a notable increase of Southeast Asian and South Asian organizing, in addition to Chinese, Filipino, Korean, Japanese, and other groups, as well as greater geographic diversity beyond the West Coast, New York area, and Hawai'i. The coalitional work in these examples moves away from a near singular focus on campaign toward reflecting on knowledge created in the process of organizing and toward more intentional movement building.

Ongoing Legacy of the Asian American Movement

I just finished listening to Karen Tei Yamashita discussing her innovative, jazzy epic novel, *I-Hotel*. Twelve years after its publication, Yamashita's *I-Hotel* became the California Book Club's selection of the month.[43] Her novel traces multiple perspectives on the Asian American movement, as presented in ten novellas, or ten "hotels," that comprise the book. The book is named after the International Hotel, or I-Hotel, that housed working-class Filipino and Chinese elders, mostly single men, who created a home in the hotel's cramped rooms in the last remaining block of San Francisco's Manilatown. We know the story. After a nine-year battle to fight evictions and resist gentrification to make San Francisco into the "Wall Street of the West," the city evicted the remaining tenants, along with their activist supporters, on August 4, 1977. But that wasn't all. The many AAM organizations in the I-Hotel's storefront offices also lost their home. Some say this marked the end of the AAM. I remember Richard Aoki telling me that he never wanted to fight anti-gentrification battles because he viewed them as impossible to win against the interests of big capital. But then his friend Harvey Dong reframed the struggle. They did lose their objective goals; they could not stop the evictions or block the elimination of working-class residence and small businesses, to be replaced by establishments that serve corporate and tourist economies. But their struggle, in this case for the I-Hotel, mattered. Their work trained organizers, built activist infrastructures, fostered political and social relationships, signaled the importance of ethnic communities, and, significantly, enabled ordinary people the chance to practice participatory democracy. The I-Hotel struggle changed people's lives. The campaign developed organizers who continued to build toward horizons of liberation through the many Asian American organizations discussed in this chapter and book. Ultimately, the site of the I-Hotel was never built into the image of the corporate owners, but thirty years later became the International Hotel Manilatown Center, with senior housing and a cultural center. The I-Hotel mobilization has been the subject of documentaries, scholarly and fiction books, and murals, and is arguably the most iconic representation of the Asian American movement itself. It continues to be discussed forty-five years after the evictions.

I wondered about the legacy of the AAM. How should we think about the frequent invocations of Yuri Kochiyama by young people today? What does it mean that young people are resurrecting, and even iconizing, AAM slogans, such as in the proliferation of "Yellow Peril Supports Black Power" signs during Black Lives Matter protests in 2020 following the police killing of George Floyd?[44] I offer a cautionary against the mere repetition of concepts and slogans and figures that took place in an earlier moment, without regard to differences in political economy (from the welfare state to neoliberal austerity) and somewhat transformed understandings of race and racism and intersectionality. What work does the invocation of AAM figures and slogans serve? What does it mean for communities without memories of their activist pasts to resurrect figures, slogans, and histories of struggle? And what work has been done through the commemorations of the fiftieth anniversary of the AAM—the exhibits, talks, and oral histories? I recognize that commemorative work can often produce nostalgic remembrances that flatten complexities of movements, that highlight the good or the aspirational and remove flaws from sight when it may be even more important to learn from the mistakes of prior struggles. What is lost or missing when we foreground particular people, places, events, campaigns, and interpretations? And what is lost if we don't?

I close this chapter by discussing three new developments in Asian American activism that were not as evident in the AAM of the 1960s and 1970s. I further argue that through theorizing and practice, the AAM of fifty years ago produced knowledge, however imperfect, that influences these newer ideas and continues to shape our understandings of Asian America and U.S. society and history writ large. First, today's organizers have advanced the intersectional analytics intertwining sexuality and gender, building on the AAM's earlier focus on race, nation, class, and gender as well as its neglect of queer issues. In the 1960s–1970s, LBGTQ-identified activists faced an Asian American movement unaccepting of LGBTQ identity and a gay/lesbian movement lacking an antiracist agenda. KDP was distinctive as perhaps the only AAM with openly LGBTQ-identified members, including some in top leadership. In the 1980s and 1990s, influenced by the U.S. Third World feminist movement and the AIDS crisis of that period, activists developed an Asian American gay and lesbian movement, as it was then called. They formed new LGBTQ organizations such as the Asian Pacific Lesbians and Gays in Los Angeles and South Asian Lesbian and Gay Association (SALGA) in New York and organized for queer politics in, for example, Unbound Feet, CAAAV, and the Asian Women's Shelter. Through the continuing influence of these and other organizations and academic and public writings, today's activists focus far greater attention to Asian American queer politics and critique.[45]

Second, today's heightened spotlight on environmental justice linked with antiracism is propelled by the urgency of ecological disaster and also builds on struggles in the 1990s, particularly the first People of Color Environmental Leadership Summit in 1991 and APEN's formation in 1993. While less in evidence, AAM activists also raised environmental concerns in the late 1960s. Asian Americans for Action, for example, printed an article on capitalist-rooted environmental destruction, and the Red Guard Party demanded that "the United States government halt the rape of the land" or risk creating "a lifeless planet of rock and dust."[46] The AAM's support for Filipino farmworkers, Japanese American gardeners, lunch programs for Chinatown seniors, anti-gentrification struggles, and labor organizing can all be reinterpreted as environmental justice issues to improve the health and well-being of workers and communities, and relations to the land itself.[47]

Third, Asian American and Native Hawaiian activists today, along with the academic fields of Indigenous, American, and Asian American studies, have sharpened a focus on settler colonialism. This expands the AAM's ideological critique of imperialism, global capitalism, and white supremacy to include an examination of the relationship between Asian migrants as settlers or "arrivants" and Indigenous peoples. The ideas of Haunani-Kay Trask, Candice Fujikane, Jonathan Okamura, Dean Saranillio, Iyko Day, and Jodi Byrd have been particularly influential in the academy and the movement. The struggle for Native Hawaiian sovereignty enables Native peoples and settler Asian Americans to find common ground in opposition to settler colonialism and in support of land and water protectors at Mauna Kea and Standing Rock.[48]

The AAM has called into being today's activists and organizers who are engaged in study and struggle to create mutual aid networks and provide services for Asian American communities; struggle for decent housing, jobs with dignity and economic sustainability, holistic health practices, and access to high-nutrient, locally grown, and culturally enlivening food; support self-determination and grassroots leadership development of those most impacted by systemic oppression; live in harmony with Mother Earth and build on the Chinese and Indigenous knowledge of healing; fight for learning and political education inside and outside of formal schooling; demonstrate solidarity with all oppressed peoples; and counter the impacts of racial capitalism, heteropatriarchy, and U.S. militarism and policing that diminish the capacities of people to imagine and fight for an emancipatory world.

There has never been a moment like the present with greater potential for Asian American movement building, in the face of growing global fascism, overt white supremacy, and a visible Asian American rightwing. We find ourselves at a historic crossroads. As organizer Alex Tom notes, "No generation has this historical view of 20th century revolutions and socialist experiments; and 21st century crises in capitalism and the complete deterioration of the earth."[49] Attending to how we study and interpret the AAM, its theories, methods, and mistakes, can shape our thinking and organizing in the present. While invoking ongoing analysis and strategic planning, the Asian American movement teaches us to prioritize the collective leadership, radical critique, solidarity, long-haul movement building, and model of "serving the people with the people" that will be required if we are to enable the survival of the planet and its people.

Notes

1. Christine Ahn, Terry K. Park, and Kathleen Richards, "Anti-Asian Violence in America Rooted in US Empire," *The Nation*, April 19/26, 2021; Bill Chappel, Vanessa Romo, and Jaclyn Diaz, "Official Who Said Atlanta Shooting Suspect Was Having a 'Bad Day' Faces Criticism," NPR, March 18, 2021.
2. Due to space constraints, I have significantly pared down citations throughout this chapter.
3. See Diane C. Fujino and Robyn M. Rodriguez's special issue of *Amerasia Journal* 45:2 (2019).
4. Diane C. Fujino, "Political Asian America: Afro-Asian Solidarity, Third World Internationalism, and the Origins of the Asian American Movement," *Ethnic Studies Review* 47:1 (2024). From the AAPA newspaper: "Draft Counseling," 1:1 (November-December 1968): 4; "The Political Settlement of the South Viet-Nam

Problem" and "Area Movements-AAPA," 1:2 (January 1969): 2, 3; "Thirdworld Roots: Bandung," 1:4 (March-April 1969): 1, 4.

5 From the AAA newsletter: positions, "Price of Assimilation," "Danger! Two Bills Set Up Concentration Camps and Police State," June 1969, 1, 3, 6; "Hiroshima Day," "Okinawa," July 1969, 1–2; Mary Kochiyama, Hiroshima-Nagasaki Week Speech, October 1969, 3–4.

6 From *Gidra*: Laura Ho, "Red Guard Party," 1:2 (May 1969): 4; Patrell, "Glad They're Back," 2:9 (October 1970): 4; Evelyn Yoshimura, "GIs and Asian Women," 3:1 (January 1971): 4, 15; Patricia Sumi, "Vietnamese Women's Union," 3:6 (June 1971): 7–9; Carmen Chow, "I Wor Kuen," 3:6 (June 1971): 12–13.

7 Glenn Omatsu, "The 'Four Prisons' and the Movements of Liberation," *Amerasia Journal* 15 (1989): xvi.

8 Ho, *Legacy to Liberation*; Fujino, "Who Studies the Asian American Movement?," 30; Michael Liu, Kim Geron, and Tracy Lai, *Snake Dance of Asian American Activism: Community, Vision, and Power* (Lanham, MD: Lexington, 2008), xvi; Daryl J. Maeda, *Chains of Babylon: The Rise of Asian America* (Minneapolis: University of Minnesota Press, 2009).

9 While space prohibits a fuller accounting, this includes Okinawa Women Act Against Military Violence, Women Cross DMZ, Comfort Women Justice Coalition, and Red Canary Song.

10 Elizabeth Hanna Rubio, "'We Need to Redefine What We Mean by Winning': NAKASEC's Immigrant Justice Activism and Thinking Citizenship Otherwise," *Amerasia Journal* 45 (2019): 157–158; also Ga Young Chung, "Dismantling the 'Undocumented Korean Box': Race, Education, and Undocumented Korean Immigrant Activism for Liberation," in Diane Fujino and Robyn Rodriguez, *Contemporary Asian American Activism: Building Movements for Liberation* (Seattle: University of Washington Press, 2022).

11 On Asian Americans advancing abolitionism, see Dylan Rodríguez, "Abolition as Praxis of Human Being: A Foreword," *Harvard Law Review* 132:6 (April 2019): 1575; Charmaine Chua, "Abolition Is a Constant Struggle: Five Lessons from Minneapolis," *Theory & Event* 23 (2020): 127–147; Jason Wu and James McMaster, "Hate-Crime Laws Are Not the Answer to Anti-Asian Violence, Abolition Is," *TeenVogue*, April 28, 2021, www.teenvogue.com. On Asian American prison and political prisoner activism, see Eddy Zheng, "Prison-to-Leadership Pipeline: Asian American Prisoner Activism," in Fujino and Rodriguez, *Contemporary Asian American Activism*; Diane C. Fujino, *Nisei Radicals: The Feminist Poetics and Transformative Ministry of Mitsuye Yamada and Michael Yasutake* (Seattle: University of Washington Press, 2020); Yuri Nakahara Kochiyama, *Passing It On—A Memoir*, ed. Marjorie Lee, Akemi Kochiyama-Sardinha, and Audee Kochiyama-Holman (Los Angeles: UCLA Asian American Studies Center Press, 2004). Influential Black feminist abolitionists include Angela Davis, Ruth Wilson Gilmore, and Mariame Kaba and organizations such as Critical Resistance.

12 Barbara Ransby, *Ella Baker and the Black Freedom Movement: A Radical Democratic Vision* (Chapel Hill: University of North Carolina Press, 2003), 188, 170–195; Maylei Blackwell, *Chicana Power! Contested Histories of Feminism in the Chicana Movement* (Austin: University of Texas Press, 2011).
13 Asian American Political Alliance, "How AAPA Works," AAPA newspaper 1:1 (November-December 1968): 4; AAPA Fact Sheet, September 1968; Craig Scharlin and Lilia V. Villanueva, *Philip Vera Cruz: A Personal History of Filipino Immigrants and the Farmworkers Movement* (Seattle: University of Washington Press, 2000), 104.
14 Laura Pulido, *Black Brown Yellow and Left: Radical Activism in Los Angeles* (Berkeley: University of California Press, 2006), 204–205.
15 Sadie Lum, "Asian American Women and Revolution: A Personal View," *East Wind* 2 (Spring/Summer 1983): 49. On IWK's platform, see Ho, *Legacy to Liberation*, 405–407.
16 Diane C. Fujino, "Grassroots Leadership and Afro-Asian Solidarities: Yuri Kochiyama's Humanizing Radicalism," in *Want to Start a Revolution? Radical Women in the Black Freedom Struggle*, ed. Dayo F. Gore, Jeanne Theoharis, and Komozi Woodard (New York: New York University Press, 2009), 294–316; Karen Brodkin Sacks, *Caring by the Hour: Women, Work, and Organizing at Duke Medical Center* (Urbana: University of Illinois Press, 1988).
17 In the 1960s–1970s, Asian American, Black, Chicano/a, and Indigenous women tended to work on women's liberation through racial or nationalist movements and feel alienated by the liberal women's movement's exclusion of race and class issues. They often did not identify as feminists. Yet, as in Chela Sandoval's deployment of "US Third World feminism," I use the term *feminism* to claim it as an expanded, politicized, and intersectional concept of liberation.
18 Susie Ling, "The Mountain Movers: Asian American Women's Movement in Los Angeles," *Amerasia Journal* 15:1 (1989): 53–55; Pulido, *Black Brown Yellow and Left*, 208, 211.
19 Pulido, *Black Brown Yellow and Left*, 186–191, 195.
20 I offer one cautionary: collective leadership is often misunderstood as completely horizontal leadership that rejects any form of hierarchy. This might work for one-off programs, but when building political movements over the long haul, organizers often find a kind of "democratic hierarchy" to be necessary, one where people have different roles and influences, but where many knowledges and skills are equally valued and indispensable to creating the whole.
21 Jennifer Jihye Chun, George Lipsitz, and Young Shin, "Intersectionality as a Social Movement Strategy: Asian Immigrant Women Advocates," *Signs* 38 (2013): 917–940.
22 Asian Americans comprised 1.5 million or less than 1 percent of the U.S. population in 1970; Historical Census Statistics, by Race, 1790 to 1990, www.census.gov.
23 Martin Luther King Jr., "Letter from Birmingham Jail," August 1963, in *A Testament of Hope: The Essential Writings of Martin Luther King, Jr.*, ed. James

Melvin Washington (San Francisco: Harper & Row, 1986), 290; Gordon H. Chang, "The Many Sides of Happy Lim," *Amerasia Journal* 34 (2008): 70–98; Diane C. Fujino, "The Indivisibility of Freedom: The Nisei Progressives, Deep Solidarities, and Cold War Alternatives," *Journal of Asian American Studies* 21 (2018): 171–208.

24 Clement Lai, "The Racial Triangulation of Space: The Case of Urban Renewal in San Francisco's Fillmore District," *Annals of the Association of American Geographers* 102 (2012): 151–170.

25 Pulido, *Black Brown Yellow and Left*, 156, 169.

26 I thank George Lipsitz for his insights into this issue. Yoko Fukumura and Martha Matsuoka, "Redefining Security: Okinawa Women's Resistance to U.S. Militarism," in *Women's Activism and Globalization: Linking Local Struggles and Global Politics*, ed. Nancy Naples and Manisha Desai (New York: Routledge, 2004), 239–266.

27 Daryl J. Maeda, "Black Panthers, Red Guards, and Chinamen: Constructing Asian American Identity through Performing Blackness, 1969–1972," *American Quarterly* 57 (2005): 1079–1103; Diane C. Fujino, *Samurai among Panthers: Richard Aoki on Race, Resistance, and a Paradoxical Life* (Minneapolis: University of Minnesota Press, 2012); Nobuko Miyamoto, *Not Yo' Butterfly: My Long Song of Relocation, Race, Love, and Revolution*, ed. Deborah Wong (Berkeley: University of California Press, 2021).

28 Scharlin and Villanueva, *Philip Vera Cruz*; Catherine Fung, "'This Isn't Your Battle or Your Land': The Native American Occupation of Alcatraz in the Asian-American Political Imagination," *College Literature* 41 (2014): 149–173; Fujino, *Nisei Radicals*; Diane C. Fujino, *Heartbeat of Struggle: The Revolutionary Life of Yuri Kochiyama* (Minneapolis: University of Minnesota Press, 2005).

29 Cherríe Moraga and Gloria Anzaldúa, eds., *This Bridge Called My Back* (New York: Kitchen Table Press, 1983); Fujino, *Nisei Radicals*.

30 Diane Wong, "The Future Is Ours to Build: Asian American Abolitionist Counterstories for Black Liberation," *Politics, Groups, and Identities* 10 (2022): 493–502.

31 See, for example, May Fu, Simmy Makhijani, Anh-Thu Pham, Meejin Richart, Joanne Tien, and Diane Wong, "#Asians4BlackLives: Notes from the Ground," *Amerasia Journal* 45 (2019): 253–270; and various online postings such as https://crossculturalsolidarity.com, www.blackwomenradicals.com,/and https://roarmag.org.

32 The most influential critique of the nonprofit industrial complex is INCITE's *The Revolution Will Not Be Funded: Beyond the Non-Profit Industrial Complex* (Cambridge, MA: South End Press, 2007).

33 Harvey Dong, "Transforming Student Elites into Community Activists: A Legacy of Asian American Activism," in *Asian Americans: The Movement and the Moment*, ed. Steve Louie and Glenn Omatsu (Los Angeles: UCLA Asian American Studies Center Press, 2001), 193; Mori Nishida, "Serve the People," in *Asian Americans: The Movement and the Moment*, 305–306.

34 Glenn Omatsu, "Listening to the Small Voice Speaking the Truth: Grassroots Organizing and the Legacy of Our Movement," in *Asian Americans: The Movement and the Moment*, 308–309.
35 Roger Kim and Martha Matsuoka, "Building a 21st Century Environmental Movement That Wins: Twenty Years of Environmental Justice Organizing by the Asian Pacific Environmental Network," *AAPI Nexus* 11 (2013): 139–158.
36 Simi Kang, "Mutual Aid & Resistance: Commercial Shrimping in Environmental Sacrifice," presentation at the Association for Asian American Studies conference, April 2021, virtual; Dean Spade, *Mutual Aid: Building Solidarity during This Crisis (and the Next)* (New York: Verso, 2020), 136.
37 Diane C. Fujino, "Drivers on the Front Lines: The New York Taxi Worker Alliance, Neoliberalism, and Global Pandemic—An Interview with Javaid Tariq," in Fujino and Rodriguez, *Contemporary Asian American Activism*; "Mayor Adams Delivers Raise for Essential Gig Workers," February 11, 2022, www1.nyc.gov and www.nytwa.org, accessed March 16, 2022.
38 Alex T. Tom, "On Movement Praxis in the Era of Trumpism," in Fujino and Rodriguez, *Contemporary Asian American Activism*.
39 I thank Audee Kochiyama-Holman and Mo Nishida for helping me think through this question; Kochiyama-Holman, email to Diane Fujino, May 25, 2021; Nishida, conversation with Diane Fujino, May 25, 2021. This is not intended as an exhaustive list.
40 Grassroots Asians Rising, "Building a Movement Family: Our Statement," 2018, www.grassrootsasians.org/; GAR, "Asian American Racial Justice Toolkit," grassrootsasians.org. GAR is comprised of, in San Francisco, the Chinese Progressive Association; in Oakland, the Asian Pacific Environmental Network and AYPAL: Building API Community Power; in Providence, RI, Providence Youth Student Movement (PrYSM); in New York City, Desis Rising Up and Moving (DRUM) and CAAAV; and in Charlotte, N C, SEAC Village.
41 "Southeast Asian Activists Urge 'Solidarity with Black People' Post Garner Non-Indictment," *Colorlines*, December 4, 2014, www.colorlines.com/.
42 Freedom Inc., Mekong NYC, PRySM, Vietlead, FIGHT, ManForward, and Minnesota8.
43 CBC's March 2022 program featuring Karen Yamashita, www.youtube.com.
44 I thank Mark Tseng-Putterman for his insightful questions. Taylor Weik, "The History Behind 'Yellow Peril Support Black Power' and Why Some Find It Problematic," *NBC Asian America*, www.nbcnews.com.
45 See, for example, Amy Sueyoshi, "Remembering Asian Pacific American Activism in Queer History," in *Identities and Places: Changing Labels and Intersectional Communities of GLBTQ and Two-Spirit People in the United States*, ed. Katherine Crawford-Lackey and Megan E. Springate (New York: Berghahn Books, 2020), 130–172; Karen Buenavista Hanna, "Being Gay in the KDP: Politics in a Filipino American Revolutionary Organization (1973 to 1986)," *CUNY Forum* 6 (2018): 30–46.

46 Asian Americans for Action, "Time to Kiss the Earth Again," newsletter, October 1969, 9–11. I thank Pam Tau Lee for alerting me to this rare version of the Red Guard Party's platform found in AION (Lee, "The Struggle to Abolish Environmental and Economic Racism: Asian Radical Imagining from the Homeland to the Frontline," in Fujino and Rodriguez, *Contemporary Asian American Activism*).

47 Julie Sze, "Asian American Activism for Environmental Justice," *Peace Review* 16 (2004): 149–156.

48 See, for example, Haunani-kay Trask, "Settler of Color and 'Immigrant' Hegemony: 'Locals' in Hawai'i," *Amerasia Journal* 26 (2000): 1–24; Candace Fujikane and Jonathan Y. Okamura, *Asian Settler Colonialism: From Local Governance to the Habits of Everyday Life in Hawai'i* (Honolulu: University of Hawai'i Press, 2008).

49 Alex T. Tom, "Asians as a Critical Force in the Movement" (unpublished, 2013), 18.

PART I

Refuge and Refusals: Confronting Migrant Detention and Deportation

Dominant U.S. immigration histories often frame the United States as a haven for immigrants and refugees seeking economic opportunity and political freedoms. Traced from the era of Chinese Exclusion and the Asiatic Barred Zone to the present, the history of Asian migration to the United States instead reflects not a progressive march toward national inclusion but a shifting dynamic of inclusion/exclusion shaped by evolving state practices of labor recruitment and exploitation, incarceration, and removal. Contemporary mainstream discussions of migrant rights have failed to present the complexities facing Asian immigrant and refugee communities. For instance, the high visibility of the so-called Dreamer movement in the Obama years solidified an approach to claiming rights that relied on appeals to innocence and the economic and social contributions of undocumented youths—often to the exclusion of adult immigrants and those with criminal records. Yet for many working-class Asian American migrant communities, arrival to the United States represents not a refuge but a new complex of structural violence shaped by the legacies of U.S. imperial wars from Southeast Asia to the Middle East. How then are migrant communities to claim rights from the very state responsible for their conditions of displacement?

Animated by this question, the chapters in this section highlight innovative research and community perspectives that challenge the liberal appeal to political belonging, foregrounding instead the power of transnational solidarity and abolitionist politics in immigrant and refugee communities facing state violence. Loan Dao examines the #Right2Return campaign, tracing how the Southeast Asian Freedom Network has forged transnational solidarities with deported Khmer Americans through the strategic deployment of a human rights framework that transcends legal appeals to the U.S. government. Lakshmi Sridaran documents South Asian Americans Leading Together's decade-long reckoning with caste supremacy and its intersections with deportation, state violence, and community politics between India and the United States—a process that ultimately led to the organization's decision to sunset in 2024. Vichet Chhuon, Ched Nin, and Jenny Srey share critical reflections on their experiences with the ReleaseMN8 campaign, which mobilized Minnesota's multiracial immigrant and refugee community to call for the release of eight Cambodian American refugees detained by Immigration and Customs Enforcement in 2016.

1

The Politics of Transnational Activism in Southeast Asian Deportation

LOAN THI DAO

In 2002, the United States convinced Cambodia to sign a Memorandum of Understanding (MOU) to receive U.S. refugees of Cambodian heritage who had been issued deportation orders. I had just left my job as the director of a youth program for Vietnamese youths in Oakland, California, and started graduate school at the University of California Berkeley. As community leaders, we were very concerned about the potential deportation of Southeast Asian Americans who had come to the United States as refugees or children of refugees. As soon as the deportations began, I knew I had to commit my time as a student researcher to the emergent campaign against deportation. I visited Cambodia for the first time in the summer of 2002, just weeks after the first cohort of deportees arrived, and I felt demoralized. There was very little in terms of a "homecoming" for Khmer American people who had been deported from the United States to a country they only knew as young children or even had never stepped foot on since they were born in refugee camps during the American war in Southeast Asia. They were in Cambodia because of a piece of paper that said Cambodia is their "legal" home, and the United States now viewed them as "surplus." After the government released them from an immigration holding center upon arrival in Phnom Penh, all the exiled Khmer Americans were initially transferred to a transitional house. The house resembled a small bed-and-breakfast compound with two stories of individual rooms laid out like a mahjong table, with a courtyard in the center. This place, Returnee Assistance Program (RAP), was run by an expatriate white American elder who had ties to the country since the Vietnam War era. The first things I noticed on my initial visit was a huge container of Folgers instant coffee, and a group of men playing cards and another group playing dominoes on the cement floor of the courtyard while feral cats wandered the premises. There was a small computer room with a few donated out-of-date computers. One man was waiting for the internet to stop buffering while others sat around listlessly. Lights were out by 10 p.m., and gates were locked for security. The transitional house—meant to provide a familiar space and orientation for exiled Khmer Americans—had instead become a reproduction of the prison system they had left behind in the United States.

Over the years, things began to change. More people arrived, and more people had diverse experiences and relationships with family and friends back in the United States. Some family members of those deported had connected to Southeast Asian American activists in the immigrant rights movement, and some of these activists themselves had friends or family members who were deported. By 2014 there was a critical mass of people in Cambodia who had the linkages, the mental and emotional capacity, and the resources and skills to coordinate with Southeast Asian American activists through a coalition called Southeast Asian Freedom Network (SEAFN). I noticed a different tone of hope and determination, a political analysis, and a readiness to act among the people in Cambodia with whom I kept in communication. One exiled Khmer American summed up what I observed: "We want to change things for people still in the U.S. We still have hope to return, too, and now we meet and we're learning about how to organize. We all have roles and responsibilities." SEAFN members had been going to Cambodia and setting up workshops to teach community organizing skills and build campaign planning initiatives with these folks within the communal spaces of what was the RAP, renamed the Returnee Integration Support Centre (RISC). The seeds of a transnational campaign to end deportation of refugees from the Vietnam War had emerged. With it, these young activists were forging a diasporic identity that shifted the cyclical pathways of "diaspora" and transnational campaigns.

Over forty-five years since the end of the Vietnam War in 1975, the question, "When does a refugee cease to be a refugee?" has resounding salience as the Trump administration (2016–2020) reinstated the deportation of Cambodian refugees and accelerated its efforts to deport refugees from Laos and Vietnam. Toward the end of the Obama administration (2008–2016), Southeast Asian American activists claimed the simultaneity of statelessness as refugees and their "right to stay" while campaigning the United Nations in 2014–2015. This chapter analyzes claims to refugeeism and human rights made by the transnational #Right2Return campaign against the deportation of refugees from the United States to Vietnam, Laos, and Cambodia. I draw on the campaign's public statements, activists' personal documentation of their work, and formal interviews and informal conversations with members of SEAFN, the coalition grassroots network of youth groups that led the campaign. While I attempt to discuss this campaign from an "objective" distance, my analysis is inevitably shaped by my own direct involvement in SEAFN between 2002 and 2006, as well as involvement with various local and national activities of SEAFN member organizations between 2006 and 2017. Drawing from these experiences as an organizer and scholar, I examine the transnational campaign and the complexities of the reliance on juridical determinants to define our human rights, and thus our humanness.

SEAFN's anti-deportation work contributes to the current discourse in Asian American studies on criminalization, detention and deportation, and the conceptualization of rights as articulated through legality in the context of Southeast Asian displacement, migration, and resettlement because of the American War in Southeast Asia.[1] Historian Sam Vong reminds us of the political strategies that have motivated the forced movements of people within and beyond national borders that serve as precedents for contemporary attitudes and policies of deportation:

> Displaced groups were classified by the United States and [South Vietnam] using ever-changing nomenclature of victims, survivors, defectors, evacuees, and refugees, among a variety of other ambiguous and malleable categories. The proliferation of these labels revealed how the category of refugee was unstable and continuously remade as American and South Vietnamese officials tried to make sense of the "refugee problem" and the experiences of displacement. Officials constantly redefined the varied meanings of displacement and sought to reconcile competing understandings of who was and was not a refugee and what these definitions meant for the larger war effort. These military policies and strategies

laid the groundwork for how the American media and military reframed them as heroically "rescuing" them afterward.[2]

Vong's analysis serves as the precursor for what Mimi Thi Nguyen refers to as the "gift of freedom"—a neoliberal relationship characterized by the debt of war and, by extension, freedom as "a revenant, a ruin, a reminder of what has been lost—but debt is also a politics of what is given in its place."[3] Nguyen refers to the contradictory role the United States played in both creating the circumstances of the refugee situation during war and its claim to be the "savior" of those same refugees. That claim inevitably reconstructs the plight of refugees and their resettlement in the United States as one of indebtedness. I suggest that the debt of war, like its memory, takes root in intergenerational transference sometimes too intricate to untangle. As refugee scholars have stressed, the notion of refugeeism as fleeting is based on the temporality and convenience of the receiving state. The notion of accountability in the legal and policy timeline are supplanted with narrative revisions of the American savior who has accepted refugees as a gift of kindness, for which the refugees must repay their debt. These reframings of Southeast Asian American communities and scholarship do more than challenge the inequities of power hierarchies. The stories reveal intersectional identities of race, class, and sexual orientation that occupied a new terrain in social movements and cyclical directions of transnational movements.

Reframing the Debts of War

Since the arrival of many Southeast Asian refugees in the 1970s and 1980s, refugee anti-deportation organizing has marked a political shift in the history of Asian American activism. The anti-war sentiment of the Asian American left during the Vietnam War era contextualized the war as part of a racist endeavor against Asians that traveled from the streets of the United States to those of the Asia-Pacific region. Framed by the ideology of a united Third World Liberation Front, solidarity with the Vietnamese people was generally shared by the Asian American Left in the anti-war movement. Particularly, international solidarity manifested in the analysis of the war as an American imperialist endeavor to control the Asia Pacific similarly to the racist colonization of other parts of the Global South. In contrast, newly arrived refugee leaders saw themselves as the "lucky" ones who had survived war, genocide, and reeducation camps, and were not willing to let go of the American ideals they sacrificed everything to live for. By 2002 these veteran refugee leaders framed their anti-deportation stance as one of anticommunism—that by sending refugees back to communist regimes, the United States was violating refugees' human rights and undermining the legacy of U.S. anticommunist intervention against in the region.

By the early 2000s, Southeast Asian American youths were negotiating discrepancies between the political agenda and messaging of their ethnic communities and their social movement mentors. The #Right2Return campaign demonstrates a new radical refugee positionality that holds both a critical politics of this early generation of activists and the reality of war, imprisonment, torture, and starvation that inform the anticommunism of many refugees in these communities. This generation's "refugee resistance" marks a third space informed by preexisting expectations mapped onto refugee bodies by the debts of war. Their resistance signifies a watershed moment of a generation rising because it marks a new opportunity for a syncretic subject-making that engages with the multiplicity of identities within their generation, remapping the Southeast Asian American diaspora, its relationship to refugee resettlement history, and the academic themes of remembering and reconciliation within the context of social movements. They align with Gary Y. Okihiro's call to return to the international frame of Third World liberation and critique of imperialism in our identity and nation-based activism as an Asian American social movement.[4] Moreover, Southeast Asian American youth activists located themselves at the crossroads of what Cathy Schlund-Vials describes as "a legible set of refugee coordinates that identifies distinct points of U.S. foreign policy, modern Cambodian history, and contemporary Cambodian American survivor memory."[5]

Background on Southeast Asian American Deportation

Out of 2.7 million refugees from Vietnam, Cambodia, and Laos, there are over 14,000 individuals with final orders of removal based on old criminal records for which they have already served their sentences in penitentiaries across the United States. Currently, many languish in Department of Homeland Security detention centers (federal prisons, private prisons, and county jails) throughout the United States. Since 2002, a total of 669 refugees have been deported to Cambodia. Their ages ranged from twenties to nineties, with an average age of thirty-six years. Twelve women have been deported, and the top states from which deportees come from are California, Pennsylvania, Massachusetts, and Washington, in that order. The number of deportations has doubled since 2017.[6] Approximately 1,900 Cambodian Americans have orders of removal. An undetermined number of people are being interviewed by Vietnamese and Laotian government officials to issue documents that would process their deportation. There have been reports of at least eighteen of the over 8,400 eligible refugees deported to Vietnam.[7]

A recent lawsuit in the wake of twelve refugees deported to Vietnam in 2017, *Trinh et al. v. Homan et al.* (2018), has forced the Vietnamese government and ICE to state they will adhere to their MOU and will release detainees after the ninety-day legal maximum for detention of an individual who cannot be removed.[8] There are currently 4,568 Laotian nationals with deportation orders, and the Trump administration threatened Laos and Myanmar with visa sanctions if they did not agree to accept deportees from the United States.[9] In recent years, SEAFN organizers have collaborated with policy and legal advocates, particularly from Asian Americans Advancing Justice and Southeast Asian Resource Action Center to vacate the criminal cases of certain individuals, which opens the door for judges to revoke deportation orders and individuals to return to the United States. Activists have worked tirelessly to advocate for pardons from governors and have effectively leveraged the political power of those eligible to vote as well as influence through coalitions to gain these victories. In many ways, they have been successful in the turn toward an internationalized campaign that includes a multipronged approach to challenge the criminal justice system as a pathway for exiled Americans to return home to the United States.

Immigration policies since the late twentieth century have removed the stigma of refugee removals by framing them as criminal immigrants who have lost the rights and protections inherent to the notion of refugeeism.[10] An estimated one-half of those with final orders of removal came to the United States as childhood arrivals.[11] Some were born in refugee camps in Thailand, the Philippines, and other first asylum countries, but were identified as Cambodian, Laotian, or Vietnamese nationals based on their parents' citizenship status, or simply by mistake in the bureaucratic application process. Many have only a minimal understanding of the vernacular language and have few or no familial relations in these countries. Approximately one-third are now in their mid- to late twenties, are parents, and are main sources of income for their families. They have all served their sentences in some form (probation, actual time, or payment of fines), and many have served or are serving extended time in immigration detention centers (state, federal, or private prisons) because they are noncitizens convicted of aggravated felonies and are deportable.[12] Their crimes range from attempted murder to violating probation by urinating in public. According to public defenders and lawyers who regularly represent Southeast Asian clients, common violations include dating a minor, welfare fraud, grand theft auto, and armed robbery. Specifically for Southeast Asian refugee youths, their new label as the model minority "stepcousin" accentuates the fickleness of the state to choose when to frame refugees as those "deserving" of rights or as those who can be disposed of through the legal removal of their inclusion within the landscape of citizenry.

Eighty percent of those slated for deportation to these Southeast Asian countries fall into the category of criminal removals, compared to just 29 percent of the overall removable population. This is due to the expansion of the 1996 immigration reforms including the Antiterrorism and Effective Death Penalty Act, which removed the authority of immigration judges to determine deportation status on a case-by-case basis through independent judicial review. The Illegal Immigration Reform and Immigrant Responsibility Act of 1996 then required all noncitizens convicted of "aggravated felony" to be mandatorily deported; it also expanded the definition of "aggravated felony" to include convictions carrying sentences of more than one year or a fine over $5,000. It also allowed the act to apply retroactively. Finally, the Welfare Reform Act of 1996 required that one be naturalized as a citizen to receive general assistance benefits.[13] The Clinton administration enacted these laws during a national wave of "tough on crime" state policies sentencing youths under age eighteen as adults, which landed many in a cycle of recidivism.[14] The post–September 11 national hysteria then became the justification for immigration constrictions that extended the hyper-criminalization of racialized bodies into the immigration enforcement system. In essence, Southeast Asian refugee youths were upheld as the embodiment of a revisionist historiography where failed U.S. foreign policy transformed into the familiar trope of the American savior. When the refugee youths were no longer politically useful, they were forgotten as remnants of war.

Refugees act as a fluid backdrop that shift from sharp focus to blurred masses in the background of a national consciousness as is expedient to the political moment. They have been disposable subjects of the state. After almost fifty years of navigating through the political waters to advocate for their communities, a new generation of Southeast Asian American leaders reject America's revisionist and victim-blaming history of refugee resettlement.

Generation Rising

The Southeast Asian Freedom Network (SEAFN) originally formed in 2002, dispersed in 2006, and reemerged in 2013. In 2002 the national policy group Southeast Asian Resource Action Center (SEARAC) held a series of national calls to educate community leaders and social service providers about the impending deportation of Cambodian nationals. These calls inspired the Committee Against Anti-Asian Violence (CAAAV) in New York to host a convening of Southeast Asian American youth groups to strategize a response to the detention conditions and deportations. The youth groups emerged from this weekend as SEAFN, a national network of organizations that would regularly communicate and coordinate activities and messaging against the deportations. By 2006 the local campaigns to halt individual deportation cases were not successful, and funders lost interest in these "losing" battles. SEAFN was no longer active due to a lack of capacity by member groups, which had turned to local campaigns. Over the next few years, some of the original youth groups disbanded, and new ones emerged with new energy and resources, including 1Love Movement in Philadelphia in 2010, which was mentored by movement elders from Asian Americans United (AAU) in the 1980s and funded by SEARAC to revitalize the anti-deportation work. In 2013, Vietnamese American Youth of Louisiana (VAYLA), a youth group that grew from organizing efforts in the New Orleans East Vietnamese American community post-Katrina, received a grant from the Kellogg Foundation to convene Asian American youth groups. During this gathering, several of the Southeast Asian American youth groups that were affiliated with the original SEAFN felt marginalized by the dominance of East Asian American, college-educated, middle-class activists. In response, they rejuvenated SEAFN over this weekend, with a vision to develop a sustained grassroots social movement led by and for Millennial and Generation Z Southeast Asian American working-class intersectional youths. SEAFN's most notable campaign, #Right2Return, has been against the detention and deportation of community members who had arrived as refugees due to American violence in their familial countries of origin.

Between 2006 and 2013, SEAFN youth groups continued to engage in member exchanges, where their youths would visit each other's organizations to build relationships and solidarity among their members. In addition, the staff and leaders would attend each other's major events or actions and would meet among themselves to strategize how to continue to support each other and share resources. Finally, individual leaders began to travel to Cambodia to meet with exiled Khmer Americans. These visits eventually led to workshops to train deportees with organizing skills, the formalization of the organized group of exiled members into 1Love Cambodia, and a documentary video where members of SEAFN, national leaders, and exiled members were interviewed, to be released in segments as a social media campaign. Simultaneously, the dialogue across these spaces led organizers to question what it would mean to challenge deportation on an international scale. SEAFN leveraged their social capital, or relationships, with distant relatives who had access to the Cambodian government and with activists across movements who were pressuring the United Nations. These events dovetailed into synchronous activities that comprised the tactics of a transnational campaign. Their strategy was to pressure the Cambodian government to reject the U.S. pressures to accept deportees and plead the UN to recognize the rights of Southeast Asian refugees to stay in the United States and the right for those deported to reopen their cases to return. Upon the completion of their international tour to create the documentary and their international trips, SEAFN launched the #Right2Return campaign with the incremental releases of their videos.

Declaring Statelessness and Rightlessness through Human Rights Law

After the newly formed United Nations put forth its Declaration of Human Rights in 1948, Black civil rights activists presented to this body a petition, "We Charge Genocide," in an attempt to ask the international body to protect against the state-sanctioned human rights violations of Black people in the United States throughout its history.[15] Social justice activists today have increasingly found inspiration in that historical petition, turning to the United Nations as an international platform for shaming the United States on its domestic policies, including incarceration and immigration enforcement. Asian Americans and Pacific Islanders (AAPI) and U.S.-based immigrant rights organizations, such as Desis Rising Up and Moving (DRUM) and the National Network for Immigrant and Refugee Rights (NNIRR), have testified at UN conventions on the state of the United States' treatment of racial minorities, immigrants, poor people, imprisoned people, and youths. After SEAFN members educated themselves on other historical campaigns that appealed to international law, they began to strategize with 1Love Cambodia on their campaign demands to the United Nations. With the support of these immigrant rights organizations, Southeast Asian American activist organizations were able to send their own representatives to the United Nations High Commission for Refugees (UNHCR) meetings. Three activists representing three different organizations within SEAFN traveled to Geneva, Switzerland, in March 2015 to represent SEAFN's transnational campaign to end deportation and allow for the return of deportees based on the claim that their rights as refugees had been violated under international laws protecting refugees. Chhaya Chhuom of Mekong in New York, Naroen Chhin of 1Love Movement in Philadelphia, and Chanravy Proeung of Providence Youth Student Movement (PrYSM) were invited to meet privately with UN representatives and share the experiences of unjust detention and deportation of Southeast Asian refugees and their demands to this international body in the hope it would pressure the United States into legislative recourse. Chanravy shared, "It was a lot. There were all these government people, and there was us. We got to talk about what it was like to be refugees and how the U.S. had forgotten about us. We wanted them to make [the U.S. government] take responsibility for what happened when we got here. And people listened, but that doesn't mean they will do anything." And in fact, the UN representatives expressed support for the plight of refugee exiled Americans from the Vietnam War, but no action was ever taken to pressure or hold the U.S. government accountable. As another part of their multipronged strategy, a small group of SEAFN members then traveled to Cambodia to meet with governmental leadership to ask them not to accept new deportees while they asked the United Nations to pressure the United States to release detainees.

SEAFN developed demands based on the UN Declaration of Human Rights to claim that the U.S. immigration system had violated their rights to protections as refugees:

> *Universal Declaration of Human Rights, Article 26. Right to Education, & Article 7. Right to Equality Before the Law*: Most Southeast Asian refugees were resettled into inhumane conditions in impoverished neighborhoods, making us vulnerable to poverty, crime, violence, structural disadvantage, racism, discrimination, and profiling. Many young people fell through the cracks in an under-resourced education system unfit to meet their needs, leaving only 65% of Cambodian-American youth graduating from high school. Many enter a highly functional and highly funded School-to-Prison Pipeline. Law enforcement agencies in cities across the country began coding Cambodian communities as "gang infested" and we were surveilled and profiled for arrest and incarceration. Over-policing of our community led to racial profiling, police brutality, and high incarceration rates, higher than any other Asian ethnic group in relation to the size of our population.[16]

The activists claimed that as childhood arrivals, they had the right to the international rights of safety, security, and education. It was a remarkable claim to correct historical injustice in the contemporary moment, posing refugee youths as global citizens worthy of rights and opportunity. Instead of providing educational attainment as a means of socioeconomic integration for refugee youths, they argued that the legal system targeted the youths in hyper-criminalized neighborhoods, as "mass incarceration served a political purpose ... served an economic purpose . . . [and] an ideological purpose" for politicians to claim to be "tough on crime."[17]

The second demand calls for the youths to be recognized as equal members of society through due process and fairness in the judiciary process:

> *Universal Declaration of Human Rights, Article 10. Right to Due Process, Article 16. Right to Family Unity, & Article 9. Right to Freedom from Arbitrary Arrest, Detention, Exile*: In 1996, the US passed the Illegal Immigration Reform and Immigrant Responsibility Act (IIRIRA) and Antiterrorism and Effective Death Penalty Act (AEDPA). . . . Deportation for "aggravated felonies" also became permanent with no right to return, and was applied retroactively, leading to international human rights violations regarding proportionality of punishment, double jeopardy, and fairness under the law.

This statement juxtaposes international human rights against national policy, with implicit weight placed on the UN articles over the U.S. 1996 immigration reforms. Ironically, SEAFN's strategy uses the same pillars of the criminal justice system, due process and fairness, that are fundamental to a democracy. The violation of one's ability to undergo fair trial, equal treatment, and due process contradicts the ability to claim democracy when those within it can legally and systematically be expelled from its defining characteristics. In fact, it is comparable to how Junaid Rana (2011) describes the use of "illegality" as "a condition of political subjectivity that places migrants outside of the law. . . . [It] is a political identity and subjectivity that is produced through the state and iterated as a social construct that establishes a moral public sphere of regulation."[18]

Finally, the activists invoke the global hegemony of the United States as itself a violation of a universal standard for respect between countries in their right to govern, and thus to exist without a forced relationality to the dominant power:

> *Universal Declaration of Human Rights, Article 21. Right to Democracy* On March 22, 2002, the US signed a Repatriation Agreement with Cambodia and began deporting Cambodian-Americans. . . . As such, the creation of such agreements must be done through transparent, open, and

democratic processes that prioritize the will of the people and insight of directly impacted communities.

The U.S.-born and U.S.-raised activists with individual or collective memory of trauma from oppressive regimes now called upon the receiving nation to respect these countries' right to self-determination. Their choice to include the argument that upholds state power and rights as an extension of refugee visibility as human subjects worthy of rights draws on the notion of self-determination across geography into a cross-border existence that embeds the person simultaneously within and beyond the nation-state. It reiterates Bill Ong Hing's interpretation of immigration policy in the post-9/11 period as a normalization of hegemonic rule: "We have come to accept the punishment and exclusion of people from other lands ... even though our better instincts tell us to recognize the interdependency of national economies, workforces, and environmental practices."[19] The connotation in Hing's assertion lays bare the very essence of the appeal to the United Nations by oppressed groups toward their governments: the experience of being denied recognition as a human subject by a hegemonic state through its enforcement arms of surveillance, courts, and policing.

Based on these articles of the Declaration of Human Rights and the UNHCR's declaration on the rights of refugees, SEAFN's campaign demanded a rearticulation of the M.O.U. between Cambodia and the United States. The activists argued that any new M.O.U. agreements between Laos and the United States should resemble the five-year pilot program with Vietnam signed in 2008, which only allows immigrants post-1995 to the United States from Vietnam—not refugees—to be deported, and that the current M.O.U. with Vietnam be renewed with the same criteria for removal. The activists believed that these new negotiations would allow for current deportees to appeal their cases for expedited return to the United States, in what SEAFN referred to as the "right to return."

This transnational campaign called for the international governing body to address the concerns of what it considered to be a basic human right of mobility. That strategy seems perfectly logical for historically marginalized people who feel they have no influence with their own governments and that those governments are in fact the perpetrators of violence. Yet, they risked relying on a judicial system to define the inherent rights of humans to rely on systems of hegemonic power to confer *human-ness*, and by the same token, also render a person more vulnerable to dehumanization by the very system ostensibly created to protect the embodiment of what constitutes humanity. From SEAFN's perspective, by employing the international body of law as a strategic rallying point for its campaign, SEAFN subversively used the arm of state power against itself. The organization upended an international arm of U.S. hegemonic power by using the myth of American exceptionalism as a morally superior government against them. SEAFN condemned both American immigration policy in the contemporary moment and the root causes that uprooted migrants in the first place— in this case, American militarism and intrusion into their homelands. However important the theoretical debate of legality and its problematic role in defining humanity, Southeast Asian American youths used international law "for the practice [of] oppositional politics [that] is squarely situated both in and against these relationships of power in [their] challenge to the duplicitous forms of domination and affirmation."[20] They viewed American immigration admissions and enforcement policies as an extension of historical imperialist tendencies that were masked as domestic policy. The youth organizers manipulated the international stage to assume a counter-hegemonic stance that at once aligned with the democratic values their co-ethnic elders held dearly as part of their new American identity, while publicly holding the United States accountable for its failed policies at the cost of human life as its movement elders had done during the Vietnam War.

The #Right2Return campaign's proposed M.O.U. would allow anyone deported to Cambodia to petition for return to the United States if their criminal cases had been vacated or due to a family hardship protection that considered the contributions and economic hardships one's deportation had on family members. The activists articulated their demands as follows regarding the most immediate issue of Cambodian deportation:

> We call for immediate recourse to begin to rectify over five decades of U.S. human rights violations that have torn Cambodian families apart from Cambodia to the U.S., and back again:

1. We call for an immediate suspension of United States' deportations to Cambodia.
2. We call for an open review process of the United States–Cambodia Repatriation Agreement, which includes and prioritizes democratic oversight and input of impacted communities in the United States and Cambodia.
3. We call for amendments to the Repatriation Agreement that tailor its impacts to consider the individual and community experience of U.S. human rights violations and will protect those with these experiences from deportation.
4. We call for amendments to the Repatriation Agreement that ensure humane, just, and fair structures of support for impacted families and individuals in the United States and Cambodia, including economic stability, human and social services, employment infrastructure, visitation rights, and the right to return.[21]

These demands represent claims for the right to exist within and beyond borders, of the right to self-expressed identities, and of the right to claim protections from those in power. To these activists, the articulation of their rights as an inherent entitlement beyond borders reasserted their humanity against a backdrop of historical imagery as blurred masses fleeing war or the criminal "stepcousins" of Asian American model minority. Both images allow for a redaction of identity to assume their disposability in the national conscience.

Over the next two years, SEAFN representatives continued to attend the United Nations conventions and travel back to Cambodia. Through their own social networks, they were able to identify new and build upon existing relationships with exiled Khmer Americans as 1Love Cambodia. They continued to organize popular education workshops with deportees in which they shared their stories and developed a critical analysis of how their individual narratives fit into the larger analysis of the U.S. historical involvement in Southeast Asia. Borom, one of the 1Love Cambodia organizers, remembers:

> Mia-Lia and her friends narrowed down about seven or eight of us, and since she's related to one of the guys [through marriage of a relative], she had a lot of legitimacy with us. She gave us a lot of structure; we each

had formal roles, like I was head of policy because I like to be behind the scenes. Wicked is the spokesperson; Sophea organizes the other deportees because she's good with people.... [Mia-Lia] knew our traits and gave us our roles like that. She channeled our energies and gave all of us a lot of hope again.

On average, they recruited between twenty and thirty deportees to the meetings. The exiled Khmer Americans, physically in Cambodia and figuratively in the hyper-criminalized neighborhoods of the United States, forged a diasporic American refugee identity beyond borders.[22] Gradually, however, the funding for their transnational trainings and visits decreased, and the shifts in governmental regimes in Southeast Asia and in the United States after 2016 forced them to refocus on the continual urgencies of a multipronged attack on progressive values and agendas, including immigration raids and aggressive enforcement.

The historic transnational coordination between the organic group of deportees led by 1Love Cambodia and SEAFN catalyzed a new generation of activists in the SEAA community beyond the anticommunist movements of the older generation of activists.[23] As the campaign dissolved, the power relations between the movement actors were never really unpacked to consider the impact of the transitions domestically, even while they were able to win individual cases for the return of some exiled Khmer Americans.[24] SEAFN's concerted efforts to highlight the voices of directly affected individuals, and its commitment to educate exiled Khmer Americans at training workshops in Phnom Penh, gestured toward a consciousness of those power relations. As members put it, it was a means to "give voice" to those rendered invisible in the immigration process. Yet, with the 2016 presidential election and the rise of human rights violations and suppression of dissent in Southeast Asia, including Cambodia and Vietnam, U.S.-based activists were forced to rethink their global strategy in ways that might contradict the political alliances or preferences of deportees in those countries.[25]

SEAFN's well-intentioned vision and the actualization of that vision places in relief the complexities of the politics of intersectional power within co-ethnic communities, domestically and transnationally. The priorities of a movement that challenged the carceral state's exploitation and destruction of racialized bodies on an international scale required a strategic alignment with a Cambodian government that has not historically expressed any radical departure from the ideologies of a capitalist state. It also meant a framing of the United States as a desired place to return to while simultaneously critiquing the conditions of refugee life in resettlement. For SEAFN and 1Love Cambodia, it risked offering a critique of the U.S. carceral state while ignoring similar issues within Cambodia to partner with the government in a relationship of interest convergence to return exiled Khmer Americans. For some of the SEAFN activists, their transnational relationship forced them to rethink their positionality for the first time. One member who went on these trips reflected that they "always shamed people in the U.S. for looking down on our neighborhoods, and here I was back in Southeast Asia acting a [diva] and not eating street food and all that." Another SEAFN activist brought up how they were "shaking" before they entered the meeting with government officials in Cambodia because "they could arrest us" at will and "no one would stop them," expressing assumptions commonly held in the West that the governments of developing countries tend not to uphold the "rule of law." When I asked how 1Love Cambodia members felt about the SEAFN organizers trying to work with them, deportees felt favorably about the relationship and the promise of a transnational movement where they were heard and had purpose. According to Borom, the relationship was positive overall:

> At least we're at the point where something is being done, something is being talked about. I tell [SEAFN], the power struggle is not with White America, it's in our own community. Now you have a younger generation [of SEAA] who want to push for equality, and we can see them coming up and more people understanding. Intrinsically, they have a lot more compassion [than the previous SEAA generation]; their hearts are in the right place. They're not willing to accept the status quo. They're willing to fight for it. And they are searching for their roots when they come here, so that shows they care. I don't get arrogance from them like a lot of the NGO people who come here.

SEAFN activists gave 1Love Cambodia the tools to organize, but they still had to overcome differences in perspectives on deportation that were critical to building a transnational campaign. SEAFN activists and exiled Khmer Americans bonded quickly because many of them came from the same or similar neighborhoods in the United States. They were entwined in communal relationships back in the United States that legitimized the activists to the exiled community and made it easier to both trust them and hold them accountable, but some people developed a different view of the United States after deportation. For example, Borom made it clear that many deportees had mixed feelings about returning to the United States: "Our goal is different from the people in the U.S. We want to stop the bleeding [of deportations], but we're also realistic about returning. I have kids here now, and I wouldn't want them to go through the judgment and racism that I did in the United States. In Cambodia, they are loved." Borom recognized the simultaneity of transnational justice through his personal experience of deportation, but his political consciousness made him critical of the American dream and the reality of what it meant to be a racialized immigrant child in America. While the exiled community and SEAFN activists came to have a shared understanding of their refugee histories and the role of the American government in their current situation, the responses required an uneasy alliance that would require putting aside such violations at the time in Cambodia to pressure the United States. Moreover, as Borom revealed, the campaign for the *right* to return is complicated by people who had begun to view the United States from an internationalist standpoint critical of race relations and racism historically embedded in the American social fabric.

Reframing Refugee Resettlement

The #Right2Return campaign forces a reframing of the savior narrative of the United States by holding the state accountable for the long-term impacts of refugee migration and resettlement. It begs the question of the responsibility of the state to its refugee populations whose refugee subjectivity is a direct result of the resettlement country's involvement in their countries of origin. To the other end of the spectrum on the discourse on state renderings on subjectivity of bodies, Lisa Marie Cacho demonstrates how people of color have been historically subjugated to a "social death" by the state's rendering of them as outside the law and its inherent protections. The forced social location of these individuals gives the state, through the legal system, absolute power to define the person and the boundaries of their humanity as a claim for protection and recognition. SEAFN's transnational campaign against deportation reappropriated this dehumanization frame in its members' efforts to stake claim to personhood in the realm of universal human rights, thus proclaiming a repudiation of the state's right to affirm or reject their personhood. Their claims to the inalienable rights of personhood require the international community to simultaneously recognize their presence, their stories, and their identities to make judgment on their "humanity." It forces the international community to question a country's legal practice of human rights as well as define rights and rightlessness at the same time; as Naomi A. Paik suggests, it points to the contradictory simultaneous invisibility and hypervisibility of those excluded from the national political imaginary in the United States through containment of embodied threats.[26] However, the same strategic frame of the #Right2Return campaign compels us to then ruminate on the potential pitfalls of relying on any legal body to define, and thus potentially reject, the concept of human-ness and its inherent "rights." Samera Esmeir compels us to examine the broader stakes of making claims for rights at all through juridical decisions, including international bodies, such that this hegemonic entity has the power to both create and destroy the bare essence of what is human.[27] The #Right2Return campaign echoes these competing implications of appealing to the legal system to claim one's human rights. While the campaign was truncated by the election of Donald Trump and his administration's explicitly racial anti-immigrant stance, it has forced a new stage of growth and reflection in how the immigrant rights movement, and particularly the movement against Southeast Asian American deportation, must strategically articulate its relationship with domestic and international legal apparatuses.

While the anti-deportation campaign became the signature accomplishment of SEAFN, its members have faced a set of ethical challenges that have come with their empowerment as transnational actors. They embarked on a new road that they needed to pave for themselves. Their social media strategy was founded on the goal of humanizing the individuals who had been or were facing deportation, as well as introducing activists as ordinary community members to counter media perceptions that activists were radical fringes of society. SEAFN grounded its campaign in the unwavering belief that collective suffering had a direct causal relationship to American human rights violations during wartime and in resettlement, thus interpreting the concept of human rights as based in a universally assumed morality rather than a manifestation and exercise of legal determination. More recently, SEAFN has formalized its structure as a national network, with many of the original leaders of member groups assuming paid leadership roles in SEAFN. They are currently leading the Southeast Asian Relief and Responsibility (SEARR) campaign, a national policy platform with two main priorities: (1) to support national legislation that holds the United States accountable for its past involvement in the war and refugee crisis in Vietnam, Laos, and Cambodia, and (2) to provide immediate relief for Southeast Asian Americans impacted by immigration policies and enforcement. These legislative priorities include support for the Victims of Agent Orange Relief Act (H.R. 3518), the Legacies of War and Unexploded Ordinance Removal Act (H.R. 9540/S. 3795), the New Way Forward Act (H.R. 2374), and the Southeast Asian Deportation Relief Act, a historic bill for refugees that provides immediate relief from enforcement policies, encourages work authorization, and establishes a pathway to return for Southeast Asian refugees who have been deported.

Conclusion

The achievements of SEAFN's transnational campaign went without much acknowledgment as a historic moment in transnational activism for Asian Americans. The Asian American activism of the 1960s and 1970s is "a usable past for Asian Americans who dream of a more just world recuperating this history of commitment and struggle." Contemporary activism "not only gives the lie to the myth of Asian American compliance but also provides building of multiethnic, interracial, and transnational sympathies and alliances."[28] SEAFN's ability to transform its campaign against detention and deportation from local and domestic foci to a transnational one adds to the trend of social movement emphasis in immigrant rights as technology and resources help build the transnational ties, skills, and resources between deportees, their families, and immigrant rights activists. The transformation of the movement inevitably changed the narrative framing of SEAFN's campaign as well as targets and allies within the campaign from local to international and multi-sited. Claims to a diasporic identity had to be coalesced with claims for rights within the United States, and the human rights approach helped organizers do this. They then had to reconsider their power analysis of allies and targets of their campaign from the perspective of international politics, to which they clearly drew from the history of Asian American internationalists of earlier generations who viewed the United States as an empire rather than a savior bestowing gifts.[29] Thus, the Southeast Asian governments became potential allies in this campaign to pressure the American government to end deportations of refugees as an exertion of its hegemonic global power. As refugees from war who fled their homelands for fear of persecution, Millennial and Gen Z activists' strategic choices to frame the campaign as one of rights protected under international law draws on Cacho's call for a response to this system of racialized rightlessness to move beyond "realistic" approaches and instead "to be critical of what makes us vulnerable to state violence *and* what makes us susceptible to the state's seductions."[30] These activists respond to Cacho's call in their claim to a persistent refugee condition as a counter-hegemonic position to uphold legal personhood as embodied humanity in the face of institutional erasure.

In the four decades since the end of the American war in Vietnam, Laos, and Cambodia, refugees who fled the war and its aftermath face a fundamental crisis of identity. Since the critical mass of refugee immigration in 1975, the narrative of gratitude toward the United States harboring stateless people fleeing persecution has dominated the national discourse and refugee community sentiment. To the United States, they have ceased to be refugees. The new generations of Southeast Asian American activists, many of whom were born and raised in the United States, have articulated a complex argument that both claims and rejects their refugee identity. In appealing to the United Nations based on their communities' rights *as refugees*, they claim a persistent social location at the margins, if not beyond, the national imaginary that ironically justifies their claims within the state legal apparatus. By framing their claims as *human rights*, they stake claim to an international institution to their humanity beyond legal appellation while simultaneously asking for their humanity to be validated and defined through the law.

Moreover, they harken back to the racial justice movements before them that helped define the uniqueness of America. They navigated between the multiplicity of the identities they collectively claim as refugees, Americans, and subjects beyond the state in their articulation of their inherent rights. Over forty-five years later, the refugee's rights become human rights that transcend legality.

Notes

Names in this chapter are pseudonyms to protect the identity of individual interviewees.

1 For further reading, see Loan Thi Dao, *Generation Rising: A New Politics of Southeast Asian Activism* (Berkeley, CA: Eastwind Books, 2020); Bill Ong Hing, *Deporting Our Souls: Values, Morality, and Immigration Policy* (New York: Cambridge University Press, 2006); Lisa Marie Cacho, *Social Death: Racialized Rightlessness and the Criminalization of the Unprotected* (New York: New York University Press, 2012); Soo Ah Kwon, *Uncivil Youth: Race, Activism, and Affirmative Governmentality* (Durham, NC: Duke University Press, 2013).
2 Sam Vong, "Assets of War: Strategic Displacements, Population Movements, and the Uses of Refugees during the Vietnam War, 1965–1973," *Journal of American Ethnic History* 39:3 (2020): 75–100.
3 Mimi Thi Nguyen, *The Gift of Freedom: War, Debt, and Other Refugee Passages* (Durham, NC: Duke University Press, 2012).
4 Gary Okihiro, *Third World Studies: Theorizing Liberation* (Durham: Duke University Press, 2024).
5 Cathy Schlund-Vials, *War, Genocide, and Justice: Cambodian American Memory Work* (Minneapolis: University of Minnesota Press, 2012).
6 Returnee Integration Support Center, Cambodia. https://risccambodia.wordpress.com.
7 Department of Homeland Security (DHS) Immigration Statistics 2016 for Removals with Criminal Records.
8 *Trinh et al. v. Homan et al.*, 8:18-cv-00316 (CA 2018).
9 Loan Dao, "We Will Not Be Moved" (PhD diss., University of California, Berkeley, 2009).
10 The UN's definition of refugee under Article 1.A.2 is "[a person] is outside the country of his nationality and is unable or, owing to such fear, is unwilling to avail himself of the protection of that country; or who, not having a nationality and being outside the country of his former habitual residence as a result of such events, is unable or, owing to such fear, is unwilling to return to it." United Nations General Assembly resolution 429(V), December 14, 1950, www.unhcr.org.
11 Dao, "We Will Not Be Moved."
12 Ibid.

13 Hing, *Deporting Our Souls*.
14 Victor Rios, *Human Targets: Schools, Police, and the Criminalization of Latino Youth* (Chicago: University of Chicago Press, 2017).
15 N. J. Lee, D. V. Shah, and J. M. McLeod, "Processes of Political Socialization: A Communication Mediation Approach to Youth Civic Engagement," *Communication Research* 40:5 (2013): 669–697; Francesca Polletta, *It Was Like a Fever: Storytelling in Protest and Politics* (Chicago: University of Chicago Press, 2006); Lauren Langman, "From Virtual Public Spheres to Global Justice: A Critical Theory of Internetworked Social Movements," *Sociological Theory* 23, no. 1 (2005): 42–74.
16 SEAFN public list of demands for the Right2Return campaign, 2014.
17 Tanya Marie Golash-Boza, *Deported: Immigrant Policing, Disposable Labor, and Global Capitalism* (New York: New York University Press, 2015), 203.
18 Junaid Rana, *Terrifying Muslims: Race and Labor in the South Asian Diaspora* (Durham, NC: Duke University Press, 2011), 140.
19 Hing, *Deporting Our Souls*, 212.
20 Soo Ah Kwon, *Uncivil Youth: Race, Activism, and Affirmative Governmentality* (Durham: Duke University Press, 2013), 129.
21 SEAFN Press Release, "Forty Years Later: U.S. Human Rights Violations & the Deportation of Cambodian-American Refugees," March 18, 2015, https://1lovemovement.wordpress.com.
22 Eric Tang, *Unsettled: Cambodian Refugees in the New York City Hyperghetto* (Philadelphia: Temple University Press, 2016).
23 For more on transnational and diasporic movements to overthrow communist regimes in Laos, Cambodia, and Vietnam, see Kieu-Linh Valverde, *Transnationalizing Viet Nam: Community, Culture, and the Politics in the Diaspora* (Philadelphia: Temple University Press, 2012); Karin Aguilar-San Juan, *Little Saigon: Staying Vietnamese in America* (Minneapolis: University of Minnesota Press, 2009); Tuyen Tran, "Behind the Smoke and Mirrors: The Vietnamese in California, 1975–1994" (PhD diss., University of California, Berkeley, 2007); Jeremy Hein, *From Vietnam, Laos, and Cambodia: A Refugee Experience in the United States* (New York: Twayne Publications, 1995).
24 Sidney Tarrow, *The New Transnational Activism* (Cambridge, UK: Cambridge University Press, 2005).
25 Santino F. Regilme Salvador, "The Decline of American Power and Donald Trump: Reflections on Human Rights, Neoliberalism, and the World Order," *Geoforum* 102 (2019): 157–166.
26 Naomi A. Paik, *Rightlessness: Testimony and Redress in U.S. Prison Camps since World War II* (Chapel Hill: University of North Carolina Press, 2016); Ana Y. Ramos-Zayas, *National Performances: The Politics of Class, Race, and Space in Puerto Rican Chicago* (Chicago: University of Chicago Press, 2003); Marjorie Orellana, Barrie Thorne, Anna Chee, Wan Shun Eva Lam, "Transnational Childhoods: The Participation of Children in Processes of Family Migration,"

Social Problems 48:4 (2001): 572–591; Herbert J. Gans, "Second Generation Decline: Scenarios for the Economic and Ethnic Futures of the Post-1965 American Immigrants," *Ethnic and Racial Studies* 15:2 (1992): 173–192.
27 Samera Esmeir, *Juridical Humanity: A Colonial History* (Stanford, CA: Stanford University Press, 2012).
28 Daryl Meada, *Chains of Babylon: The Rise of Asian America* (Minneapolis: University of Minnesota Press, 2009), 157.
29 Mimi Thi Nguyen, *The Gift of Freedom: War, Debt, and Other Refugee Passages* (Durham, NC: Duke University Press, 2012).
30 Cacho, *Social Death*, 145.

2

From Accessing Power to Generating Power

SAALT's Decade of Transformation (2014–2024)

LAKSHMI SRIDARAN

After twenty-four years in existence, South Asian Americans Leading Together (SAALT) dissolved as an organization at the end of 2024. This chapter reflects on three critical phases in SAALT's evolution during its last ten years before sunsetting, during which I served as policy director, executive director, and co-director.

1. As an organization catalyzed by the historic level of interpersonal hate violence against Muslim, Arab, and South Asian American communities following September 11, 2001, SAALT helped increase the visibility of this violence by working with the federal government to provide both resources and pathways to recourse rooted in policy reform. Working on policy reform to address hate violence allowed SAALT to understand the connection with other policy issues like racial profiling and immigration. After SAALT's first decade of gaining and maintaining access to federal policymakers to advocate for policy reform in hate violence, racial profiling, and immigration, we shifted our strategy to challenging the systems and structures of racism upheld by our government through federal policy. Federal policy on the issues of hate violence, racial profiling, and immigration have overwhelmingly focused on criminalization, whether through enhanced sentencing for hate crimes, mass surveillance programs, or increased deportations and migrant detention. This moved SAALT away from seeing the state as the solution, and instead as a primary driver of the problem.
2. Beginning in 2015, when Indian grandfather Sureshbhai Patel was brutally assaulted by a local police officer who racialized him

as a Black man, SAALT was forced to further question the state, and our organizational history of building relationships with law enforcement to create safety for our communities. Despite the overwhelming evidence, two mistrials in the case against the police officer led to an acquittal.[1] This alarming community wake-up call to the racism embedded within our legal system led SAALT to adopt a racial justice framework that placed South Asian American experiences of injustice alongside other communities of color. However, we did not integrate our adaptation of a racial justice framework with acknowledgment, inquiry, or understanding of how caste shapes the identity and privilege of every South Asian. Because we believed that caste had no impact on South Asian communities in the United States, we never confronted the oldest barrier to organizing across a deep diversity of South Asian communities. As a result, we homogenized the disparate impacts of hate violence, racial profiling, and immigration across lines of caste, failing to fully serve the organization's pan–South Asian mandate. Beginning in 2019, we finally started listening to the long-standing assertions of Dalit, Bahujan, and Adivasi (caste-oppressed) South Asian communities that caste is not only alive in the diaspora but impacts how our institutions serve and create belonging for caste-oppressed populations. In 2020 the SAALT staff committed to integrating an anti-caste lens to SAALT's policy and programming work.

3. For three years, we attempted to radically reshape SAALT's programming and policy work in hate violence, racial profiling, and immigration in an effort to align with values of caste abolition (ending discrimination on the basis of caste). However, doing this in the absence of an internal reckoning of SAALT's organizational culture forced us to question how we could engage externally with an emerging analysis of caste without first understanding caste relationally at the level of self, staff, and board inside of an organization that had always been run by high-caste South Asians. In 2022 the SAALT staff and board, which had Dalit leadership for the first time in the organization's history, voted to transform SAALT into an anti-caste institution.

This chapter analyzes SAALT's decade-long shift from utilizing a traditional legal and policy advocacy framework to a racial justice framework that connects state and interpersonal violence, culminating with SAALT's recognition of caste as a distinctly powerful, cultural construct that shapes all South Asians and the policy issues impacting our community. The chapter concludes by considering the possibilities of further transformation outside of both the state and nonprofit institutions.

The Cost of Maintaining Access to Power

While SAALT's policy and advocacy objectives following 9/11 narrowly focused on addressing individual acts of backlash by developing stronger ties to U.S. government agencies and law enforcement, grassroots organizations like Desis Rising Up and Moving (DRUM) and Justice for Muslims Collective (which has since transitioned into two separate organizations: Muslims for Just Futures and Muslim Counterpublics Lab) offered a comprehensive and rigorous analysis of America's War on Terror as not just a foreign project of war and imperialism but also a domestic project tied to the prison industrial complex.[2] Their work, firmly rooted in racial justice, shows how the U.S. government's War on Terror greatly expanded already well-developed surveillance infrastructure under the language of "counterterrorism" in response to 9/11. Therefore, relying on the very government that criminalizes our communities through foreign wars, which in turn endangers our communities in the United States, to then protect us from that hate violence can never be an effective strategy.

A clear example of this is when the Bush administration launched the notorious National Security Entry Exit Registration System (NSEERS) just months after 9/11. This program required all noncitizen, nonimmigrant men and boys above the age of sixteen from twenty-five Muslim-majority countries and North Korea to report to their local immigration offices. After hours of waiting and interrogation about their immigration status, employment, faith, political beliefs, and so on, many would be asked to surrender all their belongings and were placed into deportation proceedings. Most of the men did not have an opportunity to notify their families. Over 80,000 men were processed through this unnecessary program, and 13,000 were deported, all under the false premise of identifying "homegrown terrorists," despite resulting in zero terrorism-related convictions. Just six months after NSEERS launched, the newly created Department of Homeland Security and Guantanamo Bay opened to officially criminalize immigration and indefinitely detain political prisoners.

Despite this context, mainstream political and legal advocacy narratives led by national organizations including SAALT largely continued to paint hate violence as senseless acts of interpersonal conflict carried out by racist individuals without seeing them as outcomes of racist systems. This was evidenced by SAALT's policy recommendations to collect better data on hate crimes, advocate for increased and harsher sentencing of perpetrators, and build stronger relationships between victimized communities and law enforcement. These efforts failed to consider the War on Terror itself as the primary driver of violence aimed at those racialized as Muslim. By justifying the spying, surveillance, deportation, and criminalization of Muslim communities, War on Terror "counterterrorism" efforts are part of the state violence that underpins and empowers horrific acts of interpersonal hate violence—from murder to physical assault, arson, and verbal threats.

Under the Obama administration, the government instituted the Countering Violent Extremism (CVE) program in 2016, framed as a congressional mandate to help states and local communities prepare for, prevent, and respond to emergent threats from violent extremism. The Brennan Center describes the CVE program as a counterterrorism strategy that recruits community leaders, social workers, teachers, and public health providers ostensibly to assist the government in identifying individuals that may be "at risk" of becoming violent extremists.[3] The program almost exclusively targets Muslims and employs spurious criteria, such as religiosity and political activism and vague feelings of alienation, as proxies for violent tendencies. During the Obama administration, SAALT participated in quarterly meetings with the Department of Justice alongside other South Asian, Muslim, and Sikh, Arab, and Middle Eastern national organizations. During these meetings, organizations provided questioning and criticism, and some even accepted the CVE program as an effective means of identifying "terrorists" and an opportunity to receive federal funding from the government in return.

In 2017, President Donald Trump signed an executive order that banned foreign nationals from seven predominantly Muslim countries from visiting the United States for ninety days, indefinitely suspended entry to the country for Syrian refugees, and prohibited all other refugees from coming into the country for 120 days. Known as the Muslim Ban, it was legally upheld by the Supreme Court over one year later.[4] The Biden administration continued the bipartisan consensus to utilize the flawed framework of CVE to address the post-Trump spike in white supremacist hate violence through "domestic terrorism" charges. And in 2021, SAALT, following the leadership of grassroots organizations, publicly opposed such efforts, accepting that programs originally conceived to target communities of color will never be effective strategies to address white supremacist hate violence aimed at our communities.

After experiencing bipartisan betrayal for twenty years, SAALT finally came to understand that legal and policy reforms will never achieve liberation for communities targeted by the federal government because the federal government is able to leverage, exploit, and bend the legal system to its will.

Separate and Unequal

As a pan–South Asian organization, SAALT's adaptation of a racial justice framework assumed that all South Asians were equally impacted by the federal government's policies. But further examination into SAALT's policy work on hate violence, racial profiling, and immigration showed very disparate South Asian American experiences based on religion, class, and caste. The COVID-19 pandemic laid bare this truth, as documented in SAALT's 2020 report "Unequal Consequences: The Disparate Impact of Covid-19 across South Asian American Communities."[5] SAALT's other signature reports discussing incidents and trends in hate violence, including "Under Suspicion, Under Attack," "Power, Pain, Potential," and "Communities on Fire," showed repeatedly that Muslims and those racialized as Muslim experienced more than 90 percent of the incidents of documented hate violence, which were aimed at South Asian, Muslim, Sikh, Hindu, Middle Eastern, and Arab Americans.[6] And yet, SAALT continued its membership in national coalitions addressing hate violence among communities of color in the United States alongside groups like the Hindu America Foundation, upholding a false equivalency of victimization between Hindu and Muslim communities.

Concurrently, 2014 marked a significant political shift in India to a Hindu nationalist federal government with the election of Narendra Modi as prime minister.[7] Broadly, Hindu nationalism is a political ideology that asserts Indian national identity and culture as inseparable from the Hindu religion.[8] As chief minister of the state of Gujarat in the early 2000s, Narendra Modi already had a track record of fueling and supporting genocide against Muslims in India. During his tenure as prime minister, he has expanded and formalized this violent political agenda of Hindu nationalism to target Muslims and caste-oppressed populations across India. The past decade has revealed what caste-oppressed communities have known and lived: the greatest threat to the well-being of all South Asian communities is the violence of Hindu nationalism. B. R. Ambedkar, preeminent Dalit scholar and lead drafter of India's constitution following independence, articulated this truth with great clarity in the nineteenth century in his unparalleled text, "The Annihilation of Caste." In this powerfully foundational essay, he makes many sharp assertions, and three important and particularly relevant ones that help us understand the historical basis and current proliferation of a Hindu nationalist movement:

1. "The Caste system does not demarcate racial division. The Caste system is a social division of people of the same race."
2. "Religion compels the Hindus to treat isolation and segregation of castes as a virtue."
3. "Turn in any direction you like, caste is the monster that crosses your path. You cannot have political reform, you cannot have economic reform, unless you kill this monster."[9]

Until this point, SAALT had taken a firm stance in only focusing on South Asian communities in the United States, with no recognition of the dramatic political, cultural, and social shifts happening in South Asia. And, because SAALT had also rejected an investment in political education until this point, we did not have an analysis to help grasp how this impacted South Asian communities in the United States. Instead, by adopting a broad racial justice framework focused on the violence of white supremacy in the United States without a deeper analysis of the fractured experiences within the South Asian community along lines of caste, SAALT overlooked how the growing Hindu nationalist movement influenced the organization's focus areas of immigration, hate violence, and racial profiling.

By claiming to represent all South Asian Americans without explicitly prioritizing South Asian populations marginalized by religion, class, and caste, SAALT was largely performing a shared South Asian identity to gain and maintain access to policymakers within a U.S. construct of racialized identity politics. We were beginning to confront the uncomfortable recognition of caste, the most crucial identity marker of all South Asians. How could we continue to engage in identity politics without understanding that which is core to our identity? By doing so, we continued to present an identity we had not invested in creating. As a policy organization, SAALT's entry point to understanding caste was to begin paying attention to how the impact of policies in our South Asian countries of origin and the movements responding to them shaped the impact of policies on our populations in the United States. The following sections further discuss the implications this has on the South Asian American diaspora.

Caste and South Asian Migration

Another cornerstone of SAALT's omission of an analysis of caste among South Asians in the United States that distorts and undermines our understanding is the impact of the interconnected systems of national security and immigration. The same South Asian populations marginalized by class, caste, and religion are both the targets of hate violence and disproportionately criminalized by our immigration system and national security state—whether it be through overt policies like the Muslim Ban under the Trump administration, the harsh and punitive asylum process under all presidential administrations, or through everyday surveillance and racial profiling.

Well before 9/11, South Asians in the United States faced policies of exclusion and incarceration. Scholars such as Vijay Prashad and Vivek

Bald have documented the early waves of South Asian migration to the United States and the shifting economic and political needs that have shaped migration flows. The first recorded South Asian migrants on the West Coast, mainly from Punjab, India, were characterized as "low-caste Hindoos"—although the majority were in fact Sikh. After the Immigration and Nationality Act of 1965, migration flows from Asia, including South Asian countries, were intentionally shifted to meet specific demands for labor in particular industries, leading to the emergence of a predominantly upper-caste population from India. This changed again in the 1990s when migration flows from South Asia shifted to meet specific demands for labor in the service industry. And, since 2014 we have seen an increase in asylum seekers and refugees from South Asian countries, fleeing political repression. SAALT's recent and nascent understanding of caste in the South Asian American diaspora helped us begin to examine how political and religious repression of non-Hindus by the Hindu nationalist government in India has led to a rapid uptick in individuals from India seeking asylum in the United States since 2014. It has also become increasingly clear that these same forces of the Hindu Right in the United States are behind the efforts to pass divisive green card reform legislation.

Applying even an emerging lens around caste alongside the history of class in South Asian American history can help us to better understand contemporary political divides in our communities. In February 2018, hundreds of Indian Americans rallied outside the White House supporting the Trump administration's immigration policies, drawing attention to the green card issue. In particular, they held a sign saying, "Dreamers pay for the wall" and offered to pay additional fees toward their green card applications to finance a border wall by supporting the Fairness for High Skilled Immigrants Act.[10] These positions and actions by the Indian American community exemplify the mindset of exceptionalism and a willingness to undermine other immigrant communities for individual benefit. But even more notable are the deeply flawed arguments around merit, class, and caste engrained in this fight.[11]

The fight for citizenship for South Asian immigrants has never fundamentally challenged the premise of racist immigration and naturalization laws. In the introduction to *Bengali Harlem*, historian Vivek Bald contrasts the 1945 congressional testimonies of two men from India—Mubarek Ali Khan, a farmer in Arizona; and J. J. Singh, an entrepreneur in New York City. Speaking before the House Committee on Immigration and Naturalization, both men employed arguments that touted the contributions of Indian immigrants, highlighting the accomplishments of scientists, engineers, and scholars to justify their right to citizenship.[12] Much like today, they both also erased the experiences of the majority of Indians who were actually living in the United States at that time, who were farm laborers and industrial and service workers.

However, in Bald's extensive research, he unearthed written testimony from a third man, a Bengali immigrant from New York City named Ibrahim Choudry, who served as secretary of the India Association for America Citizenship. His letter lifted the shroud over the South Asian working-class population that Khan and Singh had overlooked and excluded in their testimonies. Choudry's testimony in part read, "I speak for the many. I am not speaking for the transient element—the student, the businessman, the lecturer, the interpreter of India's past and present, whose interests and ties in this country are temporary, the man or the woman whose roots are in India and who eventually returns home. I talk for those of us who, by our work and by our sweat and by our blood, have helped build fighting industrial America today. I talk for those of our men who, in factory and field, in all sections of American industry, work side by side with their fellow American workers to strengthen the industrial framework of this country."[13]

Ultimately, the Luce-Cellar Act, passed in 1946 during the Truman administration, made all Indians already residing in the United States eligible for citizenship. But it also solidified future immigration policy by bending the law in favor of scientists, engineers, and businesspeople. This laid the foundation for the 1965 Immigration and Nationality Act, which, while eliminating the racial/nationality based discrimination in immigration quotas, overwhelmingly favored the highly educated while largely excluding working-class immigrants. These crucial policy decisions over time shaped the trajectory of South Asian migration to the United States, but more importantly underscores the role of advocates in engaging with the state, which interprets and enforces the law at its discretion and for whom it believes are worthy.

Through slow and intentional learning of both our history and the present to inform a stronger understanding of oppression based on religion, class, and caste, SAALT shifted its focus to prioritizing the South Asian populations most marginalized by the interconnected systems of national security and immigration. As a result, we opened ourselves to a necessarily transnational analysis of South Asian communities.

Immigrant Justice Is Transnational

In 2019, SAALT began closely following issues of immigrant detention, an underexamined immigration issue in the South Asian American community.[14] Local and regional organizations like Desis Rising Up and Moving in New York City and Jakara Movement in California's Central Valley have a longer history of supporting South Asian migrants than SAALT. This shift for SAALT as a national organization meant refocusing our immigrant justice work on undocumented South Asians, DACA (Deferred Action for Childhood Arrivals) recipients, TPS (Temporary Protected Status) holders, asylum seekers and refugees, and H-4 visa holders because these populations are the most vulnerable and have the least attention, resources, and advocacy dedicated at the national level within South Asian American communities.[15] A closer look at these populations continues to show that South Asian immigrant and migrant experience varies greatly based on class, religion, and caste.

In early 2019, nine Punjabi asylum seekers in detention went on a hunger strike in the El Paso Service Processing Center in Texas to bring attention to their neglected claims for political asylum and horrific treatment inside immigrant detention facilities. It began as a joint strike with Cuban asylum seekers in the same facility and resulted in Immigration and Customs Enforcement (ICE) officials force-feeding the asylum seekers through nasal tubes and IVs. The tubes remained in their nasal passages 24/7 and led to wounds, lesions, persistent stomach pains, and other health complications.[16] While not the first incident of South Asian migrants seeking asylum in the United States, the abuses gained mainstream attention after local organizers in El Paso contacted national South Asian advocacy organizations including SAALT. This organizing marked an important shift: undocumented South Asian migrants have never been the primary population of focus for national South Asian American policy and advocacy organizations.[17]

SAALT uncovered more data on South Asian asylum seekers, prompted by reports from our local partners working directly with detained migrants and media accounts highlighting South Asian migrants to the United States. In 2008 the number of South Asian migrants apprehended at the U.S.-Mexico border by U.S. Customs and Border Protection was in the hundreds, but this number soared to over 34,000 migrants in 2019. This data was mostly gathered from Syracuse University's Transactional Records Access Clearinghouse (TRAC), which reveals the federal government's intentionally bungled and opaque data collection on migrants apprehended at U.S. borders and languishing in detention centers. It also exposes the need for more community data on the transnational nature of migration from South Asia that informs the narratives of those who are undocumented, seeking asylum, or forced into unstable and unreliable immigration status in the United States.

Connecting the uptick of South Asian asylum seekers to Modi's election as prime minister of India in 2014, SAALT reviewed major strikes of South Asian migrants in detention beginning in 2014 with thirty-seven Punjabi asylum seekers detained at the El Paso Service Processing Center.[18] Just as in 2019, they went on hunger strike to draw attention to their neglected asylum cases and inhumane treatment in detention. Many of these apprehensions have led to prolonged detention sentences of asylum seekers, who already face dangerous and abusive conditions, including inadequate or nonexistent language access, denial of religious accommodations and dietary restrictions, use of solitary confinement as a form of retaliation, and unreasonably high bond amounts—Indian migrants have the highest median bonds, at upwards of $20,000. Until 2019, mirroring our reformist strategies to address hate violence, SAALT's strategies to support South Asian migrants were focused solely on improving their conditions in detention. This included SAALT, along with our partner organizations, investing time and resources in filing numerous complaints with the Office of Civil Rights and Civil Liberties (CRCL) in the Department of Homeland Security. This involved painstakingly engaging in meeting after meeting with staff and leadership of CRCL and attempting to engage members of Congress whose districts include detention centers to demand investigations into individual facilities. This advocacy resulted in nothing; CRCL officials informed us that ICE would have to act on its own volition to improve conditions in detention. This is because the immigration system has been intentionally designed to endure with no oversight or accountability. We knew that we had to invest in transformative strategies that did not rely on a faulty, unreliable, and ultimately unjust legal system.

In early 2019, SAALT shifted to investing much more deeply in partnerships with local community organizers and organizations in El Paso, Texas, and Las Cruces, New Mexico, following the brutal force-feeding of the nine Punjabi asylum seekers on hunger strike in the El Paso Service Processing Center. These nine men had fled political repression by India's Hindu nationalist government, which has a verified track record of violently quelling dissent and opposition. Upon entering the United States to claim political asylum, they were thrown into detention facilities—and had languished for almost two years with no movement on their legal cases, forcing them to go on hunger strike to gain attention for their stalled cases. Two local organizations, Advocate Visitors for Immigrants in Detention (AVID), based in Las Cruces, and the Detained Migrant Solidarity Committee (DMSC), based in El Paso—both which primarily work with detained Latinx migrants—were the first to learn about the hunger strike. They reached out to national South Asian organizations, including SAALT, to draw greater attention and resources to support these men. In the span of one year, SAALT helped turn these initial partnerships into a successful coalition of national and local immigrant justice organizations following a visit to El Paso to meet local advocates and the men on hunger strike. This ultimately included Northwest Resistance (Resistencia) in Tacoma, Washington, and national partners—the Sikh American Legal Defense and Education Fund (SALDEF), Sikh Coalition, Detention Watch Network, and Freedom for Immigrants. The coalition met regularly to strategize legal, media, and organizing tactics that would elevate abusive conditions and force movement on asylum cases. The powerful local organizing efforts ultimately led to the release of two of the men, an exceedingly rare outcome for detained migrants.

Later in 2019, SAALT received community reports of an ICE raid at an Indian restaurant in Washington, DC, following threats from the Trump administration that it would conduct a wide sweep of ICE raids across the country. It was reported that at least nine South Asian employees were taken by ICE to a local county jail, and eventually all were released. In response, SAALT supported three Know Your Rights trainings in Washington, DC, Maryland, and Virginia led by Justice for Muslims Collective and Restaurant Opportunities Center-DC following the increased ICE targeting of South Asian restaurant workers in the area. After putting out a call for volunteers to attend the trainings and disseminate in-language Know Your Rights materials, we were astounded by the overwhelming response. In addition to the nearly 100 local Muslim, Arab, Sikh, and South Asian residents who participated in these trainings in person, we signed up 600 volunteers across the country, forming a virtual network known as the South Asian Rapid Response Initiative. We relied on this network to provide language and legal support remotely for detained South Asian migrants. This included access to lawyers with asylum expertise, translators and interpreters who could be readily deployed, and community members who could directly support detained migrants in their geographic areas. While the initiative thrived in the initial months to support individual migrant detention cases, it also exposed the reality that there was no critical mass of South Asian American attorneys with expertise or training in asylum law or deportation defense. It was not possible to rely on this network for the full support of cases beyond language interpretation and occasional referrals. But, prior to this, it was extremely challenging to even identify any South Asian lawyers and community members who would invest time in supporting South Asian migrants and asylum seekers. This rapid-response infrastructure was an experiment in political education that enabled many South Asian Americans to channel their rage at the Trump administration's notorious ICE raids, but ultimately it did not result in a surge of South Asian American attorneys investing in long-term support for detained South Asian migrants. Applying a class and caste lens allows us to understand why this dissonance exists between the upper caste and professional class South Asian American diaspora community and often working-class and caste oppressed South Asian migrants.

However, continuing to learn from our collaborations, SAALT weaved our emerging transnational lens to both support South Asian migrants in detention and understand the root causes of this forced migration from South Asia. This helped us better understand the inherently transnational nature of immigrant justice work, and also to more explicitly connect the economic, political, and religious repression that force many South Asian migrants to enter the United States through our detention system.

In an effort to sharpen our transnational lens, SAALT began work in 2021 with the South Asian Left Activist Movement (SALAM), a collective of South Asians who use their policy, research, and communications skills to support campaigns in progressive South Asian organizations. They conducted in-depth research on South Asian country conditions to help uncover the many hidden and unacknowledged push factors for forced migration from South Asia leading so many to seek asylum in the United States. Two of these significant and related push factors are caste oppression and religious discrimination through violent targeting by the Indian government—state violence just like in the United States. It was our hope that illuminating these unique transnational conditions in South Asian communities would not only improve the currently grim asylum prospects for so many South Asian migrants but also shed light on the specific South Asian populations marginalized both in South Asia and the United States.

The power of AVID, DMSC, and Resistencia's work is derived from being firmly grounded toward abolishing the U.S. detention system. To that end, they strategically leverage elected officials, regional ICE field leadership, and media in principled ways. Learning from them, SAALT began shifting our immigrant justice strategy to both support South Asian migrants in detention and understand the root causes of this forced migration from South Asia. This dialectical development marked another shift away from SAALT's historically legal and policy reform strategies.

Generating South Asian Power Must Begin with Caste

As a national organization that had been slowly transforming from reformist to progressive to movement, we finally had to confront the question of whether we could be an antiracist South Asian American organization without also being anti-caste. We faced the critical crossroads of once again employing a racial justice framework, this time with an abolitionist lens, but still absent of first confronting caste oppression within the South Asian American community. It is important to acknowledge that SAALT's political evolution did not simply emerge from internal introspection. It was greatly informed by continuously collecting and analyzing a decade of feedback from individuals and organizations serving marginalized South Asian populations, and then shifting and disrupting within SAALT, catalyzed at times by internal transition and at times by external crises. Until 2023, SAALT's leadership was exclusively upper-caste South Asians, me included. This resulted in incremental rather than transformational change that increased the visibility and representation of upper-caste and upper-class South Asian Americans while working-class, undocumented, queer, religiously minoritized (Muslim, Sikh, and Christian), and caste-oppressed South Asians in the United States continue to experience a different reality.

The journey of active learning and political education for SAALT first began with an internal training on caste supremacy for SAALT staff led by Equality Labs in 2018, bookended by additional trainings by them for two cohorts of our community development and youth leadership programs that same year. In 2019 we were proud to partner with Equality Labs on the first-ever congressional briefing on caste in the diaspora, in which Equality Labs discussed findings from their groundbreaking report and organized testimonies from American Dalit community members.[19] And in 2021, leaders of the International Commission for Dalit Rights (ICDR) and Dalit Solidarity Forum provided a training on caste open to the fifty members of the National Coalition of South Asian Organizations (NCSO). The NCSO was created in 2007 as a purely identity-based coalition of local and regional South Asian American organizations to help facilitate shared learning across the country and create a unified federal policy agenda on behalf of South Asian American communities. But it became clear at SAALT that functioning as an identity-based coalition without a set of shared values or shared political analysis was generating conflict and allowing caste-privileged and Hindu supremacist groups to overpower the discourse and even harm others.

It was no coincidence that the trainings on caste were held on the heels of the 2020 uprisings following the murder of George Floyd by police. Requests for training on addressing anti-Black racism came pouring in to SAALT from South Asian community members. In joining the calls for abolishing the police, SAALT faced the important and difficult crossroads of adapting an abolitionist lens absent of first confronting caste oppression within the South Asian American community. The decision to begin with trainings on caste was another important disruptor that provided a much-needed push for SAALT to invest in internal political education on caste and begin a values alignment process within the NCSO to first build an analysis rooted in caste abolition before making public declarations and continuing to make only programmatic changes.

A final cornerstone of SAALT's transformation was to begin embodying an anti-caste analysis internally, which started with anti-caste values practice within our organizational operations. The first step toward this internal practice of our values began in 2020 with a deeply relational board recruitment process to intentionally bring together South Asian Americans working in movements for justice who widely represented the community across U.S. geographies, caste, class, religion, and country of origin. Guided by this newly formed board with more equitable representation of the South Asian community, we began an internal journey of exploring how caste informs the positionality of South Asians in the United States. In 2021–2022, the SAALT board and staff worked with Khalid Anis Ansari, a Pasmanda Muslim scholar, who led us in a year-long, six-part series on caste, religion, and class with a focus on Islam.[20]

After an intensive board and staff retreat in early 2022, we initiated a just transition to actively shape SAALT into an anti-caste institution. We created a caste-centered values framework to help us understand how our other values (such as racial justice, gender justice, and disability justice) were informed by an anti-caste lens, and vice versa. After experimenting with applying this caste-centered values framework to our programming and policy work for three years without pausing, we voted to focus our efforts on building an analysis of caste between board and staff to inform our internal practices first, before experimenting further with federal policy and advocacy on behalf of South Asian American communities.

In 2023 we officially entered a period of chrysalis, which continued into 2024. During this time, we ceased all externally facing programming and committed to practicing co-directorship of the organization among four staff accountable to our board (collectively called the SAALT ecosystem) and prioritizing internal anti-caste study. This was the first time in SAALT's history that the majority of the staff was representing the U.S. South and the first time a Dalit person was on the leadership team. During our first year of chrysalis, SAALT staff met biweekly, and the board and staff met together monthly to reflect on our slow, thoughtful, and deep reading of Ambedkar's foundational text "Annihilation of Caste." We continued this work into 2024 with the aim of completing our first reading and reflection of this critical text, through which we begin to understand caste and our relationships to it.

Conclusion

An excerpt from SAALT's Sunset Statement:

> We chose to break ourselves open, re-imagine our organizational values, and challenge dominant non-profit and South Asian American culture. We tried reforming SAALT through a co-directorship and chrysalis, but the limitations of the structure did not allow for this transformation. We learned that we could not fully "pause." The spaciousness we needed for anti-caste political education was frequently compromised by nonprofit compliance issues, fundraising urgencies, and targeted attacks from right wing groups.
> It proved ever challenging to slow down, be relational, and have the focus required to unpack caste while simultaneously running SAALT as a national nonprofit. The work we needed to do was deeply cultural and had no "deliverables" for traditional funders. The more we built our analysis and understood what being anti-caste in this day and age means, the more clarity we gained on how necessary social reform was, and how SAALT, is no longer the vehicle for it. We decided to say goodbye to this container that could not be reshaped.[21]

SAALT in its original shape as a nonprofit was born out of crisis following September 11, 2001. Having operated for so long in a crisis response mindset, the confines of its nonprofit shape could not hold an investment in political education or operational infrastructure and systems oriented outside of a reactive framework. As SAALT went through its own shift in consciousness, the world too was churning and rejecting the status quo. The reelection of Donald Trump as president of the United States shows that we need radically new ways of doing things, because the old ways are not working. In the last ten years of SAALT's existence, we tested different strategies and approaches, and we chose to make a fundamental shift in our theory for change toward social reform at a relational level over political reform at an organizational level as the means to becoming anti-caste. As Grace Lee Boggs taught us: "Transform yourself to transform the world."

Recently, author and activist adrienne maree brown reflected on this further by saying, "When I heard those words, it made me turn and look at myself and recognize that each of those socialized systems that I was trying to fight against out in the world were rooted inside of me as well."[22] Applying this not only to ourselves as individuals, but to our institutions and specifically to SAALT: Did we ever ask if the socialized systems we were attempting to fight in the world might be showing up within our organization? How could we be an immigrant justice organization that could not hire individuals without U.S. citizenship or green-card status? How could we be a racial justice organization that had doubled down on building relationships with law enforcement for nearly two decades? And, how could we be an anti-caste organization with exclusively upper-caste leadership? These questions are not meant to elicit shame and blame. Instead of turning away from them, we used them as our entry point as board and staff into collective inquiry and courageous experimentation.

One of the greatest outcomes of SAALT's multiple phases of transformation was a culmination of investment in creating a new organizational leadership body comprised of South Asian Americans across lines of caste, class, and religion. For the first time, we studied, struggled, practiced, and internally modeled our emergent values together. This unprecedented level of internal inquiry, experimentation, and values practice necessarily made us question our external strategies and their alignment with the new organizational culture we created. Unsurprisingly, it evolved us out of a nonprofit container that required us to consistently undermine our values to guarantee its own survival.

Brushing off this values practice as "purity politics" can be an easy escape from the hard work of pushing ourselves on the application of our values where we have the greatest control, which are also the places where the outside world is not often looking—within ourselves and inside of our institutions. To really challenge the status quo, generate power, and change conditions, we must engage in this deeply relational work of study and struggle together.

We are still at the very beginning of understanding the role that caste plays in shaping South Asian American experiences. Until we collectively acknowledge and prepare ourselves to address the sharp internal divisions that obscure and willfully mask caste within the South Asian American community, the diaspora will remain severely limited in its organizing power to address the powerful threats we face from U.S. state violence alone.

The future directions that SAALT's sunset opens gives us renewed energy for completely reimagined visions grounded in a commitment to continuous transformation guided by a clear set of values rather than by advocacy at the speed of crisis or the demands of electoral change. The lesson of SAALT is not whether it survived, but how it transformed.

Notes

I would like to express my deep gratitude to Simran Noor for being a critical thought partner during this decade of transformation and to the courageous SAALT ecosystem for their labor and leadership during our time of chrysalis and transition. I want to thank my husband, Rachit Choksi, for his steadfast support, conviction, and encouragement.

1. "Sureshbhai Patel Case: Outrage in US at Second Mistrial of Cop Who Assaulted Indian," *Economic Times*, November 6, 2015, www.economictimes.indiatimes.com.
2. Justice for Muslims, "Abolishing the War on Terror, Building Communities of Care Grassroots Agenda," 2021, www.justiceformuslims.org.
3. Brennan Center, *Why Countering Violent Extremism Programs Are Bad Policy*, September 2019, www.brennancenter.org.
4. American Civil Liberties Union, *Timeline of the Muslim Ban*, www.aclu-wa.org, accessed January 19, 2025.
5. South Asian Americans Leading Together, *Unequal Consequences: The Disparate Impact of Covid-19 across South Asian American Communities*, 2020, https://saalt.org.
6. SAALT, "Under Suspicion, Under Attack," June 2013, https://saalt.org; SAALT, "Power, Pain, Potential: South Asian Americans at the Forefront of Growth

and Hate in the 2016 Election Cycle," January 2017, https://saalt.org; SAALT, "Communities on Fire: Confronting Hate Violence and Xenophobic Political Rhetoric," January 2018, https://saalt.org.
7 Krutika Pathi and Sheikh Saaliq, "Once a Fringe Indian Ideology, Hindu Nationalism Is Now Mainstream Thanks to Modi's Decade in Power," Associated Press, April 18, 2024.
8 "What Is Hindu Nationalism and How Does It Relate to Trouble in Leicester?," *The Guardian*, September 20, 2022, www.theguardian.com.
9 Quoted from B. R. Ambedkar, *Annihilation of Caste: The Annotated Critical Edition* (London: Verso Books, 2015).
10 Varghese K. George, "Indian-American Group Marches in Support of Trump's Immigration Policy," *The Hindu*, February 4, 2018.
11 Thenmozhi Soundararajan, "Why Are Some South Asian Immigrants Offering to Pay for Trump's Wall?," *Rewire News*, February 14, 2018, https://rewirenewsgroup.com.
12 Vivek Bald, *Bengali Harlem and the Lost Histories of South Asian America* (Cambridge, MA: Harvard University Press, 2012), 2–6.
13 Quoted in Bald, *Bengali Harlem*, 4.
14 South Asian Americans Leading Together, *South Asian Migrants in Detention: A Factsheet*, 2019, https://saalt.org.
15 South Asian Americans Leading Together, *A Guide to Advocacy for Legal Immigration Reform: H-1B and H-4 visas and the South Asian American Community*, 2018, https://saalt.org.
16 South Asian Legal Defense and Education Fund, "Stop the Mistreatment of Punjabi Detainees in El Paso," February 2019, https://saldef.org.
17 South Asian Americans Leading Together, April 2019, *Demographic Snapshot of South Asians in the United States*, https://saalt.org.
18 South Asian Americans Leading Together, "South Asian Migrants in Detention Factsheet," August 2019, https://saalt.org.
19 Equality Labs, "Caste in the United States: A Survey of Caste among South Asian Americans," 2018, https://equalitylabs.wpengine.com.
20 South Asian Americans Leading Together, "Khalid Anis Ansari, Visiting Scholar," accessed November 10, 2024, https://saalt.org.
21 South Asian Americans Leading Together, "SAALT Sunset Statement," October 9, 2024, https://saalt.org.
22 adrienne maree brown, "The Radical Politics of Pleasure," *Radical* Imagination podcast, April 14, 2021, https://radicalimagination.us.

3

Organizing Inside and Out

The ReleaseMN8 Campaign

VICHET CHHUON, CHED NIN, AND JENNY SREY

On October 18, 2016, a group of Cambodian families met in St. Paul, Minnesota, to plan a public event in support of eight family members who were detained by the U.S. Department of Homeland Security's Immigration and Customs Enforcement (ICE) agency two months earlier. Working with this group was Emilia Gonzalez Avalos, executive director of Navigate MN, an immigrant rights organization in Minneapolis. Emilia understood well the deportation machine that terrorized immigrant communities and joined these Cambodian families in solidarity. That evening she educated family members on political organizing and escalation tactics.

Toward the conclusion of the session, Emilia, feeling unsure about what the families were asking for, pressed: "What is your ask? What exactly do you want ICE to do?" A smattering of English and Khmer echoed across the room. One mother yelled, "I want him home! I want my son to come home!" Others chimed in with, "Let them go!" Emilia asked—"So you want ICE to release them? Is that what you want? ICE to release them?" A loud chorus of "yes!" enveloped the room. Recognizing the moment, Julia Freeman, a community organizer from Voices for Racial Justice in Minneapolis, began a chant: "Release the Minnesota 8, release the Minnesota 8, release the Minnesota 8." Soon, every person was chanting "Release the Minnesota 8." The objective became unequivocal moving forward. Since then, this campaign has been referred to as ReleaseMN8.

In this chapter we describe from our varied perspectives the emergence of the grassroots campaign ReleaseMN8. Ched Nin was detained by ICE on August 26, 2016, and spent six months in immigration detention. His spouse, Jenny Srey, was the key organizer of the campaign that fought for Ched's release. Vichet Chhuon is a University of Minnesota professor who organized with Jenny and others on behalf of the eight families. In what follows, we provide a historical context of Cambodian migration and settlement in the United States. We then discuss the deportation issue for Cambodian Americans that has been ongoing since 2002. Through our dialogue, we offer insight into how the ReleaseMN8 campaign came to be. Overall, we aim to highlight the conversations, sense-making, and negotiations between detained individuals, family and community members, and organizers amid both current and historical contexts of U.S. immigration policies that target communities of color.

Cambodian Migration and Resettlement

The Cambodian community in the United States was formed primarily through refugee resettlement in the 1980s following a decade of civil war, famine, and genocide in Cambodia. Recent Pew data reported that there are currently over 320,000 Cambodians living in the United States, with the majority having arrived following the "killing fields" period of Cambodian history (1975–1979).[1] During this grim period for Cambodia, the new communist Khmer Rouge government evacuated every city and pushed urban residents into labor camps across Cambodia's countryside. Many would perish, including children, from disease and starvation along this journey. By uprooting the country's urban dwellers in its attempt to execute a radical Marxist experiment, the Khmer Rouge regime successfully disoriented and terrorized particular populations of Cambodians that they believed were aligned with elite and bourgeoise ideologies. During the ensuing four years, the Khmer Rouge renamed the country "Democratic Kampuchea" and abolished all religion, money, and private property in order to erase remnants of capitalism in what the regime perceived as other Western influences. Children older than age seven were separated from their parents and placed into youth brigades and reeducation camps. In all, this period of Khmer Rouge rule led to an estimated two million deaths—about half of the country's population. This particular chapter of Cambodia's history ended in 1979 when Vietnamese forces invaded Cambodia.[2]

Given many years of witnessing firsthand various horrors, it is not surprising that Cambodian refugee families would have had difficulties as they settled into life in the United States. The earliest wave of Cambodian refugees, estimated at thirteen thousand, entered the United States in 1975, when the Khmer Rouge toppled the Cambodian government. Most of this first wave of asylees were the family members of military personnel, diplomats, and urban elites. After the 1979 Vietnamese invasion of Cambodia, ending the Khmer Rouge regime, tens of thousands risked their lives to cross the Thai border into United Nations–sanctioned refugee camps. In the United States, the passage of the 1980 Refugee Act served as an important mechanism for thousands of Cambodians to be eventually granted asylum. This latter wave of Cambodians (approximately 190,000) entering the United States throughout the 1980s disproportionately came from rural farming backgrounds and tended to have little formal education. The swift resettlement of so many refugees from Cambodia and other parts of Southeast Asia presented challenges for U.S. policymakers, host communities, and for the refugees themselves. The majority of Southeast Asian refugees, including Cambodians, often spent years in refugee camps prior to their U.S. settlement. They did not have much say in where they would settle, and families were frequently assigned to those locations of sponsoring churches and/or wherever available housing existed.[3]

Minnesota came to be one of the main resettlement hubs for Southeast Asian refugees in the United States. St. Paul, Minnesota, is home to the largest Hmong urban community in the world. Tens of thousands of Cambodian, Vietnamese, and Lao families also arrived in Minnesota, with the majority living in and around the Minneapolis/St. Paul (Twin Cities) metro region. Like in other parts of the country, Cambodian families were often settled into "impoverished ethnic neighborhoods that function more as traps than as platforms for upward mobility."[4] This shaped the life chances for many Cambodian youths, particularly Cambodian boys.[5] The socialization in school and communities for Cambodian adolescent males resonate with other literature documenting the discrimination and hyper-policing of male youths of color. Negative messages of "unbelonging" communicated to these young men in school, media, and other social institutions shaped the ways that young Cambodian men learn about their place in U.S. society.

Unfortunately for Cambodian refugees, mistakes made as youths often led to placement in the criminal justice system, a pathway that would deliver many into a relentless and unforgiving U.S. immigration web.

Deportation of Cambodian Americans

Until 1996, immigration judges held considerable discretionary authority in deportation proceedings where an immigrant or refugee had committed an aggravated felony.[6] For example, judges had the authority to weigh a number of circumstances in removal cases, including the person's family ties and employment. In 1996, the Anti-terrorism and Effective Death Penalty Act and Illegal Immigration Reform and Immigrant Responsibility Act fundamentally changed the immigration landscape for many communities by making removal of legal permanent residents more frequent and efficient.[7] This legislation dictated that legal permanent residents convicted of any crime classified as an aggravated felony would be subject to removal. Certainly, aggravated felonies include some of the most serious and violent offenses, including murder, rape, and assault. This category, under immigration law, also includes some relatively minor offenses including theft and dealing small amounts of marijuana.

Some of these infractions can begin as a misdemeanor but subsequently can be classified by the immigration court as an aggravated felony if the offender receives a sentence of 365 days or longer. Any conviction that involves a sentence of one year or more is considered by U.S. federal immigration as an aggravated felony. This classification holds even if the state officially categorizes the crime a misdemeanor offense. Again, what is further critical about this legislation is that it severely limited judicial discretion to consider individuals' rehabilitation, family connections, and length of time in the United States. The 1996 laws effectively expanded the deportation machine that subsequently led to mass removal of immigrants and forced separation of families.

Refugees in the United States tend to be from countries with which the U.S. government does not have diplomatic relations. The Kingdom of Cambodia did not accept deportees until March 2002, when a secret repatriation agreement was signed between the Cambodian and U.S. governments. Regular deportations of Cambodians convicted of aggravated felonies have occurred since, despite these individuals already having served their criminal sentences. At present, more than seven hundred Cambodians have been deported to Cambodia, with almost two thousand more living with orders of removal.

Ched Nin was detained by U.S. Immigration and Customs Enforcement on August 26, 2016. We learned later that Ched's detention was part of a national roundup of Cambodians by the Department of Homeland Security. In the state of Minnesota, Ched and seven other men were detained by ICE within a matter of days of one another, and each was slated for deportation to Cambodia. Ched spent almost six months in detention before being released to his family and community on February 24, 2017.

In the following pages, we describe through dialogue and storytelling the emergence of the ReleaseMN8 campaign. Storytelling can be a particularly useful way to understand conflicts, situations, and motive. Charlotte Linde noted that an important goal for individuals in storytelling, particularly when discussing their own lives, is the creation of coherence in their narratives.[8] Narrators, like the three of us here, naturally seek to establish in our stories confirmation that they were sufficient agents in our lives. Moreover, storytelling and dialogue have the critical potential to help narrators work through moral conflicts and cultivate a positive sense of self and events. Additionally, Linde contends that an incoherent narrative can lead to emotional and psychological distress within the narrator's life. To that end, we share our dialogue with healing in mind and begin with Ched's introduction as to how he became involved in the ReleaseMN8 campaign.

The Beginning: "They took Ched."

> CHED: I was six years old when we moved to the United States in 1986. Our family came as refugees from Cambodia. I was born in the [refugee] camps. I grew up in Faribault, Minnesota, which is a smaller town outside of the Twin Cities. It wasn't easy being Cambodian in a place like that. Lots of name calling and racism. It wasn't everybody, but it was enough for me to question my place. I married very young and had children too young. Things obviously didn't work out with my daughters' mom. Today my parents live with me, which

I really like. Jenny and I were married in 2015. In 2016 I was working as a carpenter with a commercial construction company. Jenny and I, together, had five children. We were leading pretty normal lives in Farmington, Minnesota. I had an immigration removal order stemming from a conviction back in my twenties. I screwed up. I lost my temper during an altercation with my ex-wife's boyfriend and fired a BB gun at their car as they drove off. That feels like a lifetime ago now, but that's what happened. I served two years in prison and was released in 2012. I feel like I've been doing really good since then, until that day in August.

That day for check-in at the ICE office (August 26, 2016), the ICE agent asked me if I had any children with me at the facilities. I said no. He told me that I needed to go to the back with him to answer some questions. I immediately had a bad feeling about the situation. But what could I do at this point? All I could say to myself is, "Shit, this is happening!" Fortunately, I brought my friend Dwayne with me to check in that day. Before heading off with the officer, I gave my car keys to Dwayne. I told him he needed to call my wife immediately.

I was booked right away. There were already other Cambodians in the holding tank. I knew some of them, and others I did not know. And right away, for some reason I asked, "Can I give you guys a hug?" I gave all of them hugs. Then we made our collect calls on the pay phone. I was trying to reach Jenny. I didn't even remember Jenny's cell phone number but I kept trying to remember and dial. Prior to being detained that day, I thought it was a myth. In my mind, I'm like, there's no way this is happening.

In the end, I was detained with the other guys: Posy, Phouey, Shorty, Sam, Ron, CNN, and C. I love these guys. Each one is so different. What's funny is that CNN's real name is Chan but we called him CNN because he always acted like he had all the news and information. We still call him that. The main jokester in our group was C. He kept us light with his sense of humor. We stayed about a week in Sherburne County Jail in Minnesota. By the time we made our first purchase of phone calls and shampoo, we were shipped out to a processing center in Louisiana. That was my first experience of being on a plane since coming to the United States at age six. I was in the back end of a 737 in shackles. The guys and I called it "Con

Air" after the Nicholas Cage movie. I kept thinking, am I really on a plane? Am I really going to Cambodia right now? We didn't know where we were going. They told our families we would go meet with the Cambodian Consulate in California. We made a few stops on our way to Louisiana. It was weird because it was my first experience meeting Khmer folks from other parts of the country. We were everywhere.

When we landed in Louisiana, it seemed like a private island. We couldn't see anything. I kept thinking that this can't be really happening. Their intake station looked like pods upon pods upon pods. That's where they received folks on buses and airplanes. It was a federal processing center that brought folks from all over the United States. Afterwards, we flew to Adelanto, California, where we met with the Cambodian Consulate to process our travel documents to Cambodia. This facility was a mega-prison where ICE detainees were mixed with prisoners doing federal sentences. That felt sketchy to me. There was tension because the folks detained by ICE are in and out, but other prisoners are doing long stretches of time. There's about eighty of us Cambodians there, and for some reason they separated us. It seemed that the corrections officers didn't like having a large group of Cambodians together. We all felt like we lost strength.

JENNY: In August 2016, I was a social worker. My dad came to the U.S. in 1976, where he met my mom in Chicago. My parents separated when I was very young, and I lived with my dad and stepmom. We grew up in a close-knit Khmer community. We did not grow up together, but I've known Ched since I was nine years old. He was a few years older than me. Later on, we found each other again, and we just connected really well. Ched and I were married in 2015. We each had children from previous relationships and blended our families. Together we had five kids. Ched had three daughters from a previous marriage, and I had two sons from a previous marriage.

I was aware of Ched's immigration status and knew that he had been checking in with ICE every six months. In the summer of 2016, Ched received a letter to check in early. We thought that they may simply do a review where he could do an annual check-in. I've been to the check-ins. They usually take two minutes. On August 26, Ched was very nervous. I didn't really get it. However, he made sure to take the day off. I couldn't go with him that day because of work. My cousin's boyfriend, Dwayne, was available to go with him. After his check-in, more than ten minutes went by. I didn't hear from him. This was unusual. The ICE officer usually just asks for his ID, his employment condition, and if his address is up to date. Sometime later that morning, I received a call from Dwayne. He said, "Jenny, they took Ched." I said, you're joking, right? Dwayne said he would never joke about this. I was in momentary shock. I told Dwayne that I would be right there. I just remember running out and catching a glimpse of my supervisor and saying that I have an emergency and to please cancel my appointments for the day.

I called my mom on the way and asked her to call an attorney. I ran into C and Phouey when I arrived at the ICE office. I saw other Cambodian people. Phouey had his sister there from Washington State and a lawyer. I was frantic in the waiting room. They asked me to step out of the waiting room, and they took me to the basement where Ched was detained. An officer with bad breath came up to me and gave me some papers. The officer told me that I should've known that this was going to happen. I asked if I could give Ched a hug. They said no. However, they let me talk to him through the glass. My mom called to tell me that she found a lawyer. We had an appointment that same day. Ched and I were both crying. I told him that we were going to figure this out. We should be okay. Ched had told me there were other Cambodians in the ICE building under detention.

VICHET: I've been a faculty member at the University of Minnesota since 2009 and quickly found connections within Minnesota's Cambodian community. I was born in Cambodia but came to the United States with my family at age three. I understood that many of the Cambodians caught up in the incarceration to deportation scheme are of my generation. We were young when we immigrated to the U.S. and pretty much "American" in our thinking, habits, and language. I was connected to the Cambodian deportation issue primarily through teaching and community service. Prior to joining the University of Minnesota, I taught Asian American studies at UC Santa Barbara, Cal State Long Beach, and UCLA. I was also connected to the movement through writing support letters and serving on the board of directors for the Southeast Asian Resource Action Center (SEARAC) in Washington, DC. At SEARAC I met fellow board member and immigration attorney Jay Stansell, who was featured in the film *Sentenced Home*. This documentary focused on three Seattle-based Cambodian refugees with removal orders due to immigration laws that do not allow for review or redress.[9] The film followed each of these men at different stages of the deportation process and highlights the painful consequences of forced family separation. After Jay's board term was up, legal scholar Bill Ong Hing joined us, which provided steady leadership on the Cambodian deportation issue.

I didn't know Jenny or Ched, but we had some mutual friends. A week after Ched was detained, I received a phone call from Jenny. She explained that her husband had been detained by ICE. Jenny requested that I join a meeting that afternoon with other impacted family members at the office of U.S. Senator Amy Klobuchar in Minneapolis. There I would meet with Jenny and other individuals whose loved ones were also in immigration detention. It was an emotional meeting of about five family members and a local immigration attorney. Senator Klobuchar did not attend. A member of her constituent services staff listened to families explain why it was unfair that their loved ones were detained and being prepared for deportation. The families asked for the senator's support. The staff member asked a few questions, expressed her sympathy, and said that she would look into the matter.

Meanwhile, outside of Senator Klobuchar's office was a growing protest that included youths, mothers, immigrant rights activists, and many others from the Cambodian community. Also present in the crowd were former Cambodian military personnel who fought with U.S. forces in Cambodia against the communist government in the early 1970s. It was poignant that these former soldiers, now older gentlemen, came to this rally in full uniform. Their attendance, in military wear, against the backdrop of this government office was a public reminder that many Cambodian people stood with the U.S. government decades ago. These individuals fled war and genocide with their families and were standing in protest against the deportation of their children back to Cambodia.

Figure 3.1: Deportation protest, September 2, 2016. Courtesy Minneapolis Public Radio.

Organizing Inside and Out: "We knew we couldn't break."

CHED: After being sent around to different facilities for a month, we returned to Minnesota. We knew we couldn't break. And at the same time, I felt like we could break at any moment. I had to constantly check myself emotionally and spiritually. I had to balance it out. In my journey I noticed folks who fell apart. I watched as their relationships fell apart. And then folks give up. There was a good check and balance between Jenny and I. We stayed in regular communication by phone and through letters. I loved getting mail from Jenny. And I loved writing to Jenny and writing to our kids back home. This was a lifeline for me, and I think it was for them too. Jenny sent me many things. Some of these included pictures and other details from supporters. This built spirit in me. I learned about the GoFundMe page and all of the people who donated money and time to helping us come home. I wrote to many people to thank them. It was a lot of writing, but not nearly enough in my opinion. I think all of that created hope for us. Whenever mail came, we always shared the news with our group of eight and then would continue to share it with whoever was around us.

Figure 3.2: "Ice monster" protest at Federal Building, Bloomington, Minnesota. Courtesy Thai Phan-Quang.

We were organizing on the inside and out. I would give relevant information to Jenny. Other guys would send along the names of relatives and friends that Jenny could get in touch with during the campaign. And then I remember when ICE flew us back to Minnesota. Other inmates were like, "Your people were at the ICE building! They were showing up on the news, channels 9, 12, 5!" It was everywhere. I saw my mom. I saw my kids. I saw people I didn't know. There was a lot of love for us. People were fighting for us. The other detainees were giving us love too. Even the corrections officers were like, "Yup, it's the MN8 guys." Others said they wished they had people fighting for them like that. Still, it showed other people in the holding tank with us that love and fight existed. People saw the "ICE monster" at one of the protests and were motivated by that.

JENNY: I gathered documents for the lawyer. Ched's brothers drove up from Iowa. They helped me locate all of his papers. I made a list of people to call for support letters. I began a text chain with Phouey's family and C's family. We found Ron's family through a change.org petition. Later on, Montha also told me that her brother was also detained.

Sometime after, I organized a meeting at the University of Minnesota Law School with [law professor] Linus Chan and community leaders to explore our options. Ched was organizing on the inside, getting information, names, and phone numbers. I was thinking about how we can share information. We know it's not just happening to one person. We are stronger as a group than just one. Right away, I was like, so many people are impacted and let's figure out what's happening. People didn't know what to do, and people were wanting to do something. I figured it was better to do it collectively. There was still a lot of information we needed to learn.

I found the Minnesota Immigration Rights Action Committee (MIRAC) and messaged them online. I met with MIRAC, and we discussed the importance of educating people. It was shared that Senator Klobuchar had a lot of influence in this area as she was on committees related to the Department of Homeland Security. That's why we decided to do an action at her building. Our demand was that she help us. MIRAC helped us with signs and invited an attorney they worked with. After that first rally we had many more actions. We also had meetings with Mijente and Navigate MN. Jacinta Gonzales from Mijente and Emilia from Navigate told us that the only way to win was to be political. People are curious about our work with organizations that were seen as Latinx focused. These were the organizations that responded right away. I think Navigate MN and MIRAC and Mijente knew firsthand what we were up against. They knew what we were going through or about to go through. I just remember that we had to make a lot of noise. We had to be loud.

VICHET: The week after the Klobuchar meeting the eight families and I met with members of Mijente, who helped explain the levers at ICE and Homeland Security for stopping the deportations. As Jenny noted, the advice by Mijente and other organizations was that the families will need to make noise if they are to interrupt these forced removals. The meeting was informative for me personally. More importantly, I could feel in the room the raw emotion of family members. Two sisters shared openly the mistakes that each of their younger brothers made and highlighted the ways these men worked hard to rebuild their lives after incarceration.

I recall in particular a conversation with one of the mothers. Speaking in Khmer, she shared with me that this was all her fault. I asked what she meant by that. She explained that her son was a "good boy." However, when he was younger, she was so busy working that she couldn't properly watch him. With little formal education herself, she was unable to help him with schoolwork. And so she blamed herself. He struggled academically and socially and turned to gangs as a teenager. He served many years in prison but was doing well after his release. He married, maintained a good job, and had not been in trouble since.

These conversations represent the kind of stories that would later anchor the campaign. As an education scholar, I understood that Cambodian children, whose resettlement communities were impoverished and crime-ridden, often did not receive proper educational support in school. Many Cambodian refugee youths struggled academically and found themselves disengaged and marginalized within their schools and neighborhood. As well, the fact that women and girls were the driving forces behind much of the campaign is hardly a discrete aspect of the ReleaseMN8 movement. The visibility and disproportionate presence of mothers, sisters, daughters, and nieces was apparent across months of organizing. Jenny, and other women, led the charge from the beginning. They made their presence felt through active participation in meetings, protests, and conversations.

This would seem inconsistent with traditional Cambodian culture, which often expects women and girls to stay in the background. Scholars have noted how Cambodian women's roles shifted at home and in communities in the 1970s as Cambodia was engulfed in civil war.[10] Cambodian women continued to redefine their positions during the Khmer Rouge regime (1975–1979) as families were often ripped apart. Men, women, and children were often taken away, sometimes never to be seen again. Pleading and negotiating with local chiefs and officials, Cambodian mothers did what they could to keep families together. Upon their arrival in the United States, Cambodian mothers and daughters were tasked with stabilizing home lives amidst settlement in poor, crime-ridden neighborhoods. As the case with the detained Minnesota eight men, fathers in many Cambodian refugee families were noticeably absent, due to a variety of factors including genocide, incarceration, and mental health struggles.

The Rollercoaster Ride: "Good news or bad news?"

CHED: In detention, there were days that one of us would go to court, and that was hard to process. Would he be coming back? Good news or bad news? Each guy had his way of processing it. They sometimes dealt with it with food, some wrote letters, and some did laps around the facility. We tried to stay supportive of each other. I had a court date in Rice County for a postconviction relief motion. This was an effort to get the BB gun charge dropped down, which could impact my immigration case. Jenny was doing the legwork. She reached out to people who went to high school with me and played football with me. Our friend Sambath Ouk was a board member of the Key Club in Rice County. We learned that the prosecutor is also a member of the Key Club. I learned that it was good to have people who they were familiar with.

I remember that the court room was packed. I was warned to not interact with anyone. They told me to not even make eye contact. This was their process, they said. But I still looked at Jenny! Unfortunately, as much support and strength in numbers that we had in Rice County, the judge denied the motion. When I returned to detention, it was important that the guys were there for me. Yes, of course I was down, but I knew that I was lucky to even have some legal options to fight my case. Others weren't as fortunate. The rollercoaster continued. It was a legal and emotional rollercoaster.

JENNY: We invited a lot of people to Ched's postconviction relief hearing at the Faribault courthouse, which was in Rice County. Sambath Ouk invited me to speak at the Faribault Key Club. We heard that the county attorney was also a Key Club member. They denied the postconviction relief, but the judge wrote a sympathetic letter that Linus [Chan] (Ched's attorney) said was helpful.

After the meeting we had with Emilia and Julia about escalation, we held a *Sentenced Home* film screening at the University of Minnesota. Emilia helped us understand civil disobedience tactics,

Figure 3.3: Flyer from October 20, 2016, film screening of *Sentenced Home* at the University of Minnesota.

and Julia helped us with the name. That meeting was also when we started calling ourselves ReleaseMN8. At the film showing, we packed the auditorium. After the film, we had the families sit up on stage with our attorney to talk about what we needed from supporters. We had call-to-action flyers with faces of the eight men, phone numbers of elected officials to call, and a script for people to follow.[11] Through this one event, we were able to create an email listserv with hundreds of names.

I kept Ched in the loop on all of this. Me and the kids wrote to him all the time. But then the guys who were locked up said they saw us on the news. Our later events had a lot of press coverage. Representative Keith Ellison [now Minnesota attorney general] wanted to champion our issue and said he would write an op-ed. I didn't even know what an op-ed was, but I agreed to it. Later we protested at the federal building in Bloomington. Black Lives Matter got involved. There was a lot of local TV coverage. We launched a digital campaign too. 18 Million Rising was helping to organize the call-in campaign. SEARAC was helping with the press, and NBC Asian America promoted our story. Later on, we took that trip to Washington, DC, with Ched and Posy's mom and Nikki.

VICHET: I recall that for the next few months, our lives were consumed by meetings with organizers, elected officials, and community members. I was warned by friends and family to not spend so much time on this. I was in the middle of a very difficult divorce. That, combined with my teaching responsibilities, and raising my young daughter, Maya, tested me in so many ways. I kept going because I was inspired. I was inspired by Jenny. I was inspired by all of these families. They just want what we all want; for our families to be home and whole.

We came to a collective decision to do everything we could to bring these men home. We reached out to all of our networks across neighborhood organizations, higher education institutions, and local nonprofits to gather support to pressure the U.S. government to stop these deportations. Jenny led the creation of a broad and racially diverse coalition of supporters. It was quite remarkable that the campaign was able to unite Latino, Asian, and Black serving organizations locally and nationally to stand with these Cambodian families. I imagine that this was effective because of the many layers involved including immigration, education, and the prison-industrial complex. Jenny and I met with a then relatively little-known Minnesota state representative named Ilhan Omar. She is now Congresswoman Omar. I lived in Representative Omar's district. We asked for her support and invited her to our next event. She said she was supportive of our efforts, and we all took a photo. However, we never heard from her again.

Like Jenny said, in November, a group of us that included mothers and sisters of detainees traveled to Washington, DC, to meet with governmental officials, advocacy groups, and the Cambodian ambassador to the U.S. himself to seek intervention. Everyone paid their own way. Our first meeting in DC was with a governmental office called the White House Initiative for Asian Americans and Pacific Islanders. I don't know if Ched knows this, but his mom, Sen Chith, really moved the room. A small elderly woman who had been largely quiet in our organizing meetings, Mrs. Chith shared why her trip to DC is more than just about Ched. Under the Khmer Rouge regime, four of her children died. She had lost them to starvation and illness during this "Killing Fields" period of Cambodia. Her story of loss was not unique for her generation but contributed to the sadness as well as the fight inside of her concerning Ched's removal order.

Across a two-day blitz, these family members met many elected officials and decision makers to share their stories. On the flight home, I happen to be seated in the row next to Ched's mother. We talked about our quick trip to DC, our families, and life in Minnesota. She continued to share stories about Ched, about his childhood and his very social personality. I remember her being quite talkative. She told me this was her first flight since arriving from Thailand some three decades earlier.

Coming Home: "The fight has to go on"

CHED: The U.S. Citizenship and Immigration Services granted our motion to reopen my case. While I was preparing for my hearing. I remember my attorney, Linus, and Jenny talking about percentages about winning. I remember vividly all of the people who attended the hearing besides family. I especially remember seeing a priest who sat in the front row. Of course, I was so nervous. Linus taught me a calming mechanism where I drew a dot on my hand. When they asked me a tough question, I would touch the dot and relax and answer the question. I did this each time. There were so many people there to support me, I was like, "damn." It felt like a movie.

I was so scared. I didn't quite believe that we won. But we did. After the judge handed down a positive decision, I just had to stay calm and get processed out. I was so nervous when they told me that someone is going to sign this and I can go. That day, after being in ICE detention for six months, I attended my son's basketball game in the evening.

It's been four years since my release. I was able to come home. So did Shorty and Sam. But I miss my other brothers—CNN, Ron, Phouey, Posy, and C. Five of us eight were deported. The fight has to go on. After my release, I attended all of the organizing meetings. I

Figure 3.4: Washington, DC, November 2016, from left, Quyen Dinh, Mari Quenemoen, Sovanna Leang, Nikki Chheourng, Deena Parseth, Jenny Srey, Sen Chith, Sokha Kul, Vichet Chhuon, Khoeun Choun, Katrina Dizon Mariategue.

want to help families be together. Before that, as a carpenter, I only knew how to help with my hands. Jenny has shown me how to help them with my stories, and help with my voice. I'm meeting with advocates, impacted families, and politicians. It's amazing to feel love from the community. Not just labeled as a criminal or as some guy in orange who was disposable.

JENNY: I was super nervous on the day of the hearing. I had Katrina [Dizon Mariategue] from SEARAC and Julie [Mao] from National Lawyers Guild staying over at my house. I had been running on pure adrenaline. We stopped by McDonald's on the way to the hearing, which somehow helped to calm my nerves. Pastor Danny Givens from Black Lives Matter led us in prayer that morning at the federal building. Jacinta [Gonzalez] sat outside the courtroom with me as I waited to testify for Ched. After my testimony, I sat in between Jason Sole and my mom, holding each of their hands. After the judge handed down a positive decision, all I could do was smile. I remember people were commenting how nice my smile was. I realized that I hadn't smiled in so long and so people were probably noticing it for the first time.

I cannot stress how grateful I am to those communities that stood with us. I've made some amazing friends through this experience. When you go through something like this, you really build trust. I took a lot of risks across the campaign with people. I felt vulnerable. Sometimes it worked out, and sometimes it didn't. You learn who you can trust. Fighting for our families required us to build deep relationships. That's what I have with many people as one result of all of this. In 2019 I drew on the strength of these relationships to co-found ReleaseMN8 as a nonprofit organization that works with families impacted by unjust immigration policies.

I also learned that I just might believe in miracles. Our lawyer told us that Ched's case is a unicorn. It is very unusual to get a positive decision. Many people told me during his detention that he was unlikely to be released. They advised me to prepare for the worst. People told me to prepare for Ched's deportation. I think I was getting ready for that, but at the same time I could not accept that for Ched and for our family. Also, after Ched and I were married, we were trying for a while to get pregnant but had no luck. Then fairly soon after his release we became pregnant. Our son is now three years old. One thing for sure is that the petty stuff doesn't bother me anymore.

VICHET: I remember well that day of Ched's hearing. Like Ched mentioned, it felt like a movie. Each moment felt heavy. Each word as part of each testimony felt important. Honestly, I was a bit numbed that morning. I had never met Ched, but I came to know Jenny, his kids, and his parents. I knew that his deportation would devastate their entire family. When the judge rescinded Ched's removal order, there was not the emotional outburst one might expect. Perhaps it was the respect for decorum in the courtroom. But I also think the quietness was because we were in shock after seven months of organizing. I would meet Ched a few days later. We've been close since.

Onward

"Stories have the power to direct and change our lives."[12]

We have described through dialogue and stories how the ReleaseMN8 campaign emerged from circumstance, tragedy, and struggle. As Polanyi noted, stories can help us see the "discrepancies between the way it ought to be and the way it (usually) is, and show the world to be even more as one thinks it is than one might have thought possible."[13] The manner in which stories are shared is certainly shaped by social and institutional context. People tell their stories differently when at their homes than at church, and differently in private than in public. Thus, context affects how and when the story begins and which characters and critical events are prioritized. The events, persons, and timelines described across our dialogue reflect the varying ways in which we located ourselves before, during, and following the ReleasseMN8 campaign. We recognize that other members of this campaign may privilege other issues, persons, and episodes. It is important to respect that others may understand the same events differently. Regardless, this chapter emphasizes the power of storytelling for honoring voice and the perspectives of those directly impacted by immigration policies.

Further, Ched's description of his detention reinforces the ways that inequality shapes the lives of noncitizens in the United States, particularly racialized immigrants like Cambodians. Ched's experience is consistent with other observations concerning the treatment of ICE detainees. It is common practice to house ICE detainees in the same unsafe facilities with those serving regular and often long prison sentences. In addition to six major immigration processing centers across the United States, scores of state and county facilities have intergovernmental agreements with the Department of Homeland Security.[14] Many of these facilities are corporately owned, underscoring the government's relationship with corporations that profit from the housing, transportation, and deportations of certain immigrants.[15] Amid these conditions, Ched and Jenny shared critical moments of hope and refusal across months of writing and struggling. For Ched, communicating through writing with Jenny and their children was a "lifeline" for him. Even with increased technology, traditional letter writing remains the most common and cost-effective way of communicating to loved ones from prison. Through the opportunity to process and edit their thoughts in writing, letters offer some healing possibility in very difficult circumstances. Ched's letters to his loved ones and those who were supporting ReleaseMN8 contributed to the campaign's cultivation of community, which in some ways subverted the carceral system's aims of disconnection and compliance for those locked up.

Over time, many local and national organizations became involved in the fight.[16] What is remarkable about ReleaseMN8 was that the families of those detained remained at the center of the campaign. At the same time, the political education we received cannot be overstated. It is critical to document ways that those most impacted by removal policies responded in defense of themselves and their loved ones. Jenny, Ched, and so many others in this campaign became fast learners of law, advocacy, and organizing. Family members navigated complex policies, economic hardship, and ever-changing social and political relationships. As we described at the chapter's onset, there were structured trainings with outside organizations. Equally important, however, were the opportunities to learn from one another in more intimate ways grounded in stories and experiences outside the courtroom. Parking lots, government buildings, and our own living rooms became sites of political action.

While Ched and others were in detention, each meeting we had with families and activists felt urgent. We were meeting at different hours on different days while responding to new developments. We did our best to work with families' work schedules, and we often met on Sundays. We understood that getting others involved was critical to our goals and often wondered: How can we draw even more people toward political action? William Gamson observed, "The trick for activists is to bridge public discourse and people's experiential knowledge, integrating them in a coherent frame that supports and sustains collective action."[17] Jenny and other family member organizers were tasked with persuading people that their participation would make a difference. However, these pleas were being offered against a history of immigration policies that have been devastating immigrant families for decades. How do we balance the push for significant action with minimal chance for success? For months, we negotiated these demands and realities.

Our goal in this chapter is to provide narrative texture to the Minnesota-based grassroots campaign dubbed ReleaseMN8. The campaign brought together families, advocates, youths, policymakers, scholars, elders, religious leaders, and activists to engage in a politic of refusal and challenge the unjust detention and deportation of Cambodian Americans. In doing so, the ReleaseMN8 campaign connected with other struggles and movements to demonstrate the power of multiracial campaigns and coalitions that generate hope and cultivate possibilities of transformative justice for all communities.

Notes

1 Pew Research Center (2017), Cambodians in the U.S. Fact Sheet, www.pewresearch.org. The phrase "killing fields" is taken from the 1984 film *The Killing Fields* (dir. R. Joffe). This phrasing is what much of the world associates with Cambodian history. Cambodians also refer to the killing fields but more regularly describe this dark period as "a Pot" (Pol Pot time).

2 There are multiple factors that led to Vietnam's invasion of neighboring Democratic Kampuchea (Cambodia), including Khmer Rouge genocide committed against Vietnamese populations in Kampuchea and strategic military concerns given that the Khmer Rouge was heavily backed by China. See Kiernan, B. (1996), *The Pol Pot Regime: Race, Power, and Genocide in Cambodia under the Khmer Rouge, 1975-1979*. New Haven: Yale University Press.

3 See Cahn, D., & Stansell, J. (2010), "1970s: Escape from War and the Creation of Refugees." In Jonathan H. X. Lee (ed.), *Cambodian American Experiences: Histories, Communities, Cultures and Identities*. Dubuque, IA: Kendall Hunt Publishing Company, 48-63; Chan, S. (2004), *Survivors: Cambodian Refugees in the United States*. Urbana: University of Illinois Press; and Tang, E. (2015), *Unsettled. Cambodian Refugees in the Hyperghetto*. Philadelphia. PA: Temple University Press.

4 Portes, A., & Rumbaut, R. G. (2006), *Immigrant America: A Portrait*. Berkeley: University of California Press, 98.

5 Chhuon, V. (2013), "I'm Khmer and I'm Not a Gangster!": The Problematization of Cambodian Male Youth in US Schools. *International Journal of Qualitative Studies in Education* 27 (2), 233-250.

6 Asians and Asian Americans occupy a critical role in U.S. immigration history, as the first persons marked for deportation by the U.S. government were Chinese immigrant workers in 1882. On the origins of the U.S. deportation regime, see Hestor, T. (2017), *Deportation: The Origins of U.S. Policy*. Philadelphia: University of Pennsylvania Press.

7 Hing, B. (2006), *Deporting Our Souls: Values, Morality, and Immigration Policy*. New York: Cambridge University Press.

8 Linde, C. (1993), *Life Stories: The Creation of Coherence*. New York: Oxford University Press.

9 Grabias, D., & Newham, N. (2006), *Sentenced Home* [film]. Indiepix.
10 See Ebihara, M., Mortland, C. A., and Ledgerwood, J. (1994), *Cambodian Culture since 1975: Homeland and Exile*. Ithaca, NY: Cornell University Press; Smith-Hefner, N. (1999), *Khmer American: Identity and Moral Education in a Diasporic Community*. Berkeley: University of California Press.
11 Sigal, B. (2016), "Families Call for Release of 'Minnesota 8' Facing Deportation to Cambodia," Fight Back News, October 21, 2016. www.fightbacknews.org.
12 Noddings, N. (1991), "Stories in Dialogue: Caring and Interpersonal Narrative and Dialogue in Education. In C. Witherell & N. Noddings (eds.), *Stories Lives Tell: Narrative and Dialogue in Education*. NY: Teachers College Record, 157–170.
13 Polanyi, L. (1981), "What Stories Can Tell Us about the Teller's World." *Poetics Today* 2, 97.
14 Hernandez, D. M. (2019), "Entangled Lineages and Technologies of Migrant Detention." In Chase, R. (ed.), *Caging Borders and Carceral States*. Chapel Hill: University of North Carolina Press.
15 Hernandez (2019).
16 We would like to thank the organizations that supported the ReleaseMN8 campaign, including MIRAC, Voices for Racial Justice, Navigate MN, Mijente, Asian American Organizing Project, Coalition of Asian American Leaders, SEARAC, National Khmer Legacy Museum, National Lawyers Guild, ACLU Minnesota, Black Lives Matter–Twin Cities, NAACP-Minneapolis, and Interfaith Coalition Immigration of Minnesota.
17 Gamson, W. (1996), "Constructing Social Protest." In Johnston, H., & Klandermans, B. (eds.), *Social Movements and Culture*. Minneapolis: University of Minnesota Press, 85.

PART II

Abolition and Decolonization: Militarism, Incarceration, and Transnational Activism

On May 20, 2021, President Joe Biden signed into law the COVID-19 Hate Crimes Act, a bill that expanded the reporting and enforcement of hate crimes targeting Asian Americans at the federal and state levels.[1] The bill came amid rising popular attention to anti-Asian violence animated by the racist categorization of COVID-19 as the so-called China virus. Yet, as critics pointed out, this framing of "anti-Asian hate" centered interpersonal acts of hate violence without naming the systemic forms of state violence enacted against Asian Americans. Even the enumeration of incidents of anti-Asian violence through data is imbued with carceral meaning, as statistics on the "surge" of anti-Asian violence are deployed by those calling for state intervention by means of policing and prosecution. Meanwhile, the bill's emphasis on law enforcement and hate crime legislation further empowered the U.S. criminal justice system as the arbiter and enforcer of hate violence rather than naming the state itself as the primary purveyor of racial violence.[2]

In this context, this section centers a different mode of engagement with violence and the state by foregrounding movements for abolition, decolonization, and demilitarization. Understanding Asian American politics as inherently shaped by overlapping carceral, imperial, and settler colonial systems, the chapters in this section embrace a political ethos of sovereignty, abolition, and transnational solidarity that transcends liberal civil rights appeals to state recognition. Candace Fujikane builds on her formative scholarship on Asian settler colonialism in Hawai'i to explore the possibilities for Asian settler allies to disrupt the structural privilege afforded under settler colonialism to stand with Kānaka Maoli and protect sacred lands. Kim Compoc explores the productive intersection of abolitionist and antimilitarist movements in the Philippines and Okinawa through campaigns for justice following the murders of Jennifer Laude and Rina Shimabukuro by U.S. military personnel. Shaun X. Lin and Yves Tong Nguyen reflect on abolitionist movements in New York City through their work with Red Canary Song and No New Jails. Drawing connections across campaigns to decriminalize sex work and oppose the construction of new local jails, they put forth a vision of community safety beyond the carceral state and its wielding of "anti-Asian hate" as a legitimizing discourse. Facing both escalating racial violence and the carceral consequences of state "protection," these case studies serve as a call to divest our politics from the boundaries of the state and the nation, and to instead create new networks, spaces, and institutions that reflect the mutuality of our struggles and our responsibilities to one another.

Notes

1 "Biden Signs Bill Addressing Hate Crimes against Asian-Americans," *New York Times*, May 21, 2021.
2 For critiques of this discourse, see Dylan Rodriguez, "The 'Asian exception' and the Scramble for Legibility: Toward an Abolitionist Approach to Anti-Asian Violence," *Society + Space*, April 8, 2021; Elizabeth Hanna Rubio, "What Is #StopAAPIHate to the Incarcerated and Deported?," *Society for Cultural Anthropology*, October 19, 2021, https://culanth.org.

4

Asian Settlers in a Decolonial and Abolitionist Movement

Honoring Mauna a Wākea and the Laws of the Elements

CANDACE FUJIKANE

Early on the morning of July 15, 2019, hundreds of Kanaka Maoli, Pacific Islander, Native American, Black, and settler land and water protectors made our way in the dark to gather at the base of the road leading up to the summit of Mauna a Wākea (the mountain also known as Mauna Kea, on Hawai'i Island).[1] Along the way, we grabbed silk-screened signs we had made at a HULI Art Build workshop organized by Andre Perez and Camille Kalama for Action Art, a critical component of a non-violent direct action (NVDA) methodology.[2] These signs showed the world that these are "Crown lands," that "We Are Mauna Kea," and "We Are Here to Protect Mauna Kea."[3] Four years earlier, on June 24, 2015, more than eight hundred people took a stand to protect the mountain from the construction of the Thirty Meter Telescope (TMT), an eighteen-story industrial complex with a footprint of five acres near the summit that would excavate twenty feet into the sacred mountain, removing 64,000 cubic yards (equivalent to 1,728,000 cubic feet) of earth. Thirty-one people were arrested in that 2015 stand. Mauna Kea hui attorney Richard Naiwieha Wurdeman stopped the construction by filing for a state supreme court stay of construction until the legal issues could be resolved, but in 2018 the Hawai'i Supreme Court affirmed the Board of Land and Natural Resources (BLNR) decision to issue a conservation district use permit to the TMT, and on July 11, 2019, Governor David Ige announced plans to close the road to the summit to enable the transport of heavy earth-moving machinery for construction.

The strategy for protecting the mauna had been kept to a small circle of Kanaka Maoli (Native Hawaiian) activists. The rest of us had been trained months in advance by HULI organizers Andre Perez and Camille

Kalama, forewarned by news reports that state and county law enforcement were arming themselves with tear gas and a long-range acoustic device (LRAD), also known as a sound cannon, used for "crowd control." Andre and Camille and other Kanaka Maoli water protectors from Hawaiʻi had flown to stand with the Oceti Sakowin, the Nation of the Seven Council Fires of the Lakota, Dakota, and Nakota speaking peoples, at the Standing Rock Indian Reservation in North and South Dakota, and they had brought back to Hawaiʻi the lessons of nonviolent direction action to prepare Mauna a Wākea protectors for similar police tactics. We arrived at Puʻuhuluhulu at the base of Mauna a Wākea on Friday night and slept in our cars and trucks for three days while organizing the stand. Over the weekend, the Royal Order of Kamehameha declared the grounds of Puʻuhuluhulu a *puʻuhonua*, a sanctuary for protectors of the mauna. When we gathered at the road that Monday morning, we watched as chairs were brought out and arranged across the road leading to the summit. We were astonished to see beloved kūpuna, silver-haired Kanaka Maoli elders and ally elders, bundled in blankets, taking their seats on the front line. They had chosen to protect the mountain and their descendants by being the first to be arrested. The kūpuna, the most physically vulnerable but most spiritually powerful among us, had chosen to stand up to these settler state tactics to show the world that we are resolute in our stand, and that we would stand in kapu aloha and nonviolence for the sacredness of Mauna a Wākea.

Two days later, on July 17, thirty-eight kūpuna and their kākoʻo (assistants) were arrested on the front line.[4] A thousand of us, with tears streaming down our faces, watched as state officers zip-tied their hands and carried them, or pushed them in wheelchairs, or escorted them as they pushed their walkers to police vans. The kūpuna had told us to stand back and to bear witness, as the whole world did, to the occupying state's criminalization of Kanaka Maoli elders protecting sacred lands. We stood in kapu aloha, a commitment to what is morally, ethically, and spiritually just.

On that first day, an ally named Gwen Kim sat on the front line with Kānaka Maoli kūpuna. Widely known as a woman who long stood with Kanaka Maoli, Gwen was one of many active Asian ally elders whose activism has been key in showing us that Asian allies have a choice: we can identify with the settler state, or we can choose to help

Figure 4.1: On the July 15, 2019, kūpuna line: Sharol Awai, William Freitas, Noe Noe Wong-Wilson, Gwen Kim, Maxine Kahaulelio, Patricia Puanani Ikeda, Hank Fergerstrom, Jonathan Kamakawiwoʻole Osorio, Mililani Trask, Sparky Rodrigues. Richard DeLeon stands behind them. Just outside of the photo: Nohea Kalima, Ranette Puna Robinson, Earl DeLeon, John Keone Turalde. Photo courtesy of Mehana Kihoi.

grow a future beyond the settler state. Gwen passed in May 2023, but visually, her presence on that 2019 front-line stand for Mauna a Wākea continues to signal to us, as other Asian ally elders like Ronald Fujiyoshi have also done, how a long history of activism *against* the settler state has also been an activism that makes possible a future *beyond* it.

In this stand for the land and Kanaka Maoli independence, Gwen and Ron are also standing for a planetary future. Lands and waters degraded by corporate, military, and settler colonial actions can best be restored if Indigenous stewardship of their land bases is restored. Indigenous economies of abundance will survive the changes on this earth that capitalist economies of scarcity cannot. In this way, the fight to protect Mauna a Wākea is allied with the stands Indigenous peoples around the world are taking to protect sacred places that are also the places of water necessary for an abundant futurity.

As Asian Americans struggled against the settler capitalist, carceral, heteronormative racial state in its various manifestations during the COVID-19 pandemic, we continue to struggle with the contradictions of standing for our civil rights without asserting a settler colonial claim to America or calling for an enforced police state. Anti-Asian racism and violence has intensified, with racist references during the pandemic as the "China virus," and yet what this has brought to the foreground are the ways that Asian Americans can easily fall into "claiming America" or into calls for increased protections from the carceral state. The long history of police brutality against Indigenous, Black, Palestinian, Muslim, migrant, queer, nonbinary, and transgender communities, the poor and the homeless/houseless, and all those who have been dehumanized by the state in all of its oppressive dimensions, however, shows us that the police state does not keep us safe. Public safety will only come about by defunding the police and redirecting those funds toward community-led safety initiatives rooted in social services and community organizing efforts led by community leaders, public health specialists, religious leaders, and survivor advocates. Beyond that, we are organizing locally around a world beyond settler states where land-based conceptions of governance foreground a reciprocal relationship with the earth in the face of global climate change.

As Gwen Kim and Ronald Fujiyoshi stood for Mauna a Wākea, two Black men also stood with Kānaka Maoli to protect the sacred mountain. D'Angelo "Gino" McIntyre had traveled to Mauna a Wākea in 2015 to stand with Kānaka Maoli, and in 2019 he helped to transport mauna protectors to and from airports and the puʻuhonua. Sheka Torrey Price is a freelance photojournalist from Delaware, and he had volunteered at the Pōpolo Project in Hawaiʻi, a nonprofit organization working to reshape the image of Blackness in the Pacific and the world. On July 13, Gino and Sheka joined Kanaka Maoli men, as well as settler allies including my brother Dean Saranillio and former student Abraham Yi, who sat on the ground behind our line of women facing state officers. Sheka was fully ready to be arrested with them.

Gwen, Ronald, and Sheka are powerful presences in our work to articulate what a decolonial and abolitionist future looks like. Settler colonialism, as Haunani-Kay Trask and Tiffany Lethabo King point out, is rooted in the interlocking histories of genocide and slavery.[5] If the U.S. settler capitalist, carceral, racial state can only function through our oppression, then our focus must be on a dismantling that state. We are being offered alternatives to that state by Black abolitionist movements and Kanaka Maoli, Native American, and other Indigenous statist and non-statist forms of land-based governance based on an ethics of reciprocity and care between humans and between humans and the natural world. The Puʻuhonua o Puʻuhuluhulu sanctuary that we saw sprout under the shelter of Mauna a Wākea is one such example.[6] To materialize a decolonial and abolitionist future, we are manifesting and enacting in the present the future beyond the settler state through intersecting abolitionist and decolonial work. In the here and now, we must continue to work toward defunding the police and the military and working toward community-led safety. As human rights lawyer, writer, and organizer Dereka Purnell writes, "Robust movements for socialism, decolonization, disability justice, and Earth justice are equally or perhaps more important than a singular movement for abolition."[7] In the here and now, we can also work toward materializing repatriation and rematriation of Native lands, as the NDN Collective is doing in the LANDBACK campaign, for a planetary future that will survive climate change.

In this chapter, I look to the struggles on Mauna a Wākea to argue that Kānaka Maoli are enacting broad solidarities challenging the unjust laws of the occupying state through their assertion that the enduring kānāwai a ke akua, the laws of the elements, supersede the arbitrary laws of humans. In this challenge to the juridical authority of the state, Kānaka Maoli are allied with the Black Lives Matter movement in seeking to grow a land-based conception of governance. I begin by considering the ways that state laws regarding Mauna a Wākea violate both human and elemental laws at the same time that Kānaka Maoli and their allies are being criminalized, as evidenced by both the 1895 arrests of aloha ʻāina, the patriots who sought to restore Queen Liliʻuokalani to the throne, and the 2015 arrests of aloha ʻāina protecting Mauna a Wākea. I then turn to a discussion of the importance of arrests in archiving a history of resistance, and I honor the work of two Asian allies: Gwen Kim and Ronald Fujiyoshi. I conclude by considering the words of one Black

Figure 4.2: Sheka Price Torrey sitting with Kanaka Maoli and allied men behind the wahine line of women standing with arms linked on the front line. Still from video by Candace Fujikane.

ally, Sheka Torrey Price, who shows us that a decolonial future must be abolitionist, and an abolitionist future must be decolonial.

To ground this discussion of the multiple ways that we are pili (connected) to each other through our shared kuleana (responsibility, privilege, purview) to care for this earth, I want to lay a foundation for this chapter by focalizing the ways that our settler activism deepens the relevance of our scholarship, broadening our archives, and teaching us to listen for theory that emerges organically from the stories of people in collective struggle. I entered into the struggle to protect Mauna a Wākea in 2011, and at that time, I thought there was little that I could offer to the struggle. I quickly realized that as a scholar-activist, I could use my research skills to present testimony against the construction of the Thirty Meter Telescope in toxic juridical state spaces. I have read through thousands of pages of the three volumes of the TMT environmental impact statement, cultural impact assessments, and archaeological inventory surveys of Mauna a Wākea, as well as moʻolelo (storied histories), oli (chants), and mele (song) about Mauna a Wākea to learn how the mauna is represented in ʻōlelo Hawaiʻi (Hawaiian language). I have spent eight years slowly learning the intricacies of ʻōlelo Hawaiʻi and learning about the relationships of people to the elemental forms and the relationships between elemental forms.

An Asian settler positioning also enables us to archive more embodied forms of knowledge necessary to activating the elemental forms and our relationships with them. In 2012, I joined Huakaʻi i Nā ʻĀina Mauna, and Kū Ching became my alakaʻi (leader) and kumu (teacher), showing me the many different expressions of Mauna a Wākea and to love the mountain as his kupuna (ancestor). Since then, we have walked the mountain for one week every year, monitoring state activities and recording the occupying state's violations of human and elemental laws. We walk Mauna a Wākea on nine-hour huakaʻi (voyages), under the sun that bites in the thin air of the wao akua (realm of the elements), spacing our breathing to capture oxygen. We bear witness to the source of water on the mountain, the mists as the elemental form Līlīnoe who meanders over the land, swirling with the figures of her water sisters Poliʻahu, Kahoupokāne, and Waiau. I have seen the paths of water, the tiny parallel ridges of beautiful, multicolored pebbles caused by rivulets of frost heave, traces of Poliʻahu's footsteps on the mauna. I have gathered water for ceremony from the sacred springs of the mauna, water dripping from moss-covered stones once collected for the aliʻi (chiefs). I have made my way across fields of giant black lava bombs spewed from the mauna in eruptions long ago, now resembling humpback whales, koholālele breaching from the brown earth of the mauna, bringing forth ancestral knowledge from the ancestral realms of Pō. As a former attorney, Kū quizzes me on the latest legal moves of the TMT attorneys, strategizing like a master of konāne.[8]

And when necessary, I have been arrested on the front lines. As scholar-activists, we feel a critical shift in our positioning when we take these risks. I hear our voices reverberating collectively from our jail cells: "E iho ana o luna, / e piʻi ana o lalo, / e hui ana nā moku, / e kū ana ka paia! (That which is above shall be brought down / that which is below shall be lifted up, / the islands shall be united, / the walls shall stand upright)." As I argue, these arrests provide us with a powerful sense of our connectedness with the kūpuna who stood for land in past generations. Expanding our conceptions of our connectedness is necessary to the relationships we grow to expand our abolitionist and decolonial imaginations, to bring about futures that we have not yet imagined but that emerge through the work that we do.

The Laws of the Elements versus the Laws of Humans

Mauna a Wākea is the maka ihe, the spear tip, uniting the different struggles to protect lands and waters in Hawai'i. As "ka makahiapo na Wakea," the sacred firstborn of the union of Papahānaumoku, She who is the foundation birthing islands, and Wākea, the wide expanse of the heavens, Mauna a Wākea is "ka piko o ka moku," the piko of the island in the many senses of the word.[9] The mauna is the sacred piko or summit where the earth meets the sky. The mauna is also the elder sibling of both the kalo plant and the Kānaka, the people, all fathered by Wākea. Through this moʻokūʻauhau (genealogy), Mauna a Wākea is the piko as the umbilicus, the cord that binds the people to their ancestors and all of their pulapula, the seedling descendants, all those who came before and all who will come after. Mauna a Wākea thus embodies a profound sense of pilina—familial connectedness—to the past, present, and future.

Mauna a Wākea is also located in what is known as the wao akua, the realm of the elemental forms. The word *akua* is popularly defined as "god," but kumu hula (hula master) Pualani Kanakaʻole Kanahele translates akua as "elemental energetics" and natural processes.[10] There are 400,000 akua across the archipelago, each representing the natural processes in particular places. The wao akua, then, is the realm where the elemental forms preside and where their laws are preeminent. The Edith Kanakaʻole Foundation and Lonoa Honua are two organizations at the forefront of a movement that approaches climate change with ʻike kupuna, ancestral knowledges. Pualani Kanakaʻole Kanahele has established the Papakū Makawalu methodology, based on her close reading of the Kumulipo, the koʻihonua chant that tells of the birth of all things out of the heat of the deep, dark night.[11] In the Thirteenth Wā of the Kumulipo, a genealogy chant chronicling the birth of all things from the ancestral darkness of Pō, we see the birthing of what would become three houses of knowledge: Papa Hulihonua, Papahulilani, and Papa Hānaumoku.

The Kanakaʻole Foundation identifies the kānāwai, or laws of the akua or elements, that they have deciphered in mele (songs) and oli (chants), amplified through the art of kilo: keen, intergenerational observation and forecasting. The four kumu kānāwai or fundamental ecological laws from which other laws are derived are:

Hoʻokikī Kānāwai: The edict of continuum. Forces of nature in cooperation for continuity and flow so that magma moves, water runs, rains fall, air and ocean currents flow unobstructed and ferns kupu, and the island body persists. It is the law of continuum.

He kuaʻā Kānāwai: The edict of the gestating landscapes. Signs in the landscape where creation is occurring, like hot spots, marshes, steaming areas, wisdom sharers, coral heads, maʻukele. It is the law of the burning back.

He kaiʻokia Kānāwai: The edict of natural boundaries. Natural boundaries and pathways are delineated by lava flow and rivers, rivers and valleys, ocean and land, kū and hina, height and depth. It is the law of natural boundaries.

He kīhoʻihoʻi Kānāwai: The edict of regeneration. Greening of a new flow by Hiʻiaka, restoration of landscapes, when allowed the opportunity—land, ocean, and kanaka return to health. It is the law of regeneration.[12]

Based on these kānāwai, we know that the TMT threatens the Hoʻokikī Kānāwai, the edict of continuum and the free flow of water. The kūpuna teach us that Mauna a Wākea is the home of the akua of water—mists, snows, rains, springs, the lake. Mauna a Wākeaʻs sacredness has protected the mountain from human activities that would contaminate the waters of the five aquifers that it sits on. One of the many threats the TMT poses is that it proposes to house two 5,000 gallon (equivalent to 18.6 tons each) tanks underground, one storing toxic chemical waste water and the other storing human wastewater.[13] There will also be a 2,000 gallon diesel tank above ground. These tanks will be located over the Waimea aquifer that feeds much of Hawaiʻi Island. The environmental impact statement for the TMT estimates that once a month, when the tanks reach 2,000 gallons (or 7.4 tons of liquid), the tanks would be emptied onto a truck that would then transport the hazardous wastes down the steep, curving, unpaved road of the mountain.

The increased risk for toxic spills occurs at the points of loading and transporting these wastewaters down the mountain. The hydrologist hired by the University of Hawai'i attorneys claims that the TMT would not have an adverse impact on groundwater, but he also admitted that he does not know where the groundwater is.[14]

Kānaka Maoli uphold the laws of the elements and thereby challenge the juridical authority of the late liberal settler state. Kealoha Pisciotta has protected Mauna a Wākea from the construction of new telescopes for over twenty years. She explains, "Mauna Kea holds a special place on earth; therefore the cultural tradition as a temple is dedicated to peace and aloha. When we walk on the sacred ground and in the sacred realms, we are bound by the laws of akua, not our own."[15] As she concludes, "State laws have no jurisdiction in the wao akua."

Yet what is even more striking is that the TMT violates *both* elemental laws and occupying state laws protecting conservation districts. Thus, in 2018, when four Hawai'i Supreme Court justices ruled to uphold the BLNR decision to approve the conservation district use permit issued to the Thirty Meter Telescope, that act was also a violation of human laws. In the majority opinion, the justices concluded that Kānaka Maoli were unable to prove that they conducted their cultural practices specifically on the proposed site of the TMT, despite the fact that the TMT environmental impact statement recognizes those practices. They wrote, "The BLNR found no evidence, however, of Native Hawaiian cultural resources, including traditional and customary practices, within the TMT Observatory site area and the Access Way, which it characterized as the relevant area."[16] The words of the settler state here illustrate what I have described elsewhere as a settler colonial mathematics of division, shrinking the "relevant area" to the narrow boundaries of the TMT site.[17] The TMT environmental impact statement, however, identifies the project area as part of a larger complex of more than 263 historic properties in the Mauna Kea Summit Region Historical District, including 141 ancient shrines in the Mauna Kea Science Reserve.[18] Yet despite this evidence that the summit is sacred, the court engaged in a mathematics of subdivision, subdividing the summit of Mauna Kea until the proposed site of the TMT in and of itself is no longer culturally sensitive, and in such ways, the laws of humans are erratic, manipulated to serve human interests, in contrast to the enduring laws of the elements.

What is even more troubling is that the Hawai'i Supreme Court ruling establishes a devastating new "degradation principle." In his dissenting opinion, Justice Michael Wilson points to the way that majority opinion is "fraught with illogic." The degradation principle that Wilson references is this contorted rhetoric in the TMT environmental impact statement:

> In general, the project will add a limited increment to the current level of cumulative impact. Therefore, those resources that have been substantially, significantly, and adversely impacted by past and present actions would continue to have substantial, significant, and adverse impact with the addition of the Project. For those resources that have been impacted to a less than significant degree by past and present actions, the Project would not tip the balance from a less than significant level to a significant level and the less than significant level of cumulative impact would continue.[19]

Wilson rightly argues that "the degradation principle dilutes or reverses the foundational dual objects of environmental law—namely, to conserve what exists (or is left) and to repair environmental damage."[20] The articulation of this degradation principle undermines environmental law by presenting a view of Mauna a Wākea as being degraded beyond repair, precisely the apocalyptic view that the earth, too, has passed a threshold of no return.

Of most concern to me is the way that the degradation principle in the TMT case erodes any basis for denying a construction permit in the conservation use district. The absurdity of this formulation is that the impacts of a project either do not degrade land enough to have crossed the threshold of impact or lands are already too degraded past such a threshold for the project to have an impact: in either case, projects are permitted to move forward. As the multinational corporation that generated this regime of rhetoric in this environmental impact statement is spread out over five hundred offices in forty countries, we are seeing capital's wastelanding rhetoric affecting all areas of the globe.

In these and many other ways, human laws are driven by profit and not by the laws of the elements that are necessary for our continued survival as humans. We can see the ways that our very survival depends on dismantling capitalist, white supremacist, settler regimes through abolitionist and decolonial visions of a radically different world that grows out of an economy of mutual aid and reciprocity between humans, and between humans and the natural world—a world that recognizes that humans, too, are rooted in and are a part of that natural world.

Aloha 'Āina Political Prisoners, 1895

Asian settlers in the Hawai'i State Legislature stand with the settler state against Kānaka Maoli on problematic legal grounds. One Japanese American state legislative House Speaker has said that he is concerned about the ways that protectors were not obeying the Hawai'i Supreme Court decision to affirm the approval of the conservation district use permit for the TMT and that they were "losing sight of the importance of law in our society. What law means and whether or not people need to abide by the law."[21] Yet we see that the history of the United States has been a series of movements challenging its own white supremacist, heteropatriarchal laws, from the abolitionist and feminist movements to the American Indian Movement (AIM), the civil rights movement, the LANDBACK movement, the Black Lives Matter movement, the movement for migrant rights, and the Stop Asian Hate movement. How can we find just laws in a racial, capitalist, carceral settler state founded on genocide, slavery, settler colonialism and occupation, imperialism, and the caging of migrants? At this historical juncture, I want us to remember that identifying as American has been a strategic move for Asian Americans in the face of racism and anti-immigrant legislation, but I want us to think about the possibilities of what a *disidentification* from the U.S. settler state means. As Asian settlers, we have a choice: we can align ourselves with the settler racial state or we can envision a different kind of future. Gwen Kim stood for the protection of lands and waters in the 1970s to stop the eviction of farmers from leased lands in Kalama Valley and in Waiāhole-Waikāne. She fought in movements ranging from students' efforts to establish an Ethnic Studies Department at the University of Hawai'i to demilitarization movements to stop live-fire training at the Mākua Military Reservation and Pōhakuloa Training Area. She was arrested for opposing the importation of the Stryker Brigade armored vehicles to Hawaiʻi, an intensification of militarism spearheaded by U.S. Senator Daniel Inouye.[22] Later in her activist career, she worked for the Queen Liliʻuokalani Children's Trust, and as the daughter of a kalo farmer on the windward side of Oʻahu, coordinated the efforts of ʻOnipaʻa Nā Hui Kalo, a revolutionary hui, or collective, of hundreds of people who flew to different islands to restore ancient loʻi kalo (taro pond fields) across the islands. The restoration of loʻi kalo has had ripple effects in a resurgence of Kanaka Maoli lifeways and the movement to affirm Hawaiʻi's independence.

When allies like Gwen stand for lands and waters with Kānaka Maoli, they are also standing with a long line of aloha ʻāina who have stood for the lāhui (nation) since the overthrow and annexation. I want to return to Gwen's stand and the words that she said at Mauna a Wākea: "When we started the sovereignty struggle many, many years ago, like 40, 50 years ago with Kekuni Blaisdell, Gayle [Kawaipuna] Prejean, Soli [Niheu]—the father of my children—we were a small group, and they thought we were kind of crazy, you know? *But look at this.* Look at them rising, look at these young people rising, these families."[23] Gwen was there at the outset of the modern Hawaiian movement for life, lands, and sovereignty. She made it clear that she was an ally, a Korean woman who grew up farming kalo and understanding the importance of Kānaka Maoli struggles for land and the global implications of the rise of Native peoples.

Gwen pointed to the fact that Kānaka Maoli being arrested today have a genealogy of aloha ʻāina and a connection to the earlier Hawaiian patriots who stood with love for Queen Liliʻuokalani, the lāhui, and love for the land:

> Like I said, you know, there are so many others who have gone before, and they have given their whole lives to this movement. It's an honor for those of us to be there to represent them. There's a whole genealogy behind us, going back to the Kūʻē petitions, the people were imprisoned for standing up for the right thing. . . . In the end, the only thing we have is our bodies, to stand against this kind of destruction. Look at Mauna Kea, how many they would have had to arrest! They don't have enough

paddy wagons for the number of people who were willing to put their bodies on the line. If that's all we can do because we are shut out from the regular political processes by those with money and greed—well, then, damn it! We're going to put our bodies on the line. And everyone who walked, had to ask, "Am I willing to risk my life for this?"[24]

Gwen recalled for us the aloha 'āina who signed the 1898 anti-annexation petitions that turned the tide in Congress and killed the proposed treaty of annexation. Without two-thirds of the vote in Congress, the United States resorted to forcibly annexing Hawai'i through a joint resolution that required a simple majority vote—a clear violation of international law.[25] When arrested for standing in protection of lands and waters, aloha 'āina are political prisoners who stand for the political autonomy of the Hawaiian nation-state. In his own research, Ronald Williams Jr. located the 1895 arrest photos of three hundred and seventy aloha 'āina in a book labeled "Political Prisoners" in the Hawai'i Judiciary Building archives.[26] As he explains, those arrested included not only the men who fought in Robert Wilcox's insurrection, but also other loyalists who refused to pledge allegiance to the new republic. Where the occupying state has criminalized Kānaka Maoli for standing for the political independence of their people, more recently leaders like Andre Perez and Kaleikoa Ka'eo arrested on Mauna a Wākea emphasize that they are "POLITICAL PRISONERS" in words emblazoned on their shirts at the time of their arrests to amplify that they were being persecuted for seeking deoccupation and decolonization.

"A hiki i ke aloha 'āina hope loa!" (Until the last aloha 'āina!) is a powerful rallying call in the fight to protect Mauna a Wākea, signaling that the pulapula (seedling descendants) will carry on aloha 'āina work of their kūpuna in an intergenerational stand. On September 6, 1897, thousands of Kanaka Maoli patriots stood at 'Iolani Palace, listening to the words of James Keauiluna Kaulia opposing the proposed treaty of annexation. He said to the people,

> He aupuni kuokoa ko kakou i nai ia e e na Kamehameha i moe aku la, a o ka pono kukulu Aupuni kuokoa a lakou i imi ai, oia ka kakou e hauoli ne i keia la, nolaila, he aha na pilikia i ulu ae i ko kakou noho kuokoa ana?

Figure 4.3: Arrest photos of Kanaka Maoli aloha 'āina who rose up to restore Queen Lili'uokalani to the throne. Three hundred and seventy men and women ages thirteen to seventy-seven were arrested in the 1895 insurrection. These photographs were found by scholar Ronald Williams Jr. in the Judiciary Building archives.

O ke kuokoa a na makua Alii i imi ai i pono hooilina no ka lahui, oia ke ake ia nei e kanu ola ia, au e olelo ae ai ina e hoohuiia kakou me Amerika, oia ka kakou ae ana aku e kanu ola ia kakou ka lahui i loko o na popilikia he nui e ho'ea mai ana ma hop o ka hoohui ia ana. No laila, mai makau, e kupaa lokahi e ka manao, e kue loa aku i ka hoohui ia o Hawaii me Amerika *a hiki i ke aloha aina hope loa!*

We have an independent government that was formed by the Kamehamehas, who are now at rest. And the right that they sought, to build an independent government is the reason for our happiness today. Therefore, what are the problems that grow out of our continuing independence? The independence that our beloved Aliʻi sought as a rightful inheritance/legacy for the lāhui Hawaiʻi of which I speak, that is what they [the occupying state] desire to be buried alive: consenting for our nation to be subsumed within America is like agreeing that we, the nation, be buried alive with the many hardships that would follow annexation. Do not be afraid! Stand firm in love for this land, and unify in this thought, vigorously protest the annexation of Hawaiʻi by America *until the very last aloha ʻāina patriot who loves this land.*[27]

Kauila's words evoke for us the great love of Kānaka Maoli for their lands and lāhui, and how they were willing to sacrifice their lives to stop the annexation of Hawaiʻi.

Those arrests mark the beginning of a long history of arrests of aloha ʻāina who have continued to stand for the lands and waters of Hawaiʻi: at Kahoʻolawe to stop the military bombing of the island, at Kalama Valley and Waiāhole against the eviction of farmers and the corporate diversion of waters, at Waokele o Puna against geothermal development, at Sand Island / Mauliola against the eviction of homeless people, at Hālawa against the construction of the federal highway over burial complexes and sacred places, at Kahuku and Kalaeloa against dangerous giant wind turbines, at Kauaʻula against the desecration of iwi kupuna (ancestral remains) by urban development, and many, many more places where aloha ʻāina are arrested for opposing the settler colonial extractivism, exploitation, and the desecration of the laws of the akua, the elemental forms.

As a settler scholar, I look to the lessons Kanaka Maoli scholars have taught us about the work that we need to do as settlers. Haunani-Kay Trask in 1997 identified Asian Americans in Hawaiʻi as "settlers," and I had helped to develop that discussion in 2000 in a co-edited special issue of *Amerasia Journal* called *Whose Vision? Asian Settler Colonialism in Hawaiʻi*, which was expanded in 2008 into *Asian Settler Colonialism: From Local Governance to the Habits of Everyday Life in Hawaiʻi*. In a conversation with Noelani Goodyear-Kaʻōpua, I asked if we could begin to think about a "settler aloha ʻāina," a settler love for the land, without it being reduced to a settler appropriation of an ethic that grows out of an ʻŌiwi genealogical relationship to land. She went on to discuss this concept in her book *The Seeds We Planted*, where she discusses the ways that settler allies can enact aloha ʻāina while recognizing settler privilege. She writes,

> Perhaps such a positioning might be thought of as a settler aloha ʻāina practice or kuleana. A settler aloha ʻāina can take responsibility for and develop attachment to lands upon which they reside when actively supporting Kānaka Maoli who have been alienated from ancestral lands to reestablish those connections and also helping to rebuild Indigenous structures that allow for the transformation of settler-colonial relations. What we see is the emergence of new modes of non-statist organizing that have made possible a return to broad-based alliances that takes into consideration that settlers, too, can stand for the Lāhui Hawaiʻi, but it is one that must be informed by an understanding of our positionality and the operations of settler occupation.[28]

Since the publication of *Mapping Abundance*, there have been very healthy conversations about the role of settlers in Native struggles for national liberation. I want to turn to one criticism that I take to heart and one that I will move with, not against. On September 12, 2022, Kanaka Maoli activist Healani Sonoda Pale gave a talk entitled "Solidarity and Settler Allies" at the HK West Maui Community Fund series in Lahaina, which can be accessed on Facebook. Sonoda Pale argues that the term *settler aloha ʻāina* enacts a settler theft of the Kanaka Maoli concept of aloha ʻāina, a concept of love for the land that is rooted in Kanaka Maoli genealogy. This is a very important critique at a time when we are struggling to find terms that define ourselves relationally and move us toward a decolonial future. Sonoda Pale's point is that aloha ʻāina is born out of a genealogical relationship with the elements: the Kumulipo traces the genealogy of Kānaka back to the emergence of life out of Pō, the deepest darkness out of which all life emerges, the animals of the sea and the land, the stars, Papahānaumoku and Wākea, their daughter Hoʻohōkūkalani, Hāloanakalaukapalili, the kalo plant, and Hāloa, the first aliʻi. In this genealogy, Kānaka Maoli are directly descended from land and are taught aloha ʻāina for their kūpuna and elder and younger siblings.

I see the problem that Sonoda Pale raises, and I no longer use the term *settler aloha ʻāina*. There are useful arguments for the terms *settler accomplice* or *settler comrade*, but in Hawaiʻi, the term *settler ally* has been more widely used by Kanaka Maoli activists and is the term that Sonoda Pale uses herself. I use *settler* to define support by describing the actions we engage in, defining ourselves by what it is we *do* instead of the terms we call ourselves.

I identify as a "settler" because it locates me in the conditions of U.S. occupation, and I can use my own positioning strategically in an Asian-dominated settler state. I identify as a "settler" because it roots our activism in a *capaciousness*, one that grapples with the social processes of settler occupation and foregrounds the fact that we are settlers who oppose U.S. occupation. We call attention to the conditions of settler occupation at the same time that we show that we can live our lives opposed to settler occupation, and this opens up the *imaginative possibilities* for our collaborative work on *ea*, a word meaning life, breath, and sovereignty for a land-based lāhui (nation). As Asian settlers, we recognizes that our work encompasses, and yet is more than, being an ally; our work focuses on materializing decolonization itself and an opposition to all forms of oppression mobilized by the occupying settler state.

The term *aloha 'āina* is rooted in the stand that patriots of the Kingdom of Hawai'i took to end U.S. occupation. When we look to the arrests of Kānaka Maoli in the 1895 insurrection against the overthrow, we can see that identifying a settler who stands for lands and waters means giving something up of ourselves in making a ho'okupu (offering) to the lāhui Hawai'i (nation, collective). As Pualani Kanaka'ole Kanahele and her team of Papakū Makawalu researchers write,

> The nature of an exchange is directly proportionate to the significance and the intention of the exchange. In other words, if I were felling a whole 'ōhi'a tree, whose life many are dependent upon, for a ki'i (carved image), my exchange would require much more effort than if I were to ask for a liko or bud to make a lei from the same tree.... The most valuable and extreme forms of exchange require a life for a life. Some forms of reciprocity require prescribed prayers, offerings, sweat, blood, muscle, or years of commitment. Whatever the case may be, the mindset and act of reciprocity and sacrifice would not be taken lightly.[29]

As settlers, we need to help shoulder the kaumaha (weight, burden, grief) of occupation and settler occupation by doing the difficult work that Native people do. More settler land and water protectors can take our places in toxic juridical state spaces, testifying against the ways that the occupying state breaks its own laws and standing on the front lines. And more of us can help to grow the foundation for a decolonial future by helping streams to flow once again so that the kalo can ripen and the fish can spawn, while supporting a form of Kanaka Maoli governance that will sustain all of us past the ruins of capital. Being a settler can mean to grow an intimacy with land that brings about more pono (just, balanced, and generationally secure) arrangements of life. It is to open ourselves to a different consciousness by which we receive an intimate understanding of land and the elements, and by which we pass this knowledge on.

And when necessary, settlers can and should help shoulder the burden of arrests. I have been arrested at Kalaeloa for standing with the people of Kahuku—largely Pacific Islander communities—to protect their homes and schools from the devastating health consequences of the giant wind turbines. I stood in the wahine line at Mauna a Wākea on July 17, 2019, facing police officers. I was fully prepared to be arrested because even though I am not Kanaka Maoli, I believe that Mauna Kea is sacred.

I want to make it clear that I am not fetishizing arrests, and leaders in the movement to protect Mauna a Wākea have discouraged people from being arrested. But when we see that Native peoples are on the front lines of movements against climate change, and when peoples under state assault are getting arrested *multiple times* to protect places, that is when settlers who can afford to be arrested can step in to hold space for those who have already been arrested or who would be excessively punished by interlocking systems of settler colonial punitive measures that would impact jobs, education, or even custody of their children.

And there is also a protocol to arrests. I have seen white settlers stand in front of Native peoples to get arrested, but although they are well-intentioned, such protocols are to be determined by Native people who are most committed to those struggles. Like the kūpuna at Mauna a Wākea, land and water protectors organizing their struggles may choose to be arrested first as an expression of love for their lands and people.

Figure 4.4: Twelve of the thirty-one aloha ʻāina who were arrested on April 2, 2015: Chase Kahoʻokahi Kanuha, Craig Neff, Dannette Godines, Lambert Lavea, Eric Heaukulani, Erin O'Donnell, Gary Oamilda, Moanikeala Akaka, James Albertini, Joseph Kanuha, Keliʻi "Skippy" ʻIoane, Ronald Fujiyoshi. Hawaiʻi Police Department photos printed in *Big Island Now* online news, April 2, 2015.

Aloha Āina, 2015

Arrests of protectors at Mauna a Wākea resonate across time with the arrest photos of the 1895 aloha ʻāina. On April 2, 2015, thirty-one kiaʻi mauna (protectors of Mauna Kea) were arrested for criminal trespass as they formed a blockade against earth-moving equipment being transported to the summit. Among the photos of aloha ʻāina was a photo of one Japanese settler man. Ron Fujiyoshi is a Japanese settler who has stood for Hawaiʻi's independence for over thirty years, dating back to the Ka Hoʻokolokolonui Kānaka Maoli, the International Peoples' Tribunal that in 1993 found the United States guilty of violations of international law.

Ron teaches us lessons about how to leverage arrests to expose the legal fictions of the occupying or settler state. When I asked Ron how he made the decision to be arrested, he told a story of two of his arrests. In 1989 at Wao Kele o Puna, he was one of 212 people who were arrested for protecting the akua Pele from geothermal drilling. He explains how he made that choice:

> One time, I was in court with Marie Beltran, a Hawaiian woman who had been arrested for being a houseless person living on Mokulēʻia Beach. She is a good friend, and she calls me "Dad." She asked me to go with her to her court hearing in Wahiawā, and when we got to the courthouse, she says to me, "Dad, come look at this." It was a poster of the court system, honoring various levels of the court except the judges, and everyone was Japanese. The Japanese have played a part in this oppressive system. In some ways it's a stereotype, but in other ways, it's a reality. In 1989, I chose to get arrested to protect Wao Kele o Puna from geothermal development because I saw that the people in struggle were all Hawaiian and haole. I saw no Japanese. Most Japanese are pro-development, and so I decided I had to be part of the movement to end this prolonged occupation of Hawaiʻi.[30]

Ron is a part of that decolonial nation-building movement, and his arrest photo is an intervention into the racialized narratives of Japanese upholding the settler judicial system, which again and again has ruled against Hawaiian customary and traditional rights. Through these kinds of material practices, we are working to redefine our positionalities.

As a Japanese settler minister invested in liberation theology, Ron wanted his second arrest to demonstrate that people who are not Hawaiian also believe in the sacredness of Mauna a Wākea. He explains,

> It shocked them because I wanted to go to jail. If they're going find me guilty, I want to embarrass them, you know, and say, Go ahead, put a minister of a Hawaiian church in jail for obstruction when he's arguing that he believes that Mauna Kea is sacred. When I was in Southeast Asia, I worked with people of all kinds of faiths, and I respected all of their religions, and when I came back to Hawaiʻi, I saw that the court system doesn't respect the Hawaiian religion. Something is wrong, right? And I'm saying, the court system is wrong. I never argued sovereignty. I never

argued conservation. I argued sacredness. Christians argue sacredness. Even when people were saying, you're not going to win on it, I said, no, it's not about winning or losing, you're going to push what you think is the right principle, and push it all the way to its logical conclusion. We argued for the principle of the sacred, not to win the court case. You gotta to change the minds of the people; you cannot just say you just want to win the court case.[31]

So often, land and water protectors find that they can only win a case on a procedural error, not on the merits of the case, precisely because the occupying state will not admit to the unjust nature of its own laws. Ron's words illustrate a true vision of justice where the arrests are a way of laying bare for the public the fallibility of human laws. In the end, the court claimed a technical error and dismissed Ron's case without his consent. Yet Ron's argument reminds us of the broader picture we need to stand for: the sacred nature of the higher laws of the elements.

In the next section, I focus on the ways that Mauna a Wākea has been an important part of how we are articulating an abolitionist future. Mauna Kea protector Andre Perez describes the importance of Kanaka Maoli alliances with the NDN Collective's LANDBACK Campaign, which is both decolonial and abolitionist.[32] Krystal Two Bulls (Oglala Lakota), the LANDBACK campaign director, stayed two months at the puʻuhonua at Mauna a Wākea. Nick Tilsen (Lakota) explains that the mission of the LANDBACK campaign is to provide funding, resources, and mentorship for front line organizing. Two Bulls makes it clear that the fight for land is a fight against white supremacy. The goals of the LANDBACK campaign are to (1) dismantle white supremacy, (2) defund white supremacy by defunding the military industrial complex, police, border police, and ICE, and (3) move from "consultation" to "consent."[33] The LANDBACK campaign honors the goals of an abolitionist future for all of us.

I want to return to July 17, 2019, when Kanaka Maoli women stood with linked arms, chanting "Mālana Mai Kaʻū," and Kanaka Maoli men and their allies sitting behind them. Sheka Price Torrey had joined them on the mountain that day. Sheka had come to Hawaiʻi as an enlisted serviceman, traveling throughout the Pacific in naval submarines. He also began taking Hawaiian and Pacific Islands studies courses, classes in hula as well as in ʻōlelo Hawaiʻi (Hawaiian language). Sheka describes traveling to Mauna a Wākea to sit with Kanaka Maoli men behind the front line of women, and he makes the most profound statement of solidarity. He emphasizes, "Our liberation has to be rooted in their sovereignty."[34] He elaborated in a recent conversation that Indigenous stewardship of the earth enables a Black future on the earth, and one where we can grow mutually caring relationships between groups of people who have been historically separated from each other by white supremacy. He explains,

> I believe there are certain values and ways that Indigenous people have, such as living with the earth, living in harmony with all elements of the earth and its animals, that we have lost, I would say that my people have lost through the mass transformation of enslavement. And I think we can have a way of healing each other. We have practices that are healing as well. But I don't think we have the answers all by ourselves. We've already been separated from each other, so why separate again? Once I got on the Mauna, the question "Are you gonna stand?" was presented. If I got arrested, that would've followed me to the continent as well. Would I want to carry a record, a scratch to my name, when going back home, to the United States? There were three brothers standing there. When we talked later, they told me their lives flashed before their eyes as well. We felt, yeah, that's what solidarity is about: you do what's necessary. This is your struggle, but I want to let you know I'm here for you.[35]

Sheka's stand illustrates the importance of our standing with each other in an embodied, relational way to learn more intimately about each other's struggles.

We now see a growing recognition of the ways that a decolonial abolitionist movement seeks to dismantle the white supremacist state, making way for a world that promotes Indigenous and Black aliveness and vitality.[36] One of the most prominent leaders who stands at the intersection of the two movements is Joy Lehuanani Enomoto, a visual artist with Black, Kanaka Maoli, Japanese, Caddo, and Punjabi ancestry. She was one of the first protectors who set up camp at Puʻuohuluhulu at the base of Mauna a Wākea on July 12, and she has been speaking about the importance of reciprocal solidarities for the movement for Black Lives and the movement to protect Mauna Kea. She speaks about the problems of anti-Black racism in Kanaka Maoli communities as an extension of the racist discourses of U.S. occupation, then points to a key moment in the 2020 Hawaiʻi for Black Lives march: "It was a pivotal moment at the rally to see a sign that said 'Kiaʻi for Black Lives.' It meant that the past five, six years of education, of having hard conversations, actually got to some folks. Something shifted in the discourse."[37] She explains,

> By supporting Black Lives Matter, we do not lose Hawaiian ways of resistance and knowing, we do not stop perpetuating our culture or lose our language. By supporting Black Lives, our ea is enhanced. As a sovereign people we are saying we will stand as an example to those that would do us all harm, that their old tricks can no longer divide us. There is nothing more threatening to the state than mass solidarity across race, class and gender differences because there are far more of us. . . . *Onipaʻa ana ka pono*—let the right stand firm. Let us stand up for Blackness and protect Black lives. BLACK LIVES MATTER IN THE HAWAIIAN KINGDOM.

Enomoto's words remind us that ea, a word meaning life, breath, and political sovereignty, is enhanced by standing for Black lives, growing relationships that only strengthen our stands for the earth.

As we continue to challenge the white supremacist laws of the U.S. settler capitalist, heteronormative, carceral, racial state, as we work to dismantle that state and its late liberal capitalist imaginary, our relationships with each other and with the elements will make possible that decolonial and abolitionist future of planetary abundance. We have had a glimpse of that future at the Puʻuhonua o Puʻuhuluhulu at Mauna a Wākea, and we do not need a comprehensive vision of that future to work toward it, to grow it, and to manifest it.

Notes

1 I use the kahakō (macron diacritical mark) to mark plural words (kupuna/kūpuna, wahine/wāhine). In the case of the term "Kanaka Maoli," I use the kahakō when referring to plural Kānaka Maoli or Kānaka (people), but not when using "Kanaka Maoli" as an adjective.

2 Andre Perez, personal communication, January 31, 2024.

3   "Crown lands" are the lands designated in 1865, formerly the King's lands. These lands were seized at the time of the 1893 overthrow, but they continue to be the land base of the lāhui, the Hawaiian nation-state. Melody Kapilialoha MacKenzie, Susan K. Serrano, and D. Kapuaʻala Sproat, eds., *Native Hawaiian Law: A Treatise* (Honolulu: Kamehameha Publishing, 2015), 17, 24.
4   For an account of the July 17 stand, see Jamaica Heolimeleikalani Osorio, "On the Frontlines of Mauna Kea," *Flux Magazine*, https://fluxhawaii.com.
5   Haunani-Kay Trask, "The Color of Violence," in *Color of Violence: The Incite! Anthology*, ed. Incite! Women of Color against Violence (Cambridge, MA: South End Press, 2006), 9; Tiffany Lethabo King, *The Black Shoals: Offshore Formations of Black and Native Studies* (Durham, NC: Duke University Press, 2019), 59.
6   From July 12, 2019, to March 27, 2020, Kānaka Maoli grew the efforts of nonstatist nation-building at Puʻuhonua o Puʻuhuluhulu, organizing themselves so that they can feed everyone, hold educational workshops on both the occupation of Hawaiʻi and traditional oli (chants), and strategize against the occupying state.
7   Derecka Purnell, *Becoming Abolitionists: Police, Protests, and the Pursuit of Freedom* (New York: Astra House, 2021), 273.
8   Kōnane is a board game of capturing stones, similar to checkers and chess.
9   J. M. Poepoe, "He kanaenae no ka hanau ana o Kauikeaouli," in "Ka Moolelo Hawaii Kahiko," *Ka Naʻi Aupuni* 1, no. 65 (February 1906): 1. For essays on Mauna a Wākea, see David Uahikeaikaleiʻohu Maile, "Threats of Violence: Refusing the Thirty Meter Telescope and Dakota Access Pipeline," in *Standing with Standing Rock*, ed. Nick Estes and Jaskiran Dhillon (Minneapolis: University of Minnesota Press, 2019); Noelani Goodyear Kaʻōpua, "Protectors of the Future, Not Protestors of the Past: Indigenous Pacific Activism and Mauna a Wākea," *South Atlantic Quarterly* 116, no. 1 (2017): 184–194; Leon Noʻeau Peralto, "Portrait. Mauna a Wākea: Hānau ka Mauna, the Piko of Our Ea," in *A Nation Rising: Hawaiian Movements for Life, Land, and Sovereignty*, ed. Noelani Goodyear-Kaʻōpua, Ikaika Hussey, and Erin Kahunawaikaʻala Wright (Durham, NC: Duke University Press, 2014), 232–243; Joseph A. Salazar, "Multicultural Settler Colonialism and Indigenous Struggle in Hawaiʻi: The Politics of Astronomy on Mauna a Wākea," PhD diss., University of Hawaiʻi, 2014. I also discuss the struggle to protect Mauna a Wākea in my book *Mapping Abundance for a Planetary Future: Kanaka Maoli and Critical Settler Cartographies in Hawaiʻi* (Durham, NC: Duke University Press, 2021). For a discussion of Mauna a Wākea as a piko, see Edith Kanakaʻole Foundation, University of Hawaiʻi at Hilo, *Mauna Kea Comprehensive Management Plan*, i.
10 Pualani Kanakaʻole Kanahele, *Ka Honua Ola: ʻEliʻeli Kau Mai / The Living Earth: Descend, Deepen the Revelation* (Honolulu: Kamehameha Publishing, 2011), 5.
11 Pualani Kanakaʻole Kanahele, Huihui Kanahele-Mossman, Ann Kalei Nuʻuhiwa, and Kaumakaiwapoʻohalahiʻipaka Kealiʻikanakaʻole, *Kūkulu Ke Ea a Kanaloa: The Culture Plan for Kanaloa Kahoʻolawe* (Hilo, HI: Edith Kanakaʻole Foundation, February 9, 2009).

12 Pualani Kanakaʻole Kanahele, Kekuhikuhipuuone Kealiikanakaoleohaililani, Huihui Kanahele-Mossman, Kalei Nuʻuhiwa, Kuʻulei Kanahele, and Honuaiākea Summit Group, *Kīhoʻihoʻi Kānāwai: Restoring Kānāwai for Island Stewardship* (Hilo, HI: Edith Kanakaʻole Foundation, September 21, 2016), 15, http://nomaunakea.weebly.com.
13 University of Hawaiʻi at Hilo, *Final Environmental Impact Statement: Thirty Meter Telescope Project*, vol. 1, Hilo, May 8, 2010, S-8, http://oeqc2.doh.hawaii.gov.
14 Contested case hearing 2 transcripts, vol. 16, December 13, 2016, 99–100. Archived at the Hawaiʻi State Department of Land and Natural Resources Office of Conservation and Coastal Lands.
15 Contested case hearing 2 transcripts, vol. 34, February 13, 2017, 37–38. For an expanded discussion, see Fujikane, *Mapping Abundance*, 90.
16 For the Hawaiʻi Supreme Court opinion on the TMT, see In re Contested Case Hearing re Conservation Dist. Use Application (CDUA) Ha-3568 for the Thirty Meter Telescope at the Mauna Kea Sci. Reserve, 431 P.3d 752 (2018), 30, www.scribd.com.
17 Fujikane, *Mapping Abundance*, 5.
18 UH Hilo, *TMT Final Environmental Impact Statement [FEIS]*, vol. 1, 3-10–3-20.
19 *TMT FEIS*, S-9.
20 Justice Michael Wilson, "Dissenting Opinion in the Matter of the Contested Case Hearing Regarding the Conservation District Use Application for the Thirty Meter Telescope," November 9, 2018, 3–4. www.courts.state.hi.us.
21 Quoted in Māhealani Richardson, "Opponents of TMT Project Protest outside Key Financial Backer in California," *Hawaii News Now*, October 15, 2019.
22 Gary Kubota, "KOKUA Hawaiʻi Oral History Project Interview with Gwen Kim," March 19, 2016, https://scholarspace.manoa.hawaii.edu.
23 Amnesty International–Hawaiʻi Chapter interview with Gwen Kim, July 22, 2019, www.facebook.com.
24 Gwen Kim, interview by Candace Fujikane, Heʻeia Uli, August 6, 2020.
25 For an account of the Kūʻē petitions, see Noenoe Silva, *Aloha Betrayed: Native Hawaiian Resistance to American Colonialism* (Durham, NC: Duke University Press, 2004), 145–159.
26 Kuʻuwehi Hiraishi, "As Mauna Kea Recalls Dark History, Stories of 1895 Political Prisoners Revived," Hawaiʻi Public Radio, October 28, 2019, www.hawaiipublicradio.org.
27 Emphasis mine. "The Kaulia Speech: An Excerpt." Translation by Jacob Bryan Kaʻomakaokalā Aki and Noelani Goodyear-Kaʻōpua, www.kamakakoi.com.
28 Noelani Goodyear-Kaʻōpua, *The Seeds We Planted: Portraits of a Native Hawaiian Charter School* (Minneapolis: University of Minnesota Press, 2013), 154.
29 *Kīhoʻihoʻi Kanawai*, 7.
30 Ronald Fujiyoshi, interview by Candace Fujikane, Berkeley, CA, April 12, 2015.
31 Ronald Fujiyoshi, interviewed by Candace Fujikane, Honolulu, April 22, 2021.
32 Andre Perez, "Land Back Campaign," Zoom webinar, November 28, 2020.

33 Krystal Two Bulls, "Land Back Campaign," Zoom webinar, November 28, 2020.
34 Sheka Price Torrey and Shabazz, "On da Block with Sheka and Shabazz" podcast, Episode #5, "Pōpolo," August 2020, https://open.spotify.com.
35 Sheka Price Torrey, interview by Candace Fujikane, Honolulu, September 13, 2021.
36 I am inspired here by Kevin Quashie's beautiful book, *Black Aliveness, or a Poetics of Being* (Durham, NC: Duke University Press, 2021).
37 Joy Enomoto, "Where Will You Be? Why Black Lives Matter in the Kingdom of Hawai'i," *Ke Kaupu Hehi Ale*, February 1, 2017, https://hehiale.com.

5

Internationalizing Abolition

Toward Transformative Justice for Women Living (and Dying) along the Fence Line

KIM COMPOC

In "From a Native Trans Daughter: Carceral Refusal, Settler Colonialism, Re-routing the Roots of an Indigenous Abolitionist Imaginary," Kalaniopua Young theorizes a Hawai'i-based vision of abolition, weaving in her own life experiences as a formerly incarcerated, working-class Kanaka Maoli transwoman who survived both police brutality and the abuse of academia. Young makes clear that the abusive criminal justice system that put her in jail as a young person is part of the same settler colonial apparatus that illegally annexed Hawai'i in the first place. The white supremacist carceral logic of the prison industrial complex (PIC) intersects with the military industrial complex (MIC) on Hawaiian land, leaving the full humanity of trans and queer people of color unrecognized and erased. She describes her own commitment to abolition: "I explore what it means to embody and be embodied by a state of carceral refusal, by which I mean an evolving state of being and becoming in which we advocate for the abolition of the PIC and the interrelated logics of police brutality and militarism that continue to disappear poor people, trans/gender queer people, Native peoples, and people of color."[1] Throughout the essay, Young expresses her solidarity with Black, Latinx, and Native communities on the continent, who are, in essence, nations under U.S. occupation as well. Young discloses that, like many of us in the demilitarization movement, her father was in the U.S. military, and her great-grandmother was a police officer. We might refuse the carceral logic of the PIC and the MIC, but our positionality is complicated. Yet even as we might be imbricated in these systems, we build solidarity across the Pacific—in both directions—to end the war economy and insist on living differently. I find it very useful that Young describes this different state of being as "evolving."

As a queer Filipinx settler engaged in feminist demilitarization activism in Hawai'i and Oceania, I take Young's lead, learning from the abolition movement to defend oppressed communities from U.S. policing in order to map how these violent systems intersect and how we can dismantle them all. Movements to defund the police and defund the military just might win major victories in the coming years, but that will require deep commitment and cooperation. The urgency of our task demands that we begin with the important work of sharing our stories and mourning the dead.

The list of dead is long, not just in the Middle East where the United States has launched multiple imperialist wars for twenty years, but around the more than nine hundred bases around the world where the United States prepares for these wars by training soldiers, bombing the land, and demanding "rest and recreation" from service and sex workers. These bases are often on islands, and women and girls living along the fence line face particular vulnerability to military violence.[2] In just two examples, U.S. military-connected personnel brutally murdered Jennifer Laude in Olongapo, Philippines, in 2014 and Rina Shimabukuro in Okinawa in Japan in 2016. While violence against women, particularly sexual violence, has been a systemic and ongoing problem of U.S. occupation in this region and globally, this chapter draws attention to two notable factors in these cases. First, these murders sparked protests both locally and internationally. Second, both perpetrators were convicted, sentenced, and imprisoned. Historically, the neocolonial Status of Forces Agreement (SOFA) has provided blanket immunity for soldiers who commit crimes around the bases.[3] In this regard, these convictions merit reflection for holding the military accountable for the crimes its soldiers commit. However, from the standpoint of real transformative justice that Young and other abolitionists envision, these "victories" are only partial, and only *carceral*, for while these individual murderers have been held to account, U.S. militarization continues to expand in the region. To paraphrase Jennifer Laude's mother, as long as U.S. militarization remains, there will be more Jennifers, and there will be more Rinas.[4]

My purpose in this chapter is threefold: first, to honor the lives of Laude and Shimabukuro as well as the transnational movements for justice that were ignited in the wake of their murders; second, to explore the continuities and disjunctures between a U.S.-based abolition movement centered on abolishing prisons and defunding the police, and a transnational demilitarization movement centered on closing bases and defunding the military; and third, to consider our positionality in Hawai'i—sitting as we do at the intersection of the prison industrial complex and military industrial complex. From this positionality, I seek to engage how a place-based analysis might help to trouble the false dichotomy between movements focused on "domestic" and "foreign" policy, drawing critical connections between movements for police abolition and demilitarization.[5]

Put differently, I ask: Can we *internationalize* abolition to include the dismantling of the prison industrial complex with its vast network of police, prisons, jails, and immigrant detention centers, as well as the dismantling of the military industrial complex and its vast global network of bases, borders, and multidomain militia? Mobilizing a Hawai'i-based analysis, this chapter highlights how the urgency of defunding the police and defunding the military might converge.

My Positionality

As a Filipinx and haole settler living in Hawai'i, I honor the movements for self-determination and sovereignty of the Kānaka Maoli, on whose lands I write these words, and who remain under U.S. occupation. Part of the motivation for my work on demilitarization and decolonization comes from my own family's hundred-plus-year connection to the U.S. military, having fought in nearly all the wars of the twentieth century, from the wars in the Philippines to the wars in the Middle East, as well as the U.S. occupation of the Marshall Islands, where my parents met. Growing up, I did not learn about the U.S. nuclear testing program in the Pacific, or the historical context of imperialist war that drove my family to leave the Philippines for Hawai'i in the first place, or the impact that settlement has meant to the Hawaiian people, who are now vastly outnumbered on their own land.[6] I began to study U.S. empire during the first war on Iraq as an undergraduate peace activist in Washington, DC, then in Filipino and Asian American theater work in San Francisco, and now in Hawai'i, where I have lived for twenty years. It is here that I was fortunate to study with the late Haunani Kay-Trask, and witness up close the beauty of Hawaiian movements for self-determination—from reclaiming Kahoʻolawe from the military to other efforts to reclaim language, navigational traditions, food ways, water ways, and sacred sites, including Mauna Kea. I have also witnessed the work of settler allies who stand in solidarity with Kānaka Maoli in the protection and revitalization of Hawaiian land.

While "allyship" and solidarity are fraught concepts in a settler colonial context, for many settlers of color in Hawaiʻi like myself, demilitarization is central to how we contribute to Hawaiian movements for independence as well as the ongoing struggle for genuine sovereignty in our own ancestral homes.[7] I have been active with Decolonial Pin@ys and Women's Voices, Women Speak (WVWS), two Honolulu-based collectives committed to building solidarity to end U.S. imperialism in Hawaiʻi and globally. Our work in both organizations is guided by Aunty Terri Kekoʻolani, who co-founded WVWS, Aunty Maxine Kahaulelio, and other long-time Kanaka Maoli leaders engaged in the work of protecting Hawaiian land from further militarization and desecration.[8] The murders of Rina Shimabukuro and Jennifer Laude were important reminders of why we do our work, and why (trans-inclusive) feminist analysis is critical to the discussion of militarism. As the U.S. empire works transnationally, so do we. We disrupt the propaganda that we must forever be dependent on the U.S. military for our "protection." We center our vision not only in what we are fighting against, but also what we are fighting for: genuine security for all our precious islands. We refuse the false compliment that we are all "strategically located" for U.S. military objectives, as if we have no strategies of our own for Moana Nui's future.[9]

While we resist the notion that Hawaiʻi must forever have its gaze on the continent, we are also inspired by the recent successes of the U.S.-based abolition movement. The 2021 police murders of Iremamber Sykap and Lindani Myeni in Honolulu were clear examples of why models of Black liberation that originate in the United States are deeply relevant to our situation in Hawaiʻi, where U.S.-style policing is intrinsic to settler colonial governance.[10] As Mariame Kaba reminds us, police and prisons are "death-making institutions" that have robbed oppressed communities for generations. In short, we want Hawaiʻi to be visible for its anti-imperialist contributions to Moana Nui, and also for its abolitionist contributions to colonized nations in North America with whom we share so much in common.

Telling Our Stories, Honoring the Dead

Like many Filipinx in and outside the Philippines, I was deeply disturbed by the particularly humiliating death Jennifer Laude suffered. Laude lived in Olongapo, near Subic Naval Base. Thirty minutes after she met a U.S. Marine in a bar, her body was found in a hotel bathroom with her head slumped over the toilet bowl. The coroner declared the cause of death was drowning. For many of us, Laude's murder is a graphic rehearsal of the colonial degradation Filipinx have been subject to since the U.S. invasion in 1898. The past 125 years have brought the Philippines only different forms of colonial extraction, from genocidal war to the reckless way World War II was fought on Philippine soil, to the ecological violence and contamination of the bases, to the joint military exercises that keep the Philippines in a permanent state of colonial occupation and economic dependence, and with no consequences for military violence against women and girls.

It has been infuriating to listen to the military's attempts to defend Laude's killer, spending over a half million dollars on his defense, arguing for a reduced charge of homicide, not murder, and justifying his crime with transphobia. The many ways her life was disrespected—the botched investigation, the incessant deadnaming of her in the media— serve as reminders of how U.S. militarization normalizes grotesque transmisogynist violence. In spite of the horror of this murder, what has been admirable is the way the Filipinx diaspora and the demilitarization movement have had to confront transphobia and the stigma of sex work.[11] As Filipina trans advocate Naomi Fantanos wrote:

> While Jennifer Laude's death is truly saddening, her case has also galvanized the LGBT community here. Not surprisingly, her death has also resonated within other social justice movements including those fighting for genuine Philippine sovereignty and freedom, nationalism, democratization, economic justice, etc. Jennifer Laude's death is turning into a historical phenomenon in itself.[12]

What Fantanos said was true for our queer and trans Filipinx community in Hawaiʻi. Not long after the murder, we held a vigil in her honor in Honolulu where local māhū wahine and transwomen recounted their own stories of narrowly escaping death at the hands of johns, cops, and soldiers.[13] None of them were surprised by Laude's murder. Also not surprising, although equally traumatizing, was President Rodrigo Duterte's decision to issue a full pardon to Laude's murderer, Joseph Pemberton, in September 2020. In Honolulu we held a rally outside Camp Smith, where Pemberton was transported before returning home to the United States. In our caravan from Camp Smith to Waikīkī, we denounced the transmisogynist and imperialist violence that ended Laude's brief life. Dozens of cars were decorated and painted to bring awareness of our outrage: "No Transphobia and No Murderers in the Hawaiian Kingdom." With every action, demilitarization movements are strengthening our intersectional analysis and making clear that Hawaiian land struggle must remain at the center.

As scholar-activists in and outside the classroom, many of us have taken Laude's murder as an important case study on the connections between imperialism and transphobia. PJ Raval's documentary *Call Her Ganda* has been particularly useful to educate our Filipinx communities toward a fuller commitment to trans liberation. Janet Mock, a journalist and transgender advocate of Kanaka Maoli and African American heritage, has spoken about her own experience doing sex work in Honolulu, and the vulnerability she felt with both police and the military.[14] Texts like these have opened up conversations about how transmisogynist militarization has impacted my students at University of Hawaiʻi West Oʻahu personally. Last semester one of my students disclosed he knew Laude's murderer; they were in the same Marine squadron together. Another student disclosed the trauma her family experienced when her māhū cousin was murdered by a soldier many years ago, her tortured body found on Sand Island. Whether in activist or academic settings, we continue to say Jennifer Laude's name, letting that anger and grief mobilize us to organize for better futures free of U.S. imperialism and transmisogyny.

The campaign for Rina Shimabukuro has not been as visible in Hawaiʻi, perhaps because no documentary film yet exists as in the Laude case, or perhaps because it is not as customary in Okinawa or Japan to foreground the names of the deceased in cases of rape and murder.[15] Like Laude, Shimabukuro's murder was particularly gruesome. She was raped, stabbed, and put into a suitcase. The press have referred to this as the "suitcase murder," and it took a month until her body was discovered.

Okinawa shares much in common with Hawai'i as a formerly independent island nation whose government was overthrown by a more powerful "mainland" colonizer. The Japanese occupation of Okinawa (then Ryukyu kingdom) began in 1879, while the American occupation of Hawai'i began with the overthrow of Lili'uokalani in 1893. During World War II, Japan and the United States fought one of its bloody battles in Okinawa for two months, leading to more than 200,000 deaths, mostly civilians. After the war, the United States refused to leave. The military destroyed farmland to build bases to launch its multiple wars, using the same imperialist logic that Okinawa, like Hawai'i, the Philippines, and Guåhan, is "strategically located." Today the bases remain in Okinawa—thirty-three of them on an island about the size of O'ahu. Ninety percent of the U.S. military presence in Japan is actually in Okinawa, an arrangement the Japanese government co-facilitates and pays for. Each rape, each abduction, and each murder by the military is another bitter reminder of the injustice of this dual colonization. As one elder put it in the local newspaper, "One cannot safely go for a walk in a private community even 72 years since the Battle of Okinawa."[16]

To honor Shimabukuro's life, vigils were held in Okinawa, Honolulu, and Washington, DC. But it was not until Women's Voices, Women Speak was invited to Okinawa for the ninth gathering of the International Women's Network Against Militarism (IWNAM) in 2017 that we were able to see the infamous anti-base movement in person, and to learn how many more women there were to mourn. IWNAM was formed in Okinawa in 1997 in the aftermath of a rape of a twelve-year-old girl by three U.S. Marines. The outrage of the Okinawan people ignited anti-base organizers in the Philippines, South Korea, Japan, and the United States to express their solidarity and "redefin[e] security from a feminist perspective to assure the security of women and children."[17] In "Okinawa Women Act against Military Violence: An Island Feminism Reclaiming Dignity," Kozue Akibayashi traces this important herstory, explaining how indebted we are as a network to the analysis of Okinawan feminists to "untangling the interlocking of patriarchal violence, military violence, and colonial violence."[18] Since then IWNAM has grown to include Hawaiʻi, Guåhan, and Puerto Rico.

Central to the movement's demands today is the protection of Henoko and Oura Bay from a mega base now under construction by the U.S. Navy. In countless referendums, 80 percent of the Okinawan people have voted against the new base. At the time of our visit, the movement to stop the base construction was twenty years old, the same age Shimabukuro was when she was murdered. President Barack Obama expressed his "sincerest regret" over the crime and made promises of doing more to prevent such crimes in the future, but Okinawans saw these as more empty promises. The same performance of apologies and promises occurred barely two months prior to Shimabukuro's murder when a different U.S. Marine raped a local tourist.[19] As I was writing this chapter, another U.S. Marine stabbed forty-four-year-old Okinawan Tamae Hindman to death in front of her eight-year-old son. It is hard to measure the emotional toll this kind of lawlessness has had on the Okinawan people, yet they continue to fight.[20]

While in Okinawa, our hosts brought us to the vigil site in Onna where Shimabukuro's body was found. We stood in silence with dozens of other heartbroken mourners who left small gifts to honor her brief life. A sign nearby read, "No Base, No Rape, No Tears," a kind of abolitionist-style "carceral refusal" of U.S. militarization and any defeatist notion that this violence is inevitable. Legendary demilitarization activist Takazato Suzuyo writes:

> Soldiers in the Battle of Okinawa, as well as the wars in Vietnam and Iraq, have been trained to use their weapons for killing those said to be their enemies. This is true of all armies. Trained to impose their will by force, they are sent to the battles. To wage war, they must lose their humanity. The perpetrators of crimes in Okinawa should be held responsible, yet the unequal Status of Forces Agreement remains in effect and U.S. troops are not reduced. Thus, the ultimate responsibility for these crimes lies with the U.S. and Japanese governments. There is no solution other than the withdrawal of troops.[21]

Where U.S. abolitionists dream of tearing down prisons and police stations, communities like this one dream of tearing down the bases and live-fire training areas. Occupied peoples refuse the imperialist logic that their islands exist only for the pleasure of the war profiteers and their insatiable appetite for land and bodies. They do not just work for conviction and sentencing in individual cases; they insist we must end this madness of war that robs us all of our humanity. They assert their right to live as free people on their own land, rather than be reduced to the irrelevant noncitizens the United States imagines them to be.

Partial Victories

There are many more murders of women around the bases, but what was extraordinary in these two cases is that the murderers actually went to prison for their crimes. Of course, all credit for those convictions must go to the transnational movements for sounding the alarm; without the international media attention, both murderers would surely have been acquitted. In my 2021 interview with Virginia Suarez, the tireless lawyer for the family of Jennifer Laude who was featured in *Call Her Ganda*, I asked her to comment on the significance of the conviction and imprisonment of Laude's murderer:

> For the very first time a U.S. soldier was convicted, a U.S. soldier was incarcerated. But it was not a complete victory. We cannot get the 100 percent victory considering the Philippines remains a neo-colony of the U.S. Duterte granted him a pardon, and that pardon extinguished the crime itself and therefore the penalty. Even that pardon will not erase the fact that this case has brought a U.S. soldier into the Philippine jail. More than that, it's the victory of the Filipino people galvanized by this issue.[22]

Suarez notes the historical precedent of sending a U.S. soldier to prison for any crime. In essence, the conviction and sentencing in both these cases were as monumental as when a U.S. police officer is sent to prison for killing a Black, Indigenous, or migrant person. However, like Takazato, Suarez cannot call this a complete victory because only through ending U.S. colonialism and militarization will there be real victory for the people. To achieve real systemic change and transformative justice requires the political solution of U.S. withdrawal, not merely a legal victory in one or two well-publicized cases. It will also require reparations to repair the harm done to the people and to the land. To get there will require bold thinking and international solidarity from similarly-occupied peoples united on what we have to tear down and a commitment to what we want to build.

Solidarity from U.S.-Occupied Hawaiʻi

Okinawa and the Philippines have much to teach us about building powerful anti-imperialist movements that honor the dead and demand transformative justice. For those of us in Hawaiʻi, we have a particular responsibility to amplify these movements given the number of Filipinx and Okinawan heritage people in Hawaiʻi, as well as our proximity to U.S. politicians and military leaders as citizens "inside" the U.S. empire. Not twenty minutes from where I write these words, the U.S. military houses the Indo-Pacific Command (USINDOPACOM), which directs operations for what it calls the "Indo-Pacific" region, an area covering over 60 percent of the earth's surface—including the Philippines and Okinawa, where Laude and Shimabukuro and many other women have been raped and murdered. Every other year, the U.S internationalizes its occupation through RIMPAC, the Rim of the Pacific exercises, a series of "war games" held over six weeks and involving twenty-six nations, some of them not even in the Pacific (e.g., Norway and Israel). Indeed, it is RIMPAC and other forms of "international cooperation" that provide a kind of diplomatic greenwashing, as nations work "shoulder to shoulder" to invade Hawaiian land, air, and sea, training for war and signing massive weapons deals with smaller nations. Meanwhile, the genocides of Palestinians, West Papuans, and Indigenous Filipinos are invigorated through RIMPAC's joint operations with Israel, Indonesia, and the Philippines. For all these reasons, demilitarization organizations like Women's Voices, Women Speak, Decolonial Pin@ys, Hawaiʻi Peace and Justice, Veterans for Peace, and Koa Futures strive to defund the military, for the survival of all of us in Hawaiʻi, in Moana Nui, and beyond.

Here in Hawaiʻi, we learn from these movements to end the bases, amazed by the numbers their anti-imperialist movements can draw into the streets. We aim to dream bigger, but in order to do that, we need to build substantially more political power. My fellow Honolulu-based demilitarization activists Ellen-Rae Cachola, Tina Grandinetti, and Aiko

Yamashiro explain how the IWNAM gathering in Okinawa in 2017 affected how they think about movements in Hawai'i:

> Though our huaka'i [transformative journey] invigorated and inspired us, we returned home and were reminded that the demilitarization movement in Hawai'i, while steadfast, remains small. Our communities are deeply targeted by, and implicated in, militarism. This drove home the need to continue to educate ourselves and our communities in compassionate and compelling ways and commit to sustained community movement building. The transformative experience of the huaka'i helped us grow as leaders able to hold space to invite more of our community, with all the complexity and fullness of their different genealogies, into the heavy process of demilitarization.[23]

The "heavy process of demilitarization" the authors refer to is evident everywhere in Hawai'i. Many of us are discouraged by how much our communities have been militarized and radicalized through right-wing public education, evangelical churches, and social media. Often we are outnumbered, which can make us feel "small," and worse, insignificant. Women around the bases in Okinawa and the Philippines are also made to feel small and insignificant. Jennifer Laude's murder is emblemized by the toilet where she was choked and drowned; Rina Shimabukuro's case is referred to as the "suitcase murder" as that is how the murderer disposed of her body. To say their murderers aimed to diminish these young women is a gross understatement. The women around the bases need and deserve solidarity movements that stand as a testament to the immense value and significance of their lives. The North American Missing and Murdered Indigenous Women campaign and the "Say Her Name" campaign for Black women killed at the hands of U.S. police have figured out ways to honor the dead in culturally specific ways that demand our attention. So too must we learn how to mourn these women around the bases. Even from our transnational context where figuring out what is culturally appropriate might be complicated, we can honor these lives, hold the United States to account, and let our mourning be a radicalizing force to dream bigger than we ever have before.

Thinking Big: Defund the Military and Reparations, Too

My desire to "think bigger" has also been fed by Black Lives Matter movement, specifically Mariame Kaba, who I had the pleasure of hearing in person at the University of Illinois Urbana Champaign in 2019.[24] It is because of her and other charismatic, dedicated Black women leaders in the United States—Angela Davis, Ruthie Gilmore, Patrice Khan-Cullors—that I have come to understand the life-and-death urgency of abolishing the police and the prison industrial complex. In the middle of the COVID-19 pandemic, solidarity actions were held across the world, police budgets were reduced, and, most importantly, moneys were reallocated to human needs. It is this kind of political muscle we need to defund the military as well.

But even before the 2020 uprising, I found myself in awe of the abolition movement's ability to secure material gains for survivors of police torture as well as a list of other demands I never dreamed possible. The 2015 settlement with the city of Chicago included a formal apology and an agreement to pay $5.5 million in reparations to more than two hundred African Americans tortured by the police, a first in U.S. history.[25] The settlement meant direct financial compensation to the victims and their families, along with a counseling center for torture survivors, job training and college tuition for the victims and their families, and an art exhibit to memorialize the trauma put into the textbooks of all middle schoolers in the city. In short, it's not just about defunding the police, but refunding the communities whose rights have been violated. As Kaba argues, we cannot get overly focused on the legal battle to convict and sentence these individual cops; we must stay centered on transformation visions of justice that will materially impact those who have been harmed: "We cannot reform our way out of this mess." With regard to the convictions of Laude and Shimabukuro's murderers, this is sage advice given that the white perpetrator who killed the transwoman has already been pardoned, while the Black perpetrator who killed the ciswoman is in prison for life with hard labor. In the Chicago torture example, the police chief responsible for the "house of screams" was not actually convicted of torture, but *perjury*. Legal battles are not irrelevant, but communities near the bases have bolder visions than making the Status of Forces Agreements "work." They demand the removal of the U.S. military, recognition of the harm that has been caused, and the compensation to repair the harm—to bodies, land, and the economy—that has been done.

Protecting Mauna a Wākea: Site of U.S.-Style Policing and U.S. Militarization

Sometimes we get "movement envy" in Hawai'i as we participate in or watch footage of anti-base actions occurring in Okinawa, or the anti–police violence actions occurring on Turtle Island. But in 2019 it became clear that Hawai'i did have the kind of political muscle it takes to make international capital grind to a halt. I was privileged to be on Mauna Kea during the standoff over the Thirty Meter Telescope (TMT) in August 2019. There is no space in this chapter to do justice to what Kānaka Maoli created during those extraordinary eight months. In the face of this multi-billion-dollar project, kia'i (guardians or protectors) asserted their refusal to let this sacred site be violated once again.[26] Mauna Kea already houses thirteen telescopes in an area officially designated as a conservation district, and the size of the TMT, if built, would dwarf them all. The decades-long mismanagement of Mauna Kea by the state, especially the University of Hawai'i, which manages the lease, has been well-documented.[27] There has not been a political uprising as large and sustained as this one since the 1970s, when the Hawaiian movement reclaimed Kaho'olawe from the U.S. military, which had used it for target practice for decades. Importantly, the political lessons of Mauna Kea extend far beyond the act of refusing. The pu'uhonua (place of refuge) created at the base of Mauna Kea became a kind of liberated zone where Hawaiians practiced self-governance, built political power, and nurtured global relations. Free education, free health care, and free food were provided to everyone, and cultural protocol was practiced three times a day. Indigenous leaders came from all parts of the Pacific to offer their support. Over social media, people from Japan to Aotearoa to Hungary raised their hands to form the triangle symbol of the mountain, shouting "Ku Kia'i Mauna!" reminding Kānaka Maoli and all of us who live in Hawai'i that we are not so small after all.[28] At the time of this writing, the TMT construction has been postponed, representing a huge loss of revenue for the investors, and a huge victory for kiaʻi. For other contemporary political movements confronting capitalist development in Hawaiʻi, what happened on Mauna Kea was truly a game changer.[29]

One of the other important lessons learned was how much the state of Hawaiʻi was willing to devote to policing Hawaiians. Over $12.2 million was spent on multiple police forces (Hawaiʻi County PD, Honolulu PD, Maui County PD, the Division of Conservation and Resources Enforcement, as well as the National Guard) in addition to military-grade equipment like long range acoustic device (LRAD) sound cannons.[30] The trauma of seeing elders, including disabled ones, being taken to jail for nonviolent direct action spoke volumes as to what Hawaiians are up against in protecting their sacred sites. The following year, during the solidarity actions for Black Lives, ten thousand people marched in Honolulu, in one of the city's largest demonstrations ever.[31]

What is less widely known is that the U.S. military still conducts live-fire bombing on Pōhakuloa on a 133,000 acre training area, a lease for which it has held for fifty-plus years at $1 per year. The traumatic sound of the live-fire bombing is so loud one can hear it while on the mountain and from many parts of Hawaiʻi Island. The training intensifies during the RIMPAC "war games" discussed earlier. For newcomers to the movement, this was quite a shock. While witnessing the beauty of Mauna Kea and the movement to protect it, one could witness the violence of U.S. occupation at both the "domestic" and "foreign" policy levels: overly funded U.S.-style policing alongside overly funded U.S. military exercises.[32] While it would be easy to hate those wearing the uniform and waving the American flag, the truth is our own family members (Hawaiians, Filipinx, and other Pacific Islanders colonized by the United Staes) are often the ones holding the gun and/or dropping the bombs. As Young points out, Kānaka Maoli are the ones who feel the trauma of these intersecting forms of violence, desecration, and cooptation, right on their own land.

In considering what it might mean to internationalize abolition, I argue we must stay alert to the brilliance of movements across the Pacific in both directions. We must learn all we can to defund these "death making institutions" and refund common-sense sustainable development to support peace and survival. Just as Kaba reminds us we must "listen to those behind bars," we must also listen to those communities along the fence lines. Just as the military and police depend on and cooperate with each other (with U.S. police inheriting millions of dollars of equipment from the military), so must we as feminist abolitionists deepen our cooperation between our movements.

The brilliant demilitarization movements in the Philippines and Okinawa share with us the necessity to remove the bases and defund the military industrial complex. Looking to the movements for Black, Indigenous, and migrant justice on Turtle Island, we are reminded of the necessity to defund the police and the prison industrial complex. In our efforts to protect Hawaiʻi from being dominated by "the mainland," we cannot overlook how the Black Lives Matter movement has much to teach us in Hawaiʻi and across Moana Nui, particularly with regard to securing reparations for communities, not just convictions. Reflecting on the twin violences of police and military that impact the full protection of Mauna a Wākea, there are Hawaiʻi lessons for us to share as well.

Notes

1 Kalaniopua Young, "From a Native Trans Daughter: Carceral Refusal, Settler Colonialism, Re-routing the Roots of an Indigenous Abolitionist Imaginary," in *Captive Genders: Trans Embodiment and the Prison Industrial Complex* (Chico, CA: AK Press 2015), 84.
2 The title for this chapter is a reference to the documentary *Living along the Fenceline*, directed by Gwyn Kirk and Lina Hoshino, 2011.
3 Brandon Marc Higa, "Unpacking Okinawa's "Suitcase Murder": Revisiting Extraterritoriality Protections for Military Contractors under the U.S.-Japan SOFA Supplementary Agreement," *Asian-Pacific Law & Policy Journal* 21, no. 2 (2019): 1–50.
4 *Call Her Ganda*, directed by P. J. Raval, 2018.
5 Christine Ahn, Yifat Susskind, and Cindy Wiesner, "Biden Should Embrace An Anti-Imperialist Feminist Foreign Policy to Heal Wounds Abroad—and at Home," *Newsweek*, November 17, 2020.
6 Kim Compoc, Joy Lehuanani Enomoto, and Kasha Ho, "From Hawaiʻi to Okinawa: Confronting Militarization, Healing Trauma, Strengthening Solidarity," *Frontiers: A Journal of Women's Studies* 42, no. 1 (2021): 204–224; Ellen-Rae Cachola, Kim Compoc, and Darlene Rodrigues, "End Military Land Leases, Militarism; Invest in Peace Instead," *Honolulu Star-Advertiser*, August 26, 2021.
7 See Ellen-Rae Cachola, Tina Grandinetti, and Aiko Yamashiro, "Demilitarizing Hawaiʻi's Multiethnic Solidarity: Decolonizing Settler Histories and Learning Our Responsibilities to ʻĀina," *Critical Ethnic Studies* 5, no. 1–2 (2019): 68–98.

8   See Moanikeʻala Akaka, Noelani Goodyear-Kaʻōpua, Maxine Kahaulelio, and Terrilee Kekoʻolani-Raymond, *Nā Wāhine Koa: Hawaiian Women for Sovereignty and Demilitarization* (Honolulu: University of Hawaiʻi Press, 2018).
9   Moana Nui ("Vast Ocean") is a Hawaiian term used to refer to the Pacific Ocean.
10 In April 2021, the Honolulu Police Department killed two unarmed immigrant men of color, sixteen-year-old Iremamber "Baby" Sykap from the Chuuk Nation (Federated States of Micronesia) and Lindani Myeni, who was a twenty-nine-year-old father from KwaZulu-Natal, South Africa. While charges were initially filed in Sykap's case, neither case went to trial. Michelle Broder Van Dyke, "'We Say It's a Racial Paradise': How Two Police Killings Are Dividing Hawaiʻi," *Civil Beat*, July 5, 2021.
11 For more on how "diasporic anti-imperialist politics intersects with queer and trans social movements" see Gina K. Velasco, "Queer and Trans Necropolitics in the Afterlife of U.S. Empire," *Amerasia Journal* 46, no. 2 (May 3, 2020): 238.
12 Quoted in Monika Kowalska, "Interview with Naomi Fontanos," *The Heroines of My Life*, November 25, 2014, http://theheroines.blogspot.com.
13 Māhū is a Hawaiian term Young defines as "trans or gender queer." Māhū wahine is loosely translated as "transgender woman."
14 Janet Mock, *Redefining Realness: My Path to Womanhood, Identity, Love and So Much More* (New York: Atria, 2014). Mock describes how while an honor student in high school, she supported her family through sex work. After she was mugged, the police "put me in my place as a prostitute unworthy of justice," 217. Despite coming from a military family (her father was in the U.S. Navy) she makes clear that the military has always been a problem in Hawaiʻi: "It's a special place, a melted and cooled lava rock in the middle of the Pacific Ocean, the anchor of Polynesia, once ruled by kings and queens before religious, military, and tourist occupation," 88.
15 Okinawan Women Act Against Military Violence has collected statistics since 1945 of the number of military rapes and murders, and how the cases were settled. The twenty-eight-page document published in 2016 contained no names, even of the murdered. *Okinawa-Beihei ni yoru josei heno seihanzai dai 12 han* [Sexual crimes by U.S. soldiers against Women in Okinawa], 12th ed. (Okinawa Women Act Against Military Violence, 2017); Mika Kuniyoshi, "Okinawa Women Document U.S. Military Sex Crimes in Book," *Asahi Shimbun*, October 22, 2020.
16 Hana Kusumoto and Matthew M. Burke, "Base Worker Sentenced to Life with Hard Labor for Slaying of Okinawan Woman," *Stars and Stripes*, December 1, 2017.
17 Kozue Akibayashi, "Okinawa Women Act Against Military Violence: An Island Feminism Reclaiming Dignity," *Okinawan Journal of Island Studies* 1 (2020): 48.
18 Ibid., 54.
19 See "Another Heinous Crime in Okinawa" (May 23, 2017), *Japan Times*, quoted in Higa, "Unpacking Okinawa's "Suitcase Murder," 117, footnote 118.
20 See Akemi Johnson, *Night in the American Village: Women in the Shadow of the U.S. Military Bases in Okinawa* (New York: New Press, 2019).

21 Takazato Suzuyo, "Okinawan Women Demand U.S. Forces Out after Another Rape and Murder: Suspect an Ex-Marine and U.S. Military Employee," *Asia-Pacific Journal*, 14, no. 11 (June 1, 2016). Translated by Emma Dalton.
22 Virginia Suarez in discussion with the author, May 2021.
23 Cachola, Grandinetti, and Yamashiro, "Demilitarizing Hawai'i's Multiethnic Solidarity," 90.
24 Mariame Kaba, "Shrinking the Prison Industrial Complex: Strategic Abolitionist Organizing in the 21st Century." Public lecture presented at University of Illinois, Urbana Champaign, September 18, 2019. See also Mariame Kaba, *We Do This 'til We Free Us* (Chicago: Haymarket Books, 2021).
25 See Chicago Torture Justice Memorials, https://chicagotorture.org.
26 Kia'i is a Hawaiian word for "protectors" or "guardians." It is often the preferred term over "activists."
27 Kanaeokana, "Fifty Years of Mismanaging Mauna Kea," *Vimeo*, 2017.
28 "Ku Kia'i Mauna" is Hawaiian for "Protect/guard the mountain."
29 See Noelani Goodyear-Ka'ōpua, "Protectors of the Future, Not Protestors of the Past: Indigenous Pacific Activism and Mauna a Wākea," *South Atlantic Quarterly* 116, no. 1 (2017): 184–194; Iokepa Casumbal-Salazar, "A Fictive Kinship: Making 'Modernity,' 'Ancient Hawaiians,' and the Telescopes on Mauna Kea," *Native American and Indigenous Studies* 4, no. 2 (2017): 1–30; see MaunaKeaSyllabus.com; also "Solidarity Works: Lessons from Mauna Kea," Youtube.com, October 20, 2020.
30 "Costs for Mauna Kea Reach $12.2 million," KHON News, December 20, 2019.
31 See Charles Lawrence, "Activist Genealogy Visions and Enactments of Solidarity across Black and Kanaka Maoli Movements," in *The Value of Hawai'i 3: Hulihia, the Turning*, edited by Noelani Goodyear-Ka'ōpua, Craig Howes, Jonathan Kay Kamakawiwo'ole Osorio, and Aiko Yamashiro (Honolulu: University of Hawai'i Press, 2021), 194–197. David Croxford and Katie Kenny, "Watch as Thousands Protest in Downtown Honolulu in Support of Black Lives Matter," *Honolulu Magazine*, June 8, 2020.
32 See *Pōhakuloa: Now That You Know, Do You Care?*, www.kamakakoi.com; also Ka La Hoihoi Ea, "Ho'iHo'i 'Āina #MilitaryLANDBACK," YouTube, July 30, 2021, www.youtube.com.

6

How Death and Crisis Are Co-Opted into Carceral Reform

Abolitionist Perspectives from No New Jails NYC and Red Canary Song

SHAUN X. LIN AND YVES TONG NGUYEN

Since the onset of the COVID-19 pandemic, incidents of anti-Asian violence have gained increasing visibility in public consciousness as Asians and Asian Americans have been scapegoated by politicians and media figures as those most blameworthy for the global health crisis. Reports of anti-Asian violence have become alarmingly commonplace, and grizzly details are frequently shared in news reports and on social media. On the one hand, coverage of these attacks have fed into growing feelings of fear, vulnerability, and anger for many Asian Americans. And on the other, the search for recognition, legibility, and justice often pulls at the familiar threads of model minority narratives and Asian American exceptionalism, followed by calls for more police protection and other carceral reforms. Along with growing unrest in Asian American communities sprung celebrities-turned-activists and longtime nonprofit activists-turned-celebrities who seized the moment and created the #StopAsianHate slogan sprawling across social media platforms. Through the slogan #StopAsianHate, these calls for justice have resulted in the expansion of the carceral state in the form of increased resources to police Asian neighborhoods, harsher enforcement of hate crime legislation, and expansion of the prison industrial complex (PIC), including politicians, city agencies, and nonprofit and cultural organizations that benefit from the resources dedicated to carceral reforms.[1]

In this chapter, we examine the deaths of Kalief Browder and Yang Song and how their deaths informed the organizing and analyses of the

No New Jails NYC (NNJ) and Red Canary Song (RCS) campaigns activated by their respective deaths. We begin with historical context on urban poverty and the divestment of New York City's communities of color from basic city services and track a few of the massive investments in police and prisons in those same communities. Then we examine how, despite progressive rhetoric, many justice-oriented reform efforts have led to expansions, rather than contractions, of carceral state capacity. We describe NNJ and RCS as abolitionist projects that seek (1) to radically shift the exploitative and violent conditions necessitating their work, and (2) to practice safety beyond police and prisons. Finally, we evaluate the abolitionist dreams of these campaigns in relation to recent incidents of anti-Asian violence, urging #StopAsianHate activists to carefully consider the varied ways in which grassroots calls for justice have resulted in increased investments made into policing, border enforcement, jails and prisons, and we encourage Asian American activists to commit to fighting for abolition of, rather than their inclusion in, these oppressive systems.

Kalief Browder and the Formation of No New Jails NYC

In 2010, days before his seventeenth birthday, Kalief Browder was arrested on the way home from a party and accused of stealing a man's backpack. Browder had not, in fact, stolen the backpack, but regardless, a New York Police Department (NYPD) officer arrested him and charged him with robbery, grand larceny, and assault. Browder was denied bail and was sent to Rikers Island to await trial. His criminal trial would ultimately last nearly three years. During that time, Browder endured brutal conditions—first at the hands of Rikers guards and other prisoners and then locked away in solitary confinement. The accumulation of these traumatic experiences took a severe toll on his mental health; Browder would attempt suicide multiple times during the time he was detained at Rikers. The charges against Browder were ultimately dropped in 2013, and he was allowed to return home, but he would never be free of Rikers Island. The profound trauma of Browder's incarceration led to his death by suicide on June 6, 2015, at the age of twenty-two.

Like most people in jail—and about 85 percent of those incarcerated at Rikers Island—Kalief Browder was not convicted of the crime he was in jail for. The three years taken from Browder's freedom raise questions about the role of policy, including cash bail and the right to a speedy trial, in driving jail populations upward. Many individuals are in jail simply because they cannot afford bail; the median bail amount for a felony is $10,000, about eight months' rent for the typical person who cannot afford bail.[2] Browder's experience at Rikers Island and his subsequent death also raise questions about punitive practices employed by the New York State Department of Corrections (NYS DOC), such as the use of solitary confinement, on the mental health of people subjected to those practices. The unfortunate truth is that Kalief Browder is far from the only working-class young person of color whose life was taken or otherwise destroyed by the carceral state. The prevalence of such stories requires us to question the institutional workings of the carceral state and state actors like child protective services, police, district attorneys, courts, jails, prisons, and nonprofit organizations; their specific contributions to Kalief Browder's premature death; and their structural roles in upholding the machinery of a carceral state that continues to receive enormous investments of public capital, at a time when most public services are forced to undertake massive budget cuts.

Kalief Browder's death elicited a massive community response. Within a few days of his death, a vigil gathered outside the Manhattan Detention Complex to grieve the loss of his young life. Mourners called attention to the many ways the state had failed Browder, decrying the system of cash bail, the denial of the right to a speedy trial, the crisis of violence endemic at Rikers Island, the detaining of minors, and widespread abuse of solitary confinement—all of which contributed to Browder's death. Relationships grown from organizing the vigil would carry into the Campaign to Shut Down Rikers, a coalition consisting of Kalief's brother Akeem Browder, Millions March NYC, and Jails Action Committee, an alliance of incarcerated and formerly incarcerated people. The campaign organized vigils, marches, and rallies calling for the full closure of Rikers Island while arguing that that money currently spent on police and prisons would be better invested in education, health care, housing, and other basic needs.[3]

In 2018 the city announced the Borough-Based Jail Plan (BBJP) and its plan to #CLOSErikers Island by building four new jails, one in every borough except Staten Island. Rikers Island is a 413-acre island on the

East River and the current site of New York City's main jail complex, where an average of 9,000 people are detained every day. When it first opened, Rikers Island had an intended capacity of 6,000 people. Since then, new facilities were built, and the prisoner population grew from 6,667 in 1954, to 9,000 in 1960, reaching a peak of 20,000 in 1991.[4] The BBJP proposed to replace Rikers Island by massively upscaling existing jails in Manhattan Chinatown and downtown Brooklyn to forty-story "mega jails" and building new jails in the Bronx and Queens, with a total capacity of 6,000 people. At a projected cost of $10.8 billion, the BBJP represents a massive investment in New York City's carceral infrastructure at a time when almost every city agency faces massive budget cuts. Decades of divestment from necessary services like housing and schools alongside investments in police and jails highlight the lethal pairing of "organized abandonment" and "organized violence" described by Ruth Wilson Gilmore as "the conditions under which prisons became the solutions to problems."[5] The BBJP operates on the misguided belief that the violence of Rikers Island can somehow be fixed by modern design and new buildings, ignoring the violence endemic to the NYS DOC and the structural violence of the PIC. Rather, carceral reforms like the BBJP ultimately legitimize the violent systems in need of that reform, while allocating more resources to their function and daily operation.

No New Jails NYC (NNJ) grew from a joint call to action by veteran organizers from the Campaign to Shut Down Rikers along with Critical Resistance, a national abolitionist organization, for people who supported the closure of Rikers Island but who opposed the BBJP. The first NNJ meeting was attended by about forty people, including members from abolitionist organizations like Survived and Punished (S&P) and Incarcerated Workers Organizing Committee (IWOC), as well as members of neighborhood-based organizations like Take Back the Bronx, Neighbors United Below Canal, Chinatown Art Brigade, Sunset Park for a Liberated Future (SPLF), and Desis Rising Up and Moving (DRUM), which were deeply rooted in the neighborhoods proposed for new borough jails.

The public announcement of the BBJP was the first step of a city review process known as Uniform Land-Use Review Procedure (ULURP), which culminates in a make-or-break New York City Council vote. As part of ULURP, the Mayor's Office of Criminal Justice (MOCJ) would host town hall meetings in each borough slated for a jail to present their BBJP. At these meetings, city council members, members of the Lippman Commission (an independent commission on criminal justice and incarceration reform led by Jonathan Lippman), and nonprofits driving the #CLOSErikers campaign would lend public support for the new jails. The degree of coordination between MOCJ, the city agency introducing the BBJP, and the nonprofit organizations supporting #CLOSErikers gives troubling insight into the terrain of the city's nonprofit sector and the capacity of a handful of well-resourced foundations to shape public policy and dictate spending priorities. At these townhall meetings, NNJ supporters organized opposition to the BBJP not by making "not in my backyard (NIMBY)" arguments, but rather by arguing that jail construction was an issue of racial justice, gender justice, and environmental justice. NNJ members shared public testimonies, created educational and outreach materials, and spoke to other town hall attendees. In its organizing efforts, NNJ won over the vast majority of people attending the BBJP townhalls, including NIMBYs and staff and members of nonprofits funded to support the #CLOSErikers campaign.

As NNJ grew in size, so did it grow in complexity. The NNJ research working group studied other grassroots campaigns to resist jail construction, such as those in California and in the Bronx in the early 2000s, as well as the ULURP process and examples of decarceration and jail closure. Over time, the working group structure was amended to meet evolving campaign objectives: Stop The Plan (STP) focused on organizing opposition to the BBJP, and We Keep Us Safe (WKUS) coordinated mutual aid organizing in Black and immigrant neighborhoods most targeted by police and prisons. Later, NNJ would release "Close Rikers Now, We Keep Us Safe: A New Yorker's Guide to Building Community Care and Safety by Closing Rikers with No New Jails," a fifty-four-page document sharing analyses, strategies, and tools to fight jail construction as well as a vision for how the billions of dollars for jail construction could be spent to build a more inclusive New York City.[6] In its STP organizing, NNJ raised important questions about the mechanisms of carceral reform, learning from previous fights to close jails in the South Bronx and Los Angeles, and sharing strategies with ongoing fights to halt proposed jail construction projects and to close existing jails in St. Louis and Philadelphia. And in WKUS mutual aid organizing, NNJ organizers raised questions about public spending on jail construction in light of the histories of divestment from Black and Brown communities across the city, and the need to allocate resources that prioritize the needs of Black communities and other communities ravaged by the carceral state.

In October 2019 the New York City Council voted 35–14 in favor of the BBJP and allocated $10.8 billion over the next decade to build the new city jails. Although the final vote did not appear to be close, NNJ organizers had significantly shifted the parameters of the discourse. Within a year of the city's announcement of the Borough-Based Jail Plan as a progressive solution to the city's existing jail infrastructure, NNJ organizers had systematically dismantled any notion that a modern "neighborhood" jail could somehow be more compassionate to its prisoners or be a "good neighbor" to New Yorkers. The BBJP's champions in the mayor's office and on the city council, who a few short months earlier might have expected BBJP's passage to be a substantial boost to their legacies, were forced to defend their positions. Many of #CLOSErikers' initial partner organizations had tamped down their public support of the plan.

Through its organizing and outreach work, NNJ revealed the BBJP as, rather, a $10.8 billion investment in and expansion of New York City's carceral infrastructure. NNJ proposed immediate solutions—like ending broken windows policing, eliminating cash bail, and guaranteeing the right to a speedy trial—for New York to decarcerate and shrink its jail population enough to close Rikers Island, as well as a vision for how the city spending could be diverted from jail construction and toward public housing, employment, education, transportation, and public health and create for a truly safer New York City. By doing so, NNJ enacted a model of prison abolitionist organizing to address both the immediate and urgent crisis of carceral violence represented by Rikers Island, and to pose prison abolition as a horizon for antiracist, anticapitalist movements and as a vision for a more equitable urban policy in New York City. Despite the fact that their organizing efforts did not successfully stop the city's plan to deepen its commitment to carceral reform or to expand its existing jail infrastructure, NNJ critiques of public investments in the city's carceral apparatus has continued to resonate in grassroots anticarceral struggle, including in resistance to the proposed hiring of twelve hundred new NYPD officers to patrol the Metropolitan Transportation Authority (MTA) in 2019 and in efforts to "Defund NYPD" in 2020. And perhaps most importantly, NNJ served as a model of prison abolitionist organizing, as it made use of a wide array of tactics and strategies to resist specific carceral reforms as well as to sustain daily radical acts of community care like in mutual aid organizing throughout the COVID-19 pandemic by groups like Peoples Bail Out NYC and Red Canary Song.

Yang Song and the Formation of Red Canary Song

Similarly, the death of Yang Song, a Chinese migrant woman and massage worker, would spark organizing rooted in abolitionist politic as well as migrant justice and sex workers' rights. Yang Song lived and worked in Flushing, Queens, where many migrant Chinese and Korean women move because economic opportunities can be limited in their home countries. Yang moved to the United States in 2013 because her husband, Zhang Zhou, had U.S. citizenship already. She acquired a green card and worked many different jobs while caring for her elderly and ailing husband in the hope that she would eventually open her own spa. Yang also cared for her family and kept in contact with her mother, Yumei Shi, and her brother, Hai Song, who both lived in China. She would recount parts of her life to them over the phone that would come to inform what we know about her death. On November 25, 2017, Yang Song died as a result of violent criminalization from the NYPD. After being sexually assaulted by a person claiming to be a police officer and being asked to be an informant against her fellow workers, Yang Song reportedly "either intentionally leapt [or] accidently fell" from the fourth-floor apartment where she worked during a vice raid on the massage business.[7] Yang had been harassed and continually surveilled for months. The NYPD officially ruled her death to be an accident or suicide in June 2018, absolving themselves of any culpability, but Red Canary Song holds that Yang Song was murdered by the NYPD. It was their continued harassment and threat of arrest that led to her either leaping or falling to her death.

The first people to organize in reaction to Yang Song's death were sex workers in New York City demanding the decriminalization of sex work. Organizers, journalists, and grieving community members activated to call attention to the violent circumstances of her death, tell her story, contact her family, and do outreach to other massage workers in Flushing. Some of those involved would go on to form Red Canary Song (RCS), named in memoriam to Yang Song and in reference to canaries in the coal mine. Red Canary Song was founded initially around the coordination of sex workers and massage workers who wanted to create a union for massage workers in the wake of Yang's death. While this union never came to be, RCS garnered support and quiet attention from allied communities and would grow its grassroots, volunteer base over the next year. The reporting on Yang Song's death done by Melissa Gira Grant and Emma Whitford went largely unnoticed by most people in New York—let alone nationally—and other publications failed to even name Yang Song or acknowledge her life outside of her death.[8] Many Asian community members in New York City shunned Yang in death and rejected Red Canary Song's work due to rampant whorephobia and continued pushes to "clean up" Queens. Many blamed Yang's death on her occupation. Even in death, many people latched onto the same racist antitrafficking narratives about Asian migrant women that directly contributed to her criminalization. So-called antitrafficking nonprofits hopped at the chance to instrumentalize her death by saying that they could prevent deaths like hers with increased policing. While Red Canary Song's work went largely unnoticed for several years, this changed in March 2021, when RCS's work received nationwide attention in the wake of the murders of Xiaojie Tan, Delaina Ashley Yaun Gonzalez, Daoyou Feng, Paul Andre Michels, Soon Chung Park, Hyun Jung Grant, Yong Ae Yue, and Sun Cha Kim, six of whom were migrant Asian women massage workers, at three massage businesses outside of Atlanta, Georgia. Media coverage of these murders became widespread partially as a result of growing public attention to anti-Asian sentiments because of COVID-19.

Now, Red Canary Song works to support and assist Asian and migrant massage workers and sex workers in whatever way they can—be it mutual aid, providing information about their legal and civil rights, finding ways to organize and unionize, advocating for workers' rights, or working toward relevant policy initiatives to decriminalize sex work by abolishing the prison industrial complex.

Red Canary Song's history as an organization is as complex as the lives of its members. They have seen many iterations, with different members at different times shaping RCS. As previously stated, RCS started around the idea of forming a massage worker union, and early RCS members were sex workers former and current, massage workers, union organizers, and organizers working in nonprofits supporting Asian communities. Early on, certain members of RCS wanted to form a nonprofit 501(c)(3) and created an advisory board of longtime sex worker organizers, which happens often to emerging groups as nonprofits overtake movement work and take away certain financial liabilities. Some of the initial members of the collective would leave, and the remaining members rejected the nonprofit model because of its top-down structure, careerism, and blunting of revolutionary political goals to meet governmental mandates. The nonprofit industrial complex also often positions itself as a rescuer of Asian and migrant sex workers, massage workers, and other systemically marginalized communities engaging in informal labor economies. RCS seeks to push against this saviorism and everything else that comes with nonprofitization, so its members formed a volunteer-based grassroots collective with a nonhierarchical structure. Due to the sensitive nature of working with undocumented migrants and other criminalized individuals, the collective has had to stay small and secure. Because of this smallness, a working group structure would almost be impossible. Most members of RCS take up multiple roles in different areas, but RCS's work breaks down to outreach, internal administration, coalition building, and legislative policy work.

Red Canary Song roots its work in an abolitionist approach and labor framework that centers the experiences of violence faced by Asian migrant massage workers. These workers are subjected to criminalization and sexualized violence stemming from the oppression of sex workers, Asian women, working-class people, and immigrants. Much of this violence, including sexual and gender-based violence, is at the hands of the police. Policing has never been an effective response to violence because the police are agents of the white supremacist patriarchy, and many anti–sex work proponents who push for policing consider sex work and other related trades to be sexual and gender-based violence, but police are routinely sexually violent with impunity, especially toward Black and other women of color. Two in five young women in New York City report having been sexually harassed by the police—of those, almost half are Black, Latine, or Asian.[9] The criminalization and demonization of sex work has hurt and killed countless individuals—many at the hands of the police, either directly or indirectly.[10] Due to sexist racialized perceptions of Asian women, especially those engaged in vulnerable, low-wage work, Asian massage workers are harmed by the criminalization of sex work, regardless of whether they engage in it themselves. Decriminalization of sex work is the only way that sex workers, massage workers, sex trafficking survivors, and anyone criminalized for their survival and/or livelihood will ever be safe, and there is no decriminalizing sex work or anything for that matter without PIC abolition. So long as the prison industrial complex exists, people will be criminalized for these very things—no matter what state agents purport. An example of this is readily available in New York City as public opinion about sex work continues to change. After the DecrimNY coalition, which included RCS, worked to repeal the "Walking While Trans" ban, which polices loitering for the purpose of prostitution through legislative policy and public perception work, New York district attorneys soon after claimed to stop prosecuting prostitution charges. Asian massage workers are not as often being charged with prostitution; now, they are more often being charged for massage licensure. Massage workers we speak to recount police entering their workplaces randomly under the guise of stopping sex trafficking and will look for signs of sex work, and if they fail to find anything, they demand massage licenses or search for building code violations. So long as there are police, people will be policed.

COVID-19 has made the position of Asian massage workers and sex workers even more precarious, especially if they are undocumented immigrants. Because of this context, Red Canary Song focuses on mutual aid work as a way of meeting peoples' immediate needs—that is, needs that are not being met by the systems that are in place today. They are meeting people's needs as workers supporting other workers toward self-determination by providing money, food, supplies, and more so that they can survive and build and transform. Numerous mutual aid efforts sprung up during the COVID-19 pandemic, but sex workers had been doing mutual aid this whole time. This mutual aid work exists in the legacy of Black, feminist, queer, and trans-led organizing that reaches back decades.

This work of building movements off mutual aid is not simply because we are all oppressed, but because we want a world where no one is left behind, and the nonprofits that co-opt our movements do not provide mutual aid but instead saviorism that leaves many people behind and blames the violence people face on misfortune and personal choices.

Co-optation and Carceral Reform

As demonstrated, both NNJ and RCS emerged as grassroots abolitionist responses to systemic carceral violence. Yet, we have seen firsthand these campaigns be co-opted, diluted, and channeled back into the carceral system itself. How did an explicitly abolitionist grassroots call to Shut Down Rikers become co-opted into a deeply resourced #CLOSErikers campaign in support of the construction of new city jails? How were calls for "Justice for Yang Song" co-opted into antitrafficking programs and assistance that functionally increase policing and surveillance of massage parlors and further the precarity of the very people they are meant to assist? The mechanisms that worked in unison to move the Borough-Based Jail Plan are an important case study of how progressive reformers continue to push regressive expansions of the carceral apparatus, and how organized philanthropy can dictate the agendas of an entire sector of nonprofit organizations to effect policy change. We hope to situate debates on jail construction and sex trafficking in New York City in the current landscape by examining the structural failures and state responses that led to and followed the deaths of Kalief Browder and Yang Song.

In November 2015, Glenn Martin, then president of Just Leadership USA (JLUSA), spoke at a conference attended by New York City comptroller Scott Stringer about the crisis of violence at Rikers Island. In the following months, JLUSA would roll out its campaign to #CLOSErikers. JLUSA had begun to receive major grants from the Open Philanthropy Project (Soros), Ford Foundation, Chan Zuckerberg Initiative (Facebook), and Google in support of its campaign.[11] When the campaign publicly launched in 2016, it had formal support from more than a hundred partner organizations, including well-established criminal justice nonprofits like the American Civil Liberties Union (ACLU), Vera Institute of Justice, Katal Center, and local nonprofit groups such as the New York Civil Liberties Union (NYCLU), Make the Road New York, VOCAL New York, Urban Justice Center, and Communities United for Police Reform. #CLOSErikers also had vocal support of celebrities like

Russell Simmons, Nas, and Olivia Wilde, as well as the support of several key members of New York City Council.[12]

In February 2016, then Speaker of the New York City Council Melissa Mark-Viverito announced the formation of A More Just NYC (aka the Lippman Commission) to identify ways the population size on Rikers Island could be reduced to ultimately close the jail complex. The Lippman Commission consisted of twenty-seven commissioners, including Glenn Martin, along with representatives from a number of nonprofits including Nicholas Turner, president of Vera Institute for Justice, and Darren Walker, president of the Ford Foundation. Among the other members of the commission were multiple judges from New York City courts, a former U.S. attorney, the director of the Open Societies Foundation, the director of the CUNY Institute of State and Local Governance, and the president of the Citizens Crime Commission. The Lippman Commission made several recommendations, including the recommendation to close Rikers Island jail complex and to build "more humane, state-of-the-art, borough-based jails."

By 2018, when the BBJP was officially announced, a near consensus of New York City's progressive establishment of elected officials and nonprofit organizations was already on board. The Lippman Commission had set the policy agenda for the BBJP, and #CLOSErikers drove public support from elected officials and community leaders in favor of the plan. The proposed sites of the new jails had been chosen, architecture and design firms had been consulted, and city council members representing districts where the jails were to be located—Margaret Chin, Steven Levin, Diana Ayala, and Karen Koslowitz—were in support of the plan. This ruthless efficiency was coordinated by funders—the Ford Foundation and Open Societies Foundation—that actively shaped the policy agenda and funded the nonprofits tasked with pushing the plan through the charade of public process toward its ultimate realization.

Similarly, Yang Song's death was co-opted by well-funded, self-proclaimed antitrafficking nonprofits who criminalize workers related to the sex trades and trafficking survivors. And despite Yang Song being assaulted by a police officer and many other workers facing similar instances of gender-based violence, many antiviolence groups, such as Sanctuary for Families, in New York City continue to leave police out of their analyses of gender-based violence and even work with the police.

This was largely unseen by the majority of the public. These nonprofits build on long-standing savior narratives about saving Asian migrant women to promote efforts that increase police violence in the name of reducing prostitution and trafficking, neither of which policing achieves.[13] These trends build on a long history: for instance, the Anti-Prostitution Act of 1870 and the Page Act passed in 1875 purported to protect trafficking survivors and "forced laborers" but in practice gave immigration officials complete authority to criminalize Asian women and forbid them from entering the United States. Likewise, contemporary "antitrafficking" nonprofits work hand-in-hand with immigration officials, police departments, and prosecutors to covertly expand policing power, as seen in then Queens district attorney Richard Brown's statement following Yang Song's death. Brown said: "My office has long been at the forefront in helping those trapped in the sex industry find an escape through programs and assistance as an alternative to incarceration." The "programs and assistance" that Brown purports as alternatives to incarceration are actually antitrafficking nonprofits that do little else besides prolong the dehumanizing process of being funneled through "rehabilitation" programs and special courts that see migrant massage workers and sex workers as nothing more than morally flawed victims while offering no real alternatives to access economic security.[14] Without economic security, workers return to the criminalized precarious labor they were engaging in, only to be incarcerated and deported if they are undocumented. These so-called alternatives are well-funded by state and federal budgets and end up funneling people into incarceration. Under the guise of tackling sex trafficking, hundreds of massage businesses across the United States have been raided by the police and have led to countless workers being moved through the PIC for protracted amounts of time. In the wake of Yang Song's death, police and antitrafficking groups have urged a crackdown on Asian massage businesses, which would only worsen the violence of policing and surveillance that massage workers face.

The murders of both Yang Song and Kalief Browder would spawn efforts by nonprofit organizations to expand the carceral state under the guise of ending the terrors they experienced. These nonprofit organizations not only use progressive rhetoric to expand the carceral state but also play on many Asian Americans' unchecked anti-Blackness and saviorism toward our homelands.

How Asian Americans Facilitate Co-optation

Over the course of the past two years, the popularization of prison abolition has been undeniable. During this same time, popular attention to anti-Asian violence has reached new heights. However, these two trends have rarely worked in tandem. Before March 2021, most people who were not in or related to the trades have been unbothered by the violence that Asian massage workers, sex workers, and migrant workers face on a daily basis. After the Atlanta spa shootings, a growing chorus of Asian Americans looked for recognition from the state in their oppression, and in doing so often reduced these murders to racist "hate" enacted by an individual.[15] Many neglect the violence of capitalism and imperialism that force people into criminalized precarious labor while also furthering dehumanizing narratives around migrant Asian women as helpless traumatized victims, depriving them of their agency. These simplistic narratives that generalize anti-Asian violence erase the complex and deeply connected histories of racialized and gendered violence, demonstrating anti-Blackness in their clammer for state recognition.[16] In response, the state jumps at the chance to identify violence of this nature as "hate" in order to introduce hate crime legislation that further legitimizes policing. There were efforts by local government and police in Georgia to paint these murders simply as sexist and targeting people viewed as sex workers because for many people violence toward sex workers is justified by their occupation; Fulton County quickly introduced hate crime legislation, which has historically been used in other states to police Black people for "anti-white" hate crimes. The underlying narratives that allow these institutions to exist are often perpetuated by Asian Americans in a scramble for legibility.[17] Very few mainstream Asian American organizations and activists pushed back on this, and in fact many called for hate crime legislation and decried that these massage workers were sex workers and therefore were "innocent" and did not deserve the violence that sex workers face. Similarly, many Asian American immigrant advocacy groups have a long history of alienating Indigenous sovereignty by seeking state recognition and again allowing way for the policing of other marginalized groups.[18] These grabs at legibility by alienating other marginalized groups fail because anti-immigrant xenophobia, whorephobia, anti-Blackness, imperialism, and settler colonialism are all mutually reinforcing each other and cannot be dismantled by grasping at one or the other. The United States wages military occupation, military sexual violence in host nations, environmental destruction, and extractive and coercive trade/economic policies abroad in countries across Asia, while Asian people face racialized labor exploitation, rampant workplace abuse, criminalization for survival, targeted sexual violence, routine refusal of language access, immigration detention and deportation, and xenophobic media attacks domestically. It is from this context that every form of violence against Asian people in the United States springs forth. By grasping at #StopAsianHate and data collection on violence that erases so much, the state is legitimized as an authority on violence and continues to be given more power to enact violence regardless of what the data says.[19] If crime data is low, then the police are doing their jobs, and if crime data is high, then there needs to be more policing.

The framing of anti-Asian violence as an exceptional crisis, separate from histories of anti-Blackness, colonialism, imperialism, and racial capitalism, has allowed for Asian American city council members to support the building of a borough-based skyscraper jail in Manhattan Chinatown. This was done with little resistance from most of the community because the expansion of the carceral state has often not been viewed as an "Asian" issue that would cause panic in the broader Asian American community. In fact, anti-Asian violence is often met with calls for more specific and intensified state involvement. In response to calls to #StopAsianHate and to respond to anti-Asian violence during COVID-19, the NYPD added plainclothes officers to patrol Asian neighborhoods and two detectives to its Hate Crimes Task Force in 2021. Instances of anti-Asian violence continue to be met with cries for perpetrators to be charged for "hate crimes," a prosecutorial term that results in harsher sentences that do nothing to address the roots of racial violence.[20] And many Asian American activists continue to make demands for more Asian representation on and funding for task forces and other institutional responses that ultimately do little but increase funding for police and prisons and reify ideology upholding the criminal punishment system.

These misguided decisions have lasting consequences for discourse but also make it ripe for carceral nonprofits to push for expansion in our names. We see carceral nonprofits taking on more covert stances to promote carceral expansion under the guise of safety and decarceration. These well-funded nonprofits perpetuate narratives of *uniquely heinous conditions* that we as PIC abolitionists know are common and normalized. Because of this, a complete dismantling and transformation of oppressive systems is necessary, not piecemeal criminal justice reform efforts. This chapter is our attempt as Asian American prison industrial complex abolitionists to engage with an audience of Asian Americans trying to navigate the carceral state and their positionality within it. This is not meant to be complete or conclusive but rather a provocation.

There is an urgent need to unravel our position within structures of U.S. racial hierarchy, and the ways Asian American identities have been deployed by white supremacist ideology to discipline Black and other marginalized communities. Asian Americans must not strive for their own relative whiteness in the United States or the expectation that police are here to serve them, but rather for the end of patriarchal racial capitalism and the abolition of the carceral state that upholds it. The years 2020 and 2021 brought largely unexpected developments to the work of police and prison abolition that we have been quietly engaging with for years prior, and that we personally did not connect to more mainstream movements for Asian Americans but are now being asked to. We don't see ourselves as exemplary of Asian American activism, nor did we do any of the work we mention alone. This chapter is a small piece of us stitching together our separate and sometimes intersecting experiences as Asian American organizers in New York City who largely have not engaged with Asian American community-based movements partially as a political choice.

Asian American activism in New York City has been disjointed and inconsistent. While there are groups rallying for supporting of racial-equity based reforms in specialized high schools and supporting NYPD officer Peter Liang, there are also groups protesting against the BBJP in Chinatown and the institutions and individuals that support it, such as the Museum of Chinese in America (MOCA). And even among the protestors of the BBJP in Chinatown, some of the movement has been defanged and focuses largely on its impact on Chinatown residents and businesses, without mentions of the prison industrial complex or the communities that would be incarcerated there. Outside of the people who remain active from NNJ, the current organizing against the BBJP in Manhattan Chinatown generally shows little solidarity with the other boroughs, a selective focus that also implies anti-Blackness. Similar groups with overlap into the groups currently organizing around the BBJP in Chinatown are also against the building of homeless shelters in the neighborhood. These groups often represent interests of an easily discernible developer or landlord class. Similarly harmful, but more insidious, are liberal-progressive politicians, nonprofit and cultural organizations, academics, and celebrity activists who view the anxieties of Asian American communities as opportunities to advance their own careers and agendas, while supporting reforms that, at best, do little to address the root causes of violence in working-class Asian communities, and, at worst, deepen investments in carceral infrastructures, expanding the reach of police and prisons while resources of antipoverty measures are simultaneously disinvested from.

Conclusion: Defining Abolition through Organizing

In a little over a year, NNJ galvanized a citywide abolitionist movement in opposition to the BBJP. Although the campaign was not successful in halting the BBJP, the work and the consciousness built through that work continues to carry forward. And while WKUS is no longer active, countless mutual aid efforts emerged across the city during the COVID-19 epidemic, many of which grew out of relationships established from the Campaign to Shut Down Rikers and NNJ. Among those efforts is COVID Bailout, a mutual aid effort that has successfully bailed out more than 447 individuals since the beginning of the pandemic.[21] Additionally, Red Canary Song continues to expand its mutual aid efforts among Asian sex workers and massage workers, including monetary support through community fundraising, ESL classes, Know Your Rights trainings, drug-use harm reduction trainings, and more. This work thrives on mutually building each other's capacity and honoring every worker's way of survival. The everyday outreach and support that Red Canary Song does is meant to keep people safe and cared for, so that workers can reduce possible harms and avoid violence as much as possible while people are criminalized for who they are and how they survive.

At its best, NNJ was an intergenerational, multisectional coalition of abolitionist organizers that included incarcerated and formerly incarcerated people, grassroots activists, lawyers, artists, and teachers. The campaign deepened relationships between individuals and organizations while producing an immense amount of research, organizing tools, and educational resources.

The work of NNJ and RCS exists in the legacy of Black, feminist, queer, and trans-led anti-carceral organizing that reaches back decades into a political legacy that has been fighting as long as there has been state enslavement and cages. We see solidarity as a shared struggle. NNJ and RCS organizers have continued to push critical understandings of prison abolition into mainstream consciousness, grounding contemporary abolitionist struggles in New York City as "not solely [about] the abolition of the buildings we call prisons, but also the conditions which gave rise to prisons as a spatial fix to socio-economic and racial issues."[22] And in the fight against the growing carceral apparatus of New York City, a new generation of organizers has put the theory of prison abolition into the practice of community building, consciousness raising, confronting the carceral state, and providing care and mutual aid.

As PIC abolitionists, we must define safety on our own terms. For NNJ, safety might mean, rather than a $10.8 billion investment building new jails, for those resources to be invested in housing, employment, health care, education, and transportation in communities that are the most policed, most surveilled, and most incarcerated. Or it could require amplifying calls for solidarity in mutual aid organizing between incarcerated people and those on the outside. Or networks of neighbors alerting neighbors to police presence on the MTA during cracking downs on fare evasion and food vendors on transit. For RCS, safety might mean decriminalization of sex work, dismantling surveillance, and an investment in mutual aid networks for workers. For us, building relationships of trust and accountability and networks of care are at the center of building the world we want to see, with solidarity not as a denial of Asian American identity but as recognition of our shared histories and the intertwined connections of oppressive systems. Abolition speaks to a multitude of possibilities available to us. We do not hope to define abolition for every community and can only speak to what is currently available to us and what we can imagine in our own communities as we build models for what we hope life can be like in the future.

Notes

1. These reforms do little to address the roots of racial or gendered violence. In addition to the fact that the vast majority of crime or violence that occurs in Asian communities is intra-racial (between people of the same racial or ethnic group), not interracial, these remedies have not proven to be an effective deterrence to violence. Further, naming these acts as "hate crimes" individualizes the violence as an isolated act by a hateful actor, rather than situating that violence within the larger context of racialized and gendered violence in the history of the U.S. empire.
2. Sawyer, Wendy, and Peter Wagner, "Mass Incarceration: The Whole Pie 2022," *Prison Policy Initiative*, 14 March 2022, www.prisonpolicy.org.
3. Rakia, Raven, and Ashoka Jegroo, "How the Push to Close Rikers Went from No Jails to New Jails," *The Appeal*, 29 May 2018, https://theappeal.org.
4. Shanahan, Jarrod, and Jack Norton, "A Jail to End All Jails," *Urban Omnibus*, The Architectural League of New York, 1 Feb. 2018, https://urbanomnibus.net.
5. Gilmore, Ruth Wilson, "Ruth Wilson Gilmore Makes the Case for Abolition," *Intercepted Podcast*, 10 June 2020, https://theintercept.com.
6. No New Jails NYC (2019), "Close Rikers Now, We Keep Us Safe: A New Yorker's Guide to Community Care and Safety by Closing Rikers with No New Jails (Version 2.0)," 10 Oct. 2019.
7. "The NYPD's Vice Enforcement Division is, in theory, tasked with policing so-called quality-of-life offenses such as consensual sex work, narcotics use, and gambling. But in reality, over the last 50 years, Vice officers have used their badges to exploit, sexually harass, and otherwise terrorize sex workers and their clients, massage workers, and survivors of trafficking. Nearly all of those victimized by Vice are LGBTQ+, people of color, and noncitizens." See New York Civil Liberties Union, "Defund NYPD's Vice Squad," *NYCLU | ACLU of New York*, 22 June 2021, www.nyclu.org.
8. Whitford, Emma, and Melissa Gira Grant, "Family, Former Attorney of Queens Woman Who Fell to Her Death in Vice Sting Say She Was Sexually Assaulted, Pressured to Become an Informant," *The Appeal*, 15 Dec. 2017; Whitford, Emma, and Melissa Gira Grant, "Queens DA Releases Final Report on Massage Worker's Death, Calling Sex Work 'Degrading and Humiliating,'" *The Appeal*, 22 June 2018, https://theappeal.org.
9. Fine, Michelle, et al., ""Anything Can Happen with Police Around": Urban Youth Evaluate Strategies of Surveillance in Public Places," *Journal of Social Issues* 59.1 (2003): 141–158.
10. See, e.g., Arrington, Monsello, et al., "Move Along: Policing Sex Work in Washington, D.C.," Alliance for a Safe and Diverse DC, 2008, https://dctranscoalition.files.wordpress.com; Sex Workers Project, "Behind Closed Doors: An Analysis of Indoor Sex Work in New York City," *Sex Workers Project | Urban Justice Center*, 2005, https://sexworkersproject.org; "Revolving Door: An

Analysis of Street-Based Prostitution in New York City," *Sex Workers Project | Urban Justice Center*, 2003, https://sexworkersproject.org; and BAYSWAN. "The San Francisco Task Force on Prostitution: Final Report," *Sex Workers Education Network*, March 1996, http://www.bayswan.org.

11 Rakia, Raven, and Ashoka Jegroo, "How the Push to Close Rikers Went from No Jails to New Jails," *The Appeal*, 29 May 2018, https://theappeal.org.
12 JLUSA is currently leading similar campaigns to #CLOSEmsdf in Milwaukee, #CLOSEthecreek in Philadelphia, and achieve #JusticeLA in Los Angeles.
13 Shih, Elena, *Manufacturing Freedom: Sex Work, Anti-trafficking Rehab, and the Racial Wages of Rescue*, Berkeley: University of California Press, 2023.
14 Shih, Elena, "Opinion: How to Protect Massage Workers," *New York Times*, 26 March 2021, www.nytimes.com.
15 See Whitlock, Kay, "Reconsidering Hate: Policy and Politics at the Intersection," Policy Research Associates, 2012; and Whitlock, Kay, and Michael Bronski, *Considering Hate: Violence, Goodness, and Justice in American Culture and Politics*, Boston: Beacon Press, 2016.
16 See Beutin, Lyndsey, *Trafficking in Antiblackness: Modern-Day Slavery, White Indemnity, and Racial Justice*, Durham, NC: Duke University Press, 2023.
17 See Rodríguez, Dylan, "The 'Asian Exception' and the Scramble for Legibility toward an Abolitionist Approach to Anti-Asian Violence," *Society and Space*, 8 April 2021, www.societyandspace.org.
18 See Coulthard, Glen, *Red Skin, White Masks: Rejecting the Colonial Politics of Recognition*, Minneapolis: University of Minnesota Press, 2014.
19 See Nopper, Tamara, "Anti-Asian Violence and Black-Asian Solidarity Today. In: Asian American Writers' Workshop," YouTube, 29 March 2021; Nopper, Tamara, "Digital Character in "The Scored Society": FICO, Social Networks, and Competing Measurements of Creditworthiness," in Benjamin, R. (ed.) *Captivating Technology*. Durham, NC: Duke University Press, 2019, pp. 170–187; and Kuo, Rachel, and Matthew Bui, "Against Carceral Data Collection in Response to Anti-Asian Violences," *Big Data & Society* 8.1 (2021): 20539517211028252.
20 These reforms do little to address the roots of racial or gendered violence. In addition to the fact that the vast majority of crime or violence that occurs in Asian communities is intra-racial (between people of the same racial or ethnic group), not interracial, these remedies have not proven to be an effective deterrence to violence. Further, naming these acts as "hate crimes" individualizes the violence as an isolated act by a hateful actor, rather than situating that violence within the larger context of racialized and gendered violence in the history of the U.S. empire. See "A Response to Hate Crime Charges from Red Canary Song and Survived and Punished," Survived and Punished, 23 Nov. 2021, https://survivedandpunished.org.
21 Total number as of March 2024. See "Peoples Bail Out NYC," *COVID Bail Out NYC*, www.peoplesbailoutproject.org.
22 Gilmore, "Ruth Wilson Gilmore Makes the Case for Abolition."

PART III

Radical Representations: Movement Art, Narrative, and Cultural Production

Cultural work has always been foundational to the political project of Asian America. As Chris Iijima of the formative Asian American band/movement troubadour group Yellow Pearl put it: "The basis of Asian American culture was simply the construction of a counternarrative—an oppositional voice—to the white supremacist narrative and culture about the inferiority of people of color and Asians in particular."[1] Heeding this oppositional definition of Asian American culture, this section emphasizes the role of aesthetic, material, and cultural modes of production in shaping political coalitions, community safety, and narrative change in Asian American communities. Following Lisa Lowe and David Lloyd's description of culture as "the field on which economic and political contradictions are articulated," the chapters in this section examine Asian American cultural identity as a site in which a diverse array of actors negotiate and contest the overlapping fields of race, class, gender, nation, and empire.[2]

Beginning with the premise that Asian American political identity is itself an imaginative project, the following case studies foreground innovative forms of Asian American cultural production and reveal the ways in which cultural change often precedes political change. The members of the New York City–based Asian American Feminist Collective reflect on the use of discursive and visual media practices to build the political imaginations and cultural expressions of an Asian American feminist movement. From public statements against police violence to community talk circles about sex and love, their chapter highlights the important role of Asian American media making in the mobilization of collective power. Rekha Malhotra (aka DJ Rekha) revisits the 1997 formation of Basement Bhangra, a South Asian dance party in New York City, and its two decades of providing a community space for South Asian youths and movement activists amid the War on Terror. Sally

Chen, Douglas H. Lee, OiYan A. Poon, and Janelle Wong explore the use of narrative, testimony, and storytelling by Harvard Asian American students in support of affirmative action in the context of the 2019 Supreme Court hearings on *Students for Fair Admissions v. Harvard*. Together, the case studies in this section importantly expand our sense of *where* Asian American politics unfolds on the ground to include campuses, dance halls, digital zines, and other interstitial spaces.

Notes

1 Chris Iijima, "Pontifications on the Distinction between Grains of Sand and Yellow Pearls," in Steve Louie and Glenn Omatsu, eds., *Asian Americans: Movement and the Moment* (Los Angeles: UCLA Asian American Studies Press, 2014), 7.
2 Lisa Lowe and David Lloyd, eds., *The Politics of Culture in the Shadow of Capital* (Durham, NC: Duke University Press, 1997), 31.

7

Asian American Feminist Roundtable on Media for World-Building

Documenting, Archiving, Amplifying

ASIAN AMERICAN FEMINIST COLLECTIVE (SALONEE BHAMAN, JULIE AE KIM, RACHEL KUO, SENTI SOJWAL, AND TIFFANY DIANE TSO)

In this roundtable, the Asian American Feminist Collective (AAFC) recollects our history as it has been encompassed and communicated through various forms of media. This roundtable reflects notes, commentaries, and discussions from various workshops and events that we have assembled on feminist media and histories, as well as from less visible archives of meeting notes and draft documents. Our conversation came together in the spring of 2021 in the midst of multiple ongoing and unrelenting crises. Our various communities continue to experience grief and loss throughout the COVID-19 pandemic while also reckoning with the tenuous politics of solidarity. Leading up to this roundtable, we hadn't seen each other in over nine months. We have a group text thread where we chat with each other daily. Our messages range from discussions about projects we're working on, to news articles on local and national politics, and general check-ins. "I'm so tired." "Exhausted." "I'm so sorry, I haven't been able to do anything." "Accountability, I'll add to the document after work." Starting (and finishing) this roundtable was difficult given time constraints and individual and group capacity for production and collaboration. We needed the time and space to pause and reflect. To move us forward and begin the process of collectively writing, Tiffany started a Google document where we began to pose questions to one another—*How did we get to where we are? What has shifted since we started?* Salonee organized a Zoom call where we spent several hours together on a document, murmuring to one another as we wrote. The questions we asked of one another emphasize transformation and growth as we reflect on our politics and practices in relation to our media projects.

In our first zine, "Building an Asian American Feminist Movement," published later in 2018, we offered a definition of Asian American feminism as "an ever-evolving mode of knowledge, politics, and practice." In our initial zine, we also described Asian American feminism as a "world-building project."

> The beauty of the Asian American feminist movement is that we can continue to shape and evolve it. We can (and must) constantly reflect upon and refine a political agenda that works for all of us. In the spirit of producing different spaces and stories and also stronger coalitions, we look forward to connecting and building community with you to produce new ideas and better worlds.[1]

Our emphasis on growth is integral to the idea of world-building—that we can continue to create alternative ways of being and thinking together. Rather than linear progress, we focus on collective process. Through ongoing and consistent dialogue and practice, we can generate and imagine different liberatory possibilities and visions. Since our initial offerings, while we remain committed to dismantling structures of violence and building toward collective liberation, we continue to grow in how we can better show up for our communities, for instance through building worker solidarities and committing to abolition.

A roundtable in New York City was one of the first places we began. While we first came together to organize an event series on Asian American Feminism in the Age of Trump, after wave after wave of crisis in the aftermath of the 2016 elections, we began to think longer-term on what other possibilities could emerge. In February 2018 we gathered a close group of feminist organizers, scholars, cultural workers, and writers—some of whom are also included in this anthology—for a roundtable about resurfacing Asian American feminist political identity and movement building.[2] Here, we again use the roundtable format to reflect on some of our political education and community building projects over the past few years to highlight the political imaginations and cultural expressions of an Asian American feminist movement.

Our projects use different discursive and visual media forms and practices, and have included digital workshops on feminist history, community talk circles about sex and love, public statement letters against police violence and carceral expansion, creative storytelling formats, and graphics for Instagram and social media platforms. Our projects interrogate politics grounded within our communities, including those whose backgrounds encompass East, Southeast, and South Asian, Pacific Islander, multi-ethnic, and diasporic Asian identities. In the following roundtable exchange, we each discuss our visions for the future in connection with particular projects, collaborations, and events as well as reflections on lessons learned and cultural politics as a community process. Together, this roundtable brings together our analyses of political power through feminist media-making practices and emphasizes the relationship between cultural production, community building, and political mobilization.

Why Feminist Media-Making?

We see our work as building up an Asian American feminist public and informed by histories of feminist media, including anthologies such as *The Bridge Called My Back* and the Combahee River Collective Statement. Catherine Squires's model of publics emphasizes the sociopolitical and historical contexts in which groups circulate counter-discourses surrounding racial positioning.[3] We use different forms of media and distribution channels, from intimate workshops to social media posts, to produce an internal discourse about Asian American feminism, as well as to challenge dominant messages and narratives. Asian American media matters for the mobilization and production of collective politics.[4]

Our current media landscape continues to be one in which there is uneven access to and control of media platforms and channels. Feminist media-making has been a means to push back against the mainstream media and information ecosystems that have historically and currently excluded our communities and where inclusion into mainstream representation has also rendered our communities apolitical. Additionally, there are often limitations to individualized identity-based recognitions, such as the production of narrow solidarities or ways identity can be rendered into a commodity. Beyond the naming of differences to witness how power operates, feminist media-making practices and processes as well as the final output and content gives us the opportunity for ongoing analysis of how mechanisms of exclusion are replicated and re-created.[5] We bring our histories to feminism as a way to orient and position ourselves in ways that build toward collective struggle.

I—Manifesting and Building a Collective

SALONEE BHAMAN: A theme that has animated our work, from zines to structured gatherings, has been the importance of Asian American feminist archives and their role in connecting our present moment to a longer legacy of movement building. Our zines have benefited from what we could call a community-based archival practice. This practice works in two ways: we like to share the pieces of research we encounter in traditional archival repositories that are difficult to access but also reframe collecting and sharing stories, writing, and family history as a form of archive-building. Both in tandem have offered our zines a meaningful structure. The impact of an archival practice is something that some of our other collaborators have also surfaced; one example that comes to mind is the role that the digitized archives at CAAAV are playing in ongoing struggles against gentrification and police.[6] How might we describe ourselves in a Finding Aid for the Asian American Feminist Collective? Perhaps we could start by thinking through how we came to think about Asian American feminism as a kind of movement space or discrete conversation that we wanted to be part of.

JULIE AE KIM: The Asian American Feminist Collective began as an event series after the 2016 presidential election and the Women's March. At the time, I was a part of NAPAWF's (National Asian Pacific American Women's Forum) New York City chapter and starting my master's in gender and women's studies at the CUNY Graduate Center, which is where I was able to ruminate on the term "Asian American feminism": what should it mean, and where are Asian American feminists situated in the larger context of the current feminist movement? Through organizing the event series, Asian American scholars, artists, and writers came together to collectively volunteer their time. The first event in the series was called "Asian American Feminism in the Age of Trump," where thousands of people expressed interest in attending and workshopping the question, *What is an Asian American feminist?* The event led to my realization that there was a dearth of spaces for discourse around the intersection of Asian America and feminism and that public dialogue around this was needed.

After months of organizing, we came to the realization that while events were a great way to raise awareness and bring people together in conversation, ultimately, they are hard to sustain long-term, and it can be difficult to accommodate the immense interest. The information we shared also felt short-lived, as people continued to ask the same questions. That is how the idea of creating an Asian American feminist manifesto came about. We wanted to pivot from one-off events to creating longer-lasting, more widely accessible and shareable work. Ultimately, the event series enabled the current Asian American Feminist Collective to find each other. This was the most important thing to come out of the event series: a group of Asian American feminists committed to doing this work together.

RACHEL KUO: We wanted to start something independent from a formal organization that focused explicitly on Asian American feminism and explore different approaches and practices for building feminist politics. So often, new formations begin with attempts to define who we are, what we do, why we're coming together. Feminist formations like the Combahee River Collective and Third World Women's Alliance all used communal forms of writing to express political visions through statements, manifestos, and zines. In that vein, one of the first things we wanted to do was write an Asian American feminist manifesto to offer an initial definition. How do we talk about alignment across differences and articulate uneven formations of power? More importantly, how do we do so in a way that offers a set of commitments for how we do political work?

The process of articulating what Asian American feminism meant to us was a collective one. I remember sitting in my apartment with Julie and Tiffany to begin writing our manifesto on a Google document. After an initial draft, Julie circulated a shared link on Twitter to invite more people into the project to share comments, feedback, and suggestions—the "final" version of this draft ended up being our first zine, which we shared at our launch in September 2018. The collaborative process of trying to write a collective definition revealed a lot about the limits of language as well as demonstrated that what became more important was process: not "who we are" but rather "how we are together." The summer before we formally launched, I spent time in the archives of the Sophia Smith Collection of Women's History immersed in organizational documents of different feminist collectives and organizations. There was one piece of paper, a faxed document of a statement of purpose, that marked the beginning of an Asian and Pacific American women's network in the 1990s (this network eventually became NAPAWF). While the original typed text was fading, the filmy piece of paper included annotations and comments in different inks and handwriting styles—a predecessor of a shared Google doc, with people faxing a definition back and forth. In our first zine, we laid out some political principles and commitments including actively dismantling structures of anti-Blackness and settler colonialism, transnational frameworks, a politics of class solidarity, and taking down patriarchy and centering queer, trans, and gender nonconforming Asian Americans. One of the things I've observed from the archives of previous feminist formations has been different transformations; formations may come to an end over time or reemerge as something new. AAFC is a new formation, and since the manifesto, our analysis and how we ground ourselves in feminist politics continues to co-evolve as we navigate putting into practice the different principles we laid out. We're constantly growing, learning, and unlearning. For example, we have worked to evolve our understanding and practice of abolition as part of our commitments. The process of collective media-making together has also helped shift and grow my own politics, and these acts of creative making also help us evolve as a collective in our political analysis and practice. How have you seen our work grow along these commitments?

SALONEE: As someone who joined this formation sometime after that first manifesto was written, I think that those initial commitments have been incredibly useful as we have navigated the turbulent political and ideological waters of the past several years. Framing the Asian American experience, or Asian American-ness, as relational and forged in coalition with other groups, shaped and enmeshed in the politics of gender and sexuality, and situated within racial

BUILDING AN ASIAN AMERICAN FEMINIST MOVEMENT

"A COLLECTIVE IS WHAT DOES NOT STAND STILL BUT CREATES AND IS CREATED BY MOVEMENT...A MOVEMENT COMES INTO EXISTENCE TO TRANSFORM WHAT IS IN EXISTENCE." - SARA AHMED

Figure 7.1: AAFC's first zine, "Building an Asian American Feminist Movement."

capitalism has pushed us to search for connection and meaning across difference as a rule.

Negotiating the boundaries of community and racial identity as both a world-building project and political praxis can be challenging when you're working within existing digital media forms, like Instagram and Twitter [now X]. There's a prioritization of visually appealing and text-light content that often doesn't lend itself to the slow and nuanced explorations of who was part of the large, disparate coalition of Asian America. I find that a recurrent question in many Asian American spaces, both activist and academic, in the past few years has been around whether or not there is still utility in using "Asian American" as an organizing category. At its best, it offers a structure for political coalition that makes room for enormous heterogeneity of experience, prefiguring a solidarity that is beautiful if we live up to it. However, often it homogenizes, flattens, and obscures the nuances and particularities of certain experiences and identities. Feminism, in many ways, functions the same way. So, both parts of our kind of collective charge: "Asian America" and "Feminist" are loaded terms that we're trying to collectively define the course of.

JULIE: When I first started thinking about my feminist politics, it centered on my identities as a queer Asian American woman, as that was the first point of entry for me. It was also invigorating to read about groups like the Unbound Feet Collective, which included members like Mitsuye Yamada, Nellie Wong, Genny Lim, and Kitty Tsui, that also thought about similar issues in the 1970s and '80s. As I continued grappling with feminist identity and organizing around this category of "woman," there were a lot of pitfalls. First, the feminist movement as it was first known and popularized was through the lens of white supremacy and class privilege. As Alok Vaid-Menon says, "White feminism is racism." I started to recognize that the feminism that I wanted to organize on was not about identity per se, but about dismantling patriarchy and sexism, which affects everyone. I credit trans feminists and activists for bringing me to this realization and realizing that part of our work as feminists is ending the gender binary. I have a lot of respect for the Asian American feminist organizing that happened during the 1960s and '70s with the advent of the term "Asian American" and the intersectional organizing that happened with the Black Power, anti-war, and feminist movements. However, there was still so much sexism and homophobia during that time—I hope to continue the work of feminism that combats systems over individuals and to continue to develop my analysis around that.

II—Feminist Storytelling and Media Forms

SALONEE: Our collective interest in those early intersectional feminist works and groups like the Kitchen Table Press and the Combahee River Collective made the connection between literary projects, storytelling, and political imagination feel clear and vital when we were thinking about which collaborations to take on. Some of my favorite projects that we've worked on have been about holding space for community stories and experiences. Everything from Tiff's loving stewardship of the *First Times* series to Senti's commitment to making space to talk about pleasure and sexuality during our annual sex and love talk circle seems connected to those commitments. The idea that storytelling about our experiences, families, and fantasies was a really important part of feminist world-building was not new to us because of the rich and inspiring work of those intellectual ancestors. I think a lot of our work has been to hold space for people to articulate the vast diversity of the Asian American experience. And then, a lot of our political education work has been to try and continually make connections between the diversity of our stories and struggles for freedom, justice, and equity. How do you think media-making and storytelling has fit into these projects?

TIFFANY DIANE TSO: As a journalist, my goal has always been to allow stories about people and communities to be told by the sources themselves. I try not to co-opt others' stories, and I try to ensure that each narrative I help usher through is controlled by the subjects themselves and reflective of their truths. It's about agency. This is something we try to instill within our storytelling work, and what better way than to give people platforms to tell their own stories? Using digital storytelling across different types of media and platforms, we attempt to expand what "Asian America"

Figure 7.2: Image from storytelling series and the Hear Us Rise exhibit.

encompasses, educate folks on how we're situated within cross-racial BIPOC organizing, and allow people platforms for creative expression as we continue to interrogate what this Asian American feminist movement looks like. It feels good to publish stories, writing, art, and archives from folks in ways that are reflective of people's individual and collective truths. Editing our digital storytelling series on our website—the first theme being "First Times," the second "Real/Imagined"—gave artists and writers the opportunity to publish their dream pieces—poems, stories, and artwork told from their unique Asian and Asian American feminist perspectives—on our digital platform. When we began publishing the storytelling series, part of the impetus was opening up our community to feminists across the diaspora. For many contributors, this was their first published work. When I ended up serving on the curatorial committee for Hear Us Rise: APA Voices in Feminism, an exhibit for Seattle's Wing Luke Museum, I made sure to reach out to collaborators of ours to submit their own photos, stories, and voices to be featured in the museum. As a collective, we also coedit the multimedia Black and Asian Feminist Solidarities project with Black Women Radicals, published on Asian American Writers' Workshop's *The Margins*. These projects helped us connect with people outside of New York City. As another example, our #ThisIsAsianAmerica series lends people our social media platform to tell their family stories and share their archives, giving audiences a more intimate understanding of how diverse our communities are and how transnational frameworks impact our experiences.

SENTI SOJWAL: We started AAFC's #ThisIsAsianAmerica Instagram series so we could tell stories—these little but huge slices of our lives that encompass years of complex history, migration, relationships, generations of movement, and struggle and joy. Because I'd never felt totally at home in the conception of "Asian America," where South Asian voices have been historically excluded, I wanted to show the wide breadth of our stories, lives, and histories. As a mixed-ethnic Indian American, I don't often see my identity reflected in media—Indian, Western, or otherwise. My dad is Maharashtrian, from Nagpur. He was one of four in a Christian family, and spent his childhood flying kites with his brother in the streets and stringing garlands of popcorn around the Christmas tree. His father was stern, and his mother was a warm delight who would drop everything to feed anyone who walked through the door. My mother, second eldest of five, is from a tight-knit Indigenous community in the mountains of Nagaland, in northeastern India, bordering Myanmar. She looks like she could be Chinese or Tibetan, with light skin, long, straight hair, and gently slanting eyes. When I look at photos of her from the 1980s, dressed in cool metallics, traditional woven fabrics, or rocking pearls, she is the most luminously beautiful person I've ever seen in my life. My parents didn't grow up speaking the same languages (their common tongue is English), eating the same food, or practicing the same cultural traditions. They met and fell in love as seminary students in their twenties in Pune. My parents and I moved to the United States in 1994 so my dad could study theology at Princeton Seminary. He washed dishes in the student dining hall to make extra money while my mom babysat other people's children for $3 an hour. I think often of that part of their life—how strange

Figure 7.3: Photo of Senti Sojwal's parents from #ThisIsAsianAmerica Instagram series.

and difficult it must have been, but also how exhilarating, to cross an ocean for some great adventure. I'm used to explaining myself and why I look the way I do (mixed, ambiguous) after explaining that yes, I'm Indian, and no, there's a billion of us, we don't all look the same. I get asked routinely, "Are you Filipina? Mexican? Hawaiian? Are you half Asian? I can't believe you're Indian."

There's no singular Asian American identity, and no singular Asian American story. I put together a series of photos of my parents that I love—smiling in the back of a car on their wedding day, wearing a suit and a sari at a party in their twenties, in hats at a picnic table on my sibling's first birthday in the sweltering heat of a Florida summer—and told their story with the hashtag #ThisIsAsianAmerica. We invited our community to contribute to the project on Instagram and message us with their photos and family histories, asking, *How did your people come to this country? What is home to you? What stories do you wish we could tell?* The response was a diverse and deeply meaningful exploration of what it means to be Asian in America, shining a light on all the different ways our communities have navigated trauma, colonialism, and travesty, and created home and belonging.

As part of the Instagram series, Megan told the story of her great-great-great-grandfather, who smuggled himself on a freight ship to the United States and worked on the Transcontinental Railroad. He opened a laundromat in lower Manhattan, but wasn't able to bring his family overseas when the Chinese Exclusion Act passed in 1882, even as he'd helped build this country with his bare hands. Amirah told the story of her survivor parents, who fled the Khmer Rouge regime in Cambodia to raise a family in Seattle, working hard and making sacrifices so their children could flourish in "the land of dreams." Anna told the story of her grandmother, a botany professor, who left the impending civil war in Sri Lanka with three young children to Queens, New York, in the 1960s, not knowing a soul. Tiff told the story of her mom, the only one of eight siblings to leave Taiwan. She raised her family in Texas, beginning a new career at almost age forty in integrated design after taking a class at Austin Community College. Rachel told the story of her parents, adventurous journalists who spent time in Singapore and ran a mail supply store as a small family business, where Rachel's mom would spend hours writing books about colonialism, art, and politics in the backroom.

RACHEL: As another media format, zines have been a way we engage in community storytelling and political education. At the beginning of March 2020, given the racialization of the COVID-19 pandemic as "Asian," we started our third zine project with Bluestockings, a radical feminist bookstore in Manhattan's Lower East Side. The project documented incidents of anti-Asian racism as they were emerging, particularly as they were experienced by front-line service workers, health care providers, educators, and other community members. This zine was a moment of "bringing our histories to feminism," where we looked back at the racist and colonial legacies of health discourses, xenophobia, and state and institutional failure and neglect, to "move beyond narrow bids" for inclusion.[7] While incidents of anti-Asian violence became more publicly visible during the pandemic, we wanted to expand an understanding of racial violence beyond the individual desire for recognition and redress and toward bringing people into collective struggle. We connected these firsthand stories to analysis by different organizers in contemporary movements to highlight the need to decarcerate prisons and jails where COVID was spreading rampantly, for disability justice activism, and for labor and economic justice for domestic workers, caregivers, and sex workers. These different writings contributed to ways we can theorize Asian American feminism and care and also became one starting point for our collective to offer frameworks to understand anti-Asian violence beyond the predominant discourse of hate.

Following the zine and during the pandemic, we experienced a shift in the scale and pace of our work. Many of our previous events and projects have been local to New York City. However, the scale of the zine's circulation across Asian American digital publics, as well as moving most of our work online given social distancing as a public health necessity, meant that our work had a different reach and heightened visibility. The number of workshops and events we were participating in also increased threefold. We started working at an increased pace and volume while remaining in physical isolation from one another. We also started the longer-term project Black and Asian Feminist Solidarities with Jaimee Swift at Black Women Radicals and working closely with the Asian American Writers' Workshop, which gave us a different timeline and platform to think through bigger-picture questions we were grappling with surrounding questions of feminist solidarity.

While we work closely in collaboration and coalition with other people and groups in our projects, the current structure of AAFC is five people. We are not a "formalized" organization with a fixed governance or financial structure. On the one hand, not having a rigid structure gives us the nimbleness and flexibility to pursue a range of projects, continue to transform and grow, and move a set of politics without needing to appease institutions or answer to a fiscal sponsor. On the other, a lack of formalization can make it both difficult to sustain work and easy to replicate hierarchies if we're not intentional about *how* we do our work. We are currently seeking alternative ways to sustain ourselves without becoming a 501(c)(3), including prioritizing relationships as a primary resource. We continue to experiment with our internal infrastructure and negotiate ways to put ideals of feminist solidarity into practice. That work is hard. Additionally, because the broader scope of our work is community building and political education, we continue to reflect on how our projects can invite people into feminist movement building by encouraging different entry points and ways of engaging with Asian American feminism. I'm curious to know from everyone else, what do you see as forms of practice for feminist solidarities?

III—Practicing Feminist Solidarities

SENTI: We talk a lot about solidarity and what it means in practice. To me, solidarity depends on how we come together and is defined by how we understand and enact our responsibilities to, and relationships with, each other. To share our stories, to expand the notion of what it means to be Asian American or a feminist or an activist, to create media and art that celebrates our histories and illuminates the ways we're intertwined and not, is an invitation to grow together, and part of the healing and liberatory work of solidarity. To be in solidarity is to ask to be seen and realized by another. I'd love to think that the way we approach our work and art reflects this kind of powerful tenderness.

In the solidarity letter we wrote with Black Women Radicals we asked, "What are the radical possibilities of catalyzing cross-racial feminist solidarities, imaginations, and substantive realities? What revolutions must we create within ourselves to dismantle our prejudices, discrimination, and silences to create the world we want to see?"[8] I love this part of our solidarity letter because it reminds me that creating new worlds is a project of boundless imagination and creativity. We are encouraging ourselves and each other to dare to dream of a future in which borders and barriers are lifted, our people are celebrated, and we live in communities that radiate with love and opportunity. Queer artist Tourmaline calls this process of engaging with radical possibility "freedom dreaming." In a piece for *Vogue*, she wrote:

> The world that I dream of is filled with ease. I'm not satisfied with Black trans lives mattering; I want Black trans lives to be easy, to be pleasurable, and to be filled with lush opportunities. I want the abundance we've gifted the world—the art, the care, the knowledge, and the beauty—to be offered back to us tenfold.[9]

As activists, as feminists, as dreamers and movement builders, we are used to being told no. That we want too much too soon, that the world isn't ready, that it's not time yet for prison and police abolition, or health care for all, or gender self-determination. I love our work at AAFC because the invitation here is always to dream bigger, bolder; to be soft, to luxuriate in possibility, and to say yes. The way we choose to be with one another reminds me that the revolution is equal parts thousands of people marching in the street and our own quiet moments of self-love and acceptance. Our work together is a place to freedom dream, to create what we don't yet see, and to build on the dreams of all those who came before.

SALONEE: Senti reminds me of the really hopeful energy that thinking in terms of connection and building can imbue onto the sometimes devastating struggles that we're engaging in. The process of collaborating on making our Care in the Time of Coronavirus zine felt really communal, warm, and urgent despite unfolding during an extremely difficult time. What had begun as an exploratory call grew into something more complex at the same time that New York City weathered some of the darkest days I have ever lived through. As we tried to think about the different meanings of care work, taking care, and ways of caring during moments of crisis that were making themselves slowly visible, we had to work so quickly to include everything and reach out to a lot of people, while trying to hold and treat each other with the grace required by a world-altering pandemic. While the experience of a stay-at-home order really intensely reshaped my world, it was valuable to start thinking about the experience as something that many in the disabled community had been navigating and thinking about for a long, long time.

That zine was also meaningful to me as a space where we were explicitly framing what was happening around us as an instance of racialized state abandonment with precedent and ample historical context. It felt important to disrupt the narratives of a news ecosystem incentivized to discuss crises as exceptional moments or unprecedented phenomena. So, it was really an experience that both felt like it was about creating a specific piece of content and like it was about bringing together different people into conversation and into community. I'm curious about what makes some digital spaces feel like a community. What kinds of media make people feel like they are part of a movement?

IV—Feminist Community Building through Media

JULIE: Digital spaces can translate into community in real life as well. There were times I would meet activists, artists, and organizers that I'd interacted with on Twitter or Instagram, and when we met in person, we would continue conversations we'd already had. I find that connecting online is a tiny web that through repeated interaction or taking the next step to meet online, lays the foundation for calling on each other for help or to collaborate that wouldn't exist through just cold calling or emailing. This felt evident when Tiffany and I gathered Asian American feminists from our online and offline networks for an Asian American feminist photo shoot. Through an online friend, I met the photographer, Marion Aguas, and asked if they would be interested in photographing Asian American feminists. We spent an entire day shooting with Marion, and while this was without a plan for how we would utilize these photos, there was a powerful energy present as people came by throughout the day who believed that it was important to document as a group that identified as both Asian American and feminist. The photos and the people in it depicted the start of a burgeoning Asian American feminist community in New York City. While the photos eventually became published in the online publication *Broadly*, I feel that the friendships and connections I made that day spending time together laid the groundwork for further activities and organizing.

Creative writing was another way that I experienced how feminist ideas and conversations can be shared in a way that is much more accessible to a broader public, as a lot of feminist theory and discourse are in academic contexts. In addition, creative writing taps into the *feels* and our hearts as opposed to purely the headspace/thinking that organizing spaces may bring out in us. I was a part of Kundiman's inaugural Mentorship Lab fellowship, where I was mentored by T Kira Madden. That was transformative for me, and it unlocked a different form of expression of the feminist political ideas. Through that relationship and experience, AAFC partnered with Kundiman to produce the Asian American Feminist Writing Workshop in 2021. One of the aims of the writing workshop was to cultivate community with the twenty participants, culminating in a

Figure 7.4: Image of Asian American feminist community from photo shoot for *Broadly*. Photo by Marion Aguas.

zine. We tried to do that through small groups and through biweekly small-group meetings. I think this is where there are limitations to creating community purely through digital means, because I do wonder if having in-person, more spontaneous interactions with the cohort would have created more opportunities to build deeper relationships. In addition, 2021 was a truly difficult and devastating time for so many of us. The final zine created through the workshop is called "To Us & Ours," featuring the participants' work and lives permanently on our website.

SALONEE: More recently, we've done a few different events that were in direct response to anti-Asian violence amid the COVID-19 pandemic, including the mass shootings targeting Asian-owned spas in the Atlanta area on March 16, 2021, and they have made me reflect on the intimacy created by shared grief, even if it is a brief and fleeting intimacy. We have also worked to build spaces such as workshops and teach-ins to think through community safety and care outside of law enforcement responses as we were seeing the deaths of Asian women being instrumentalized to expand policing. For example, Tiffany and I led a workshop that put into practice a kind of "care-mapping" or "resource-mapping" in collaboration with some other groups in response to a spate of violent attacks on Asian elders across the country. Even though we were on Zoom, the digital space felt really raw, and emotions were running high for everyone; people were sharing vulnerable things about what they were experiencing and how they were feeling. I think there's often not a lot of room for vulnerability in digital space, and holding that kind of space is really challenging for organizers.

TIFFANY: I've been thinking about resource lists as a form of feminist media and care practice. Whether they're published on journalistic platforms, self-hosted blogs, or collaborative Google docs, the care work that goes into compiling and sharing resources for mutual aid, safety, or mental health is feminist praxis. There was a huge spike in this type of mutual aid/resource sharing during the pandemic. We included some of these resources in our Care in the Time of Coronavirus zine, and like many others we were sharing countless lists and community resources during this time. One of the pieces included in the zine was the article I wrote for Rewire News Group on how to help sex workers through COVID-19. Making lists in general has always soothed me, so when faced with so many crises, creating and passing on resource pages can sometimes temporarily take away that feeling of impotence against all the world's strife. I like to add resource and donation lists to the end of workshop and presentation slides. I have compiled a COVID-19 mutual aid resources page for our website and made a collaborative national "cop-free" resource list, specifically addressing violence against Asian American communities.

Collaborating with our community members—sometimes people familiar to us, other times Anonymous Otters on Google—also brings us back to the roots of our collective making. Not only was there that collaborative document for the manifesto but as we began having these conversations during the Asian American Feminism event series, we also began to document them with the hashtag #aafeminism, which serves as a social media archive of our early dialogue around building this movement.

SALONEE: I think that naming world-building and imagination as explicit parts of our work and then engaging in imagining a world without certain forms of carcerality really allowed me to commit to and understand the necessity of prison and police abolition. When we first began organizing together, I was relatively new to a conversation about what abolition might look like, whereas Rachel had been doing a lot of organizing around it in other formations. As we worked together, I felt able to ask questions and challenged myself to imagine alternatives to our current reality because we had built a relationship grounded in trust and mutual respect. That relationship was a container for those leaps of faith. Over time, our collective politics have similarly become unambiguous about naming abolition as one of our values. I'd like to think that the work we have done in facilitating spaces where people who are coming with different kinds of knowledge and awareness can have conversations, share stories, and make work/art together has helped move various conversations about feminism into a space that interrogates the structures of capitalism, imperialism, and carcerality more critically. I also hope that we have helped people feel welcomed into the project of building that new world.

Conclusion

Three years after our initial roundtable convening and event series, we have grown a lot and are continuing to learn different lessons. One clear takeaway has emerged: as a formation trying to push a larger conversation and movement, we may always be in the midst of transformation and transition. We will always be shifting and growing—in our political analysis, how we do our work, and how we are with each other and in relation to communities around us. These transformations are necessary moments as well as vulnerable ones, and this elasticity, adaptability, and fluidity is at once both exciting and also exhausting. In order to sustain, we are trying to move more slowly and build in less reactive ways. Part of this building means formalizing our financial structuring and governance models. Another part of this building means taking time to rest—increasingly, we have observed other collectives around us needing to take a break. This does not mean that we are passively inert, but that we are practicing collective care and resisting impulses to always respond with urgency.

This roundtable serves as a way to intentionally archive and document a particular moment of change. It is important to acknowledge that as we compile our gathered insights, we are not sure what the future holds. The Asian American Feminist Collective came together with the intention of creating intimate and open spaces for dialogue, togetherness, and mobilization for social change. Over several years, we have stretched ourselves and our organization in order to explore new ways of being together while physically apart. We have met new collaborators, learned a great deal about ourselves, and realized that we face a series of open questions about the scale at which this work functions best and how we can encourage others to create intimate feminist formations of their own. There is no ready-made model to do this work. What we are sure of is that doing this work requires a willingness to be vulnerable and show up for one another, as friends first. From that place, we continue to imagine the transformational possibilities of what an Asian American feminist movement can collectively accomplish—of where we might go together.

Notes

1. Asian American Feminist Collective (2018), "Building an Asian American Feminist Movement."
2. Tiffany Tso (2018), Why Do You Need It? A Roundtable on Asian American Feminism, *Feministing*, 19 April, http://feministing.com.
3. Catherine Squires (2002), "Rethinking the Black Public Sphere: An Alternative Vocabulary for Multiple Public Spheres," *Communication Theory* 12(4): 446–468.
4. Lisa Lowe (1998), "Work, Immigration, Gender: New Subjects of Cultural Politics," *Social Justice* 25(3) ; Lori Kido Lopez (2016), *Asian American Media Activism: Fighting for Cultural Citizenship,* NYU Press; Lori Kido Lopez and Vincent Pham (2017), "Introduction: Why Asian American Media Matters," in Lopez and Pham, eds., *Routledge Companion to Asian American Media*, Routledge, 1–8; Rachel Kuo, Amy Zhang, Vivian Shaw, and Cynthia Wang (2020), "#FeministAntibodies: Asian American Media in the Time of Coronavirus," *Social Media + Society*.
5. Jennifer Nash (2010), On Difficulty: Intersectionality as Feminist Labor," *Scholar and Feminist Online*, http://sfonline.barnard.edu.
6. Minju Bae and Vivian Truong (2025), "A Movement to Stay," in Diane Wong and Mark Tseng-Putterman, eds., *Asian America Rising*, NYU Press.
7. Asian American Feminist Collective (2020), *Care in the Time of Coronavirus*.
8. Black Women Radicals and Asian American Feminist Collective (2020), "Black and Asian Feminist Solidarity Letter," Asian American Writers' Workshop, 30 July, https://aaww.org.
9. Tourmaline (2020), "Filmmaker and Activist Tourmaline on How to Freedom Dream," *Vogue*, July 2, www.vogue.com.

8

The Party Is Not Just a Party

Reflections on Basement Bhangra

REKHA MALHOTRA

Just a few feet from the stairs to the uptown No. 1 subway, at the southeast corner of New York City's Houston and Varick Streets, are two sets of darkened windows and a door. The view outside gives no indication that you will walk into what feels like a cavernous yet intimate space: Sounds of Brazil (aka SOB's), a former print factory attached to a narrow coffee shop that was converted into a live music venue and restaurant. On the first Thursday of every month for ten years, the space transformed into Basement Bhangra, an energy-packed room filled with the New York City and global Desi diaspora and their friends dancing to Punjabi, dancehall, and hip-hop beats, walls saturated with projections of bhangra videos, urban landscapes, and political incitements. A bhangra dance lesson and free frozen mojitos before 8 p.m. started the party that kept going as long as was legally permitted. Outside, the line running down the block signaled the space inside: bouncers and BIPOC millennials with clipboards would turn away eager clubbers hoping to skip the line.

Four years after its inception and nine days after September 11, 2001, the space that held Basement Bhangra at Houston and Varick—located just a mile and a half from ground zero—was blocked off, and armed military personnel were perched across the street. New York City streets were quiet at night, with the gravity of what had happened still settling in. Two niche groups—the CMJ music festival and New York Fashion Week—were supposed to be guaranteed money makers for that second week in September. But nightlife was a ghost. Local bars were crowded, but clubs, lounges, and live music venues were empty. SOB's was slated to hold a Basement Bhangra bonus night on September 20. But how do you party when it feels like the world is falling apart?

The club owner's wife was against holding the event, fearing a racist backlash like those that targeted other Muslim and South Asian community spaces in the wake of the attack. Turbaned Sikh men had long been a noticeable segment of Basement Bhangra's core audience. Unlike most local clubs, SOB's door policies did not enforce gender parity or strict dress codes and welcomed anyone with a willingness to get down—and a passable ID if needed. Her concern was irritating and surprising to me, but she rightly recognized the sentiment held by many: that the attack was perpetrated by Muslim terrorists, and that Sikhs were visually identifiable as "Muslim." Even the beloved, culturally savvy, and politically astute Brian Lehrer, a morning talk show host on New York's NPR station, mistakenly thought Sikhism was a sect of Islam. The first direct case of violence in response happened four days after 9/11 when Balbir Sodhi was gunned down in Arizona. Several other incidents would happen in the months to come.

But the question remained: do we open? Do we advertise and promote an event that relies on good spirits and a room full of people who want to dance? The answer is, you always open, because the party is not just a party. Basement Bhangra was a community space, and even though we had little or no expectation of what the night would hold, we felt like we needed to open. On that night, a total of twenty-eight people showed up. I am not sure what we charged at the door. I am sure we closed early, and the night was a financial loss. But the following month, the place was full—not as full as usual, but respectable. The backlash by then had grown, but there was a feeling of safety on the dance floor.

A Desi DJ Origin Story

The first time I remember seeing a DJ was when I was watching the 1984 Grammy Awards on TV and saw Herbie Hancock perform a live version of his track "Rock It." A *New York Times* write-up of the performance, published the next day, stated that it "featured synth drums, a stacked keyboard rig and a D.J. behind a set of Technics 1200s—Grand Mixer D. ST—whose scratching made him the track's breakout hero." The performance was all that we seventh graders could talk about at school the next day. I was moved by that performance, and soon I became immersed in hip-hop music. But I did not yet envision the possibility of being "behind the decks"—of being a DJ myself.

I grew up in Westbury, Long Island, a suburb twenty-five miles from Manhattan, where my father ran numerous small businesses. There I was exposed to the rich culture of second-generation Caribbean Americans. This "Village," as it was designated, was racially and economically diverse, but the school system was segregated. White families primarily sent their children to private schools, and the public school system was largely attended by Black students. After one year of private school, due to economic hardship I entered public school as a sixth grader. During this time, I also witnessed the birth of hip-hop, because we were in close proximity to the Queens hip-hop scene. At school, hip-hop was the dominant topic of conversation; the music as well as its five elements of graffiti, breakdancing, DJing, MCing, and knowledge. Many of my classmates were actively engaged in breakdancing, graffiti, and composing rap lyrics.

In 1986, when I was fifteen, my mother traveled to England to attend the wedding engagement celebration of a family friend my parents were close with when they lived there. She brought me back a cassette tape of Birmingham-based Punjabi singer Malkit Singh's album *Upfront*, as it was very popular at the event. The music was revelatory. It was a departure from the South Asian popular music of Hindi language films—the term "Bollywood" was not yet in parlance—with which I was familiar. The vocals were in Punjabi, my parents' mother tongue, but in a different dialect. The rhythms were electrifying. Singh's voice was distinct and melodic. It moved me in a way that the Hindi film music soundtracks we would listen to didn't. The music was also less cluttered, and you could hear what I later learned was the tumbi, a single-stringed instrument, and the dhol, a two-sided worn drum played with sticks, accompanied by other percussion instruments.

A few years later, two of my male cousins, Nitin and Deepak, moved from India to the States with the intention of settling here. They were four and six years younger, and our age difference felt significant at the time. But since I was attending Queens College on the same plot of land as their high school, our proximity to each other fostered a relationship. Our growing bond over music deepened our connection. Through their South Asian classmates, they were getting remixes of Punjabi songs layered and mixed with hip-hop, dancehall, and electronic beats. The vocals of Malkit Singh, the artist I fell in love with a few years earlier, were now embedded in an eleven-plus-minute track, "Golden Star U.K. Ragga Muffin Mix" (1991), by U.K.-based Punjabi producer Bally Sagoo. Sonically, this medley embodied the Caribbean sounds of dancehall that I was exposed to in Westbury but incorporated a DJ aesthetic of blending in the various songs from Malkit Singh's band Golden Star. The style of music is referred to as Bhangra, a musical style that emerged in the Punjabi countryside that was brought to Great Britain by migrants, so it became known as UK Bhangra.

During this time in the early 1990s, my cousins and I saw the emergence of DJs in the Indian community at cultural events and social gatherings. We felt our combined musical knowledge of Indian and American music and my unused credit card would be enough for us to form our own DJ crew. On June 26, 1992, Sangam Sounds was formed, and we worked our first gig as the DJ crew for a little boy named Ankush's first birthday party at Bombay Harbor restaurant in New Hyde Park, New York. Our set-up consisted of two consumer CD players, including one that I pulled out of my parent's hi-fi rack system, a Radio Shack Public Address System mixer, a tape deck, a receiver (also from the parents' hi-fi rack system), and a set of low-quality carpeted DJ speakers. We had only fifteen CDs, which caused us to repeat several key tracks—a DJ no-no. Our inexperience with the technology did not account for the receiver, which was powering the speakers, overheating. This necessitated borrowing a fan from a college classmate who lived close by. We made $51 that night.

From there, the gigs became more lucrative. We slowly amassed music in the form of several crates of physical vinyl records and CDs. Within a couple of years, we also had two turntables, a professional mixer, a commercial-grade amplifier, and DJ speakers. Meanwhile, due to family circumstances, Nitin returned to India. A few months later, Deepak followed. In retrospect, my role in the crew was gendered. Being older, owning a car, and having a credit card established me as the informal head of operations. Nitin took on the actual act of DJing. Then, when he left, Deepak took on this role. In fact, when Nitin left, Deepak had very little experience on the decks, but we worked out a system where I would select the music and he would be the one to play it. Upon

Deepak's departure, I was left with several thousand pieces of music and a slew of bookings. But I still had not actually DJed.

Through my networks, I was introduced to Joy Bhattacharya, another college student, who DJed at his school's radio station. He agreed to help me on my next booked gig on August 4, 1995, a fortieth birthday party for one of my parents' friends, seventy miles from my home in Westbury. Joy was also living at home a few miles away from me. That summer Friday, I picked him up after his car died, and we made our way through rush-hour traffic. After many of the guests arrived, we set up on a multi-shelf computer table, putting the different pieces of gear on various shelves. I had given Deepak many of the CDs we accumulated as a parting gift, so I had to resort to using cassette tapes for some of the tracks at the party. Over the next year, I improved my rudimentary DJ skills by spending hours in Joy's parents' basement, where the gear was set up on a ping-pong table. He was adept in spinning and patiently imparted his technical knowledge. We bonded over our love of hip-hop, and I caught him up on the Bhangra tracks in my repertoire.

Socially and creatively, we became immersed in the burgeoning South Asian party scene in New York City. Competing crews would rent out different venues, usually on holiday weekends when the mainstay club crowds were out of town and the clubs had an extra day to fill. This was one of the only ways that South Asians could get access to mainstream venues. We were often hired to DJ these events, pejoratively called Indian or Desi Parties. The competition extended to securing choice spaces on coveted weekends. Meanwhile, the aim for many party promoters, then as now, was to get a moneyed professional crowd in the door. As Joy and I were gaining a reputation for playing good music, our bookings increased—but so did the directives on what to play. We were frequently told not to play too much hip-hop or Bhangra, the styles of music that had brought me to DJing in the first place. One year later, on August 4, 1996, Joy and I performed in front of five thousand people at Central Park's SummerStage to support Qawwali singer Abidha Parveen and Pakistani rock band Junoon.

A few months later in that year, Joy and I were asked by Ethnic Folk Arts, an organization dedicated to immigrant arts, to participate in a program celebrating the range of Indian dance styles. We were there to represent the Desi party scene and its embrace of South Asian dance music and club culture. Also on the bill was the Toronto-based band Punjabi by Nature. Ethnic Folk Arts tried to get the band a second gig since they were driving fourteen hours to perform in New York City. They reached out to SOB's, which was known at the time to program Brazilian music and the invented and now-dated-sounding genre of World Music. The bookers at SOB's did not have any openings at the time but offered the band a gig the next February, the slowest and coldest month of the year. When the time came, Joy and I were hired to help promote the night. We were paid in part by the number of people who brought discount flyers to the door with our hand-marked initials. That cold February night, the venue was packed, and the booker at SOB's asked us to come up with a concept for a monthly night. Since this was a music venue and not an off-season nightclub, SOB's managers were interested in the style of our music, which fit SOB's brand as a place for global sounds. SOB's was also one of the few clubs that embraced hip-hop at that time, as hip-hop was still seen as niche music for a Black audience and was not yet part of mainstream radio play.

Joy and I had been feeling increasingly frustrated by the creative directives we got from Indian party promoters. We were told not to play Black music because they believed it would attract a more unruly crowd. We were told not to play Bhangra music because it was associated with cab drivers and seen to draw a working-class or nonprofessional Punjabi crowd. So, when SOB's asked us to come up with a concept for a monthly event, I wanted to defy the constraints of DJing for other party promoters and envisioned a night dedicated to showcasing the two genres that we loved: hip-hop and Bhangra. The idea that certain kinds of music would draw "undesirable" people was not a concern for SOB's, which saw commercial potential in serving a new audience that liked to party and, more importantly, drink, fortifying the revenues of a given night. The club's managers had experience with weekly events marketing to the Haitian American community and did a lot of programming that focused on New York's many underserved immigrant and diaspora communities. Basement Bhangra was conceived as a night where we would spin Bhangra music with a hip-hop sensibility. SOB's also freed us from dress codes, gender parity, and other gatekeeping requirements used by many venues and promoters to filter the patrons by class, encouraging a heteronormative, "upscale" professional crowd, effectively de-queering club spaces and tending toward a banal monoculture more interested in dating prospects than dance-floor connection.

The first official Basement Bhangra night was launched with Bally Sagoo as the headliner. As luck would have it, Bally Sagoo, whose productions had sparked my cousins and me to form a DJ crew several years earlier, had signed a worldwide record deal with Columbia Records, a division of Sony Music. The label was looking for places to promote his two albums, *Rising from the East* and *Bollywood Flashback*. Our about-to-be launched club night was a perfect fit for Sagoo to get in front of a South Asian club audience in New York. The crowd that night consisted of Joy's and my social circles, record label professionals, and New Yorkers who looked to SOB's as a place to discover and listen to non-mainstream music. Also present were people from activist circles, many of whom were writers, artists, organizers, teachers, and people in queer circles, some coming to the party in drag. The next first Thursday, and for the next twenty years, this monthly happening was the root of my artistic career. Joy gave up DJing in 2000, but, for me, it became a viable and fulfilling way to realize my artistic self, build community, and grow into curating other artists.

The creative freedom to play whatever I wanted also supported my commitment to create an inclusive space. At the time the Basement started, I was active in several South Asian community organizations. Galvanized by a wave of violence by a group that called themselves the "Dotbusters" as they targeted Indian immigrants in the Jersey City area in the late 1980s, second-generation South Asian law students in New York City formed an organization called Yaar. I found out about Yaar when they organized an action to support Dr. Kaushal Saran, a victim of a hate crime whose attackers were on trial and were later acquitted. As a means to raise funds to continue the work for civil rights education, I suggested that we start hosting a monthly event. From an ad in the local arts paper, the *Village Voice*, I found a club space that could be rented out for $500. This monthly night brought together different intersections of academics, members of the LGBTQ community, and social justice activists. This moment in New York also witnessed the formation and rise of other South Asian community organizations, including the New York Taxi Workers Alliance and Sakhi for South Asian Women.

Coming from an activist mindset and experience, I created the night not just as a place to dance but to foster an inclusive and liberatory space that had an accessible entry fee, no dress code, and could be a forum for established U.K. and emerging U.S. artists. Many of the artists we booked for bonus nights were from the United Kingdom, as North America did not have a strong pool of Bhangra musicians given the size and age of the community. These bookings were challenging in that the acts would want the same fees they were accustomed to getting at large weddings, which was their primary source of income. In addition, we had to navigate the bureaucratic world of artist work visas, which was both time consuming and expensive. The bands and talent that did see the appeal at playing in New York were the ones we established long relationships with and kept booking through the years. Over time, we also were able to give a platform to emerging New York City–based artists.

The voluminous press attention Basement Bhangra generated during its tenure contributed to greater visibility for South Asians as part of American society and culture. Its success was a springboard for many great creative opportunities in sound design and remixing. It also provided a secure foundation to launch other club nights like Mutiny, Bollywood Disco, and Lipstick Optional. Basement Bhangra taught me how to create and hold space, to reimagine how community could look, feel, and sound. The act of presenting the night encompassed curating the performers, the design and production of physical and digital flyers used for branding and information, projection of visuals that were mixed live during the event, and the use of various DJ methods to disseminate sound to a room of dancing bodies.

"Everyone Loves a Funeral"

The year is 2017—twenty years since the first time an event called Basement Bhangra took place. Bouncers and South Asian millennials with clipboards wave away entitled club goers hoping to avoid the wait. Once again, the line of attendees continues down the block, and even the stanchion ropes cannot contain the eager crowd. There is nowhere in the world, including India, Mumbi, or London, where so much South Asian art takes place on any one given night. In New York City, there is something about the city that breeds this kind of art. And that's why in so many ways Basement Bhangra could only happen here. Basement Bhangra was now coming to a close. But it was a good place to stop, to know that that's out there.

It had been a while since SOB's was this packed for Basement, as it is affectionately called. But as the owner likes to say, "Rakker, everyone loves a funeral."

9

Sounding the Alarm and Reclaiming an Asian American Politics for Racial Equity

SALLY CHEN, DOUGLAS H. LEE, OIYAN A. POON, AND JANELLE WONG

Deafening chants echoed out over handmade protest signs bearing equally bold proclamations: "Yellow Peril Supports Black Power," "Diverse Campuses = Better Campuses," and, most telling of all, "We will not be silenced—we will tell our stories." In the fall of 2018, the battle for affirmative action on Harvard University's campus was a kaleidoscope of moments like these. Coauthor Sally Chen was a student organizer for affirmative action who ultimately took the witness stand in the federal lawsuit *Students for Fair Admissions (SFFA) v. Harvard*. Both through on-campus organizing and participation in the legal process, students spoke to the salience of race in their lives and voiced the importance of race-conscious policies, campus diversity, and solidarity between communities of color.

Although the student testimonies presented at trial in *SFFA v. Harvard* are now part of the court record, narrative agency remains an imperative. Across campuses, student activists continue to draw lessons from the events that occurred through various forms of storytelling, such as art, interviews, editorials, reflections, and documentaries. During the lawsuit, Sally wrote a creative reflection, part of which is offered here (see figure 9.1) to situate her testimony in the context of the fight for affirmative action to draw attention to how testimony has been and continues to be a powerful tool in the genealogy of Asian American movements.

Asian American activist and filmmaker Renee Tajima-Peña emailed Sally's evocative words of encouragement before her oral testimony: "Knock 'em dead tomorrow. Remember Yick Wo, Wong Kim Ark, Mamie Tape, Fred Korematsu [sic] and all our ancestors who spoke truth to power in the courtroom."[1] Tajima-Peña linked Sally's efforts to

Figures 9.1a–b: Illustration series from Sally Chen's original document.

a lineage of Asian American civil rights struggles, illustrating a proud history of progressive activism, litigiousness, and resilience. While this paints a powerful story in its own right, Sally's own experience with testimony led her to explore a less triumphant narrative frame. In her depiction of each case, including her own, she highlighted aspects of

Figures 9.1a–b (cont.)

personal sacrifice, self-interest, complacence, and even complicity with dominant systems of power.

Opening this chapter with Sally's reflections on student protests during her time as an undergraduate student at Harvard reminds us that stories like these are critical. They are vehicles through which we make sense of the world. People come to understand political issues and their significance through storytelling.

To understand Asian American politics in the context of racial justice, and through how we tell our stories, we must also grapple with the role that Asian Americans play in conservative and racially regressive activism. Equally litigious in their methods, historic cases like *Ozawa v. United States* (1922) and *United States v. Bhagat Singh Thind* (1923), in which Asian immigrants laid claim to whiteness to prove their eligibility for citizenship, demonstrate the capacity for Asian Americans to align with white supremacy.[2] The historical similarities to present-day conservative Asian American activism and testimony against affirmative action in *SFFA v. Harvard* are impossible to ignore. Throughout this chapter, we unpack mobilizations of narratives in Asian American activism across the political spectrum.

Since 2014, some Chinese American immigrant activists have created and sustained an antiracial equity policy movement, starting with the 2014 defeat of SCA-5—a state ballot measure that would have reinstated race-conscious policies for admissions in educational institutions in California. These activists arguably represent one of the most visible cases of Asian American political activism.[3] Although evidence suggests that Chinese American activists who oppose racial equity policies are a small minority of the Asian American population, they represent a dangerous and growing phenomenon in the United States that threatens cross-racial coalition work for civil rights progress.[4] As Chinese American interdisciplinary scholars and activists, we offer insights into the emergence and evolution of the Chinese-led racially regressive political activist movement, which started with the debate over race-conscious admissions and has grown to other areas of policy, such as opposition to disaggregated ethnic data collection by state agencies and the U.S. Census, gender-inclusive restrooms, and decriminalization of marijuana. In sounding the alarm on this movement, we present possible strategies to reclaim Asian American politics for racial equity.

Research has long recognized an Asian American affirmative action divide, but impassioned mobilization against race-conscious admissions is not simply about who gets into highly selective educational institutions like Harvard.[5] The active mobilization of Chinese Americans against racial equity policies in K-12 and higher education highlights a potential shift in contemporary U.S. racial politics. While past research recognizes co-optation and tokenism of non-white opposition to race-conscious equity policies (e.g., Ward Connerly and Proposition 209, the Japanese American Citizens League, and the League of United Latin American Citizens at certain periods), contemporary Asian American opposition to affirmative action and other equity policies is fundamentally distinct from any non-white conservatism in the past.[6] Today's Asian American conservative activism is larger, more grassroots in nature, and more effective than previous instances of non-white conservatism. Although most Asian Americans support affirmative action, there are significant numbers of Asian Americans willing to assert a false equivalency between race-conscious admissions and anti-Asian racism, allying Asian American and white opponents of these policies to circumvent charges of racism typically levied at them.[7] This emerging mobilization engenders new forms of both racial power and resistance. It also brings into focus ideological diversity, which tends to align with generational differences, underscoring the importance of producing analyses of Asian American community politics that brings multiple dimensions of diversity among Asian Americans into focus. This diversity calls for new theories and analyses to inform the Asian American agenda for racial justice.

In the following sections, we briefly summarize the state of legal precedent and debate over race-conscious admissions. We then present a theoretical model to highlight how divergent racial ideologies and frameworks lead to clashing theories of change between Asian Americans. Next, we analyze anti–affirmative action Asian American organizations that submitted amicus briefs in the federal lawsuit *SFFA v. Harvard* and show their connections to Chinese American population centers and communities, revealing their false claim of representing either Asian Americans or students writ large. Finally, we highlight Harvard student and alumni efforts to build cross-racial solidarity between Asian Americans and other communities of color to defend affirmative action in *SFFA v. Harvard*. Through testimonies and organizing, this coalition reclaimed both the legal record and public narrative for racial justice in education. Inspired by these testimonies that demonstrate the importance of narrative in culture-shifting work, we end with strategies to reinvigorate racially progressive Asian American activism for racial justice.

Affirmative Action Debates as a Site of Asian American Ideological Conflicts

Affirmative action began in the 1960s as a voluntary policy to open college access to populations that had long been barred or limited from participating in U.S. higher education.[8] Prior to the 1978 Supreme Court ruling in *Regents of the University of California v. Bakke*, some postsecondary institutions administered quota programs, reserving a minimum number of admissions offers for students of color, acknowledging the need to redress the legacies of systemic racism. In the *Bakke* case, the UC Davis Medical School had reserved a minimum of sixteen admission offers to applicants of color, including four for Asian Americans. The Supreme Court declared such racial quota programs unconstitutional. In the same ruling, Justice Lewis Powell replaced the remedial rationale (i.e., to redress past discrimination) with the diversity rationale (i.e., everyone benefits from a diverse learning environment) as primary legal justification for including the consideration of race in admissions.[9] Since 1978, the Supreme Court has reaffirmed the diversity rationale precedent twice—in the 2003 case *Grutter v. Bollinger* and the 2016 *Fisher v. UT Austin*. Additionally, each ruling has further restricted how race can be considered in admissions. In *Gratz v. Bollinger* (2003), the Court declared point systems (i.e., automatic points for applicants based on racial/ethnic demographics) unconstitutional. Additionally, the Court has ruled that race can be one among many factors considered in the evaluation and selection of students (*Grutter v. Bollinger*, 2003) through holistic review when there is campus-based evidence showing the need for increasing racial diversity, so long as no "race neutral" practices are found effective. Race can never be the primary or only factor in admissions, and it can only be considered if other "race neutral" practices, such as those based on class, prove to be ineffective at advancing racial diversity.[10]

Since 1978, Asian American civil rights groups have actively submitted amicus briefs (i.e., friend-of-the-court briefs) to offer their perspectives on questions presented in each case.[11] In 1978, the Asian American Bar Association of the Greater Bay Area submitted the lone brief on behalf of Asian Americans in the *Bakke* case—in support of affirmative action. Starting with the *Grutter* and *Gratz* cases, submitted briefs from Asian Americans were split: two supported the policy, and one opposed. This split in submitted briefs on behalf of Asian Americans has continued to grow, with briefs submitted by Asian Americans for both sides in the *Fisher* cases.[12]

Although research shows that the majority of Asian Americans support affirmative action, there remains an impassioned divide between Asian Americans along racial ideology and framing.[13] These divisions can be understood through a critical analysis that recognizes racial capitalism—the ideological and systemic intersections of racism and capitalism—as central to shaping divergent positions on race-conscious policies among Asian Americans.[14] The most significant marker between Asian American affirmative action supporters and opponents is whether they frame, or understand, racism as a systemic problem.[15] Policy supporters understand racism as a system that maintains white dominance, requiring race-conscious policies, that is, solutions that problematize and seek to dismantle racial hierarchies. Policy opponents view racism as a problem of individual attitudes and interpersonal dynamics. They may also view race-conscious policies as the same as racist policies. Guided by an antiracist systemic analysis, policy supporters advocate for a theory of change that calls on social institutions (e.g., higher education) to disrupt systemic racism. They are ideologically grounded in notions of "linked fates" and solidarity with other communities of color that have been targeted by systems of white dominance.[16] In contrast, policy opponents reject the call for institutions to consider how their practices and routines can reproduce intersectional racial disparities, because it goes against their ideologies of individualism. This individualism ideologically positions them to reject notions of linked fates between Asian Americans and other communities of color. Their theory of change places the problem with individuals. Informed by this perspective, opponents can view policies and practices with racial equity in mind, such as affirmative action and race-conscious admissions, to be racist in themselves.

A large segment of Asian American opponents to affirmative action are Chinese American, many of whom may possess a limited understanding of, or refusal to acknowledge, the systemic nature of the reproduction of social inequalities—including those suffered by Asian Americans.[17] Their framing of racism as an individual problem motivates their political activism to oppose structural solutions. An active segment of the Chinese American population has been catalyzed into racialized political engagement through debates over race-conscious admissions. Moreover, they falsely claim to represent the Asian American majority.

Who and What Do Anti–Affirmative Action "Asian American" Groups Represent?

Public narratives and strategic storytelling have been crucial in the legal battle over race-conscious admissions, in large part because much of the fight was waged in the court of public opinion. In this lawsuit, Students for Fair Admissions (SFFA) and Ed Blum, who is white, situated Asian Americans as a racial wedge against other communities of color.[18] They argued that race-conscious admissions harm Asian Americans applicants and that Asian Americans oppose the policy. Despite research and polling that proves otherwise, this public narrative has consistently captured mainstream media attention, sparking rampant misinformation about college admissions.[19] SFFA's targeting of Harvard, whose name bears cultural significance, created a media spectacle instigating a barrage of media attention that centered on Blum and SFFA's claims.

In July 2018 the Asian American Coalition for Education (AACE) and Asian American Legal Foundation (AALF) filed an amicus brief against race-conscious admissions in the *SFFA v. Harvard* federal lawsuit.[20] According to the brief, signatories included 156 affiliated Asian American organizations, which are each listed as opponents of affirmative action and race-conscious admissions. The brief's authors claimed to represent "Asian American community leaders, business leaders, and most importantly, parents." AACE suggested that they and the 156 organizational signatories were more legitimate in representing Asian American interests than "professional 'civil rights advocates.'" Further, they claimed that they were "forced to become civil rights advocates to stop and prevent the discrimination against their children that the 'professionals' ignore, downplay and facilitate."

Troublingly, some mainstream news outlets also framed the AACE coalition as representative of Asian American interests. To examine this claim, we conducted an interpretive content analysis along various organizational dimensions. Throughout the analysis, we focused on organizational types, ethnicity, geography, and stated organizational mission and activities. Although the authors claimed to represent diverse groups within the Asian American community, the brief represents a much narrower segment of the population. We illustrate that this coalition of Chinese American organizations does not represent Asian Americans in terms of national origin or viewpoints.

Organization Type

Our analysis of AACE's signatories shows that few appeared to have expertise on education, Asian Americans, and policy. In table 9.1 we classified the organizations by type. In table 9.2 we delineated the numerous interests among the seventy classified associations. The largest organization consisted of twenty-nine culturally based organizations, twenty-seven of which were Chinese-identity-related. Another segment of signatures represented private businesses that were owned or operated by Chinese and Chinese Americans. Only fourteen of the 156 organizations articulated a direct connection to educational interests or activities in their organizing documents. They included Chinese-language schools (e.g., Huaxia Chinese School of Greater New York) and

Table 9.1: Organizational Types (n = 156)

Type	Count (#)	Type	Count (#)
Association*	70	Civic Engagement	9
Private Businesses	20	Media	4
Education	14	Religious / Community Center / Athletic	9
Political	14	Unknown	16

Table 9.2: Association Interests (n = 70)

Association Interests	Count (#)	Association Interests	Count (#)
Cultural	29	Community Service	2
Alumni	8	Foreign Relations	2
Workers/Professional	8	Housing	2
China	5	Women	2
Business	4	Education	1
Parents	3	LGBT	1
Civil Rights	2	Medical	1

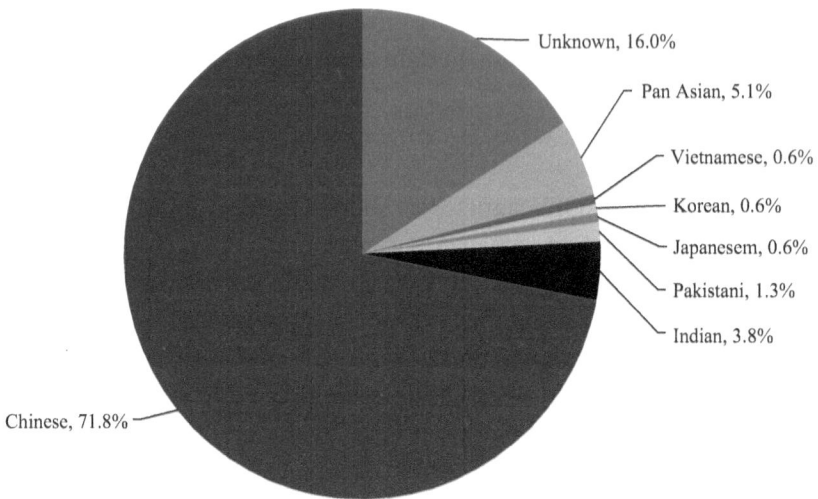

Figure 9.2: Predominant ethnic/national origin of organizations (n = 156).

parent organizations (e.g., Emerald Parents Association). Many of the parent associations' websites refer to advocacy for educational programs for children and selective high school admissions processes.

There were twelve political organizations, which mostly represented Republican or conservative interests. Several of the partisan organizations had links to Chinese or Chinese American identity (e.g., Chinese American Alliance for Trump) or took on a pan-ethnic identity but were led by Chinese Americans (e.g., Asian American GOP Coalition).

Ethnic/National-Origin Breakdown

We also found that the AACE and AALF amicus briefs do not represent the ethnic diversity among Asian Americans. Figure 9.2 illustrates the ethnic identities of the organizational signatories. Although less than 25 percent of Asian Americans are Chinese, we identified over 70 percent of the organizations as primarily Chinese American. Several organizations claimed to be pan-Asian in orientation, but after examining the board members and the leadership contact information, surname analysis determined that these groups' leaders were predominantly Chinese. For example, the leadership and members of organizations such as Asian

American Voters and Asian American GOP Coalition were primarily Chinese American. Many of these organizations also offered a Chinese-language portion of their website, and some of these "Asian American" organizations' websites were only in Chinese.

Promoting Chinese America

We also examined the mission statements and histories of the Chinese American organizations that signed the AACE legal brief for insights into their ideologies. Across organizational mission statements, the three most common themes we found were promoting and preserving culture, fighting for racial equality, and ensuring some form of transparency and consistency in different political processes. These articulations demonstrated collective interests in fighting for a Chinese American place in society, as well as protecting and expanding their access to socioeconomic resources, particularly education. Their publicized activities varied from cultural activities (e.g., lion dances, Lunar New Year festivities, and Chinese-language exchange), but also included voter registration drives, which were consistent with the first and third themes. Many of these organizations articulated the importance of protecting, promoting, and improving the voice of Chinese American or Asian American voices to fight for racial equality.

Unlike traditional advocacy for racial justice, the positions these groups adopted demonstrated conflict between the interests of Chinese Americans and of other communities of color. Several organizational websites discussed their histories of opposing affirmative action by fighting SCA 5 and supporting Proposition 209 in California.[21] They also argued for class-conscious policies over race-conscious ones. Further, they demonstrated their interests in protecting and promoting Chinese American status through their support for Peter Liang, decrying what they felt was the injustice of holding the NYPD officer accountable for the killing of Akai Gurley, an unarmed Black man in Brooklyn. According to these organizations, these cases and issues galvanized their engagement and exemplified the need for their groups' existence and activities to protect Chinese Americans. This language makes it clear that these Chinese American groups felt a need to safeguard their place in society, and do not represent a cross-section of Asian Americans.[22]

Next, we take a closer look at the organizing efforts led by students to defend diversity in *SFFA v. Harvard*, and how these efforts align with a long tradition of storytelling and counternarratives in movement building.[23]

Reclaiming the Narrative on Asian American Inter-ethnic and Cross-Racial Solidarity

Neither AACE, the SFFA, nor Harvard truly represented the voice and interests of Asian American students and other students of color. In fact, SFFA did not bring forward a single prospective or current student to make their case.[24] Though claiming to represent student interests, SFFA relied on highly suspect statistical analysis and nonstudent witnesses to argue against race-conscious admissions. Harvard's administrators and lawyers also claimed to represent student interests in defense of their race-conscious policies but did not make an effort to include student perspectives and voices. In fact, Harvard's legal team stood *with* SFFA in opposing the participation of Harvard students as direct intervenors representing their own interests.[25] Amplifying stories from directly impacted students was an effective progressive intervention to refute the co-optation of student voice and to re-center the issues most critical to current students. Through both testimony and direct action, this narrative-shifting work gave evidence to the importance of race-conscious admissions policies and strengthened cross-racial solidarity.

Diverse student and alumni voices in support of race-conscious admissions provided a progressive counternarrative on the legal record during the federal District Court trial proceedings. Through pro bono legal advocacy from the Lawyers' Committee for Civil Rights Under Law, Arnold & Porter, Asian Americans Advancing Justice, and the NAACP Legal Defense Fund, students and alumni from Harvard were able to join the lawsuit under "amicus plus status," which granted the ability to submit declarations, speak at hearings, and provide direct testimony.[26] The only student testimony recorded during the trial came from supporters of diversity and race-conscious admissions. The individuals who testified represented both Asian American ethnic diversity (Chinese American and Vietnamese American) as well as broader racial diversity (indigenous Mexican American or Chicana, African American and Mexican American, and Black).

Their testimonies gave direct evidence to the crucial role of race and racial diversity to student experience, and thus the importance of race-conscious programs. Multiple individuals testified to how their applications and admission to Harvard would not have been possible without affirmative action. Sarah Cole, former president of the Harvard Black Students Association, powerfully stated in her testimony: "Race-blind admissions is an act of erasure. To try to not see my race is to try to not see me, simply because there is no part of my experience, no part of my journey, no part of my life that has been untouched by my race."[27] Racial identity is core to student experiences, and to deny this aspect of a student's life is unthinkable. Vietnamese American student Thang Diep, who grappled with experiences of marginalization as a Southeast Asian student, was no stranger to this erasure. Diep described the exhaustion of distancing himself from his immigrant upbringing and how choosing to write about his identity became an act of reclamation: "I was also just tired of erasing my identity for so long and feeling like my identity has been erased. And so I took like the power back and wrote about that on my college essay." Race-blind and "race-neutral" admissions can devalue students' experiences and identities, whereas race-conscious policies are a tool to counter the disempowerment of students of color.

Student and alumni testimony also highlighted the necessity of race-conscious policies as foundational for positive and diverse learning environments for all students. In her testimony, African American student Madison Trice critiqued the isolation of being tokenized in the absence of diversity and the overwhelming pressure during what she described as "times where you felt like a representative for your entire race."[28] Students and alumni testimonies indicated that the presence of a critical mass of different student groups of color can allow for deeper engagement and understanding of issues beyond the interpersonal. For example, Catherine Ho, co-president of Harvard's Asian American Women's Association (AAWA), described events the group co-hosted on topics including anti-Black racism. In describing her motivation for leading AAWA's involvement in the lawsuit, she emphasized the importance of these dialogues: "Solidarity is so important.... There are differences in our lived experiences, but by recognizing those differences, we can be stronger together." Moving beyond multicultural celebration, ethnic affinity groups can build cross-racial solidarity around issues that impact students of color across the board.

In her testimony, Chicana alumna Itzel Vasquez-Rodriguez gave a direct example of how cross-racial student dialogues evolved into joint efforts to address systemic racism on campus through her work with the Harvard Ethnic Studies Coalition (HESC). HESC is a multiethnic student advocacy group fighting for the establishment of an ethnic studies department. Vasquez-Rodriguez described working in tandem with other students of color through the coalition: "We had so many different perspectives and world views and we were all coming together to fight for a common cause.... That's what made our work worthwhile and, in the end, very powerful."[29] HESC's mission centers on the diversity of experiences as well as the shared struggles between students of color, building an understanding of linked fate at the foundation of their work. Through joint organizing and coalition building, HESC has been successful in advocating for both an undergraduate ethnic studies track and faculty hires in Latinx studies, Asian American studies, and Native American studies.[30]

Through their testimony, students and alumni were also able to advocate for policies beyond admissions, advancing student activism at Harvard for racial justice more broadly. Though aligned with Harvard in defense of its baseline race-conscious admissions policy, students and alumni were adamant that race-conscious policies were the minimum response to institutional racism at Harvard.[31] All eight students and alumni witnesses not only provided their strong support for race-conscious admissions in defense of campus diversity, but also uplifted other issues that were important for addressing systemic racism that their own organizations were working to advance. In her oral testimony, Chinese American alumna and Coalition for a Diverse Harvard member Margaret Chin urged the university to "hire more admissions officers, learn about demographic differences within the Asian-American community ... [and] have implicit bias training."[32] Chin outlined the university's responsibility beyond the legal minimum of disallowing intentional nondiscrimination in admissions and offered recommended actions. Multiple student testimonies referenced the incident of campus police brutality against a Black student in 2017 and uplifted ongoing student demands for change. Embedded in each testimony were indictments of Harvard, calling attention to multiple areas in which institutional racism continued to fester on campus.

With six of eight student and alumni witnesses involved in ethnic studies advocacy at Harvard, the five-decade devaluation of ethnic studies without an undergraduate major or department also came to a head with the lawsuit. In her testimony, former co-coordinator of the Task Force for Asian American Progressive Advocacy and Studies (TAPAS) and coauthor of this chapter Sally Chen argued for the importance of ethnic studies "for all students . . . to have the language and the skills to really grapple with the critical issues, particularly around race and ethnicity that are so salient in communities beyond the gates of Harvard."[33] In a case so entwined with concepts of race and racism, many of the advocates articulated the stakes of affirmative action and situated their own stories within historic context because of their ethnic studies education. Student organizers carried the momentum and public attention of the lawsuit and published op-eds such as "We Testified, It's Time for Action," calling for the university to resource support for students of color, not merely use their stories as props for campus diversity.[34] The students rallied for the establishment of a community-centered ethnic studies department under the chant, "Out of the courthouse, into the classrooms!"[35] Ethnic studies advocates leveraged their testimonies outside of the courthouse onto the streets to call for institutional change.

Organizing with the Local Boston Community

Students and alumni in support of affirmative action seized the opportunity to tell their own stories via legal testimony and also organized locally to show multiracial solidarity with groups outside the university. At the start of the lawsuit, there was no existing organization on Harvard's campus focusing on affirmative action. As legal outreach to organize amicus briefs began, groups with strong community ties took initiative to facilitate discussion and sustained participation. These groups include TAPAS, the student-led public service organization the Phillips Brooks House Association, and the alumni organization Coalition for a Diverse Harvard.[36] Students, alumni, amicus brief legal staff, and representatives from community-based organizations began to meet regularly to co-host events and share resources in the face of mounting media attention.

In the weeks leading up to the trial, local activists who had previously organized around conservative opposition on data disaggregation learned that AACE was planning a rally in Boston's Copley Square to oppose race-conscious admissions and celebrate Ed Blum as a champion of "Asian American" civil rights. Recognizing the need for a narrative that was both representative of Asian America and relevant to the wider public, this coalition of students, alumni, and community advocates joined together to respond. In order to draw greater attention to the supporters of affirmative action, the group focused on organizing a week of action including a photo campaign, multiple speaker events with cosponsoring organizations, and a culminating counter rally dubbed the #DefendDiversity Week of Action and Solidarity Rally for Opportunity and Equality.

Rather than accept SFFA's false framing of race-conscious admissions as anti-Asian racism, the coalition of student, alumni, and community advocates purposefully sought a diverse representation in support of affirmative action, including Asian Americans across a range of ethnicities, age groups, and sectors. In direct opposition to SFFA's narrative, Chinese immigrant parents of both Harvard and Boston-area high school students flanked the #DefendDiversity rally, proudly carrying their custom banner emblazoned with the words, "Chinese Americans for Affirmative Action."[37] Local organizations such as the Asian American Resource Workshop and the Chinese Progressive Association lent crucial support, including outreach to grassroots networks, rally marshalling, and speaker engagement to represent Asian American students, residents, and workers in the Greater Boston Area. Finally, organizations represented in the Harvard student and alumni amicus brief supporting race-conscious admissions, including the Harvard Islamic Society, Harvard-Radcliffe Black Students Association, Native Americans at Harvard College, and Fuerza Latina of Harvard, turned out their members and alumni across undergraduate and graduate campuses as well as other local universities, including Wellesley and Amherst College, to join the rally and week of action.[38] With the support of Asian Americans Advancing Justice, the composition of rally

Figure 9.3: Chinese American parents of Harvard and Boston high school students attended a rally to stand for affirmative action in October 2018. Photo courtesy of Alexander Zhang.

speakers also reflected an ambitious range of cross-issue solidarity, with representation from the Boston Teachers Union, Temporary Protected Status Coalition, and UNITE HERE Local 26.[39]

In culmination of the rallies, organizing, court hearings, and testimonies, U.S. District Court Judge Allison Burroughs ruled in favor of Harvard in 2019. In 2020 a panel of federal judges in the First District Court of Appeals also ruled in favor of Harvard. At both federal court stages, the judges found no evidence that Harvard had violated the law, nor did they find intentional anti-Asian discrimination in the university's race-conscious admissions practices and approach to creating incoming classes. In June 2023 the Supreme Court overturned the lower courts' rulings and forty-five years of legal precedent in its 6–3 decision against race-conscious admissions for diversity in *SFFA v. Harvard/UNC*.

The multiethnic coalition of students and advocates that initially came together to defend diversity in response to the lawsuit have continued to build their alliances to further the movement for racial justice and educational equity across the country. While advocacy has led to

Figure 9.4: Insert photo: Students from the Harvard Black Student Association attending a pro-affirmative action rally in October 2018. Photo courtesy of Alexander Zhang.

commitments from Harvard's administrators to invest in an ethnic studies program, student and alumni advocates continue to fight as progress flags in the face of ongoing institutional racism in tenure decisions, curriculum building, and faculty hiring.[40] Allied coalitions continue fighting ongoing battles at selective public high schools in Boston, particularly in the context of COVID-19, to remove structurally inequitable barriers for applicants to these high schools.[41] Coalition members have also worked in both the state of Washington and California to champion efforts to repeal state affirmative action bans across public education, employment, and contracting.[42] Numerous advocates and organizations in this multiethnic, multiracial, intergenerational coalition continue to advance ambitious campaigns, taking the movement beyond in defense of diversity to equity for all.

Strategies for Reinvigorating Racially Progressive Asian American Activism

We assert the need to continue building on leadership of diverse students and centering student-driven narratives in debates over race-conscious admission policies in highly selective educational institutions. Although Asian Americans as a whole support affirmative action, with 70 percent of Asian American voters saying they support "affirmative action programs designed to help Black people, women, and other minorities get better access to higher education" in recent polls, support tends to be strongest among younger compared to older people and among those born in the United States compared to those who are foreign born.[43] For example, among Chinese Americans, the Asian American national-origin group that is least enthusiastic with regard to race-conscious admissions policies, 68 percent of those Chinese Americans of college age (18–24) said affirmative action programs designed to increase numbers of underrepresented minorities were a "good thing" versus a "bad thing," compared to just 46 percent among those over age thirty-five.[44] The 2020 Asian American Voter Survey shows that among Asian Americans registered to vote, 73 percent of those ages 18–34 believed affirmative action was a "good thing," versus 67 percent of those over fifty years old. Similarly, support for affirmative action programs were higher among the U.S.-born (72 percent) compared to those born outside the United States (69 percent). As illustrated by youth-led movements for racial justice across the nation, young people and students are at the forefront of digital activism to promote narrative change.[45] As we have illustrated in our analysis, the coalition of Chinese American opponents of affirmative action and race-conscious admissions does not represent the diversity of Asian Americans. Moreover, not only do they dismiss independent students' voices, but their views also contradict those of the very young people whose interests they claim to represent.

In addition to following the lead of young people and students, contemporary Asian American activists who support the ideals of a shared racially diverse society and fair institutions can capitalize on strengths that remain unavailable to affirmative action opponents. First, these strengths include the ability to align with and draw support from a multiracial coalition as Asian American student organizers at Harvard did. Multiracial coalitions are essential to both organizing and public narrative leadership. Asian American advocates in the Harvard case were part of a broad, multiracial coalition of students and civil rights activists. Their presence as Asian Americans disrupted the narrative that Asian Americans were uniformly against affirmative action. At the same time, their position in a larger coalition that included not only Asian American students but also Black and Latinx student leaders and organizations stood in sharp contrast to the Asian American opposition, which was notably homogenous and mostly Chinese American. As such, Asian American proponents of affirmative action were able to show broad support among a range of diverse stakeholders.

A second strength includes cultivating trust and building on long-standing relationships with elected officials, journalists, local activists, and community leaders. Established civil rights organizations, including the NAACP Legal Defense Fund, the Lawyers' Committee for Civil Rights Under the Law, and members of the Asian Americans Advancing Justice consortium provided legal representation and support to Asian American and other student activists in the Harvard case. Working with these trusted organizations was critical. First, these organizations have deep experience and expertise in the area of affirmative action, having defended the policies for decades. Second, they have legitimacy in the public and legal spheres due to their advocacy for racial justice and immigrant rights more broadly and over time. Finally, each organization had long-term relationships with other civil rights organizations, academics, journalists, and elected officials. These relationships created an ecosystem of support for the students' advocacy that was less available to more newly organized Asian American groups mobilized against affirmative action. That said, Asian American opponents of affirmative action have also been able to tap into well-established conservative legal activist organizations and foundations.

Finally, contemporary Asian American social justice activists can leverage resources in the form of a network of well-established Asian American and Pacific Islander ethnic advocacy organizations with full-time staff and organizational infrastructures. We learned that many organizations listed as signatories of the amicus briefs submitted by Asian American affirmative action opponents were small in scope, and the day-to-day operations of those organizations were not focused on national policy or educational policy. Some were small businesses, specialty professional associations, and realtors. These organizations' presence allowed people like Ed Blum and white conservative organizations like SFFA to prop up the idea that there were more Asian Americans opposed to affirmative action than there actually are. Finally, much of the work of progressive Asian American organizations that collaborated with and supported student activism in the Harvard case is focused on a broader agenda to advocate for social and policy changes for immigrant rights, health-care accessibility, language access, and policy representation. These issues go to the heart of Asian American civil rights and help to cement the group's broader legitimacy in the sphere of education and offer long-established community foundations and interests from which to renew interconnected political agendas and engagements.

Sally's Story, Continued

We started this chapter in the highest decibels of organized student voice: fierce, collective, and demanding to be heard against a backdrop of twisted representation and co-opted narrative in the days leading up to the start of the trial. However, the solemn halls of the federal courthouse would set the final stage for students and alumni to ultimately make their own case. We now turn to the following recollection provided by coauthor Sally Chen:

As the last student scheduled to testify, I was not allowed to attend any of the prior court proceedings, nor hear the testimony of any of my peers. Reading the court transcript in full, you would hardly believe that was the case. Through a dozen different resonant journeys, each of us emphasized racial solidarity and the urgent necessity of being seen and heard in full. Just as we explained how our identities and stories made us so much more than flat numbers on our college applications, we breathed life into the legal record through the power of our own voices—vulnerable, courageous, and deeply compelling. On the day I testified, though I walked up the steps to the witness stand alone, the hard work of coming together as both a community and a movement, listening and learning together, was already well underway. All I had to do was take a deep breath and speak.

Notes

1 Renee Tajima-Peña, email to author, October 2018.
2 Angelo N. Ancheta, *Race, Rights, and the Asian American Experience*, 2nd ed. (New Brunswick, NJ: Rutgers University Press, 2006); Ian Haney López, *White by*

Law: The Legal Construction of Race, 10th anniversary ed. (New York: New York University Press, 2006).
3   Janelle Wong and Sono Shah, "Convergence across Difference: Understanding the Political Ties That Bind with the 2016 National Asian American Survey," *RSF: The Russell Sage Foundation Journal of the Social Sciences* 7, no. 2 (April 2021): 70–92.
4   Jennifer Lee, Janelle Wong, and Karthick Ramakrishnan, "Asian Americans Support for Affirmative Action Increased since 2016," Data Bits, a blog for AAPI Data, February 4, 2021, http://aapidata.com.
5   Paul M. Ong, "The Affirmative Action Divide," in *Asian American Politics: Law, Participation, and Policy*, eds. Don T. Nakanishi and James S. Lai (Lanham, MD: Rowman & Littlefield, 2003), 377. Affirmative action refers to a set of policies in public contracting, employment, and education. In college admissions, Court rulings we review in this chapter have rolled back affirmative action, which has evolved into race-conscious admissions practices. It is important to note that contemporary race-conscious admissions is not the same as affirmative action.
6   C. J. Kim, "Playing the Racial Trump Card: Asian Americans in Contemporary U.S. Politics," *Amerasia Journal* 26, no. 3 (2000): 35–65; Dana Y. Takagi, *The Retreat from Race: Asian American Admissions and Racial Politics* (New Brunswick, NJ: Rutgers University Press, 1992); B. Marquez, "The Politics of Race and Assimilation: The League of United Latin American Citizens 1929–40," *Western Political Quarterly* 42, no. 2 (1989): 355–375.
7   OiYan A. Poon and Megan S. Segoshi, "The Racial Mascot Speaks: A Critical Race Discourse Analysis of Asian Americans and Fisher vs. University of Texas," *Review of Higher Education* 42, no. 1 (2018): 235–267.
8   OiYan A. Poon and Liliana M. Garces, "Asian Americans and Race-Conscious Admissions: Understanding the Conservative Opposition's Strategy of Misinformation, Intimidation, and Racial Division," in *Civil Rights and Federal Higher Education*, eds. Nicholas Hillman and Gary Orfield (Cambridge, MA: Harvard Education Press, 2022), 53.
9   For more on the evolution of case law from the remedial rationale to the diversity rationale and how the latter has also changed over time, see Liliana M. Garces and Uma M. Jayakumar, "Dynamic Diversity: Toward a Contextual Understanding of Critical Mass," *Educational Researcher* 43, no. 3 (2014): 115–124.
10 Julie J. Park, *Race on Campus: Debunking Myths with Data* (Cambridge, MA: Harvard Education Press, 2018).
11 Ideally these briefs are substantiated by robust research, but many anti–affirmative action briefs use op-eds and news articles, rather than refereed research, as their evidence. Catherine L. Horn, Patricia Marin, Liliana M. Garces, Karen Miksch, and John T. Yun, "Shaping Educational Policy through the Courts: The Use of Social Science Research in Amicus Briefs in Fisher I," *Educational Policy* 34, no. 3 (2020): 449–476.

12. For an analysis of the Fisher briefs, see Poon and Segoshi, "The Racial Mascot Speaks."
13. Rossina Zamora Liu, William Ming Liu, Janelle S. Wong, and Richard Q. Shin, "Anti-Black Racism and Asian American Local Educational Activism: A Critical Race Discourse Analysis," *Educational Researcher*, OnlineFirst (March 2023).
14. C. J. Robinson, *Black Marxism: The Making of the Black Radical Tradition* (Chapel Hill: University of North Carolina Press, 1983).
15. OiYan A. Poon, Megan S. Segoshi, Lilianne Tang, Kristen L. Surla, Caressa Nguyen, and Dian D. Squire, "Asian Americans, Affirmative Action, and the Political Economy of Racism: A Multidimensional Model of Raceclass Frames," *Harvard Educational Review* 89, no. 2 (2019): 201–226.
16. M. C. Dawson, *Behind the Mule: Race and Class in African-American Politics* (Princeton, NJ: Princeton University Press, 1995).
17. Marc P. Johnston-Guerrero and Kai Zhao, "Is Affirmative Action Interfering with the Chinese Dream in America? Exploring WeChat Users' Views on Affirmative Action in U.S. College Admissions," *Race, Ethnicity and Education* 25, no. 7 (2022): 939–957.
18. Sarah Hinger, "Meet Edward Blum, the Man Who Wants to Kill Affirmative Action in Higher Education," *ACLU News & Commentary*, October 18, 2018, www.aclu.org.
19. Kimmy Yam, "70% of Asian Americans Support Affirmative Action. Here's Why Misconceptions Persist," *NBC Asian America*, November 14, 2020, www.nbcnews.com.
20. AACE, "Over 150 Asian American Organizations Jointly File Amicus Brief Opposing Harvard's Discriminatory Admissions Practices," press release, July 31, 2018, https://asianamericanforeducation.org.
21. SCA 5 was a proposed initiative in 2012 to consider eliminating California Proposition 209's ban on the use of race, sex, color, ethnicity, or national origin in recruitment, admissions, and retention programs at public universities and colleges in California. It passed the California Senate but was withdrawn due to strong opposition. California's Proposition 209 passed in 1996 and prohibited public institutions in California from considering race, sex, and ethnicity.
22. Lee, Wong, and Ramakrishna, "Asian Americans Support for Affirmative Action Increased since 2016."
23. Haivan V. Hoang, *Writing against Racial Injury* (Pittsburgh: University of Pittsburgh Press, 2015).
24. "SFFA did not present a single Asian American applicant who was overtly discriminated against or who was better qualified than an admitted white applicant when considering the full range of factors that Harvard values in its admissions process." Allison D. Burroughs, *Students for Fair Admissions, Inc., Plaintiff, v. President and Fellows of Harvard College (Harvard Corporation), Defendant*, Findings of Fact and Conclusions of Law, U.S. District Court, District of Massachusetts, September 30, 2019.

25 *SFFA v. President & Fellows of Harvard Coll.*, 308 F.R.D. 39 (D. Mass.), *aff'd*, 807 F.3d 472 (1st Cir. 2015).
26 "Students for Fair Admissions vs. Harvard University," *Lawyers' Committee for Civil Rights under Law* (blog), accessed March 27, 2021, https://lawyerscommittee.org.
27 *SFFA v. President & Fellows of Harvard Coll.*, U.S. District Court of Massachusetts, Day 11 Transcript, https://lawyerscommittee.org, 83–84.
28 *SFFA v. President & Fellows of Harvard Coll.*, U.S. District Court of Massachusetts, Day 11 Transcript, 168.
29 *SFFA v. President & Fellows of Harvard Coll.*, U.S. District Court of Massachusetts, Day 11 Transcript, 19, 17.
30 See the Harvard Ethnic Studies Coalition, https://harvardethnicstudies.wordpress.com.
31 "Coalition for a Diverse Harvard: Join the Week of Action 10/8–10/14, 2018," Diverse Harvard, accessed March 27, 2021, https://www.diverseharvard.org; "Task Force for Asian American Progressive Advocacy and Studies," Harvard TAPAS, accessed March 27, 2021, www.harvardtapas.com; PBHA, "Phillips Brooks House Association: Our History," June 1, 2015, accessed March 27, 2021, http://pbha.org.
32 *SFFA v. President & Fellows of Harvard Coll.*, U.S. District Court of Massachusetts, Day 11 Transcript, 47.
33 *SFFA v. President & Fellows of Harvard Coll.*, U.S. District Court of Massachusetts, Day 11 Transcript, 208.
34 Sally Chen, Thang Q. Diep, and Catherine H. Ho, "We Testified, It's Time for Action," *Harvard Crimson*, February 25, 2019, www.thecrimson.com.
35 Amanda Su, "Harvard Students Rally for Ethnic Studies Outside Alumni Conference," *Harvard Crimson*, accessed March 27, 2021, www.thecrimson.com.
36 Camille G. Caldera and Amanda Y. Su, "'We Will Tell Our Stories': Students of Color Build Coalitions in Face of Threat to Affirmative Action," *Harvard Crimson*, May 28, 2019, www.thecrimson.com.
37 Alexander Zhang, "Chinese American Parents of Harvard and Boston High School Students Attend Rally to Stand for Affirmative Action in October 2018," Alexander Zhang (cred: @tea.haus)—Google Drive, October 14, 2018, https://drive.google.com.
38 Ivy Yan, "Defend Diversity! Solidarity Rally for Opportunity and Equality," Facebook, October 14, 2018, www.facebook.com.
39 Yan, "Defend Diversity!"
40 Graciela Mochikofsky, "Why Lorgia García Peña Was Denied Tenure at Harvard," *New Yorker*, July 27, 2021, www.newyorker.com.
41 Carolyn Chou et al., "Asian-American Activists Voice Support for Suspension of Exam School Test," *Bay State Banner*, October 29, 2020, sec. Opinion, www.baystatebanner.com.
42 Vincent Pan, "Building Upon Prop 16: A Letter from Executive Director Vincent Pan," *Chinese for Affirmative Action* (blog), November 6, 2020, https://caasf.org;

Mike Baker, "Voters Narrowly Reject Affirmative Action in Washington State. What's Next?," *New York Times*, November 12, 2019, www.nytimes.com.
43 "Asian Americans Support for Affirmative Action Increased since 2016," AAPI Data, February 4, 2021, http://aapidata.com.
44 Lorrie Frasure, Janelle Wong, Edward Vargas, and Matt Barreto, "Collaborative Multi-racial Post-election Survey (CMPS)," Inter-university Consortium for Political and Social Research, May 3, 2022, www.insidehighered.com.
45 Danielle Allen and Cathy Cohen, "The New Civil Rights Movement Doesn't Need an MLK," *Washington Post*, April 10, 2015, www.washingtonpost.com.

PART IV

Rooting Resistance: Perspectives on Environmental Justice and Ecological Politics

From extreme heat to rising sea levels, billions of people around the world are facing the uneven impacts of the climate crisis. Like other communities shaped by the forces of racism and imperialism, Asian Americans are disproportionately impacted by climate change and experience some of the greatest health risk factors.[1] Yet despite increased attention to the intersections of race and environmental justice, national environmental organizations remain overwhelmingly white.[2] In this context, Asian American perspectives on environmental justice provide an opportunity for critical intervention. Contemporary Asian American ecological politics shifts our attention to the slower, accretive, and temporal dimensions of violence, weaving the intimate to the structural, the personal to the political, and the past to the present. Given the longstanding perception of Asian American communities as sites of disease and degradation, Asian American ecological politics also provide a necessary corrective to the historic roots of the American environmental movement in eugenics and colonialism.[3]

This section examines case studies of environmental justice organizing that Asian American communities are engaged in to address questions related to ecological concerns that include land degradation, residential segregation and planned shrinkage, housing precarity, food sovereignty and contamination of foodways, and pandemic politics. As each of the chapters in this section remind us, there are a multitude of ways in which Asian migrants, youths, women, and elders are contesting the capitalization of human loss and the necropolitical workings of ecological violence that negatively impact their communities. Vivian Shaw, Jacqueline Leung, and Julie Sze explore the "changing same" of climate injustice facing Asian migrant, refugee, and Pacific Islander women and at the same time reflect on what the COVID-19 pandemic has taught us about Asian American, Native Hawaiian, and Pacific Islander solidarities in the face of environmental harms. Ja Bulsombut and Kristin Chang discuss the W.O.W. Project's Resist Recycle Regenerate program, through which Manhattan Chinatown queer, trans, nonbinary, and gender-expansive youths in New York City engage with a politics of sustainability—both in the creative reuse of confetti from Lunar New Year parades and in sustaining youth-centric leadership as Manhattan Chinatown confronts new waves of displacement. Frances Huynh explores the power of community gardens in Los Angeles Chinatown as a platform for food security, community resilience, and intergenerational healing in the face of structural displacement and gentrification.

Notes

1 Sara Grineski, Timothy Collins, and Danielle Morales, "Asian Americans and Disproportionate Exposure to Carcinogenic Hazardous Air Pollutants: A National Study," *Social Science & Medicine* 185 (1982), 71–80.
2 Dorceta E. Taylor, "The State of Diversity in Environmental Organizations," Green 2.0 (July 2014), accessed February 5, 2024, https://orgs.law.harvard.edu.
3 On historical perceptions of Asian Americans as sites of environmental toxicity, see Nayan Shah, *Contagious Divides: Epidemics and Race in San Francisco's Chinatown* (Berkeley: University of California Press, 2001); Mel Y. Chen, "Toxic Animacies, Inanimate Affections," *GLQ* 17, 2–3 (June 1, 2011): 265–286.

10

Messy Solidarities

Asian American, Native Hawaiian, and Pacific Islander Environmental Justice in the Pandemic and Beyond

VIVIAN SHAW, JACQUELINE LEUNG, AND JULIE SZE

COVID-19's disproportionate harm to people of color and other systemically disenfranchised communities across the globe has underscored the sobering reality that racism is fundamentally a matter of life and death.[1] We write this chapter from within the United States, where public health data shows that legacies of systemic racism converge to produce vastly disproportionate outcomes, with Native Americans, African Americans, and Pacific Islanders hit far harder than white and Asian Americans in the United States.[2] According to the Native Hawaiian Pacific Islander (NHPI) Covid 19 Data Policy Lab, COVID-19 cases among Native Hawaiian and Pacific Islanders are the highest: up to nine times higher in Washington State.[3] This pattern is similar in fourteen other states and Washington, DC.[4] The stark asymmetry of the pandemic—the dissonance of what it means to live through or die from COVID-19—has compelled many of us to examine the pluralities of crisis. As Ash-Lee Henderson, co-executive director of the Highlander Research and Education Center, put it at a 2021 summit, racism and the pandemic are "intersecting and compounding, not parallel."[5] Echoing these insights, we hope that by reminding readers of some lessons from environmental justice scholarship and movements, we can collectively better understand this moment. We situate the pandemic as a problem of environmental justice not merely due to speculation of the virus's zoonotic origins, but rather to emphasize how the manners of how we move through and interact with the physical world—from the air we breathe, to the toxins in our bloodstream, to the food we eat—are molded through histories and continuing politics of extraction and resource allocation that undergird racial capitalism.

In reframing COVID-19 and climate change as co-constitutive within what public health experts have begun calling a global "syndemic," we consider how the legacies that have positioned Asian bodies as diseased and contaminated intertwine with the parallel logics of war and coloniality that have rendered them simultaneously exploitable *and* disposable. In this chapter, we pivot toward a critical analysis of Asian American lives during the pandemic through the lens of environmental justice activism and scholarship.[6] Within this discussion, we wrestle with what we believe is a fundamental dilemma. That is, while it may be impossible to understand present and future trajectories of Asian American environmental justice without considering broader connections within the Pacific, Asian American studies perpetually erases, even as it purports to claim, Native Hawaiian and Pacific Islander people, stories, and resistance.[7] Rather than attempting to escape this obstacle, we infuse our scholarly analysis with candid conversations, interweaving interview excerpts with prose. Our excerpts come from conversations between the authors—Vivian, who is Taiwanese American; Julie, who is Chinese American (from Manhattan Chinatown); and Jackie, who is Micronesian. Through this dialogue, we reflect on what our time of writing has taught us about Asian American, Native Hawaiian, and Pacific Islander solidarities in the face of environmental harms—as well as what we do not know.

Lessons from Environmental Justice Movements

How can an environmental justice perspective help us confront multiple emergencies that simultaneously unfold through distinct processes but also converge and exacerbate each other? Why is environmental justice important for how we understand contemporary Asian American politics? These questions are the points of inspiration for this chapter. To answer the first question—environmental justice and climate justice movements reject the idea that environmental problems are divorced from social and racial inequalities. Environmental "issues," such as air and water pollution, pesticides, toxicity and siting, and drought, are neither separate from each other nor separate from the structures of political and economic domination.[8] Environmental justice movements also prioritize the voices and perspectives of those *most impacted* and *least responsible* for environmental pollution and problems, what some scholars call "fence-line/front-line" community perspectives.[9] In matters of climate, for instance, the United States is responsible for 25 percent of cumulative carbon emissions since 1750 (until 1882, the largest emitter was the United Kingdom).[10] The U.S. military, with more than eight hundred military bases around the world, would by itself be the fifty-eighth highest carbon emitter if it was its own country.[11]

Environmental justice toggles multiple fields, as a type of praxis that takes shape at the cross-sections of community organizing, public policy, and critical scholarship. Environmental justice organizing and scholarship aims to spotlight histories of harm. Structural power imbalances between state and corporate entities and the already marginalized communities upon which they inflict harms contribute to rendering them "invisible," especially when perpetuated over decades and centuries. Environmental justice movements and allied scholarship fundamentally engage with this task of making such power dynamics visible, while contextualizing the human and socially disparate costs of racial and colonial violence that has become normal and quotidian. Building from this conversation, our impetus for bringing together conversations about Asian American life and death during the present pandemic emerge from our view of disasters as an omnipresent challenge for environmental justice. In contrast to mainstream framings of disasters as exceptional, disasters are, in fact, *already* everyday and "normal" experiences for marginalized populations across the globe. Disasters, in other words, are simultaneously already here and imminent. While we hesitate to reproduce an oversimplified narrative of disasters as socially transformative moments, the current pandemic may be a moment that elucidates how disasters become everyday battles. Whereas disasters such as hurricanes, earthquakes, and tsunamis frequently get narrated as disruptive external shocks, the long duration of the pandemic—entering its fifth year at the time of writing—underlines how easily environmental crisis evolves into stasis. Yet this is precisely what environmental justice advocates have told us for years.

In the face of environmental racism, Asian immigrants and refugees have grasped opportunities for political resistance within and across communities.[12] Asian Pacific Environmental Network (APEN), through its Laotian Organizing Project (LOP), focuses on Laotian resettlement and youth activism in Richmond, California, where Laotian and Black communities face elevated toxic exposures as well as police and school violence.[13] Asian American environmental justice activism dovetails with Asian American critique that has continually emphasized how global white supremacy is multi-sited and enacted through the entanglements of empire "abroad" and systemic exclusion and exploitation "at home." Colonialism and imperialism reside at the core of Asian American political critique, with this analysis enabling activists and scholars to contextualize contemporary anti-Asian violence within racist histories of displacement and resettlement. Historian Simeon Man underscores that "Asians were not 'immigrants'"—rather, their arrival in North America came as a consequence of Western economic and militaristic expansions that rendered their "lives unlivable."[14]

Numerous public figures have blamed President Donald Trump's antagonistic stance toward China and stoking of white nationalism as a primary driver of anti-Asian racism, which gained attention as a national problem since the early days of the pandemic and conspicuously manifested as 11,409 incidents of anti-Asian verbal harassment, threats, and intimidation, and in some cases physical violence, as of 2023.[15] These critiques of Trump have provided a political opportunity for Asian American activists and scholars to connect acts of violence on an interpersonal scale to state violence. A bracketing of the timeline of anti-Asian racism to the Trump administration and the language of "the Wuhan virus" and other COVID-era epitaphs, however, occludes the perpetuity of U.S. empire and its interventions in Asia that have systematically relied on environmental destruction. Writing on ecological warfare through Agent Orange and other cases, literary scholar Cathy Schlund-Vials reminds us of the continuity across time in forgetting and disregarding the devastating environmental impacts of U.S. militarization.[16] Omitting environmental racism within this history serves the function of disconnecting imperialism from ongoing and accelerating problems, such as climate change and toxicity. Amid continual toxic exposure, including regular chemical accidents, environmental justice activism offers a site of negotiation and identity-making around ethnicity, gender, youth identities, class, immigrant status, and refugee legacies of war and contamination.[17]

Guåhan scholars Michael Bevacqua and Isa Ua Ceallaigh Bowman demonstrate how the project of ostensible environmental repair following military occupation can rationalize continued U.S. military presence in Guam.[18] The rendering of geographies as unlivable through environmental destruction during and in the aftermath of empire operates in collusion with other forms of political violence that dictate the displacement and resettlement of Asian people. Such processes drive not only migration but also the environmental conditions into which Asian communities resettle. As Eric Tang highlights across the cases of Cambodian refugee resettlement in the Bronx and Vietnamese post-Katrina communities in New Orleans, environmental precarity—in the form of disinvested housing stock and proximity to toxic threats—factors significantly shape Southeast Asian communities' experiences of poverty in the United States. Similarly, the histories of war that connect colonialism, the pandemic, and anti-Asian violence knit together the disproportionately high illness and mortality rates of Filipina nurses who care for patients with COVID-19 and meatpacking workers in factories across the United States who suffered astonishingly rates of infection and mortality due to COVID-19.[19]

Any conversation bringing together Asian American, Native Hawaiian, and Pacific Islander lives to explore the politics of environmental justice during the COVID-19 pandemic is unavoidably fraught, given tendencies within Asian American studies to simultaneously erase and appropriate Native Hawaiian and Pacific Islander stories and perspectives. Our response to this dilemma, which became clear to us through our writing process, is to *center* the tensions in our analysis. Thus, one of the guiding philosophies for this chapter is a commitment to exploring how messiness and contradictions can generate new possibilities. In other words, rather than immediately rushing to resolve tensions, we consider what lessons we might learn from sitting deeply with them. As we contend with environmental violence on a planetary scale, how can we move toward solidarity while also thinking of the specificities of our communities and histories? What does environmental solidarity look like for Asian Americans, Native Hawaiians, and Pacific Islanders during and after COVID-19? How do we navigate such interconnections ethically and restoratively—and why think about solidarity at all? As we begin answering these questions, we must examine what it is about the *now* that necessitates reinvesting in the project of environmental solidarity.

At present, we are enfolded in a political moment that requires us to explore the meanings of solidarities across communities. The fluctuating visibility of different forms of racial violence has generated new conversations and reignited older attempts at articulating solidarity and inclusion. Asian American communities have found truth in the narrative that the pandemic has exacerbated and accelerated anti-Asian racism, grasping upon a sudden uptick in attention as an opportunity for redress for Asian American communities, which they feel have been long overlooked. Yet within these attempts to gain and leverage recognition for community restoration, Asian American activists and scholars often have mis-stepped. Hashtags such as #StopAAPIHate have been vital for raising care and concern for Asian Americans, but they have also occluded differences within Asian America—particularly among ethnic communities—as well as those between Asian Americans and Native Hawaiians and Pacific Islanders. Moreover, such approaches have largely ignored the disproportionate burden of illness and death that so many Native Hawaiian and Pacific Islander communities have endured because of the virus itself and the ways that it has become compounded amid profound structural inequality. Our call to rethink the meanings of Asian American, Native Hawaiian, and Pacific Islander environmental solidarity, therefore, is rooted in our concern that existing efforts to articulate solidarity so frequently reinscribe the very violence and erasure they seek to remedy. Following a brief discussion of our pathways into this conversation, we will focus on some of the themes we find most salient for environmental justice now and in the future—health, the pandemic, climate change, and solidarity.

Entering at the Edges

The process of writing this chapter highlights the tensions of Asian American and Native Hawaiian and Pacific Islander intellectual and political solidarities—as well as potential avenues for restorative collaboration. Each of the authors came to this project with distinct backgrounds, interests, and motivations for exploring Asian America, Pacific Islander, and Native Hawaiian environmental justice. Vivian arrived at her research on disasters and crisis through her personal and political interests with cultural trauma. One of the earliest stories of her family that she learned was of her mother's loss—at the age of one—of her own mother and two brothers as the result of an aerial attack on her hometown of Taipei, Taiwan. Vivian's approach toward understanding the environment, thus, has always taken interest in the pluralities of histories, systems of power, and biographies as people rebuild themselves and their communities while grappling with devastating material and social losses. Julie has spent decades researching and collaborating with immigrant environmental justice movements. Her scholarship helped pave the way for interdisciplinary research at the intersections of American studies and environmental studies, particularly for Asian American environmental scholars. Julie's contributions to this chapter draw from her perspective as someone who has witnessed dramatic changes in the landscape of environmental justice scholar-activism over the past twenty-eight years since she began her research. Our friendship and collaborative writing of this piece developed after Vivian cold-emailed Julie asking her to serve as a mentor for a postdoc.

In the early genesis of this chapter, when Julie and Vivian were the only two authors, we imagined a conversation about Asian American environmental justice that took inspiration from Marshallese activism around climate change and COVID-19. But we quickly recognized our own hypocrisy on "borrowing" from Marshallese political and intellectual histories as Asian American scholars with limited direct collaboration with Native Hawaiian and Pacific Islander communities. We sought external guidance from scholars and activists such as Vicente Diaz and received generous feedback that made clear that we could not proceed with our original plan. To discuss these issues ethically and accurately, we needed to entirely restructure our conversation.

Vivian reached out to Jackie, the executive director of the Micronesian Islander Community (MIC), a nonprofit organization serving Micronesians, and Compact of Free Association (COFA) citizens in Oregon.[20] MIC serves approximately fifteen hundred of an estimated seven thousand people living in Oregon who are COFA citizens. MIC formed in in 2011 and officially incorporated in 2012.[21] Jackie's involvement in MIC grew out of an accident. In 2012 she was working on a radio show as a DJ. Her show, "From Different Shores," focused on the Asian and Pacific Islander communities. As she was searching for more Pacific Islander events, Jackie learned about MIC's "Taste of Micronesia." She decided to attend and, after meeting some of the organizers, was invited to join MIC's next board meeting. By the following year, she had become MIC's unofficial chair. At the start of the pandemic, she steered MIC into an independent 501(c)(3) status, formally separating from its fiscal sponsor. Through this process, MIC went from a zero-budget organization that relied solely on volunteers and donations to an organization with eight paid staff and an annual budget of $2 million. MIC has focused on community outreach and engagement, including COVID-19 wraparound services, enrollment into the Oregon Health Plan (the state's Medicaid program), and celebratory cultural events. MIC was one of the organizations that spearheaded legislation within the state of Oregon, ensuring that COFA citizens would have a driver's license or Oregon identification card for seven years, like other Oregon residents. Before the law's passing, COFA citizens were only able to hold a one-year license.

In our restructuring conversations, Jackie highlighted the need to avoid lumping together different communities and the necessity of recognizing differential marginalization even within already marginalized demographics. With this principle in mind, we toggle between the *specificity* of Jackie's work through MIC and the broader theoretical questions around environmental justice that Julie has excavated through her research. The architecture of this chapter, moving between prose and interviews, takes inspiration from other parts of this book and aims to be candid and accessible. We believe our direct approach to talking about transparency and process speaks to questions around representation, inclusion, erasure, and solidarity that are fundamental to the future of Asian American studies. These concerns mirror similar contentions around power and privilege "within" Asian America, especially alongside public debates about the usefulness of *Asian American* as an identity.

We hope that this conversation can help guide conversations with students, teachers, and engaged members of our communities alike. The style we have adopted in this process of restructuring also reflects the logistical challenges of writing—or doing work—during a worldwide and as-yet-unended pandemic that has impacted our lives in various ways. Like so many others, we have navigated the everyday violence of the pandemic itself and the encroachments of neoliberal academic labor expectations alongside grieving painful personal losses. Thus, both the content and form of this chapter represent many of the complexities, compromises, and opportunities we have personally encountered in working through this moment.

Compounding Health

As Karina Walters et al. put it, "contemporary physical health reflects the embodiment of historical trauma."[22] When the United States ended nuclear testing on the Marshall Islands in 1958, it left the Marshallese with high radiation levels, which led to birth defects, cancers, and destroyed crop harvests for decades afterwards.[23] These communities live and die under what literary scholar Rob Nixon calls conditions of normalized "slow violence," which echoes what Indigenous health scholars suggest when they write that "bodies contain stories."[24] Slow violence and intergenerational bodily trauma contrasts with, but is intimately connected to, conditions of "fast violence," whether in police killings or the coronavirus.[25] As scholars who teach and research on the politics of the environment, we build upon critiques of racial capitalism from the literatures of critical refugee studies, ethnic studies, and environmental justice to recenter legacies of environmental ruin within systems of imperialism and settlement. Exposing such connections is crucial for understanding the historical development and present conditions of our syndemic crises.

> VIVIAN: Can you explain why health migration is such a crucial issue for Pacific Islander diasporic communities, particularly for COFA citizens?
>
> JACKIE: Many of the COFA citizens who are coming here [to Oregon] for health reasons are Marshallese, and their migration is connected to the atomic bomb testing that took place in the 1940s and 1950s.[26] Members of these communities are coming here to get treatment for different types of cancers. We're seeing the long-term impacts of nuclear testing, where even people who weren't directly exposed— but have parents or grandparents who were—are now presenting with cancers. Other COFA citizens are also coming over for other

health reasons. Some are developing cancers of unknown origin, even though cancer had not historically been an issue in their communities.

Insufficient access to health care on their islands, a by-product of decades of colonial occupation, compound the biological vulnerability COFA citizens have experienced as a result of radiation. Health-care access differs across islands, particularly for issues that require specialty care. I hear from people specifically in the Marshall Islands that if you have dental needs you just pay five bucks [for those services].... But that's *if* you have five dollars. A lot of people can't afford to pay that for dental treatment. If you don't even have those five dollars, you're still kind of stuck in a situation where you can't access that care. Diabetes and obesity are also on the increase. A major reason for this is increased reliance on processed foods, resulting from lack of access to land on their own respective islands to grow their own food or to go fishing. MIC has worked with local and state health-care providers in Oregon to develop culturally informed strategies for addressing health disparities that disproportionately impact COFA communities, such as diabetes.

In addition to health migration, COFA citizens often move to the Oregon region to support family with day-to-day responsibilities, such as childcare. These family relationships often shape how COFA citizens interface with health-care providers and other institutions. While working with directly impacted community members, healthcare providers must also communicate with their family members or other people with whom they are cohabitating. Elderly community members frequently rely on other people in their household for rides and experience discomfort with using public transportation or rideshare services due to language and financial barriers and cultural norms.

Forced and coerced migrations resulting from the unlivability of war, environmental degradation, and poverty operate in tandem with labor inequalities in the continental United States. Such histories offer one point of connection between Pacific Islander and Asian American health inequalities. For instance, Marshallese resettlement in Arkansas grew as an outcome of the community's disproportionate employment in the poultry industry. Significant proportions of Laotian immigrant communities also work in the meatpacking industry.[27] With meatpacking and poultry industries being well-documented hotspots of COVID-19, these communities have suffered a disproportionate vulnerability to the virus.[28]

VIVIAN: One of my goals for the AAPI COVID-19 Project is to expand conversations about anti-Asian racism—namely, to talk more about how labor conditions shape the differentials by which people are exposed to violence. The economic conditions that lead to workers interfacing regularly with members in the public in front-facing industries contribute to their vulnerabilities in a very physical sense. In the case of 2021's Atlanta massage parlor killings, gender, immigration, and sexuality all factored into these women's physical proximity to this person who then decided to come into their business to kill them. This is why I have a hard time identifying something that's *not* environmental. I see these labor and working conditions as fundamentally environmental.

JULIE: That's what Pam Tau Lee said! About labor and occupational health issues as a central part of Asian and immigrant refugee communities. She was looking at the barrio, but you could say the same thing.[29] That's what all the research on Vietnamese nail salon workers is about, their exposures in so many different forms.[30] For people who do environmental justice or environmental work and have a justice worldview, yes, everything is connected.

Chronicling COVID-19

MIC's strategy for addressing health disparities shifted considerably during the pandemic. Prior to the pandemic, the nonprofit's central focus was on addressing diabetes and maternal child health; increasing community access to health, vision, and dental insurance, screenings, and care; and improving provider service through job training. Since the start of the pandemic, much of MIC's work has shifted to COVID-19 relief efforts. Staff assist community members with rental, mortgage, and utilities payment assistance; supply food and other groceries; and organized testing and vaccination outreach events.

JACKIE: This past year we were able to return to in-person events, following social distancing safety protocols. Last August [of 2021], we had our third annual back-to-school resource event. We had around eighty people who had registered; in total, around four hundred people came. We gave out forty-two vaccines that day. We only had seventy backpacks [with school supplies and other educational materials] because we weren't expecting that many people—so we ran out really fast. But what that tells us is that next year we'll have two hundred backpacks.

One issue many people are facing right now is difficulty with keeping or getting a job. Or they may have a job that's very low paying. They will usually have to move into multiple-family households. For example, three or four different families might live together in one home—with some of these being multigenerational families. Before the pandemic, I've been in homes where there are sixteen or seventeen people living together in a three-bedroom house. Some people work, some don't, but everyone is trying to chip in to pay for the expenses. They may or may not be close relatives. Some are, while others are like, "Oh, we're not related, but that's so-and-so's relative, and so they're staying with me."

Alongside disproportionately high rates of illness and mortality related to the virus, the pandemic has produced an undue social burden for COFA citizens by preventing reunification among members of the diaspora. At the time of this writing, the Marshall Islands was the only COFA nation that had reopened and was permitting people to reenter. Jackie describes how many COFA citizens have been stuck in Guam, Hawai'i, or in the continental United States.

JACKIE: One of the biggest issues affecting the community is that there's this huge diaspora where people are having to leave their islands. But some of them wanted to go back home during the pandemic, or at least have their family members who have died during the pandemic be buried back home. The cost of funeral arrangements has increased significantly. As people want to be buried on the islands (and not cremated and remains returned in an urn), when individuals die off-island, the cost to pay for the funeral arrangements varies, from anywhere from $15,000 to $20,000 a person. These costs do not include the expenses to maintain the body in the hospital or other facility until the funds are raised to bring the person's remains back home. During the pandemic, when entry into the islands were restricted, MIC worked alongside other Micronesian partners to advocate for permission of the deceased to be repatriated. This was denied for most of the pandemic. Some families opted to wait until the islands reopened, while others opted to cremate and return the remains when they could do so.

Considering Climate Change in Context

Nuclear testing has left an ongoing legacy of toxic contamination, exacerbated now by drought and sea-level rise from climate change. Philosopher Olúfẹ́mi Táíwò , drawing on scholars of "climate colonialism," argues that we are at a crossroads—of "climate apartheid" or "climate reparations."[31] He and Beba Cibralic define climate reparations as "a systemic approach to redistributing resources and changing policies and institutions that have perpetuated harm—rather than a discrete exchange of money or of apologies for past wrongdoing." As Neel Ahuja writes, the hegemonic discourse of climate refugees ignores the historical and ideological constructions of racism and capitalism, and it ignores the forces of war in favor of liberal humanist accounts of "human security." Instead, Ahuja positions "climate change as a racial ecology of capitalism."[32] This critique of home and of climate refugee discourse thus allows for a political and analytic connection between climate refugees, including Pacific Islanders, with Southeast Asian refugee communities facing elevated pollution and health risks.

> JACKIE: What's happening back home on the islands is that with the warming of temperatures and the melting of ice, ocean levels are rising—specifically around the islands. Areas of land that used to be able to grow crops can no longer be used for growing. So, people now have to try and find other areas on their islands. It's harder for them to catch fish now. Before, they would be able to fish and get plentiful fish. Now, there are less fish, or they aren't as big. This is also

in combination with overfishing—not by them, but by illegal fishermen who are coming in and taking up all their fish.

Another consideration is typhoons, which are now a lot stronger, and what that means for their islands. On the northwest beach of the outer islands, a typhoon came about two or three years ago. Normally during typhoons people are fine. They could just go deep into the forest and avoid it—nothing too bad would happen. But this particular typhoon bleached out all their coconuts. Instead of losing maybe a few coconuts, all of their trees rotted. Areas where they normally would be able to grow their taro patches and other crops became contaminated with seawater. Extreme temperature changes and weather events are taking place that they haven't seen before—which is in effect affecting their ability to have access to food.

JULIE: A number of scholars are working on climate apartheid: Olúfẹ́mi Táíwò most prominently, in a piece on the coming police crisis.[33] There's also Neel Ahuja's recent book, *Planetary Specters*, which discusses the figure of the climate refugee as the racialized figure moving, for example, in Bangladesh.[34] Ahuja explores state-centered discourse that focuses on climate migrants' border crossing as a security threat—simultaneously rationalizing the militarization of borders and obscuring the extractive economies, such as oil, that drive much of transnational migration. This emergent scholarship further contextualizes policing in the context of climate change and policing in the context of borders. In other words, as the impacts from global climate change become more intense, those in the Global South bear the disproportionate burden of problems that they did little to create. Coastal communities and nations (such as Bangladesh) and small island nations (in the Arctic, the Caribbean, and the Pacific) are particularly vulnerable, although they are the least responsible.

VIVIAN: It reminds me of the expression, "We're here, because you were there."[35] The policing of migration is connected to the fact that places in the world are being made uninhabitable, or extremely difficult to live in because of all these other issues, including as a result of war, because of changes to the environment.

JULIE: In "The North Pole," which I've written about as an abolitionist climate justice narrative, one of the characters uses the same exact quote.[36] And that's why Neel Ahuja's critical ethnic studies take on the *figure* of the climate refugee is so important. Because it situates that question of why people are leaving within this very political issue and within the context of the afterlives of colonialism and racial capitalism. For me, Movement Generation has an incredible strategy document for a just transition where it talks about the extractive economy and how we need to move from the bad to the good.[37] And it discusses bad things, like militarism. Justice movements really look at that sense of scale, not parts per million, or degrees burned, or number of COVID cases. They engender a capacious sense of history and responsibility.

Solidarities in Practice

When reimagining the political project of environmental justice, a fundamental challenge that remains is developing solidarity and recognition of shared experiences across different communities while also confronting the power differentials that have impacted solidarity in the past and present. As allied scholars and community members, we have noticed tendencies to regard social movements as ideas and causes foremost, and people secondarily. In our teaching and writing, we attempt to invert this assumption by reminding our students and readers that social movements are made from people doing labor. And people are, by definition, very complex and multifaceted.

> VIVIAN: One of the challenges of doing politics in a disaster or moment of crisis is that the urgency creates a feeling like there's no time to deal with the messiness. We're in this moment of tension, where we can see the crisis of anti-Asian racism getting invoked to justify the policing of Black and Brown people. At the same time, many Asian Americans, particularly younger ones, *do* see themselves in solidarity with movements like Black Lives Matter.[38] This dilemma has made me think about policing as an environmental issue, which I know Laura Pulido, David Pellow, Elizabeth Bradshaw, and others have written about.[39] In this way, I view the recent revitalization of attention to Asian American issues as an opportunity for political amplification that remains incredibly fraught.

As Abigail Echo-Hawk, who is the director of the Urban Indian Health Institute, said, we need to start getting comfortable with the discomfort.[40] Sociologist Jodi O'Brien, a queer white woman who grew up Mormon, talks about teaching her predominantly white, middle-class students.[41] As they learn about social problems, they often immediately imagine ways to "fix" the problem. This impulse functions alongside the assumption that those who are most directly impacted themselves don't have their own knowledge or solutions. I want to sit on that and think about amplification, solidarity, and then this principle from environmental justice organizing of, "We speak for ourselves." How do we proceed with this as scholar-activists? Amplifying, while not speaking for others.

JULIE: Charles Hale's idea of engaging contradictions in scholar-activism argues that there is going to be messiness and there's going to be contradictions. They were there historically and are still there now. You have to engage with the messiness and violence, the swirling patterns of history. It's connected to Gloria Anzaldúa's sense of the messiness of the borders or the frontiers, which she describes as *neplanta*.[42] From Jackie's view as a community service provider, wrestling with such messiness requires an understanding that diversity exists even within a "single" demographic. She points out differences in languages, cultural practices, and customs among the three COFA nations and between main islands and outer atolls.

JACKIE: Alongside data disaggregation, which we see as a clear path and impetus for public health, public-serving providers, social movements, and other institutions must look inwards—with honesty and self-critique. Rather than treating diversity as an issue of numerical accounting, meaningful inclusion requires an active effort to create working conditions that enable people from different communities to participate. The problem that I still see, especially with some researchers, is the lumping together of AAPI. Even other terms like AANHPI still don't address the heart of the problem. Looking at the different demographics between Asian Americans or even Asians across different groups, like Southeast Asians and other areas of Asia, you can still see there are major health disparities. And when you're now lumping in AANHPI, and including MIs under PIs, you're not only diluting the information, but also missing what the actual health disparities are between the groups.[43] There's a way to be inclusive without being so inclusive that you pretty much bury the other groups.

Let's just say it's a coalition of different groups who are together. In that coalition, who are the main leads? Is there actual representation from the different Pacific Islander or Micronesian groups? Leaders from those communities who are playing a significant role? Or are they just sitting there and being talked to? You could be a group that says that you're AAPI, but if your leadership is primarily Asian and your staff is all Asian except for maybe one or two PI, I really can't say that it's an AAPI-serving organization. If you're going to have something with a Micronesian and/or Pacific Islander perspective, you need to do more than just like, "Oh, we have one token person!" as the answer.

That requires doing actual authentic outreach, and not just serving the interests of the organization. If you expect us to be at the table, don't expect us to do it for free or outside our work hours. Take into consideration that some of us are doing this voluntarily. I've been in spaces where the white leaders are saying, "Oh, we don't have enough people from different communities here, where are they?" And I kind of shot back with, "Why are you expecting them to come to you during *your* time? Like, do you think during this lunch hour there's a way for people to get off from work, come over here, then go back to work? Within an hour?" What efforts are *you* taking to go out there, to tell people about this opportunity? Why should they care about coming to this space?

Conclusion

As feminist geographer Farhana Sultana points out, COVID-19 and climate change are *co-produced crises*, which necessitate intersectional analyses of overlapping and uneven conditions of great harm.[44] Likewise, those communities that are most impacted by these crises often offer the most incisive analysis. Feminist and intergenerational Marshallese climate justice activism and responses to COVID-19 offer important lessons for environmental justice more broadly, including for Asian American activists and scholars. Their justice perspective is not solely about remediation (nuclear or otherwise), but *refusal* of the conditions of violence that shape their lives, homelands, and bodies.

Marshallese health and justice activists' calls for repair and refusal are important *emergent* examples of restorative and reparative climate and health justice. Ultimately, these calls point to the importance of thinking historically and systematically about how decarbonization and demilitarization are linked, in addressing historical and structural violence and vulnerabilities across time and space. Where justice movements matter is in rejecting the naturalization of conditions of disproportionate harm, and in rejecting never-ending death and destruction through a framework of normalization and shifting baselines of acceptable COVID-19 rates, or in the degrees the temperature warmed.[45]

Imagining new directions for Asian American politics from the lessons of Marshallese activism require us to engage with the challenges and potentials of solidarity alongside disaggregation and continual violence, both fast and slow. We believe that at the center of this process is the ethical imperative to broaden our definition of anti-Asian violence to extend beyond the space of hateful incidents to examine structural racism more broadly. Disproportionate death and illness from COVID-19—which hit particularly hard, among others, Southeast Asian factory workers, Filipina nurses, and communities already living with residential and bodily toxicity. Moreover, responses to anti-Asian racism must similarly problematize assimilationist solutions that seek to harness state violence in the name of political recognition. Such refusal is not merely theoretical. The consequences are clear when we consider the push for anti–hate crimes legislation. While seeking to "protect" certain Asian bodies, such policy initiatives overlook the impacts of over-policing on Asian immigrants who are undocumented and working in informal and/or stigmatized industries.[46] Yet as we offer these critiques, we also acknowledge that the labor of critical refusal already exists within Asian American activism networks that emphasize mutual aid and care and in the long-standing struggles of Pacific Islanders, Native Hawaiians, and Indigenous communities for their rights to collective continuance and survivance.

Notes

1 We take inspiration here from Ruth Wilson Gilmore's definition: "Racism, specifically, is the state-sanctioned or extralegal production and exploitation of group-differentiated vulnerability to premature death."

2   This demographic trend does not disaggregate for ethnic, socioeconomic, and other social differences among Asian Americans.
3   In Washington State, for example, Pacific Islanders had COVID-19 cases at nine times the white population, with hospitalization rates ten times higher. Jackson, Lagipoiva Cherelle, "Pacific Islanders in US Hospitalized with Covid-19 at Up to 10 Times the Rate of Other Groups," *The Guardian*, July 26, 2020.
4   Ramirez, Rachel, "How Pacific Islanders Have Been Left to Fend for Themselves in the Pandemic," *Vox*, December 14, 2020, www.vox.com.
5   2021 Unity Summit, "Plenary: Parallel Pandemics," October 27, 2021, https://2021unitysummit.us2.pathable.com.
6   Environmental humanists Joni Adamson and Steven Hartman argue that "in our present COVID-19-affected world, we believe (syndemics) helps illuminate the entangled, rhizomatic connections between climate change and contagions of various kinds, both biological (in the conventional sense of epidemiology) and psychosocial." Adamson, Joni, and Steven Hartman, "From Ecology to Syndemic: Accounting for the Synergy of Epidemics," Bifrost Features, June 8, 2020, https://bifrostonline.org.
7   There is a vast scholarship on these topics. Two places to start are Vicente Diaz's classics: "'To 'P' or Not to 'P'?": Marking the Territory between Pacific Islander and Asian American Studies," *Journal of Asian American Studies* 7, no. 3 (January 2004): 183–208; and Lisa Kahaleole Hall, "Which of These Things Is Not Like the Other: Hawaiians and Other Pacific Islanders Are Not Asian Americans, and All Pacific Islanders Are Not Hawaiian Hall," *American Quarterly* 67, no. 3 (September 2015): 727–747. Diaz was generous in talking to Sze about how to ethically situate this research, which led to restructuring of it entirely.
8   "Bali Principles of Climate Justice," EJnet.org, August 29, 2002, www.ejnet.org; "Principles of Environmental Justice," presented at the First National People of Color Environmental Leadership Summit, Washington, DC, October 24–27, 1991, www.ejnet.org.
9   Irfan, Umair, "Why the US Bears the Most Responsibility for Climate Change, in One Chart," *Vox*, December 12, 2019, www.vox.com.
10 Crawford, Neta, "Pentagon Fuel Use, Climate Change, and the Costs of War," Watson Institute, Brown University, November 13, 2019.
11 Shaw, Vivian, "We Are Already Living Together," *Precarious Belongings: Affect and Nationalism in Asia* (2017): 59–76; Shaw, Vivian, "Strategies of Ambivalence: Cultures of Liberal Antifa in Japan," *Radical History Review* 2020, no. 138 (2020): 145–170; Kuo, Rachel, Amy Zhang, Vivian Shaw, and Cynthia Wang, "#FeministAntibodies: Asian American Media in the Time of Coronavirus," *Social Media + Society* 6, no. 4 (2020): 2056305120978364.
12 Tang, Eric, "A Gulf Unites Us: The Vietnamese Americans of Black New Orleans East," *American Quarterly* 63, no. 1 (2011): 117–149; Kim, Nadia Y., *Refusing Death: Immigrant Women and the Fight for Environmental Justice in LA* (Stanford University Press, 2021).

13 Tai, Stephanie, "Environmental Hazards and the Richmond Laotian American Community: A Case Study in Environmental Justice," *Asian Law Journal* 6, no. 189 (1999): 189–207.
14 Man, Simeon, "Anti-Asian Violence and US Imperialism," *Race & Class* 62, no. 2 (2020): 24–33, 26.
15 STOP AAPI HATE, *Community Reports to Stop AAPI Hate: 2020–2022 Key Findings*, 2023, https://stopaapihate.org.
16 Schlund-Vials, Cathy J., "Silent Spring and Biological Annihilators: Re-seeing America's Pacific Century through Environmental Catastrophe," *Verge: Studies in Global Asias* 7, no. 1 (Spring): 21–31.
17 Shah, Bindi V., *Laotian Daughters: Working toward Community, Belonging, and Environmental Justice* (Temple University Press, 2012).
18 Bevacqua, Michael Lujan, and Isa Ua Ceallaigh Bowman, "9. I Tano'i Chamorro / Chamorro Land: Situating Sustainabilities through Spatial Justice and Cultural Perpetuation," in *Sustainability: Approaches to Environmental Justice and Social Power*, edited by Julie Sze (New York University Press, 2018), 222–245; see also Sisavath, Davorn, "The US Secret War in Laos: Constructing an Archive from Military Waste," *Radical History Review* 2019, no. 133 (January 2019): 103; Nguyen, Viet Thanh, "From Colonialism to Covid: Viet Thanh Nguyen on the Rise of Anti-Asian Violence," *The Guardian*, April 3, 2021, www.theguardian.com.
19 Hunte, Tracie, and Gabrielle Berbey, "4 Percent of Nurses, 31.5 Percent of Deaths: Why Filipino Nurses Have Been Disproportionately Affected by the Coronavirus Pandemic," *The Atlantic*, February 25, 2021, www.theatlantic.com; Choy, Catherine Ceniza, *Empire of Care: Nursing and Migration in Filipino American History* (Duke University Press, 2003); Nasol, K., and V. Francisco-Menchavez, "Filipino Home Care Workers: Invisible Frontline Workers in the COVID-19 Crisis in the United States," *American Behavioral Sciences* 65, no. 10 (September 2021):1365–1383.
20 Jackie and Vivian had already been working together for several months on a separate research project related to COVID-19.
21 The dearth of demographic data makes it difficult for the organization to know a more precise number of the population of COFA citizens in the region.
22 Walters, Karina L., Selina A. Mohammed, Teresa Evans-Cambell, Ramona E Beltrán, David H. Chae, and Bonnie Duran, "Bodies Don't Just Tell Stories, They Tell Histories: Embodiment of Historical Trauma among American Indians and Alaska Natives," *Du Bois Review* 8, no. 1 (April 2011): 179–189.
23 Wong-Padoongpatt, G., A. Barrita, A. King, and M. Strong, "The Slow Violence of Racism on Asian Americans during the COVID-19 Pandemic," *Frontiers in Public Health* (2022): 1–15.
24 Slow violence is "a violence that is neither spectacular nor instantaneous, but rather incremental and accretive, its calamitous repercussions playing out across a range of temporal scale." Nixon, Rob, *Slow Violence and the Environmentalism of the Poor* (Harvard University Press, 2011), 2; Dillon, Lindsey, and Julie Sze, "Equality in the Air We Breathe: Police Violence, Pollution, and the Politics of

Sustainability," in *Sustainability: Approaches to Environmental Justice and Social Power*, edited by Julie Sze (New York University Press, 2018), 246–270.
25   Ibid.
26   Hilgers, Lauren, "How Two Waves of Coronavirus Cases Swept through the Texas Panhandle," *New Yorker*, July 10, 2020, www.newyorker.com; Little Laos on the Prairie, "APAHM and the Erasure of Laotian America," May 21, 2020, https://littlelaosontheprairie.org; Berta, Ola Gunhildrud, Elise Berman, and Albious Latior, "COVID-19 and the Marshallese," *Oceana* 90, no. S1 (December 2020): 53–59.
27   Hilgers, How Two Waves of Coronavirus Cases Swept through the Texas Panhandle."
28   Martinez, Doreen E., "The Right to Be Free of Fear: Indigeneity and the United Nations," *Wicazo Sa Review* 29, no. 2 (Fall 2014): 63–87.
29   Tau Lee, Pam, "The Struggle to Abolish Environmental and Economic Racism: Asian Radical Imagining from the Homeland to the Front Line," in *Contemporary Asian American Activism: Building Movements for Liberation*, edited by Diane C. Fujino and Robyn Magalit Rodriguez (University of Washington Press, 2022).
30   See the work of the California Health Nail Salon Collaborative, www.cahealthynailsalons.org.
31   Táíwò, Olúfẹ́mi O, "Our Coronavirus Failure Will Be Our Climate Failure," *Aljazeera*, April 22, 2020, www.aljazeera.com; Táíwò, Olúfẹ́mi O., and Beba Cibralic, "The Case for Climate Reparations," *Foreign Policy*, October 10, 2020, https://foreignpolicy.com.
32   Specifically, he rejects "racial capitalism's ideological double-move that extracts the climate refugee from the broader histories of colonial war and migration, fixing the refugee as a figure that is both a risk and a supplement to the political order." Neel Ahuja, "Race, Human Security, and the Climate Refugee," *English Language Notes* 54, no. 2 (2016): 25–32.
33   Táíwò, Olúfẹ́mi O., "Climate Apartheid Is the Coming Police Violence Crisis," *Dissent*, August 12, 2020.
34   Ahuja, Neel, *Planetary Specters: Race, Migration, and Climate Change in the Twenty-First Century* (University of North Carolina Press, 2021).
35   For more on the British immigrant rights slogan, see Patel, Ian Sanjay, *We're Here Because You Were There: Immigration and the End of Empire* (Verso Books, 2021).
36   Sze, Julie, "Climate Justice, Satire, and Hothouse Earth," in *The Routledge Companion to Contemporary Art, Visual Culture, and Climate Change* (Routledge, 2021), 173–181.
37   Movement Generation, "From Banks and Tanks to Cooperation and Caring: A Strategic Framework for a Just Transition," 2016, https://movementgeneration.org.
38   Wong, Diane, "The Future Is Ours to Build: Asian American Abolitionist Counterstories for Black Liberation," *Politics, Groups, and Identities* 10, no. 3 (2022): 493–502.
39   Pulido, Laura, "Flint, Environmental Racism, and Racial Capitalism," *Capitalism Nature Socialism* 27, no. 3 (2016): 1–16; Pellow, David N., "Toward a Critical

Environmental Justice Studies: Black Lives Matter as an Environmental Justice Challenge," *Du Bois Review: Social Science Research on Race* 13, no. 2 (2016): 221–236; Bradshaw, Elizabeth A., "Do Prisoners' Lives Matter? Examining the Intersection of Punitive Policies, Racial Disparities and COVID-19 as State Organized Race Crime," *State Crime Journal* 10, no. 1 (2021): 16–44.

40 Echo-Hawk, Abigail, "Data Justice," presentation for the National Academy of Medicine, 2023, https://nam.edu.

41 O'Brien, Jodi, "Sociology as an Epistemology of Contradiction," *Sociological Perspectives* 52, no. 1 (2009): 5–22.

42 Anzaldúa, Gloria, "Chicana Artists: Exploring Nepantla, el lugar de la frontera," *NACLA Report on the Americas* 27, no. 1 (1993): 37–45.

43 Nguyen, K. H., K. P. Lew, and A. N. Trivedi, "Trends in Collection of Disaggregated Asian American, Native Hawaiian, and Pacific Islander Data: Opportunities in Federal Health Surveys," *American Journal of Public Health* 112, no. 10 (October 2022): 1429–1435.

44 Sultana, Farhana, "Political Ecology II: Conjunctures, Crises, and Critical Publics," *Progress in Human Geography* 45, no. 6 (2021): 1721–1730.

45 Roberts, David, "The Scariest Thing about Global Warming (and Covid-19)," *Vox*, December 4, 2020, www.vox.com.

46 As sociologist Elena Shih documents, within an incarceration-to-deportation pipeline, police raids on Asian massage parlors have led to violence, and in some cases, death, for low-income immigrant women. Shih, Elena, *Manufacturing Freedom: Sex Work, Anti-trafficking Rehab, and the Racial Wages of Rescue* (University of California Press, 2023).

11

Resist Recycle Regenerate

A Conversation around Sustainable Leadership and Regenerative Art Practices

JA BULSOMBUT AND KRISTIN CHANG

Confetti explodes into the sky and rains down onto the pavement, gathering in the gutters as lion dancers roll their drums through the street, preparing to bless the next storefront. Children trail after them, followed by their elders, both pointing at the dancers as they work together as one, maneuvering the lion head as it bows and flits its eyes. Every year, the Lunar New Year parade symbolizes a cycle of renewal—the demons of the old year are left behind, and the new year is ushered in, with an understanding that the cycle will continue to repeat itself. The five fellows of the Resist Recycle Regenerate (RRR) program gather at this celebration to enact a cycle of their own: with our brooms, red jumpsuits, and butterfly nets, we go out onto the streets to sweep confetti and envision it in new forms. By centering Chinatown youths in the collection and recycling of confetti and other reusable materials, the RRR program refuses the narrative that Manhattan Chinatown and other working-class immigrant neighborhoods are disposable and sites in need of cleanup and investment. RRR sees Chinatown not in these static, quantitative terms but rather as fluid and alive, comprised of communities and their livelihoods. By including multiple generations in the process of creating art through recycled materials, RRR seeks to imagine an intergenerational future where the existing residents of Chinatown are its innovators. Though sustainability and ecological justice is typically represented as a raceless and classless issue, the program draws from the existing knowledge and livelihoods of Chinatown's residents to inform sustainable art-making.

We have joined this cycle of celebration as undergraduate students from Sarah Lawrence College seeking a way to connect with and learn from place-based organizing and joyful community-building. At Sarah Lawrence, we co-led a student organization for Asian American students and found that the institutional environment was often at odds with our goals and values. After a fellow Sarah Lawrence student urged us to apply to an open call for Resist Recycle Regenerate fellows, we found a grassroots space of intergenerational dialogue and belonging.

Resist Recycle Regenerate

Resist Recycle Regenerate is a program for women and nonbinary folks aged 16–21 that intersects art and activism through building youth-centric leadership within the Chinatown community. RRR was founded by artist Juliet Philips and Mei Lum of the W.O.W. Project, a community-based initiative in Chinatown that seeks to reinvent, preserve, and encourage Chinatown's creative culture and history through arts, culture, and activism. Formed in 2017, the RRR program addresses and subverts the history of patriarchal leadership in Manhattan Chinatown. RRR's youth mentorship model promotes young women as leaders and mentors to inspire growth and leadership development in their peers through art-making. Through the years, fellows can become program leaders, mentoring and guiding the next cohort of younger fellows.

The program is organized into three main phases: in the first phase, former fellows teach the incoming cohort how to make paper out of recycled confetti collected during the annual Lunar New Year parade. In its first two years, RRR invited volunteers to help collect discarded confetti fireworks, engaging the community to join in the process of recycling confetti into new creative materials. The first phase also consists of inviting guest practicing artists to teach various art-making skills such as paper-cutting and calligraphy, as well as guest speakers who lead workshops on the history and lineage of Asian American activism and Chinatown movements. In its third year, RRR fellows worked collaboratively to build a lion head for the Lunar New Year parade, using confetti collected by fellows from previous years.

In the second phase of the program, the program leaders teach the current fellows how to facilitate and lead papermaking workshops for the community. In the past, we have conducted fellow-led workshops for seniors at Henry St. Settlement's Abrons Art Center,

LGBT+ organizations including Q-Wave, and other community institutions. Fellows have also applied their acquired knowledge on the history of Chinatown and Asian American activism by participating in actions and rallies in the community. For instance, RRR participated in a protest in the fall of 2019 with members of the Chinatown Art Brigade (CAB) to advocate against the construction of four new jails in Manhattan Chinatown. For the protest, RRR fellows created posters with recycled paper and participated in No New Jail protests in Chinatown, linking the youths' use of recycled materials in their art to direct action and political impact. In 2021, youth fellows participated in rallies and spoke against rising anti-Asian violence.

The third phase of the program synthesizes the skills, experiences, and interests fostered throughout the year. Program leaders guide the current cohort through the process of creating final projects that incorporate the handmade confetti paper and the art-making skills learned during the first phase of the program. These final projects engage with themes of personal and collective migration stories, Chinatown history, daughterhood, and diasporic un/belonging. Fellows have the unique opportunity to share and discuss their projects with the community by displaying their work in the store during the final showcase, and by hosting a digital showcase. The showcase provides a space for the fellows and program leaders to collectively reflect on their growth and development as artists, young mentors, and community members who are invested in the past, present, and future of Chinatown. Our leadership model is based on the idea that relationships are long-term and sustainable, and that no one is disposable.

The three tenets of RRR are Resist, Recycle, and Regenerate, all three of which guide the program. The fellows participate in political action that resists gentrification, forces of displacement, and state-sanctioned racial violence. By centering unwanted and typically forgotten materials in their personal artwork and political projects, RRR foreground the tenets of recycling and sustainability as a creative and innovative practice, necessary for sustainable and intergenerational futures. The program also highlights the idea of recycling by incorporating collected and "unwanted" materials and reinventing them for new purposes, creating a cycle of regeneration rather than disposability. Similarly, RRR's leadership model mirrors this idea of sustainability, longevity, and lineage, as fellows are given the opportunity to return as leaders and each generation of fellows shapes and leads the next. Regeneration is embodied by the program's structure, as well as by the act of alchemizing discarded confetti into community-centered art that interacts with, sustains, and empowers the community.

In April 2021, during the fourth year of the RRR program, former fellows and program leaders Ja Bulsombut and Kristin Chang met in Wing On Wo's basement studio, the site of many RRR workshops, to discuss the personal and collective impact of the RRR program on their own growth from student activists to movement artists, the importance of regeneration in art-making and interpersonal relationships, and the radical possibilities of community spaces that are led by youths. We have chosen the format of a recorded conversation because it is the dynamic form of storytelling that RRR is based on. Throughout the program, oral storytelling and oral histories are a community-building practice that bridges generations and fosters closeness among the fellows. For example, one of our first sessions is a walking oral history tour of Chinatown led by Gary Lum, Mei Lum's father, in which memory and place live through dialogue. Furthermore, the fellows give oral storytelling presentations of their own lives to share with the rest of the cohort, creating a space of fluidity and porosity, in which experiencing the story and the memory in community with others is as important as the story itself. A conversation eschews the authority and rigidity of written conclusions and instead seeks to be more inclusive, collaborative, and open to possibility and new directions.

Storytelling as a Lineage-Building Practice

In the first part of our conversation, we discuss the significance of storytelling in empowering our youth fellows, as well as the core tenet of recycling that threads through all of RRR's work, both in its art-making practices and in building a lineage of youth leaders who mentor and guide the next generation, allowing the program to be sustained entirely by its youths. In centering youth narratives about their relationship to Chinatown, the program looks at the neighborhood through a lens of intimacy and familiarity rather than othering it as dirty and uncared for.

KRISTIN: In the first phase of your first year of the program, we invited teaching artists who were all women and all part of this diaspora. And then during the Lunar New Year, we went out and collected confetti from the streets and then drew new sheets of paper from it. We taught paper-making workshops to the community. For the final project stage, we used the handmade paper and incorporated it into our own personal projects. I remember that the first time we recycled confetti into paper, it was very exciting. We didn't expect that color! I remember that all our paper was purple, this very specific purple that I'd never really seen elsewhere and that couldn't be replicated except with that specific mixture of confetti. In terms of how the community responded, I think the first year was quite intimate.

JA: We did all our community workshops in W.O.W.'s basement studio.

KRISTIN: I think people responded well; they were super interested in our work. I think when we went out that first year during the parade, there was a lot of curiosity about what we were doing.

JA: There was a lot of engagement, and even children helped us collect discarded confetti.

KRISTIN: Oh, yeah. The children helped us scoop confetti, and we recruited people at the parade to help us in this process. It felt like a communal process of recycling. That was also the first time we were more outward facing, and we were trying to engage with other people in the work. I remember a mom and her young daughter filling plastic bags for us and just having fun with it, tossing the confetti on the ground into the air. It really reminded me of the woman-centeredness of RRR, and how celebration and joy was as important as what we were collecting.

JA: The program began as kind of introspective, with community-building among ourselves, and then that transition to more community-facing work felt really important. We knew we had this skill to create paper from confetti, and we wanted to teach it to someone else. We're giving back to the community in this way and recycling the knowledge back out. But the program was also building our leadership, our sense of being part of a practice and part of a community.

KRISTIN: That's really beautiful. How do you see the program in relation to the idea of recycling and regeneration?

JA: The most obvious part about recycling is that we literally recycle confetti and regenerate it into new forms. Regeneration is also related to the intergenerational aspect of the program and how RRR fellows return each year to become leaders and then can return again to be program coordinators. And so we're all tethered to each other in some way.

KRISTIN: Yes, you're right. Our leadership model emphasizes that we're all interconnected, that none of us can be discarded: leadership as care. The fact that we take a material that's seen as useless or as waste and think about new ways of using it to engage our community through art-making and to give it new life [reflects that interconnectedness]. I remember that when we first picked up the confetti, we were surprised to see that when it was soaked in water, the dye washed off the confetti and revealed itself to be newsprint. We realized that the confetti itself was already a recycled material from Chinese newspapers. We were recycling a material that had already been recycled many times, and we were just one part of its many transformations. Chinese newspapers are such an important part of the community, and to think of its lifespan from conveying knowledge to being thrown in celebration to being recycled again into new paper for the youths to shape is fascinating. We are creating just one more iteration of this material that has a life of its own again and again and again and again.

JA: What do you think about our decision in the third year to use the confetti to make a paper lion head for the parade?

KRISTIN: It was such a collaborative process, it was so much about accountability to each other. Because we were all building the lion head together, it was so communal. The eyes, the ears, the skeleton frame, all of it had to be created in concert with each other. It was about communication and unity and feeling like we were collectively giving birth to this beautiful object. To me, accountability is emotional, and not just about being obligated or having to finish the assignment. It's a way that we care for each other and respect and listen to each other's wants and needs.

JA: I agree. If I remember correctly, the lion head took around five months to build, and it took commitment beyond the three hours allotted each week on Saturdays. Even when we didn't require it, all the fellows took turns staying behind to work on the lion head as well as coming in on other evenings of the week. Commitment, then, is not simply a matter of just showing up when you're asked to, but rather an understanding of knowing what needs to be done and putting in the work in order to make it happen. An agreement was made to build the lion head together, and that was something we all knew we had to honor. I think that sense of collective investment also applies to W.O.W. as a whole: it's not like we do our parts in our respective positions and programs and then leave, but instead there is this sense of long-term investment. We all feel like we have a stake in W.O.W.'s future and either stay on or remain involved in some way. I think this feeling is cultivated by W.O.W.'s ethos that people aren't disposable and are always welcome back, which I believe is so integral to creating a sense of belonging that is rooted in collective practice, in building together.

KRISTIN: There's something really beautiful about building it together—I think rather than an individual sense of ownership, which is how we are taught to relate to the world and to objects, we were collectively shaping the confetti and making decisions about the lion head. It's not owned by any one person. And the fellows used confetti collected entirely by previous years' fellows, so this lion head relied on a lineage of past fellows. It's a collaboration with the previous generations of fellows who collected the confetti, and there's a sense of collective ownership.

JA: That lion head will also be passed down through the generations. Every year that RRR goes out onto the streets to celebrate Lunar New Year, we get to be part of that new cycle. It feels especially important and empowering that the fellows were building something to perform in together, since lion dancers are typically men. That RRR, as a group of young women, are performing the lion dance felt subversive.

KRISTIN: Yes, I agree! It's because Chinatown is historically patriarchal, and cleaning is a gendered form of labor, so going out onto the street to sweep up confetti and reuse the material felt like we were making Chinese American women visible in a very public way. The parade usually has many crews of young men performing lion dances, and RRR's presence, along with our partnership with an all-women lion dance crew, subverted the traditional makeup of the festival and the visibility of folks in the parade where the confetti is thrown. While building the lion head together, it felt like relief from academic or institutional spaces. We could tell stories about ourselves and shape what we wanted to include in our narratives. We held space for fellows and leaders to give personal presentations on their histories and their families' histories, and it allowed for vulnerability, connection, and community-building.

JA: I've always loved how communal lion dances are. I thought the fellows' performance in front of the W.O.W. storefront offered a different way of interacting with the community than our papermaking workshops—it facilitated collective celebration and joy. The communal is literally embodied in the performance itself. And this sense of the collective is emphasized in every other aspect of the program too. Like you said, RRR holds space for us to tell our own stories, and I think it matters that these stories are shared communally. Storytelling has always been a communal practice: our lives don't exist in isolation but are deeply intertwined, and are always part of broader narratives and histories. In their performance, the fellows are telling the story of defeating Nian together.

KRISTIN: The lion head felt like a culmination of our growing collaboration over the years. To perform a lion dance, you have to literally share a body. Someone is the head and someone is the tail, and you have to move in sync and have a bodily connection to each other. It shows how symbiotic the fellows were, and that interconnectedness defines the fellows' relationships not only to each other but to their environment and to the confetti collected from the neighborhood.

Rethinking Leadership as a Practice of Holding Space

In the following part of our conversation, we discuss how RRR's intergenerational and nonhierarchical leadership model differentiates it from other institutional and community spaces, and how the cultivation of such a model is informed by the program's emphasis on community relationships and place-based work and art. This speaks to the idea that people, places, and objects are not disposable, and that sustainability and environmental justice requires a reframing of how we value and relate to one another.

JA: I've always liked what you said about how there are different kinds of leadership styles, as opposed to the traditional idea of leadership that celebrates authority, confidence and assertiveness, traits that we are often told to measure ourselves against. Right from the start, when we were still fellows ourselves, the program never demanded that of us. I thought Mei and Juliet, as the founders of RRR, gave us such a good example of what leadership could look like. It's not just one person running the whole show, you know? And I do think that we also complemented each other really well—we each brought something different to the space. I wanted to make sure that we in turn were also cultivating a warm and open space for the later fellows, where they didn't feel like they had to be a certain way. I was also conscious of the fact that we were also modeling leadership for the fellows ourselves.

KRISTIN: I always thought of leadership as very hierarchical—like a position you have to earn and deserve. And then when you're in that position, you have this earned power over other people, which I think is kind of dangerous. But like you said, that's the way we're taught leadership, and I think with RRR it's different. It's more like care. It's like, I care about this program. That's why I'm here, not because I have the best resume, and I took the most AP classes, and I have the highest GPA, and therefore I have earned this position of power. It is still challenging for me to think about leadership as a kind of service because it's very hard to reverse the idea of leadership that's been cultivated in us.

JA: Even thinking about having to TA [be a teaching assistant] next year, I keep asking myself, God—do I have to put myself in a position of authority? How do I come across as someone who is authoritative and knows what they're doing? These were questions I didn't really have to ask when we were running RRR—there wasn't any pressure to have to embody that, even if we inevitably felt that way in the beginning. It felt like we were in a casual and informal space among peers. By the time we became coordinators, we were already very comfortable in the space and in the position we occupied, which to me is the beauty of RRR. But I like what you said about leadership as care.

KRISTIN: Yeah, I wish it was like that in other spaces. But speaking of moving onto the coordinator role in the third year of the program, I guess what was exciting was the fact that every year is unpredictable and new, because we were placed into this new completely undiscovered role. As coordinators, it was interesting to be a little bit distant or removed from the fellows, because while we're still part of the weekly sessions, we took a step back, and we had to trust that the helm of this program and the vision for it will be guided by this next generation.

JA: Yes! Angela Chan and Bonnie Chen transitioned into program leaders. It was also interesting to see how they grew into the role, how they complemented each other, and what their version of leadership looked like.

KRISTIN: Yes, that kind of growth and confidence, I felt like Mei and Juliet were conscious about building it into the structure of the program. I think a lot about "Asian American" as an intentional identification rather than this kind of passive thing that we just *are* from purely a demographic standpoint—which obviously affects how we think about solidarity. That was part of the issue for us when we ran APICAD (Asian Pacific Islander Coalition for Action and Diversity) during our time at Sarah Lawrence. It was a struggle, and we faltered a lot. We weren't sure what our vision was, and joining RRR—it was like night and day, because there was a real connection to the community. W.O.W. is very place-based, very situated within the Chinatown community. There's a strong mission and ethos behind us, whereas what we were doing with APICAD felt a little detached and ungrounded.

JA: I felt like I was floundering a lot, and that was definitely because of what you described—feeling detached. I also didn't feel like we had a model to look up to learn from in terms of leadership, which I think is maybe an outcome of trying to organize without being grounded in context or community. Joining W.O.W. and RRR, because both were so grounded in the context of the Chinatown neighborhood and had such a strong mission, I felt like we had so many people to look to, and it was meaningful to see how they did and talked about their work. We're not from Chinatown, but forming those kinds of connections and being able to model our intentions and agendas after folks who have been doing this work for years was really important for me. Having movement elders is so key.

KRISTIN: That's true. You're right that RRR created a model for a space where you could be vulnerable. It fostered a deep sense of connection, compared to what we were used to in a more institutional setting. I think that being within an institution really limits what you're able to do, because of funding, and therefore inevitably part of your ethos is attached to the institution. I think with RRR there was more room to create your own visions for what's possible in terms of building a sense of a collective. Creating leadership models or leadership pipelines for young people to be outside of an institution allows for much more freedom, and the work ends up being more interesting and more innovative, because you aren't limited or tied to bureaucracy or academic institutions.

JA: Yeah, that's a great point. I felt like our conversations at Sarah Lawrence, at APICAD, sometimes felt a little abstract, whereas at W.O.W. your personal experiences are tied to larger histories, and rather than talking about "gentrification" and "displacement" from within the academy, you get to learn—with a much greater sense of urgency and understanding of the stakes—about present-day issues from people who have been on the ground and doing the work for a very long time.

KRISTIN: The fact that W.O.W. as a whole is tied to community arts is really important. That the program created this low-stakes experimental arts practice as a way of exploring all these issues is super important. Again, it doesn't feel abstract or like something we're just simply intellectualizing. We're together in this space, and there's an actual creative product that's coming out of it, which allows us to explore these topics more deeply. It's a very tactile way of interacting with these materials within the context of the community.

JA: Yeah, definitely—that also made me think a lot about youths, and youth leadership. I think nowadays it's really important that you can come into the RRR space without having had to be tuned into social justice jargon or discourse beforehand. Of course that language is important and helps us make sense of the world, but the program, in only asking you to be open and committed, highlights that you don't really need discourse or theory to understand what's happening in your neighborhood and community.

KRISTIN: I'm also thinking about the first year where we did those personal presentations, which wasn't part of the curriculum but spontaneously kind of happened. I thought it was important that everyone who was involved in the program did those, including the visiting artists who spoke about themselves, their work, and practice in a very open way. There weren't guidelines. What's so beautiful is that it's come to be incorporated into future years as an actual part of the art-making and exploring. I love that you're bringing your full self into the space, that in other spaces would be kind of pushed away or put under and caged into very specific terms of labels. I remember thinking that our community is so incredibly diverse and that we each have our own stories. I think storytelling as the center of our program is also really important and allows for nuance in a way that other spaces might shy away from. When we invited the fellows to make personal presentations with photos and slides about their lives, I loved hearing about how they related to their lineage and to Chinatown. Everyone's migration history and relationship to art and art-making was so different and yet unified by the desire to pay homage in some way. It was really moving to hear about the silences in our histories, and what our families didn't talk about. The RRR space could hold those silences and help us approach our stories and the absences in our lineages.

JA: I agree. Through collective storytelling, we learn how our own personal histories and experiences fit within both the broader context of Manhattan Chinatown and Asian America. In this way, we're able to speak from a place of community and knowledge of our collective histories and lineages, rather than just empty discourse.

KRISTIN: That's how I feel about how RRR addresses ecological justice. Sometimes, that discourse can feel very removed from immigrant experience and from working-class communities. The idea of environmental justice is very white-washed in the mainstream. But RRR brings ecological concerns into discussions about our relationship to the community, and grounds ecological justice in the realities of race and immigrant communities. It also centers youth and intergenerational relationships in those conversations and practices.

JA: Chinatown's association with dirtiness isn't inherent, but rather because Chinatowns in the United States have historically been allocated fewer resources. People often say this about neighborhoods of color, that they're "dirty" or "run-down," but the reality is that they've received less support from the city. Gentrification and displacement are products of city neglect, and sanitation problems are a product of city neglect. The city doesn't have the solution. It's the ethos of RRR to think about community-based solutions and being in conversation with all of these issues because their causes are all one underlying problem: political systems are inadequate and Chinatown is marginalized within it. By really centering the community in RRR and interacting with the neighborhood during confetti collection, the program pushes fellows to engage with the streets and the neighborhood itself in a really concrete way.

KRISTIN: That's an aspect I hadn't really thought of before, that stigma of waste and dirtiness being inherent to Chinatown. It reminded me of Omer Fast's exhibit at the James Cohan Gallery that RRR fellows protested in the first year, where the artist created a caricature of Chinatown inside the gallery, and there was an installation with newspapers and a broken ATM. It's really meaningful that RRR was there to protest against this caricature of Chinatown as a place full of "junk" or "cheap things," to engage in this way, where broken or old things aren't just necessarily disposable. It really showcases resourcefulness in a way, working with found objects. And they were resisting this image of Chinatown shaped by historical racism and classism in a very physical, embodied way by being present and exercising their voices and becoming a new generation of leaders who are trying to conceive of and use traditional materials in a generative and community-centered way. Our action against the gallery was protesting the displacing force of white-box art galleries that see Chinatown purely as cheap real estate, and it was also them drawing from their identities as young immigrant women to reverse power dynamics and racist perceptions.

JA: It pushes back against the white-washing of ecological justice because it's not just applying policies that are so completely removed from the reality of the neighborhood; it's not a top-down process. It's about going into the community and seeing at the ground level what's available and what's important, and creating from there. We've also integrated that into the community's celebratory process by collecting confetti during the parade. It makes the process of recycling part of the festivities and part of celebration rather than centering the narrative of uncleanliness and hopelessness.

KRISTIN: I agree! It makes an act of recycling into an act of joy and celebration. My perception before RRR was that ecological justice only happened in wealthy neighborhoods. It was tied to the word "clean." But RRR demonstrated that actually, it's the neighborhoods that are most vulnerable that are most affected by ecological issues.

JA: There's a sense of reclamation—reclaiming Chinatown as a space of joy, community, and collective action—and that's where the concept of recycling and regeneration came out of: the specific context of increasing gentrification within Chinatown, the displacement of families and businesses that not only have been in the neighborhood for generations but have also made the community the way it is! The program, in bringing together the process of collecting and recycling confetti with its contemplation of diasporic belonging, collective migration histories, and displacement, points to the fact that such questions are inseparable from that of ecological justice. Racial justice, immigration justice, and ecological justice are intertwined: by taking part in No New Jails marches and other protests in Chinatown, I think RRR highlights that structural inequalities make some people more vulnerable to displacement and to environmental disasters. It's a matter of who is most deeply affected and will be displaced by climate change. Marginalized communities in the United States and countries in the Global South will and already are bearing the brunt of climate change. It's their homes, communities, and livelihoods. A good friend of mine in my PhD cohort, Ki'Amber Thompson, is doing research on bridging abolition with environmental justice. She argues that prisons and policing, as toxic and harmful institutions, should also be brought under the purview of environmental justice.[1] How can sustainable communities develop and thrive when people are treated as disposable? I think a lot can come out of RRR exploring its relationship to abolition. Ki'Amber and I also talk about the necessity of imagination, of the work of world-building, after critique. We want to dismantle systems, but we also have to build: what do we want to build? I think W.O.W. and

RRR have always been engaged with that kind of visionary work in some way.

KRISTIN: I totally agree, and love that RRR approaches this work with a sense of creativity and community. It's about regeneration and holding onto hope and imagining our future. It's not apocalyptic or pessimistic, and it's intergenerational. I'm thinking about the recycling practices our elders do. I think typically we tend to dismiss ecological justice as something that only young people have to deal with and find the solutions for, but I love that idea of it being intergenerational, and drawing from our elders' way of life. It challenges the idea that innovation is only for the young.

JA: One hundred percent! RRR challenges the temporality of ecological justice as something that is in the future tense. What is being done right now? The way RRR recycles confetti during the Lunar New Year parade is very communal and celebratory. I like that it's culturally specific and the way it cultivates this sense of collective ownership among the fellows. There is so much possibility for this program as it continues to expand.

KRISTIN: There is so much more room to think about solidarity practices and how RRR can show up on an even larger scale. It's already made such an impact on us, and I'm excited to see similar programs implemented in other Chinatowns in the future. I don't think I've ever been in an environment like RRR, where the leadership is sustainable, and everyone is treated as integral to the program and to the community. It was very much an experiment, and it felt like we were forging a new model of what leadership and learning could look like.

JA: Yes, definitely. RRR and W.O.W. as a whole cultivate and nourish long-term relationships, even if we're not directly involved with the core activities anymore. It still feels like we're part of a lineage, and that we are still growing and learning alongside new fellows. Our first-year showcase was titled "Roots," and that idea still resonates. RRR allowed me to set down roots.

KRISTIN: Same here. It's transformed the trajectory of my own life and how I think about sustainability. Not only in thinking about materials, but how we can work sustainably to envision our futures.

JA: Yeah, and to think about sustainability and ecological justice in the *now*. Not as a part of some far-off utopian future but rather as work that is currently being done in the moment. In a way, it asks us to be accountable: what am I doing now?

Looking toward the Future

In the wake of the pandemic, RRR had to pivot to the digital space. Though our work is still place-based, centering Chinatown youths in the creation of installation artwork for Wing On Wo's storefront, we were limited in the ways that we could gather and hold physical space. Furthermore, concerns about anti-Asian hate crimes and the desire for political education shifted RRR's conversations and increased a sense of urgency in our work. Due to economic hardship for Chinatown's residents, the importance of collaboration and collective action have been more important than ever. Accountability and collaboration have sustained the community through business relief funds and free meal programs. Tackling environmental justice draws from those same communal relationships and the sense of interconnectedness to one another. The coronavirus has shown us that none of us are isolated individuals, and that there are limits and dangers to Western ideas of individualism. Chinatown's communal responses to the pandemic and its crises demonstrated the essential nature of collaboration for our collective survival.

COVID-19 has raised important questions about environmental justice and about who society has decided is essential and worthy of saving, and who is considered expendable. Many Chinatown residents are essential workers who have had to work in life-risking conditions. It feels increasingly important to center the residents whose labor is constantly rendered invisible, especially when it is that labor that keeps the city running.

Youth conversations about anti-Asian narratives, how they fit into larger structures of racial oppression, and the importance of political education to ground our understanding of these incidents have led RRR into a crucial new direction. As the program continues to evolve to address the needs of young people and encourage them as leaders who are making important connections between all these issues, we hope to see the program collaborate even more with other organizations and direct political actions. RRR has always been about long-term investment in and relationship with youths, and we hope to balance the work of addressing precarity and urgency in the Covid era with building sustainable solutions for the future.

Note

1 Thompson, Ki'Amber T., "Prisons, Policing, and Pollution: Toward an Abolitionist Framework within Environmental Justice," Senior Thesis, Pomona College, 2018.

12

Creating and Sustaining Chinatown

Gardens and the Right to Los Angeles

FRANCES HUYNH

Tòhng Yàhn Gāai was what we once called where we lived: "China-People Street." Later, we mimicked Demon talk and wrote down only Wàh Fauh—"China-Town." The difference is obvious: the people disappeared.
—Excerpt from "Translations" by Wing Tek Lum

In front of Pauline's apartment sits a raised plot of dirt overflowing with the green leaves of sweet potato plants. Vivian and I stand there, holding onto reused plastic grocery bags from her kitchen. Pauline starts to slowly cut off different sections of leaves with a large pair of scissors. "These are the pretty ones," she points out to us in Cantonese, "because they have no 窿 (holes)." To cut the leafy greens, you get rid of the hard part of the stem, or you can keep the stems to eat with the leaves. In a few days, they will all grow back. While she gifts us her garden's harvest, I am reminded of something she often says during our walks throughout Los Angeles Chinatown: "你幫人. 人幫你. (You help people. People help you.)" It seems so simple: I help you, and you help me. Yet, these words highlight the importance of compassion, accountability, and mutual aid, particularly in a neighborhood where socioeconomic and health disparities and the threat of gentrification grow. To embody this line of thinking and have it manifest in everyday life can be truly transformative in ensuring communities are sustainable and equitable. It serves as both a reminder and a call to action, especially when we are confronted with the question: what is the future of Chinatown?

A Gentrifying Los Angeles Chinatown

Gentrification threatens Chinatown's existence as a working-class immigrant neighborhood. Chinatown where it stands today is a historical ethnic enclave that the Chinese American community (re)built in the 1930s after being displaced from its original 1880s location by Union Station. In a rapidly industrializing Los Angeles in the 1930s, the construction of this railroad terminal came at the expense of the "old Chinatown" community. In a rapidly gentrifying Los Angeles today, the development of market-rate projects, rent increases, and evictions threaten to displace Chinatown's working-class population and their community spaces. The displacement happening in Chinatown today is not new but reflects a history of racist and classist policies that have oppressed and segregated communities of color. While acknowledging the histories of displacement that many communities of color continue to face, it is important to recognize that they are rooted in even earlier histories of displacement: government policies rooted in settler colonialism have displaced Indigenous peoples from their land. Chinatown and the rest of Los Angeles occupy unceded Tongva territory.[1]

Geographically bounded by the Interstate 110 Arroyo Seco Freeway (I-110), the Los Angeles River, and Dodger Stadium, Chinatown today is a multiethnic, multigenerational commercial and residential neighborhood. Over the years, it has grown to house a large population of multiethnic working-class immigrants (64 percent foreign born, of whom 82 percent are Asian and 17 percent are Latinx) and tenants (95 percent).[2] The fastest growing segment of the U.S. population, a significant number of seniors (age sixty-five and older) live in the neighborhood (20 percent).[3] Chinatown has a history of disinvestment and marginalization by the city, but it has been recently marked as a prime location for real estate speculation and increased investment from wealthy developers due to its proximity to the urban center of downtown Los Angeles. With an influx of middle-to-upper-class residents and development projects that cater to them, rising commercial and residential rents, and the displacement of working-class residents, Chinatown is being gentrified.

Rooted in a History of Exclusion

Gentrification's threat to Los Angeles Chinatown is not a "random event" but a "systematic process" rooted in a history of exclusionary laws and policies that specifically barred Asians from immigration and naturalization.[4] The first immigration legislation to explicitly exclude people based on nationality and race, the 1882 Chinese Exclusion Act, prevented skilled and unskilled Chinese laborers from immigrating to the United States. Not long after, the Asiatic Barred Zone Act was enacted in 1917 to bar immigration from countries in the Asia-Pacific zone, targeting the significant number of South Asians immigrating at the time.[5] The Immigration Act of 1924 was designed to target Southern and Eastern Europeans, but amid growing anti-Asian sentiment, a provision barring the immigration of "aliens ineligible for citizenship" was added.[6] While this provision aimed to exclude Japanese in particular, it excluded all Asians except for Filipinos, who were considered nationals up until the Tydings McDuffie Act of 1934.[7] As a political gesture toward China, a U.S. ally during World War II, a quota system based on nationalities and regions was established in 1943, allowing 105 Chinese immigrants to enter the country every year. The Immigration and Nationality Act of 1952 ended blanket exclusions of immigration from Asia and allowed Japanese to naturalize but continued to uphold quotas. It was not until 1965 that this national origin quota system was abolished by a new Immigration and Nationality Act. This opened the doors for immigration from Asia as well as other countries through two pathways: (1) *family reunification* of the immediate relatives of U.S. citizens and permanent residents, and (2) *occupational preference* for skilled workers to fill labor shortages in the United States.

Nevertheless, anti-Asian racism persisted in laws such as racially restrictive covenants that prohibited people of color, particularly African Americans and noncitizens, from purchasing or leasing homes in certain neighborhoods. The California Alien Land Laws of 1913 and 1920 prohibited Asians, who were considered "aliens ineligible for citizenship," from owning or holding long-term leases for land.[8] The 1930s Home Owners' Loan Corporation (HOLC) and homeowner programs of the Federal Housing Administration and Veterans Administration explicitly used race to determine where they would approve mortgages.[9] HOLC redlined almost every majority-Black neighborhood in the United States, preventing Black people from receiving loans.[10] Through racist planning policies, the federal government deliberately created suburbs for the white and wealthy and disinvested from "dense, mixed-use, and diverse" inner cities deemed undesirable, such as Los Angeles Chinatown.[11]

Los Angeles Chinatown has wavered between existing outside and inside the state. Following Union Station's dismantling of Old Chinatown in the 1930s, New Chinatown in Los Angeles emerged out of middle-class Chinese American businessmen's vision of a business-oriented district self-funded by the community. The adoption of sanitized and industrialized ideals of American spaces included modern buildings "correctly engineered for earthquake, fire safety, and sanitation," Chinese architectural designs, wide streets, and no "houses of vice, such as gambling."[12] The move to re-create Chinatown as clean and modern reflects Chinese Americans' resistance to racist discourse and its material manifestations, which include the state's economic disinvestment in the community. At the same time, it calls attention to the community's desires to incorporate into white America in attempts to avoid further socioeconomic and physical exclusion.

Unpacking Gentrification

A multifaceted process resting on the notions of urban redevelopment and economic growth, gentrification restructures communities of color that have historically experienced disinvestment from the state and developers but are now found to be profitable. It is a process that represents "cycles of investment and disinvestment in urban centers."[13] Where land is perceived as cheap and buildings are underfunded or declining, developers speculate they will have the biggest potential for profit.[14] In other words, wealthy developers buy real estate at lower values and sell them for exponentially more. All the while, rising commercial and residential property costs spatially and economically exclude working-class residents and small businesses that cannot afford to participate in a city's economic growth. The poor and their community spaces are deemed deviant given their inability to be productive or profitable in a system of capitalism that prioritizes profits over people. According to Peter Moskowitz, it is "a system that places the needs of capital (both in terms of city budget and in terms of real estate profits) above the needs of people." Cities transform from being spaces that provide for the poor and middle classes into spaces that primarily generate capital for the rich.[15]

The process of gentrification pushes out poor, immigrant, and elderly people of color in favor of corporations and the wealthy elite. It is an extension of racist and classist structures that work in tandem with individuals—such as real estate developers, upper-class Chinese Americans who participate in both state and market processes that drive gentrification, and a demographic of upwardly mobile professionals, artists, and consumers—to restructure Chinatown. As "the spatial expression of economic inequality," gentrification disrupts "existing social structures of support and exchange within communities, most dramatically among people such as the elderly, the poor and non-white racial and ethnic groups."[16] These groups are at risk of losing not only their physical homes but also the support networks that give them a sense of community. Ultimately, gentrification is unfettered privatization of land that threatens Chinatown's existence as a multiethnic enclave and does not benefit or prioritize low-income communities of color.

Functions of Gentrification

While the city's elite profits from investments in market-rate developments and a rebranding of Chinatown, the community's most marginalized residents face illegal rent increases, poor housing conditions, and the loss of important community institutions. Which story gets heard and centered in conversations and planning processes? Chinatown's low-income immigrant residents are often ignored by developers, politicians, and community leaders. This is reflected by more development proposals for market-rate housing than for low-income senior housing, by more mainstream media coverage of Chinatown's rising hip food scene than on the longtime family-owned restaurants hustling to serve noodle soups and stay in business, and the elders being served eviction notices and rent increases by landlords.[17]

There is a growing economic and social divide between working-class community members and the new wealthier, often white, professionals and "creatives" in Chinatown. This speaks to the ways in which the state and state-like private and public institutions, such as the nonprofit

Chinatown Business Improvement District, render certain people visible (and valuable) and others invisible (and not valuable) through the promotion of neoliberal economic development. Business Improvement Districts are a tool of gentrification, participating in the increasing criminalization and privatization of urban cities. Working closely with both local governments and private investors, they play a large role in the decision-making processes of urban redevelopment. With property owners sitting on their boards and a lack of engagement with, and quite possibly, exclusion of, working-class residents, they are far from representative or accountable to the needs of the rest of the neighborhood.

A key and inherent element of gentrification is the displacement of low-income people of color and homeless communities through increased rents, evictions, criminalization, and aggressive policing, the latter of which disproportionately impacts Black and Latinx communities. In Chinatown, gentrification threatens to indirectly and directly displace existing informal economies, small family-owned businesses, cultural institutions, and the significant population of seniors, tenants, and immigrants. Although more than 41 percent of the population lives in poverty, more spaces are made inaccessible and unaffordable for residential and commercial tenants, forcing them to leave Chinatown because of rising rents.[18] Public spaces are also increasingly being policed by private security who are hired by the Chinatown Business Improvement District. Working closely with the Los Angeles Police Department to "keep crime down in the neighborhood," they have harassed street vendors, musicians, and homeless individuals who make up the community.[19]

Gentrification is an intentional process of racial, spatial, and economic segregation that manifests within the epistemological and political structures of neoliberalism. With neoliberalism comes the defunding of social programs that serve poor people of color, the deregulation of market forces that enable elite interests and corporations to flourish, and the increased commodification of places and people. Affluent East Asian property owners, developers, and young professionals who constitute some of the drivers of gentrification in Chinatown are part of these former groups who now have "access to capital and citizenship in ways that were previously unimaginable."[20] This ranges from property owners who serve on the board of directors for the Chinatown Business

Improvement District to middle- to upper-class entrepreneurs opening artisanal coffee shops in the neighborhood.[21] Gentrification works within a neoliberal framework to disavow the social, economic, and geopolitical violence it enacts on poor bodies of color and their physical and social constructions of space in favor of whiter, financially wealthier bodies and spaces. It physically and figuratively erases the bodies, community spaces, and narratives of working-class people of color.

Gentrification as a manifestation of neoliberalism functions to violently disrupt and displace the livelihoods of those deemed deviant in a system rooted in capitalism and white supremacy. The process of gentrification (re)produces forms of economic development and discourse that are inherently inequitable and unaccountable. Land continues to be rendered as property ripe for real estate speculation and transactional exchange rather than as communal space driven by collectivity and the production of joy. Gentrification perpetuates socioeconomic and health disparities for poor communities of color. It works to physically uproot and exclude working-class people of color, all the while figuratively erasing their narratives and experiences in historical and everyday discourse. In Chinatown, this looks like increased policing, rising evictions of commercial and residential tenants, dismantling of social networks, loss of resources and cultural institutions, and rapid privatization of housing, education, and health care.

Physical and Figurative Erasure: Who Are These Spaces For?

Gentrification creates spaces inaccessible to working-class residents of color, physically erasing their bodies by limiting their ability to afford, feel welcomed, or exist in these spaces. In Chinatown, gentrification most visibly manifests as residential and commercial projects that range from luxury mixed-use apartment buildings to art galleries to hip coffee shops and eateries. From Jia Apartments on Broadway to the isolated galleries on Chung King Road to the chef-driven restaurants in Far East Plaza, these projects all function together to drive and sustain gentrification by catering primarily, if not solely, to the younger, upwardly mobile demographic of professionals and "creatives" that developers, such as Tom Gilmore and Izek Shomof (two of Los Angeles's biggest gentrifiers), market to and profit from. These are the commercial spaces that line developers' visions of trendy urban destinations and the people who can afford market-rate studios and goods that are too expensive for most of Chinatown's residents. As both the executive director of the Chinatown Business Improvement District and vice president of Macco Investments Corp. (the investment company that owns Far East Plaza), George Yu is frequently credited for bringing these new businesses into Chinatown.[22]

Gentrification disregards the livelihoods of existing working-class immigrant residents and the need for culturally competent health care and social services, community gathering spaces, grocery markets, and quality low-income housing. Despite these increasing demands, developers seek to build more market-rate projects in Chinatown that the majority of residents cannot afford to live in. Jia Apartments and Blossom Plaza are two luxury mixed-use (retail and commercial) buildings with monthly rents starting around $1,903 and $1,845 for 571- and 436-square-feet studios, respectively.[23] As a superficial attempt to fit within the neighborhood, these buildings feature facades with red accents, lanterns, and certain names (jiā means "home" in Mandarin) to evoke an exotified Chinatown aesthetic. Yet, in Chinatown, where the median household income is $18,657 and 95 percent of the population are renters, who can afford to call these places home?[24]

A significant number of Chinatown's residents already struggle to pay rents that fall far below those of Jia Apartments and Blossom Plaza Apartments. From 2012 to 2016, 23 percent of residents paid between $100 and $499, and 30 percent paid between $500 and $999 in gross rent, while 47 percent paid more than $1,000.[25] The median gross rent for different parts of the neighborhood ranged from $653 to $1,560 (where the market-rate apartment development the Orsini is located).[26] Many residents are rent burdened, spending more than 30 percent of their household income on rent. Even worse, a growing number of tenants are considered severely burdened, paying more than 50 percent of their incomes on rent.[27] High housing costs limit how much they can afford to spend on healthy food, transportation, and health care. In 2016, 60–67 percent of the population faced these financial strains.[28] This is a significant increase compared to prior years. In 2013, 49–57 percent of the population was already rent burdened.[29] The degree of rent burden and the percentage of those who are rent burdened can be expected to rise as wages continue to stay low and rents continue to rise with the construction of unaffordable housing projects. These luxury apartments are not built to house people, especially the poor, but to generate capital. When housing and businesses are developed solely to attract "a younger, more privileged and upwardly mobile demographic," gentrification is economic investment in a new affluent community at the expense of the existing working-class one.[30]

The language that journalists, restaurateurs, and investors use to describe Chinatown evokes unsettling references to colonialism.[31] Painting cities as "urban wilderness" that needs to be cleaned up and developed, especially by those who are wealthy and white, the language of gentrification incorporates frontier imagery reflective of European colonialism in the Americas.[32] Chinatown is seen as both a "fringe neighborhood," unconventional and "egalitarian," and holding much potential for economic growth. Jonathan Gold once described the former Starry Kitchen as almost qualifying as a Chinatown "pioneer" in "a brave new culinary world."[33] It would be unsurprising if Gold also used this word to describe Roy Choi, who believes Chinatown is a "great area for growth because it's like an island. . . . You can create your own wonderland over there because it's all encapsulated.[34] Similarly, Derrick Moore, a principal with the commercial real estate services firm Avison Young, calls Far East Plaza a "destination project in the works."[35] Most articles on Chinatown highlight narratives such as these, barely, if at all, scratching the surface of the culinary scene's relationship to residential displacement. By centering narratives of upwardly mobile entrepreneurs and their clientele, these frameworks decenter and erase the narratives of those most threatened by gentrification: the existing small businesses and working-class residents.

If people change the ways they talk about Chinatown and gentrification so that they center working-class immigrants, what individual actions, policies, and collective grassroots organizing could this manifest materially? Across Los Angeles, collectives such as Defend Boyle Heights, Los Angeles Tenants Union, and Chinatown Community for Equitable Development challenge gentrification through direct actions and tenant organizing. In Boyle Heights this ranges from boycotting corporate-funded art galleries to protesting wealthy white landlords who attempt to evict longtime community members such as the mariachis who perform at Mariachi Plaza.[36] In Chinatown this includes building deep relationships with low-income tenants and working with them to develop their self-efficacy and agency around their rights. These groups imagine and fight for communities in which housing is respected as a human right and working-class communities of color continue to exist and thrive. Gentrification is not inevitable. It is a process that can be interrupted.[37]

Tam Gong Gong's Garden

One hot summer day in late June 2017, Annie and I met Tam Gong Gong, a Chinatown resident and avid gardener, for what I thought was the first time. My friend Tim, who I had talked with the week prior, had mentioned to me over pastries and *baos* at KBC Bakery that he had noticed an older woman gardening outside the apartment building next to where he and his grandparents lived in the neighborhood. A large garden flourished in the front yard of the building. Vines peppered with yellow flowers wove themselves around the white yarn strung across the front gate. A pathway cut across the middle of the garden, leading to a door painted evergreen. It was locked. Annie and I stood outside for a few minutes until an auntie who lived there happened to come home. "Do you know who gardens here?" we asked her in Cantonese. Unlocking the door, she shyly said no and pointed to the first door in the hallway facing us. It was the unit where Tam Gong Gong and his family lived.

When we arrived at this building, everything looked familiar to me, but I wasn't quite sure why. When Tam Gong Gong opened his door and we asked about the garden outside, it gradually dawned on me that I had talked with him before. It had been a brief doorway conversation that took place during one of the monthly neighborhood outreaches that I helped coordinate for Chinatown Community for Equitable Development (CCED). The weekend prior, some CCED volunteers had also talked with Tam Gong Gong and his wife Tai Tai about tenant rights and housing issues. The landlord who had purchased their building in 2016 had been attempting to force tenants out through "cash for keys," a common tactic used to pressure low-income tenants to *voluntarily* move out of their apartment units by offering them money. Despite the building being protected by the Los Angeles Rent Stabilization Ordinance, the tenants are vulnerable to landlord harassment and such tactics of displacement. Because of the statewide Costa-Hawkins Rental Housing Act, which severely limits municipal rent control and prohibits vacancy control, the landlord can rent to new tenants at any price once units are vacant.

In a capitalist economic system that prioritizes productivity and profitability, the livelihoods of working-class seniors such as Tam Gong Gong are disposable. Tam Gong Gong and Tai Tai share a two-bedroom apartment with their son and his wife and children. The $1,000 monthly rent is too expensive to afford on their own because of their fixed income. If they were not splitting costs with their son's family, the majority of this elderly couple's Supplemental Security Income would be spent on rent, leaving them with approximately $400 for food and other living costs. Their monthly rent feels high and increases by 3 percent each year, but it seems that for their landlord, it is not high enough. If the existing working-class tenants leave, their vacant apartment units can be rented for any amount at the landlord's discretion. Thus, the landlord seeks to displace them for higher-income, higher-paying tenants. Lacking the financial and social capital recognized as valuable by the property owners and developers who gentrify Chinatown, Tam Gong Gong and his family are devalued for their inability to be profitable. Similarly, spaces that serve working-class residents are also devalued because of their role as sites that sustain the livelihoods of minoritized life. This includes Tam Gong Gong's garden.

Gardens such as Tam Gong Gong's are viewed as deviant because of their inability to be profitable for the city, developers, property owners, and nonprofit institutions that operate as extensions of the neoliberal state. Like the working-class residents who tend and rely on them, they are vulnerable to displacement. According to Henri Lefebvre, contradictions in society, such as those between the forces and relations of production, emerge in space and at the level of space.[38] He points to a contradictory process that degrades and eventually destroys urban space: "the proliferation of fast roads and of places to park and garage cars, and their corollary, a reduction of tree-lined streets, green spaces, and parks, and gardens."[39] The contradiction itself lies in the clash between a consumption of space that produces surplus value and one that produces only enjoyment."[40] In Chinatown, gardens and informal street vendors produce enjoyment and sustenance for working-class residents rather than profits for the elite who control the means of production in a capitalist system. Thus, they are rendered unproductive and disposable.

When we spoke in July 2017, Tam Gong Gong had never met his new landlord. Instead, he had been introduced to a handful of individuals whom the landlord hired to tell him and his low-income neighbors to move out so that the apartment building could be renovated. According to Tam Gong Gong, everyone refused to leave because they knew they wouldn't be able to find an affordable place to live elsewhere. Whatever amount of money the landlord offered would not be sustainable, especially for those relying on government assistance. "Even if they gave me $100, the government would take away $100 from my SSI," he explained. For the tenants, this is their home. Yet, by using cash-for-keys tactics and refusing to meet with them directly, the landlord disregards their livelihoods. This lack of interpersonal interaction between the landlord and the tenants exemplifies the dehumanization of certain racialized and gendered groups that occurs within gentrification.

Given Chinatown's proximity to downtown Los Angeles and inequitable economic capital-generating projects such as the Metro transit system, tourist destinations, and arts districts, land that was once disinvested in is now ascribed with capitalist value because it is profitable. While the state does not recognize the gardens of Chinatown's working-class senior immigrants as valuable, it unarguably recognizes the land that these gardens occupy as holding great potential for profitability. This rent gap, "the disparity between how much property is worth in its current state and how much it would be worth gentrified," is becoming larger in Chinatown.[41] As real estate speculation and profit-driven urban development increase, property values in the neighborhood, such as where Tam Gong Gong's apartment building stands, will increase. Developers seek to build development projects that can better generate financial capital. Gentrification is further commodification of land by neoliberal forces. The value of land is narrowly measured by its financial worth in the present and in a speculative future.

The sites of gardens and informal street vendors are consumed by local residents in ways that contrast with the consumption of neoliberal economic development, such as the new wave of eateries and boutiques, art galleries, market-rate mixed-use residential and commercial buildings, architectural offices, wineries, and breweries. In Chinatown, this clash in consumption grows as gentrification leads to the creation of more profit-generating spaces and the hastened removal of public communal spaces. The process of creation and removal extends to include the different bodies who occupy and consume each space. Valued and protected groups, such as middle-to-upper-class professionals and creatives, are welcomed, while racialized and gendered groups, such as the low-income senior immigrants, are displaced from the spaces that serve them. The existence of Tam Gong Gong's garden is tied to his ability to continue living in his home. Without him, who will sow the vegetables and water the plants as they grow?

On Gardens and Self-Sustenance

Throughout the neighborhood, seniors huddle in corners around tables playing Chinese games, stop in the middle of sidewalks to talk with friends they run into, and wait at bus stops to go grocery shopping. These seniors nurture and sustain Chinatown as a working-class immigrant neighborhood with their social networks, physical and emotional labor, and cultural practices. They play a large role in making Chinatown what it is today, but the fact that they are poor, elderly, and immigrant makes them vulnerable to displacement at the hands of neoliberal economic development. Their existence is a reminder of Chinatown's past, its present, and the possibility of its future as a community that continues to serve some of those who have been devalued by the state.

Gardening is part of a larger progressive history of Chinatown's self-determination and self-sustenance. When the state has failed to provide for Chinatown, community members have advocated, organized, and provided for themselves. In 1971 the Chinatown Service Center formed in response to the lack of culturally competent health care and social services in the neighborhood.[42] According to Phyllis Chiu, a longtime organizer in the neighborhood, a group of politically conscious students from UCLA created the Chinatown Youth Council (CYC) in the late 1960s to address the lack of services and access to education for immigrant teenagers. CYC initially ran a summer youth employment program that provided bilingual education and job development. Soon, it grew into an umbrella group that housed many programs that served the neighborhood's wider working-class residents. Given that major newspapers in Chinatown did not publish daily, they produced and distributed the monthly 覺華報 (*Chinese Awareness Newspaper*) to share community news and news from China. They would sell it in restaurant kitchens and sewing factories for about twenty-five cents each. On Saturday mornings, Chinatown Food Co-op purchased fruit and vegetables from a wholesale market downtown and distributed the food to residents outside someone's home in Chinatown. Although the community had many markets at the time, including the former Ling's Market (now closed Ai Hoa), Yee Sing Chong, Kwan Lee Lung (now closed JC Market), and BC Market, the Food Co-op was formed to provide low-income residents another means of accessing affordable fresh produce.

According to Monica White, "gardening becomes an exercise of political agency and empowerment" when "members of the community face harsh economic realities."[43] In Detroit, Michigan, a city with a deep history of working-class resistance to housing discrimination and racial segregation, Black women have used food to reclaim land and resist social, economic, and environmental injustice. They have transformed vacant land into urban gardens, creating a community-based food system that "allows them to be able to feed themselves and their families."[44] In the context of a gentrifying Chinatown, gardening has the potential to transform from a hobby and necessity to an act of resistance. Gardening offers insight into the ability of the community's working-class senior immigrants to exist uninterrupted by neoliberal forces, at the same time that it reflects their increasing vulnerability to neoliberal forces in the midst of gentrification. To engage in activities that sustain them and bring them joy while living in a system that aims to physically and figuratively erase them speaks to the transformative power of gardens in challenging oppression that manifests in poverty, poor health, and displacement. At the intersection of food and space, seniors produce knowledge, which include gardening practices, cultural beliefs, traditional recipes, community news, and land use, that foster the possibility of "a politics of difference that radically rethinks self and community."[45]

Although the gardens and the informal street vendors stand in opposition to forces of neoliberalism and capitalism, they also embody the potential to produce the politics that can challenge the inequitable manifestations of these oppressive systems. Through the site of the garden, land is reimagined as a space for enjoying one's time, nurturance, and social interactions. Thus, land is decommodified. Seniors occupy apartment balconies, front lawns, and pathways in Chinatown to tend soil, grow food, and hold conversations with neighbors. Working as informal street vendors, some seniors take their harvests and sell them to make modest incomes. They occupy parking lots and public streets, interacting with acquaintances and passersby. In contrast to spaces produced by neoliberal development, gardens do not solely function to produce surplus value. They function to serve working-class immigrants finding ways to sustain their livelihoods. At the same time that working-class residents rely on these communal spaces, they sustain them. They enable their own continued existence in the community with the joys, uses, and knowledge produced in gardens. Community-oriented and community-driven spaces are alternative models of economic development that stand in the way of the hyper-privatization of land that accelerates with gentrification. Thus, they have the potential to actively challenge this process. How working-class residents relate to these spaces and each other provides a framework that imagines land not as property that produces surplus value, but as community that produces enjoyment: communal sites to exercise agency and self-determination, take care of oneself and others, and exist equitably. In this vision of Chinatown, the working-class community as a whole, rather than a few rich interests, controls the means of production, distribution, and exchange.

Flourishing Community Gardens

Gardens of various sizes and varieties speckle Chinatown's residential neighborhood. They can be found in the backyards of family homes and on empty plots of land. Many of the neighborhood's tenants cultivate gardens in apartment balconies, communal front yards, and patches of dirt lining the side of buildings and pathways. Chinatown's working-class residents depend on these gardens in various ways. Representative of other social and physical spaces that serve working-class immigrants in the community but holding potential for their own unique political possibilities, they are sites for growing food, sharing knowledge, and socializing with neighbors and passersby.

In these gardens, one can find an abundance of different varieties of 菜 (vegetables). This includes leafy greens commonly used in Chinese cuisine such as 莧菜 (red amaranth), 白菜 (bok choy), a-菜 (a-choy), and 番薯 (sweet potato leaves). In the late fall to early winter months, 冬瓜 (winter melons) are ready to harvest according to Tam Gong Gong. Popular in both Chinese and Southeast Asian dishes, herbs such as 韭菜 (chives), mint, basil, and lemongrass seem to grow effortlessly in the California sun. Common fruits such as 火龙果 (dragon fruit), 金橘 (kumquat), 枇杷 (loquat), 紅棗 (jujube), tangerine, guava, grapefruit, persimmon, and pomegranate, are grown, gifted, and sold at different points of the year. Some of these plants require long-term cultivation. Their growth speaks to the gardeners' persistence and patience, qualities that are also essential to seeing the fruition of grassroots organizing and the movement of building working-class power.

Everyday Joys

Tam Gong Gong, Tiffany, and I stand outside in the shade of a pomegranate tree. It is now early September. Although the open space between the apartment and its front gate is fairly small compared to the spacious front yards of many of Los Angeles's suburban homes, the garden is quite large. Greenery fills nearly every square inch of dirt on both sides of the central concrete walkway. The space belongs to all of the tenants in the building, but only a few of them garden. Tam Gong Gong, who claims to garden the most of all of his neighbors in the building, grows and tends one side of the apartment's garden.

After retiring, Tam Gong Gong began gardening as a way to pass the time. He waves off the labor of his hobby as easy. "All you do is throw the seeds in the dirt and water them," he says modestly. "When they bud, you spread them and replant them further apart." In early September, Tam Gong Gong's garden flourishes with 茼蒿 (edible chrysanthemum) and the bulbous 球茎甘蓝 (kohlrabi). In one section, a large winter melon peeks out from the cool shade of its broad leaves. Planted in March and harvested in October, these winter melons are almost ready for Tai Tai, who makes all the meals at home, to chop up and cook into nourishing winter soups.

Tam Gong Gong spends most of his time gardening. Aside from allowing him to pass the time during retirement, it brings him joy. To see something he has planted grow and to eat it uplifts him. Each morning and early evening, he goes outside to water the plants. However, as he's grown older, the laborious nature of gardening has impacted how much Tam Gong Gong can do physically. In the past two years, he hasn't been gardening as much as before because of his aching back and knees. In addition to Tai Tai, who will sometimes water the plants, his adult children help him tend the garden.

In contrast to Tam Gong Gong, Pauline doesn't readily see herself as a gardener. There's nowhere for her to grow food, she tells me, because she lives in a first-floor apartment. As quickly as she insists that she isn't a gardener, she also says that she grows 番薯 (sweet potatoes). "是 garden! (That's a garden!)," I exclaim in a mix of English and Cantonese. But she waves it off as something that's done casually and requires minimal effort. This is because gardening came by chance to Pauline, who, at age twenty-six, immigrated to Chinatown from Hong Kong with her husband and five-year-old daughter over fifty years ago. Growing up in the city, she didn't have the opportunity or space to plant fruits and vegetables. "我唔識種. 我是香港出世. 乜野都唔識. (I don't know how to grow things. I grew up in Hong Kong. I don't know anything.)," she claims. One day, her neighbor who had sweet potato plants but no 地方 (space) to grow them came over and planted the vines in the empty plot of dirt in front of Pauline's apartment in Chinatown. Pauline watered them, and they just grew. Now her garden is full of 番薯 (sweet potatoes) and a lone 辣椒 (chili pepper) plant that sits in one corner. Peanut shells used for compost are scattered in the dirt.

Fostering Community

Gardens, alongside the public streets that street vendors occupy, provide spaces for informal conversation and interaction that help create and sustain the community's social networks. While Vivian and I stood outside on the street with Pauline, an auntie walking by noticed our gathering around Pauline's garden and stopped to comment. They didn't know each other but spoke with familiarity. This was a common scene in Chinatown: strangers striking up friendly conversations in shared languages on bus rides, in small grocery stores, and at Alpine Park, all spaces that are accessible to them. On this neighborhood street at dusk, it was no different.

Similar to the rest of the community spaces that serve the neighborhood's working-class residents, gardens serve as "a forum to build connections and reciprocity of social capital among groups of people."[46] Working-class immigrant residents can be found exchanging community news, resources, and greetings. Where neoliberal development practices create less socially cohesive neighborhoods and dismantle existing working-class social networks through displacement, having the spaces for these interpersonal connections are powerful. Within capitalism, lives become increasingly isolated and commodified, so saying hello to your neighbor can be considered a radical act because it is unprofitable and uncommodifiable.[47] Gardens can function not only as spaces for enjoyment but also as sites for building a stronger sense of community among working-class residents.

Residents take care of one another through the community's social networks. Through gardens and the relationships they foster, residents share food with each other, in addition to tips about the best deals on fresh affordable groceries, how to navigate the city and government institutions as immigrants, and how to grow and cook sweet potato leaves. Although their neighborhood and relationships are increasingly threatened by gentrification, working-class immigrants in Chinatown have social networks that can provide them the power to effect change within their community.[48] When it comes to grassroots organizing, they are better equipped to mobilize one another around issues of inequity because of a developed sense of mutual support. According to Mrs. Mar, "有相信 (there's trust)" when she, someone with a deep relationship to Chinatown, having lived and worked here for many years, talks with other residents. Collectively, working-class residents can wield immense power with their social capital, sense of community, and shared experiences as marginalized people.

Shaping and Redefining Land through Knowledge Production

Working-class knowledge shapes the land that gardens occupy in Chinatown, producing spaces that are central for relationship building, enjoyment, and community health. They are vulnerable to displacement compared to the spaces produced by recognized modes of expertise that are valued in neoliberal development practices. Yet, working-class senior immigrants have the power to challenge the elite's control of space that occurs within capitalism. Stemming from the community cultural wealth produced and sustained in gardens, the politics of difference arising from these spaces enable the possibility of transforming land as "private commodity" back to "common use."[49] They enable the possibility of recovering and holding onto land in the form of equitable, community-oriented production and control of spaces, thus imagining systems of economic development alternative to capitalism.

Tucked away at the end of a cul de sac, Pang Baak's garden is easy to miss when walking or driving by. A narrow dirt pathway scattered with old clothes and sporadic concrete steps leads to his garden. The backsides of homes and apartment buildings, one of which has been spray-painted with graffiti, surround it on one side, while a panoramic view of Chinatown's commercial district surrounds it on the other. Leafy greens and herbs grow out of Styrofoam containers, plastic buckets and crates, and old produce boxes filled to the brim with dirt. Over forty empty tofu storage containers sit side by side on the ground, ready to be reused. While we talk, Pang Baak tends his plants. He plucks two bright red cherry tomatoes and hands them over. Their vines stretch across the top of a well-crafted wooden archway; dragon fruit plants grow at the bottom. After retiring from work at a Panda Express restaurant, which he refers to as "Panda," he began gardening several years ago. He immigrated from Taishan, China, and has lived in Chinatown for more than twenty years. "唔識打麻將. (I don't know how to play mahjong.)," he admits in defense of his garden. He goes on to name several other activities that other seniors in Chinatown commonly engage in to pass the time but that he doesn't know how to do. His sense of purpose and fulfillment comes solely from gardening.

The informality of the seniors' gardens complicates notions of ownership that are tied to property rights. Pang Baak does not legally own the property that his garden occupies but stakes claim to the land with the labor, food, and joy he produces. While the seniors' creative and resourceful use of land is usually ignored or tolerated until it stands in the way of profitable development, in Pang Baak's case, the property owner supports his gardening. Pang Baak used to live in one of the adjoining apartments. Although he moved to another location a mile away some years ago, he continues to return every day, driving over in a car that he uses to transport tools and supplies. The land that his garden occupies is part of the property of one of the adjacent apartment buildings. "佢知道你種嘢嗎? (Does he know you're planting things?)," I ask. Pang Baak's plot of fruits and vegetables is the largest of several in this space. He exclaims that the property owner wants him to garden, otherwise someone would have to be hired to take care of the land. In what appears to be an informal arrangement, Pang Baak is able to utilize the space, while the landlord receives some tax benefits from the presence of a garden on his property. Their relationship speaks to the ways in which informal land use can both challenge and coexist with formality.

Where Chinatown and Solano Canyon meet lies an undeveloped plot of land. The 110 North freeway separates it from Chavez Ravine,[50] a historical neighborhood home to generations of Mexican Americans who were forcibly displaced by the city of Los Angeles and replaced with the Dodger Stadium in the 1950s.[51] In the middle of the plot, a garden of green herbs and vegetables flourishes, contrasting greatly with the empty space of dry grass and dirt surrounding it. Two small raised beds of dirt sit to the side, closer to the shade of the bordering apartment's trees. These gardens aren't gated, unlike the formal Solano Canyon Community Garden across from them, to which access is only allowed to those who can pay the monthly fee to own their own plot. According to a young Latino artist who recently moved into the neighborhood and exhibited work at an art gallery at Blossom Plaza Apartments, the middle-aged Spanish-speaking Latino immigrant caretaker who he befriended through shared language watered and cared for most of these plots. The caretaker's own garden sat to one side, green, loved, and thriving.

The gardens that occupy the open space across from the Solano Canyon Community Garden are shared by several immigrant residents from the neighboring rent-controlled apartment building: the Yu family, Lim Yee, and another Chinese family. At a glance, this informal space appears to resemble values truer to the concept of community gardens as communal space. Community gardens are increasingly institutionalized, overseen by nonprofit organizations. They are also capitalized on by developers given their ability to often increase property values. However, the informality of this particular garden speaks to immigrant creativity and a sort of renegade quality: community members seeing empty land and reimagining it as food and joy, a space unrestricted by property rights and zoning laws. It stands ungated, its plants seemingly vulnerable to being ravaged or stolen, and it stands open, as a space for others to help tend, contribute to, and borrow from, in exchange for labor, more plants, or simply, a deep appreciation of its abundance or a need for its nurturance. A degree of trust surrounds this open space. The way it has been constructed and how it exists openly speak to a form of land use and design that contrasts greatly with current development. The informal communal garden produces a knowledge and framework that shifts how communities are built.

As rice paddy farmers in China, Yu Sook and his family are skilled at cultivating land for food. Although they have lived here for twenty years, they have only been gardening on what he says is government-owned land for six years. According to him, it costs around $20 to $40 to garden at the Solano Canyon Community Garden, and there is a waiting list. With access to this land next to their home, why pay to use that community garden? The family's middle plot flourishes with sweet potato plants, cilantro, chives, and A-菜 (a-choy) that are enough for the family to eat. Yu Sook says that he and his neighbors help each other "斟水 (pour water)" on the plants when they get home from work. If anyone picks some of their vegetables without asking, he says that they wouldn't mind. The biggest issue seems to be the birds and rodents who eat all the fruit from Lim Yee's loquat tree. Even then, Lim Yee, who immigrated here from Cambodia over thirty years ago, seems content with her gardening. At eighty-nine years old, she gardens for fun but finds it harder to do nowadays as she's getting older. "*Bhoi lak* (No energy)," she says in Teochew, walking me slowly to her plot of lettuce that she calls "Cambodia salad." She finds it difficult to carry containers of water outside, as has been required since the landlord complained about the tenants using too much water and locked up the hose. Yet, her garden, however small, is lush. Her neighbors help her water the plants.

Similarly, Pauline's garden symbolizes collectivity and mutual aid, speaking to the ways in which working-class senior immigrants nurture and sustain Chinatown. While her neighbor started the garden, Pauline waters it to ensure its growth. It sits in front of her apartment, openly facing the residential sidewalk. Sometimes people she knows will come over and take without asking. She tells me that someone once pulled the vegetable from its roots because they didn't know the proper way to pick it. However, she doesn't mind. She would have shared her harvest regardless because sweet potato leaves "很快出啊! (grow really fast!)." Community members, both acquaintances and strangers, are welcome to take what plants they need from it, giving back to her their own garden harvests and resources: a gift of grapefruits from a neighbor's tree that she then gives to me, and snacks they bought at the market. Tam Gong Gong also shares his garden's harvests with "很朋友 (good friends)." During these moments, food becomes more than a commodity; it's a form of appreciation and care.

In Pauline's garden, older women transmit knowledge of Chinese foodways through the sharing of gardening practices and recipes. Pauline's neighbor happened to be home when she noticed us standing outside. Joining us, she grabbed the scissors from Pauline and cut the leaves at a quick pace. Our bags filled with leafy greens. "She knows much more about gardening than me," Pauline shrugged. Her neighbor cut specific leaves and stems for Vivian and me to replant. "返回種. 插落去. (Go back home and grow it. Plant them into the ground.)," Pauline said. Believing that we didn't know how to garden, she told us "問你的媽點得啊 (You can ask your mom how to do it.)." Agreeing, her neighbor said matter-of-factly in a mix of Cantonese and Toisan, "媽識整啊. 老人素識整. (Moms know how to [garden]. Old people usually know how to do it.)."[52] Their insistence that our mothers knew how to garden speaks to women's role in knowledge production.

As street vendors, waitresses, caretakers, gardeners, cooks, aunties, mothers, and grandmothers, women play a significant role in transmitting traditions, guidance, and beliefs among each other and intergenerationally through food. With many tasks taken up by women, labor around food is often gendered. While these gender roles reveal sexual divisions of labor that can be unfair and uncompensated, they also speak to women's agency in producing knowledge. Wong Po Po's garden occupies multiple patches of green space found on the public sidewalk in front of her apartment building. Commonly eaten in Toisan-style soup, 大白菜 (big bok choi) hang on the bars of her window to dry. When she shares how to cook different vegetables from her garden with Desmond and me, second-generation Chinese Americans, she both preserves and shapes Chinese diasporic culture. For 韭菜 (chives), she stir-fries them with eggs. For the bitter 枸杞 (goji berry leaves), she cooks it in soup. 茼蒿 (crown daisy or edible chrysanthemum) leaves are added to hot pot soups. We recognize the vegetables, remembering their taste in our mouths, their images in homecooked meals, but she teaches us names and practices. She bends down to pick handfuls of 麥菜 (Indian lettuce, also known as a-choy) to gift us, telling us in Toisan to boil and sauté, then add soy sauce or oyster sauce. At home, I give the 麥菜 to my mother, who then sautés them in a large pot. The process of growing, harvesting, cooking, and eating is powerfully shaped by the women who nourish us.

Cooking can reflect immigrants' cultural maintenance of habits and knowledges learned from their homeland and cultural adaptations that are made in new places. Pauline learned how to cook while growing up in the Kowloon region of Hong Kong. In order for her to learn how to make meals on her own, her mother asked the domestic worker who helped their family not to cook anymore. Pauline has carried these skills into old age. Now retired and living with her 先生 (husband) in Chinatown, she cooks all the meals at home. Some of them include her garden's sweet potato plants.

Sweet potato plants can be cooked in various ways similar to other Chinese leafy greens. Pauline likes to sauté or stir-fry the stems and leaves together with fried onions, then add 蝦米 (small dried shrimp) or 腐乳 (fermented bean curd), both common ingredients in Cantonese dishes. To balance the saltiness of these two ingredients and the slight bitterness of the leafy greens, a distinct taste that her neighbor says is liked by some and disliked by others, she suggests adding a small amount of 糖 (sugar). Boiling the leaves in a pot of water also creates a nutritious soup. When we finish eating ours, she told us, we can come back for more. The sweet potato leaves would have all grown back in a few days. "一個禮拜, 很多. (After one week, there will be a lot.)," her neighbor said.

The Power of Everyday Practice

Organizing spaces fostered by Chinatown Community for Equitable Development, to a great extent, mirror what many working-class senior immigrants already do throughout the community: build deep relationships with neighbors, share resources and information, and envision more housing, markets, and jobs. In the gardens, they grow food and preserve traditional knowledge. In the streets, they play the erhu, sell fruits and vegetables, and socialize with friends. They also lead protests against greedy landlords, whom seniors such as Pauline emphasize we need to fight and keep accountable, talk with the press about working-class needs in the neighborhood, and outreach to neighbors about tenant rights. The seniors show us that grassroots organizing can take different forms, all of which work together to fuel the larger fight for social justice and a stronger resistance against gentrification in Chinatown.

Working-class senior immigrants hold the power to challenge gentrification in their everyday practice. The social networks, knowledge, cultural practices, and mutual aid they produce in sites, such as those of gardens, provide the tools and epistemological frameworks to address the growing affordable housing crisis, widening income gap, and other issues worsened by gentrification. To focus on their community cultural wealth is not to ignore the reality of displacement and poverty happening in their lives, but to highlight their power while also confronting issues of race, class, gender, and capital and holding the state accountable for these injustices. Working-class senior immigrants' foodways are sites of resistance that embody radical potential for fundamental social change in a gentrifying Chinatown.

Notes

1 This chapter does not do justice in fully exploring ongoing efforts for Indigenous sovereignty. By recognizing that Chinatown rests on Indigenous Tongva land, I hope to take one step toward fighting the continual erasure of Indigenous peoples as relics of a colonial past. For working-class immigrants in Chinatown to fight for their right to stay in the neighborhood, it is important to have deeper discussions of what anti-gentrification movements look like in relation to and in solidarity with Indigenous communities. See "Mapping Indigenous LA: Place-Making through Digital Storytelling," UCLA, https://mila.ss.ucla.edu.
2 Wendy Chung, *One Chinatown* (Los Angeles: University of Southern California, 2016), 18.
3 "2010 Census Shows 65 and Older Population Growing Faster Than Total U.S. Population," U.S. Census, November 30, 2011, www.census.gov; Chung, *One Chinatown*, 18.

4 Brooke J. Havlik, *Eating in Urban Frontiers: Alternative Food and Gentrification in Chicago* (Eugene: University of Oregon Press, 2013), 30.
5 Shelley Sang-Hang Lee, *A New History of Asian America* (New York: Routledge, 2014), 143–144.
6 Ibid.
7 Ibid.
8 Ibid., 133.
9 Peter Moskowitz, *How to Kill a City: Gentrification, Inequality, and the Fight for the Neighborhood* (New York: Nation Books, 2017), 113.
10 Ibid., 111.
11 Ibid., 114.
12 Suellen Cheng and Munson Kwok, "The Golden Years of Los Angeles Chinatown: The Beginning," reprinted from the *Los Angeles Chinatown 50th Year Guidebook*, June 1988, accessed May 6, 2017, http://oldchinatownla.com.
13 Havlik, *Eating in Urban Frontiers*, 32.
14 Moskowitz, *How to Kill a City*, 37–39.
15 Ibid., 9.
16 "What We Don't Understand about Gentrification," YouTube.com, TEDx Talks, January 15, 2015, accessed July 1, 2017, www.youtube.com; Havlik, *Eating in Urban Frontiers*, 13.
17 One group of tenants organizing around their rights includes the majority senior and low-income residents at 651 Broadway who have been fighting against illegal rent increases and poor habitability issues. See Brittney Le, "Los Angeles Chinatown Tenants Protest 'Illegal Rent Increases,'" October 15, 2017, https://asamnews.com.
18 Randy Mai and Bonnie Chen, *The State of Los Angeles Chinatown* (Los Angeles: University of California Press 2013), 11.
19 Jean Trinh, "The Past, Present, and Future of Chinatown's Changing Culinary Landscape," KCET, February 28, 2017, www.kcet.org.
20 Ibid., 11.
21 Chinatown Business Improvement District, "Boardmembers & Staff," March 15, 2016, www.chinatownla.com; see Javier Cabral, "Meet the Former Molecular Biologist Who Fought Cancer and Now Makes Amazing Coffee," February 26, 2016, https://munchies.vice.comffee; Allyson Escobar, "Coffeehall Chinatown: Brewing Community and Rotating Roasters in the Heart of Los Angeles," KCET, July 7, 2017, www.kcet.org.
22 Katherine Spiers, "Chinatown's Far East Plaza Is a Dining Destination Thanks to George Yu," *LA Weekly*, May 3, 2017, www.laweekly.com.
23 "Jia Apartments," Equity Apartments, Equity Residential, accessed January 29, 2018, www.equityapartments.com; "Floor Plans," Blossom Plaza Apartments, accessed March 26, 2017, www.blossomplazala.com.
24 Chung, *One Chinatown*, 18.

25 Chinatown is made up of U.S. Census Tracts 2060.10, 2071.01, 2071.02, and 2071.03. See U.S. Census Bureau, 2012–2016 American Community Survey 5-Year Estimates.
26 Ibid.
27 "The State of the Nation's Housing 2017," Joint Center for Housing Studies of Harvard University, 5.
28 U.S. Census Bureau, 2012–2016 American Community Survey 5-Year Estimates.
29 Ibid.
30 Chung, *One Chinatown*, 11.
31 Some anti-gentrification groups call gentrification the new colonialism. However, this fails to acknowledge settler colonialism and disregards Indigenous communities who continue to face the violences of colonialism. Gentrification targets communities already marginalized by the state, but it is a process that is very different from colonialism. See Wakíŋyaŋ Waánataŋ (Matt Remle-Lakota), "Gentrification Is NOT the New Colonialism," July 29, 2017, https://lastrealindians.com.
32 Neil Smith, *New Urban Frontier: Gentrification and the Revanchist City* (New York: Routledge, 1996), xxiii–xiv.
33 Kim, "How an Aging Chinatown Mall Became a Hipster Food Haven"; Jonathan Gold, "Chinatown Emerging as LA's Hottest Restaurant Destination," January 16, 2015, *Los Angeles Times*.
34 Trinh, "The Past, Present, and Future of Chinatown's Changing Culinary Landscape."
35 Kim, "How an Aging Chinatown Mall Became a Hipster Food Haven."
36 Jacob Woocher, "Mariachi Plaza, Evictions, and the Bullsh*t Ideology of Capitalism," medium.com, November 15, 2017, https://knock-la.com.
37 Havlik, *Eating in Urban Frontiers*, 76.
38 Henri Lefebvre, *The Production of Space* (Oxford, UK: Blackwell Publishing, 1991), 358.
39 Ibid., 359.
40 Ibid.
41 Moskowitz, *How to Kill a City*, 38.
42 Chinatown Service Center, "History," accessed April 15, 2018, www.cscla.org.
43 Monica M. White, "Sisters of the Soil: Urban Gardening as Resistance in Detroit," in *Race/Ethnicity: Multidisciplinary Global Contexts* (Bloomington: Indiana University Press, 2011), 19.
44 Ibid.
45 Hong, *Death beyond Disavowal*, 8.
46 Havlik, *Eating in Urban Frontiers*, 63.
47 Moskowitz, *How to Kill a City*, 216.
48 Havlik, *Eating in Urban Frontiers*, 63.
49 Donald A. Krueckeberg, "The Difficult Character of Property: To Whom Do Things Belong?," *Journal of the American Planning Association*, 1995, 302.

50 Independent Lens, "The History of Chavez Ravine," PBS.org, accessed April 14, 2018, www.pbs.org.
51 Through the statewide Urban Agriculture Incentive Zone Act (2013), Los Angeles County provides reduced property tax assessments to property owners who transform eligible vacant or unimproved land into an agricultural use. See Los Angeles County Urban Agriculture Incentive Zone Program, http://planning.lacounty.gov.
52 Pauline and her neighbor assumed that my mom would know how to garden and were right! Not only does my mom garden, but my dad does too. They grow a wide variety of fruits and vegetables at our home.

PART V

Looking Back, Moving Forward: Community Memory, Archives, and Institutions

This section probes the role of community memory in shaping how we interpret and remember Asian American activism. With the majority of Asian Americans being first-generation immigrants, the experiences that catalyzed Asian America as a political identity over fifty years ago require constant rearticulation and renegotiation. Meanwhile, the silences and ruptures caused by war, colonialism, and displacement have created deep narrative ruptures across different generations of Asian Americans. Drawing from a feminist praxis of memory work as care work, this section foregrounds grassroots approaches to community memory as a future-oriented conduit of Asian American political identity.

Through oral histories, community archives, and testimonial narrative—practices that exceed traditional institutional repositories of knowledge—the case studies in this section document the process of movement meaning-making from moments of intergenerational rupture to the joyous moments of Asian American life. Vivian Truong and Minju Bae discuss the processing of CAAAV Organizing Asian Communities' organizational archive, exploring the parallel precarity of this community archive and the organizational commitment to "a movement to stay" for low-income Asian tenants in New York City. Eric C. Wat addresses the AIDS crisis as an intergenerational rupture in the gay Asian American community, probing how the lessons learned from Asian American AIDS activists of the Reagan era might provide useful for younger generations. Amber Lee, Linda Luu, Mimi Khúc, Kevin Park, and Lawrence-Minh Bùi Davis provide an insurgent how-to manual for establishing Asian American studies, building on diverse experiences as student organizers and contingent faculty fighting for institutional commitments to Asian American studies while navigating the neoliberal logics of the university.

13

A Movement to Stay

The Grassroots Archive of CAAAV Organizing Asian Communities

VIVIAN TRUONG AND MINJU BAE

In January 2018, a snowstorm overwhelmed New York City. The snow accumulation, high wind gusts, and bitter cold of this "bomb cyclone" hobbled the city's infrastructure. Schools were closed, and subways and buses were delayed, while the Department of Sanitation suspended trash pickup to repurpose trucks for snow removal. For some low-income tenants and other vulnerable New Yorkers, the storm exacerbated existing challenges and social inequalities. Thousands of residents in public housing were left without heat and hot water as temperatures fell into the single digits.[1] The elderly and disabled were homebound as ice covered sidewalks. Workers who could not stay home were forced to contend with long and dangerous commutes. But bomb cyclone or not, the city's infrastructural shortcomings during severe weather events, as well as mounting hardships for working-class communities of color, were certainly not new.

As a grassroots organization working with immigrant tenants in Manhattan's Chinatown and Astoria, Queens, CAAAV Organizing Asian Communities braced for the worst. Founded in 1986 as the Coalition Against Anti-Asian Violence, CAAAV has been organizing low-income Asian immigrant and refugee communities in New York City for over three decades. The organization had navigated severe weather events before. During Hurricane Sandy in 2012, Lower Manhattan experienced a blackout for almost a week. Through conversations with tenant members in Chinatown, CAAAV staff realized that there was a complete absence of emergency aid in the immediate aftermath of the storm. The organization stepped in to distribute meals, water, batteries, blankets, and other resources for New Yorkers living in precarious conditions.[2] Hurricane Sandy revealed how CAAAV's tenant organizing against displacement could not be separated from the escalating climate crisis.

Despite its recent history with severe weather, CAAAV did not expect the impact that the 2018 bomb cyclone would have on the headquarters of the organization itself: its office in Chinatown. At CAAAV's storefront on Hester Street, a frozen pipe burst and set off the sprinklers, soaking computers, floors, and files. The office had been closed for the winter holidays, and thankfully, no one was in the space when the flooding occurred. As public historians who had been working with the organization's archives since 2014, we—Vivian and Minju—were worried about the state of the irreplaceable documents and archival materials stored in CAAAV's back closet.[3]

The day after the storm, Vivian visited the office to assess the damage. It was pitch black. None of the lights were on or working. The wet wooden floorboards were peeling off from the ground. We became most concerned about one set of materials in particular: the archival records of one of the organization's co-founders. Mini Liu's papers sat in a cardboard box directly under a sprinkler. When Vivian picked up the soaking box, its bottom disintegrated and the folders slid to the floor. When Minju arrived, we piled the documents, along with photographs that had also been water damaged, into her car. That evening, Minju laid out the materials to dry in her apartment.

Luckily, we were able to salvage almost all of the papers and photographs that were soaked in the storm. But the flood had thrown the goals and values of the CAAAV archive project into stark relief. Over the following days, as we carefully peeled wet papers from each other, separated them with paper towels, and hoped for the best, doubts and questions rose to the surface. What was our responsibility as public historians who had taken on the task of working with the organization to document its history and preserve its archives? The event demonstrated the environmental and structural conditions that complicate archival sustainability, especially in an era of escalating ecological crisis. A singular event could threaten both neighborhoods and the archives that document their histories.

Prior to the flood, we had made the decision with the CAAAV board and executive director to house the materials with the organization rather than with an institutional repository. As we surveyed the water-damaged papers and photographs, we asked ourselves whether we had made the right choice. Instead, the archive could have sat in a climate-controlled repository with paid staff to steward this collection. The most viable institutional archive was the Tamiment Library at New York University, a special-collection repository that collects materials regarding New York's leftist politics and labor history. But, while the Tamiment is where much of New York's Asian American records are accessioned, New York University is one of the city's top-ten most land-owning landlords, incongruous with CAAAV's anticapitalist agenda to ensure "housing for all."[4] Like so many grassroots organizations and community-based archives, resource allocation and adequate funding were among our central concerns; but CAAAV's grassroots archive also had to align with CAAAV's organizational mission.

In our work with CAAAV's grassroots archive, we have had to choose between prioritizing preservation for the future and the archive's accessibility for the organization's ongoing work. Preservation of the materials is indeed vitally important. As the flood revealed, the precarious housing and climate conditions that threaten the sustainability of grassroots archives are not separate from those that confront their communities. In the face of displacement and erasure, the archive stakes the place of poor and working-class migrant residents in the city's past, present, and future. But even in the face of precarity, we have insisted on the practice of self-determinative archiving. For CAAAV, documenting and engaging with community histories of resistance is a critical part of the organization's fight against gentrification. Consequently, housing the archive at CAAAV—in binders, the office closet, its server, and on hard drives—has become our commitment. The self-determinative politics of the archive, made useful for political organizing and embedded in its current location, decenters preservation as the primary goal of archival practice.

We argue that CAAAV's archival practice is principally a demonstration of a political agenda to "stay" in an era of displacement. In a city that deprioritizes the well-being of low-income tenants and public housing residents, CAAAV organizes to hold landlords and government officials accountable for untenable housing conditions and extreme inequalities. CAAAV's tenant members have fought for the right to stay in their homes in Chinatown and Queens as part of a citywide movement against rising rents, landlord harassment, unsafe public housing conditions, and the predatory urban changes of gentrification. The same archive that documents these struggles over urban space has also faced its own displacements. In the context of these displacements, the archive contributes to the movement to stay, to change the conditions of precarity rather than solely attempting to survive within them. Through practices of self-determination, we illustrate that archives are not only for the documentation of the past and preservation for the future, but also can be a part of struggles for justice in the present.

Developing a Self-Determinative Archival Practice

CAAAV's grassroots archive is a living history and testament to a social movement to stay. In this chapter, we establish the centrality of historicization in grassroots organizing efforts. During the Asian American movement, activists conducted historical research, amplifying experiences of internment, labor struggles, wars, and militarism, as well as campaigns for social change.[5] Through a study of CAAAV's founding years and subsequent campaigns, we situate CAAAV's archival collection in this tradition of memory reclamation. We highlight the significance of engaging these pasts with youths, activists, and the organization's members. To facilitate these engagements, housing these materials with the organization has been central to our praxis. But the archive project has not been without challenges and obstacles. It confronts many of the same conditions that CAAAV grapples with as an organization. Multiple forms of precarity, questions about archival sustainability, and the status of repositories in New York City have informed our practice of self-determinative archiving. We conclude the chapter with some "lessons learned," with commitments to constantly reflect, adapt, and shift our assessments of the relationships among the archive, the organization, and the city.

We situate the CAAAV archive project within a growing movement toward the maintenance of archives by the very communities that produced them. Traditionally, professional archivists have led archives with the intent to collect and preserve materials in an institutional repository for future research. In contrast, archival studies scholar Andrew Flinn defines community archives as "the grassroots activities of documenting, recording, and exploring community heritage in which community participation, control and ownership of the project is essential."[6] As a community archive project, we are not only changing *what* histories are documented but also shifting the *who, when, where,* and *why* of archives. At CAAAV, we have involved community members in maintaining the materials within the organization and engaging the archive to support the everyday work of an organization that continues to live out the legacies documented in its histories.

Certainly, CAAAV's collection is not the first grassroots archive to reclaim the historical pasts of Asian communities in the United States. The Densho Digital Repository is home to thousands of photographs, magazines, newspapers, and other primary documents, preserving the experiences of Japanese American incarceration and the legacies of World War II. The repository's administrators not only are dedicated to the documentation and preservation of these histories but have an expressed agenda of using their collections as "tools for social change," which includes reshaping the way Japanese American incarceration is taught in K-12 education.[7] The South Asian American Digital Archive (SAADA) preserves and shares the long history of South Asian American communities—and, notably, most of these materials are born digital. Co-founder and archivist Michelle Caswell notes how SAADA addresses the "symbolic annihilation" or erasure and marginalization of South Asian experiences in broader narratives of U.S. history.[8] There is also the Southeast Asian Archive at the University of California, Irvine, which is the repository for primary and secondary materials regarding Southeast Asian diasporic communities. Asian American studies scholar Dorothy Fujita-Rony contends that projects such as the Southeast Asian Archive do not just add multicultural difference to the national discourse, but also highlight how archives have been shaped by "militarized rupture" and the historical erasures created by U.S. imperialism.[9]

The grassroots archive at CAAAV presents a few differences from these projects. Centrally, the archival collection at CAAAV does not stand alone. Neither accessioned at an institutional repository nor an independent project, the grassroots archive lives with and for the organization. Aimed to bolster ongoing organizing campaigns and political education, as well as to ground the organization in time and place, the archive is intentionally embedded in CAAAV. We challenge the tendency to view community archives as "stepping stones" before materials are transferred to a more traditional archival institution.[10] Beyond the ethical concerns of donating the records of an anti-gentrification organization to a large landowning university, housing the CAAAV archive at an institutional repository may actually be counterintuitive to the aim of the project to be useful for current organizing. A self-determinative practice allows us to rethink the location, use, and temporality of archives beyond those that are circumscribed by mainstream institutions.

Through an examination of CAAAV's archive, we show that social movement archives do not solely reflect histories of activism, but also have the potential to shape them. They guide current organizing, act as a site of community-building, and root community members in a politically and historically grounded sense of identity and context. Our approach to the project aligns with Michelle Caswell's provocation to move beyond a linear understanding of time and progress that locates the ultimate purpose of archives in the future. She suggests that we "reconceptualize archival *use* . . . shifting our imaginary about use from some vague, more-just future that might never come, *to now*. What does it mean to activate records to end cycles of oppression in the current political moment?"[11] Produced by an organization dedicated to community organizing, the CAAAV archive project illustrates how historical work, specifically the production and maintenance of records, has long been part of Asian American movement-building.

Historicizing Movement Roots

From the Asian American movement of the 1960s and 1970s to CAAAV's community organizing since the 1980s, archives and historical awareness have been central priorities in struggles for justice. The production and interpretation of historical records about Asian American communities have not been processes solely led by outside scholars looking to the past; rather, activists and organizers have documented historical moments as they lived and created them. As public historians who have played various roles in CAAAV and other community organizations, we have developed the CAAAV archive project with an attention to the ways that history has, and continues to, contribute to movement work.

In the 1960s and 1970s, Asian American activists embarked on historical recovery projects as a form of self-determination through the reclamation of knowledge about their own communities. One of the movement leaders who has been credited with coining the term "Asian American," Yuji Ichioka—of the Asian American Political Alliance at Berkeley—was a historian of prewar Japanese American experiences, interested in reframing the past.[12] Movement activists also published anthologies, such as *Roots* and *Counterpoint*, which compiled early writings of the movement and included articles on Chinese, Filipino, and Japanese American histories.[13] In 1969 the New York–based Asian Americans for Action (AAA)—the first Asian American organization on the East Coast—wrote in their first newsletter, "The price we have paid for . . . assimilation is the loss of our community, the sense of group identification with our fellow Asians."[14] They then situated Asian Americans' common experiences of migrant exclusions and their role as cheap laborers within a broader politics of Third World liberation.[15] Asian American activists also connected the detonations of the atomic bombs in Japan to the rising body count in the Vietnam War to demonstrate the disposability of Asians in U.S. wars. For leaders of the early Asian American movement, a sense of shared racial identity was rooted in historicizing a collective past.

Then and now, historical work has been a critical part of building "Asian American" as a unifying political ideal.[16] CAAAV is directly tied to the legacy of pan-ethnic Asian American movement-building in New York that began with AAA. Co-founders Mini Liu and Monona Yin met as members of the Organization of Asian Women (OAW), which emerged from AAA to create a space to discuss and address Third World women's issues. Kazu Iijima, a Japanese American camp survivor who was one of the co-founders of AAA and OAW, was also an early member of CAAAV, board member, and contributor to the organization's newsletters. Iijima, Liu, and Yin carried the pan-ethnic coalitional ethos of the 1960s and '70s Asian American movement into a new decade.

The 1980s were a particular flashpoint in the history of Asian American organizing for racial justice. In 1982 two white autoworkers,

Ronald Ebens and Michael Nitz, fatally beat Chinese American Vincent Chin on the night of his bachelor party. Resentful of the Japanese auto industry's rise, auto workers in Detroit blamed East Asians and Asian Americans for their recessed economic prospects, as workers faced layoffs and joblessness. In the wake of Vincent Chin's murder, the pain and rage felt by Asian Americans across the country politicized and galvanized new community formations. In 1986, with a parallel rise in violence against Asian Americans in New York, Mini Liu and Monona Yin brought ten organizations together to create a forum to discuss and organize around anti-Asian violence. The Coalition Against Anti-Asian Violence was founded at this 1986 forum. And then, the coalition became its own organization in 1988: the Committee Against Anti-Asian Violence.

In the early 1990s the organization began to shift from responding to individual cases of violence to addressing the systemic roots of racial, economic, and gender injustice.[17] CAAAV organized South Asian taxi drivers and Filipina domestic workers for labor rights, Vietnamese and Cambodian families for access to social services, and Chinatown-based youths and tenants against police violence and gentrification. Several of its former programs have developed into autonomous organizations, including the New York Taxi Workers Alliance, Mekong NYC, and Domestic Workers United.

All of these campaigns produced records, photographs, films, ephemera, and notes. Preserving, filing, and utilizing these materials in the everyday work of the organization created the groundwork for retelling the history of New York's Asian communities and the significance of CAAAV's programs. Through thirty-five years of history, CAAAV has become one of the most prominent Asian American grassroots organizations. These archives are a testament to that history, revealing its model of community organizing and its commitment to leftist politics, working-class membership, and multiracial coalition-building. Through these records and historical reclamation, CAAAV is trying not just to survive in precarity, but to affirm life in the city through self-determinative practices.

CAAAV has undergone significant transformations in the past few decades. What began as a coalition addressing individual cases of anti-Asian violence became an independent organization focusing on grassroots community organizing. Its name, constituencies, program areas, and issues of concern have changed throughout the decades. Dozens of staff and board members have come and gone. Despite these major shifts, the organization's commitment to its values, particularly to intersectional and multiracial coalition-building, has stayed consistent. Referencing the organization's stance against homophobia in the 1980s and addressing anti-Arab violence during the Gulf War, co-founder Monona Yin stated, "The way that people talk now about making those connections, we made all those connections in the beginning. We always had this very stable worldview, and we always knew which side we were on."[18] Since its early years, CAAAV held fast to a broader vision of justice that did not only mean securing rights and privileges for Asian Americans, but also to understand their struggles in relation to other communities of color. The organization also prioritized the concerns of those marginalized within the category of "Asian American," including immigrants, refugees, the poor, women, and low-wage workers. Institutional memory has been a central part of maintaining this worldview and guiding CAAAV through these dramatic contextual changes in its organizational life.

An attentiveness to the importance of the organization's history in its ongoing activities has guided our work with the CAAAV archive project. Vivian, having worked on the organization's staff as a youth organizer in the previous two years, initiated the archive project in the summer of 2014. That August, Minju responded to a call for volunteers to digitize the organizational archives. At the time, we were both students in our respective graduate programs in American studies and history. Since then, we have worked together on multiple phases of the archival project beyond the newsletter digitization, archiving the organization's papers, photographs, audio and visual media, ephemera, and other materials.[19] We began the archive project not as outside professional archivists, but as student volunteers who were part of and hoped to continue to contribute to the communities and movements whose histories were recorded in the archive.

Rather than approaching the project through the lens of "discovering" neglected records, we began with an understanding that the organization was already embedding its history in its everyday work. For instance, orientations for new youth and tenant members often began with recounting the organization's founding and key moments in its past, and lessons learned from the organization's history also influenced decisions about new campaigns. In spite of the historical lessons that were instrumental for the organization's political agenda, there were few resources and limited capacity among staff members to sustain the archive. Consequently, a significant trove of documents, photographs, audiovisual materials, and other archival media sat mostly unused in the office's back closet and off-site storage unit. We took on this labor in order to coordinate, organize, prioritize, and catalog materials at the organization—and in particular, to support their process in creating a living history that exists in the past and present.

Record-keeping and documentation had been a long-held practice in the organization and among its members. One of CAAAV's first projects in its work against anti-Asian violence was to produce a centralized record of "hate incidents" against Asian Americans across the country. The organizational newsletters began as an effort to update and distribute this documentation. Notably, CAAAV co-founder Mini Liu meticulously collected papers on the organization's activities from its beginnings in the 1980s, organized into a box of forty-two folders. In 2017, Liu donated materials and ephemera to the grassroots archive—materials about founding campaigns, banners, memos, and notes from meetings—and these materials play a central role in locating the collection alongside the organization's beginnings.

In addition to Liu's personal papers, CAAAV has intentionally collected a broad scope of archival materials in many forms. In the organization's storage closet, boxes of VHS tapes, DVDs, and audio cassettes were labeled "to be converted," signaling the archiving impulse of a previous member of the organization. In yet another instance of record-keeping, CAAAV produced documentaries on the issues its members faced and the organizations' efforts to address them: *Eating Welfare* focused the campaign against welfare reform in the 1990s and its impact on Southeast Asian families in the Bronx, while *Our Homes, Our Rights* followed tenant organizing against gentrification and housing insecurity in Chinatown. Additionally, record-keeping was a routine practice. CAAAV had a ritual of buying copies of the next day's newspapers and tucking news clippings into a binder of plastic sleeves after every rally, press conference, or media event.

Since its founding, for organizers and activists of CAAAV, an understanding of a shared history has been part of the process of building the organization and connection to a broader movement. Many of the items in the grassroots archive, including newsletters, documents, photographs, VHS tapes, and audio cassettes, were produced with the intention of creating a lasting record of the issues facing Asian immigrant and refugee communities and the organization's efforts to address them. Our work has focused on increasing capacity and attention to the archive, weaving it into the ways the organization was already engaging its own history.

Building a Living Grassroots Archive

Working with the history of an ongoing organization, we have as much obligation to respond to the present as to document the past. With the goal of being attentive to coterminous organizing campaigns, the project exists in multiple temporalities and engages many constituencies. The project follows Maria Cotera's formulation of the archive as a process of *encuentro* (encounter) that shifts from building collections to building the collective.[20] Collaborating with youth members to conduct oral histories and tenants to develop a timeline of the organization's history, we have approached our work with the archive as a living process of intergenerational encounter and transfer of institutional memory. These encounters reflect the duality of efforts for the archive to survive and "stay," and to contribute to a dynamic process of movement-building.

The duality between moving and staying was evident in the summer of 2014, when we began to digitize the organization's newsletters as police violence became a central contention in Asian American politics. Printed biannually from 1988 to 2008, the *Voice* was widely distributed to supporters, and together, these newsletters summarize a comprehensive overview of the organization's history. The newsletters detailed CAAAV's organizational activities as well as members' analyses of issues affecting Asian Americans and other people of color in New York City and beyond.

As the newsletter digitization was underway, CAAAV became center stage for another major flashpoint in the history of Asian American organizing in New York. In November 2014, Chinese American New York Police Department officer Peter Liang was convicted of the fatal shooting of African American public housing resident Akai Gurley in Brooklyn. Continuing its commitment to organize alongside the families of police violence victims, CAAAV supported the Gurley family in their demands for accountability. After Liang's indictment and conviction in 2016, the organization faced severe backlash from Chinese Americans who claimed that Liang served as a scapegoat for all NYPD misconduct. Citing this unprecedented moment of police accountability, many conservative Chinese Americans argued that Liang's conviction was unjust. In meaningful contrast, CAAAV organizers identified a long history of systemic violence, identifying that white officers like Daniel Pantaleo, the NYPD officer who killed Eric Garner in 2014, were not indicted.[21]

As CAAAV organized with the families of police violence victims, the organization invoked its history, particularly its role in the movement against police violence during Rudy Giuliani's mayoral administration in the 1990s. Evident in the organizational newsletters, one of the critical cases that CAAAV organized around in that era was the NYPD killing of sixteen-year-old Chinese American Yong Xin Huang in Brooklyn. In 2016 his sister Qing Lan Huang published a public statement that addressed why she supported Akai Gurley's family in their pursuit of justice. She wrote, "Twenty-one years ago, my younger brother, Yong Xin Huang, was killed by an NYPD officer and my family never got justice. Our family's story and grief are not so different than that of Akai Gurley's family. The injustice his family now faces at the hands of the justice system is not so different than that my family faced 21 years ago."[22] CAAAV's commitment to coalition-building in the era of Black Lives Matter was grounded in an understanding of the organization's roots in multiracial and intergenerational movements against police violence in New York City over the past decades.[23]

While this critical debate was unfolding, CAAAV staff and members honored the organization's past. In 2016, CAAAV was preparing for its thirtieth-year anniversary gala, a moment to reflect on the organization's past, present, and future. Historically, CAAAV's youth members played a critical role in the organization, prioritizing intergenerational relationships and memory work in organizational politics and movement to stay in place. CAAAV recognized that youth members—particularly the "1.5-generation" or the second-generation children of immigrants and refugees—served as translators and navigated state bureaucracies, uniquely situated as organizers. For many youth members, CAAAV became a place for them to "cut their teeth" as leaders and organizers, eventually moving on to political work elsewhere. Celebrated in May 2016, the event honored more than a dozen women who had led the organization, as well as various movements for racial, economic, and gender justice in New York City and beyond. Many of the honorees had been working with or alongside CAAAV for many decades, and some of them began as youth members and organizers.[24]

In 2016 the organization activated its living archive with youth members, cultivating historical awareness of its place in movement history. That summer, Vivian coordinated an oral history project in which members of the organization's youth program Asian Youth in Action interviewed women leaders who were honored at the thirtieth-year anniversary event. She specifically trained youth members who were part of the organization to conduct interviews, with a focus on learning from the lessons of multiracial coalition-building of the past to apply to organizing in the present. Among the histories discussed in the interviews and shared in the youth-led event were the organization's work against police violence and multiracial solidarity in the aftermath of the Rodney King verdict in 1992. The summer oral history project concluded with a multimedia event that drew more than seventy community members and incorporated the audio and video of the interviews into youth art, poetry, and performance. The oral history project offered a way for the organization's members and supporters to make sense of the responses to Liang's conviction and CAAAV's role in this critical and unfolding moment in Asian American history.

After the oral history project, we continued to engage youth members and volunteers in the archive to facilitate the intergenerational transfer of institutional memory. We shifted gears to focus on the digitization of organizational photographs and audiovisual materials, including VHS tapes and audio cassettes. Over the summer of 2018, four members of Asian Youth in Action scanned more than a thousand photographs, entered metadata, and transferred photos into archival preservation boxes and folders. The photo digitization efforts took place immediately before CAAAV welcomed a new executive director. While Asian Youth in Action paused its usual organizing activities that summer during the leadership transition, the archive project allowed for youths to continue to engage with the organization and its past. At another organizational event, the youth members shared favorite archival photographs and research, bringing members and supporters together for another opportunity to reflect on CAAAV's history during a time of leadership transition.

The "encounter" among generations and between past and present was made evident again in 2018. We were finalizing a timeline banner, part of a storefront exhibition developed in collaboration with the Chinatown Art Brigade, a collective of culture workers supporting the neighborhood's campaigns against displacement. The timeline featured photographs digitized by the youth members and incorporated feedback from members of CAAAV's Chinatown Tenants Union. Previous iterations of the timeline, used to introduce new members to the organization's history, were written in colored marker on pieces of butcher paper taped together. As with other aspects of the archive project, the timeline emerged out of a specific need from the organization, with attention to the way that CAAAV was already engaging its history. The organization had been grappling with the question of how its programs—the Chinatown Tenants Union, Asian Youth in Action, and the Asian Tenants Union in Queens public housing—related to the organization as a whole. Tracing CAAAV's history from its founding in 1986 was part of developing a sense of shared organizational identity. The timeline showcased more than thirty years of CAAAV's most significant campaigns, from organizing against police violence to creating worker centers for lease drivers and domestic workers. But the last panel on the timeline was still unfolding.

In 2018 the notorious Seattle-based company Amazon was looking to expand. Cities throughout North America hummed with the question of where the new "Amazon HQ2" would go, encouraging locales to start a bidding war for tax breaks and other corporate incentives. After a prolonged process, the corporation announced that it would settle one of its new headquarters in Long Island City, a neighborhood in Queens known for its warehouses, taxi depots—and, an emergent scene of high-rise luxury apartments, hotel development, and gentrification.

The economic and racial disparities of this part of Queens were not lost on many New Yorkers. Since 2015, CAAAV has worked with Bangladeshi, Chinese, and Korean tenants of Queensbridge Houses in Long Island City to demand language access, better living conditions, and an end to the privatization of public housing. Just across the way from where Amazon had announced its new territory is the largest housing project in North America, where the median income is far below the federal poverty line.[25] Amazon was preying on poor New Yorkers, threatening to intensify inequalities and deepen unaffordability in the neighborhood. In response, a coalition of tenants, housing justice activists, and anti-gentrification organizations fiercely mobilized to fight and realize a New York City without HQ2. Building cross-racial alliances with Black and Latinx tenants in the face of Amazon's expansion plan, CAAAV members joined the coalition of housing justice activists to make their case for public housing residents' right to stay in their homes and fight for a more affordable city. In late 2018, the city council began to hold hearings, as activists, public officials, and New Yorkers voiced their claims against this corporate giant and the deleterious impact Amazon would have on affordability in New York.

The last panel on the timeline documented the ongoing campaign against Amazon's HQ2. Shortly after we picked up the nine-foot banner from the printers, we heard the news of the tenants' successful efforts against one of the world's largest corporations: Amazon withdrew its plans to build a headquarters in Queens. CAAAV and the coalition of anti-gentrification organizations had defeated one of the wealthiest corporations in the world. In the midst of this victorious moment for the organization and poor and working-class residents of Queens, we realized that our freshly printed and unfurled banner was already outdated. This moment was emblematic of one of the core questions we have confronted in our work with CAAAV's grassroots archive: how do you preserve and archive a living history?

The "Housing for the People" exhibit opened in February 2019. In addition to the timeline of CAAAV's history, it featured a map of Manhattan's Chinatown and interviews with members of CAAAV's Chinatown Tenants Union. The materials situated the organization's campaigns in space and time, while the stories provided context of low-wage and migrant Asian New Yorkers' struggle against gentrification. The timeline now hangs as a banner in CAAAV's storefront office in Chinatown, physically accessible for active engagement. Alongside archival and recent photographs, the timeline contextualizes the office and gathering space with a history of organized struggle and resistance.

Figure 13.1: CAAAV members at a rally after the murder of twenty-three-year-old Trinidadian American Michael Griffith in Howard Beach.

The final panel on the timeline still reads, "Tenant leaders of CAAAV's NYCHA Organizing Project speak out against Amazon's plan to open a headquarters in Long Island City." As a snapshot of the campaign while it was still in progress, that panel demonstrates CAAAV's living archive. In this chapter, we have suggested that the purpose of grassroots archives go beyond preservation for an ill-defined future—even in the face of precarious conditions that threaten that future. In fact, the fight against the Amazon headquarters shows how these archives can actually *resist* preservation. At the very moment when we tried to capture the history of an ongoing organization into a static timeline, that organization continued to make history. Living histories require us to rethink the tools and goals of archive projects.

Conclusion

The wrinkled documents from Mini Liu's collection—water-damaged from the 2018 office flood at CAAAV—are a testament to a "movement to stay." As of the writing of this chapter, CAAAV has been active for almost forty years, a point of immense pride for its founders and staff. Co-founder Mini Liu, who had been part of the organization in formal

Figure 13.2: CAAAV archival materials laid out to dry after the 2018 storm in New York City.

and informal roles since 1986, declared at the thirtieth anniversary celebration in 2016, "I don't burn out on issues. Issues burn out on me." The leadership of women like Mini Liu has sustained CAAAV and broader movements for racial, economic, and gender justice through the decades. Against conservative ascendancy and neoliberal retrenchment of the 1980s and 1990s, these women leaders have built the organizational infrastructure that has done the daily work of movement-building between and through moments of mass mobilization. While we lamented the damage to Liu's papers, she reassured us that the files belonged to CAAAV. "I had let go of my attachments to the documents when I passed them to you," she said.[26] Liu's wisdom demonstrates her commitment to the movement, redirecting ownership of the archives to an organization that continues to carry on the work of the Asian American movement.

In an ever-precarious city, where infrastructural neglect and the local effects of a global climate crisis are the environment of archival collections, we consider the urgency of rethinking the logic of archival work. What is the purpose of archives?[27] For community organizations and activist groups that may be grappling with the question of how to engage with their archives, we offer the following lessons learned from our work with CAAAV.

1. *Determine how the organization already engages with its past.* This evaluation of how staff, members, and other stakeholders use their organization's history in their everyday work provides an important basis for understanding the purposes and direction of an archive project.
2. *Approach archive-building projects as a collective.* The work of building, preserving, and engaging the archive can be part of the process of creating community, not just documenting the history of a community that already exists.
3. *Negotiate tough decisions with the organizational mission in mind.* When confronted with dilemmas regarding where and how to maintain archival materials, consider how these choices might be guided by the ongoing needs and purpose of the organization to which the materials belong.
4. *Rethinking preservation as the primary goal of archives.* While archives are typically preserved for future use by researchers, our

movements need archives to support struggles for justice in the here and now.

Over fifty years have passed since the beginning of the Asian American movement. We are at a critical juncture. Asian American organizations have now accumulated decades of records. It is time to assess the state of movement organizations' commitment to historical memory, especially as grassroots archives often face the same precarious conditions as the communities in which they are located. In the face of uncertain futures, self-determination in archival practice can be a tool to build and sustain movements to stay.

Notes

1. Edgar Sandoval and Greg B. Smith, "Thousands of NYCHA Residents without Heat as Winter 'Bomb Cyclone' Prepares to Pummel City," *New York Daily News*, January 3, 2018, www.nydailynews.com.
2. Sukjong Hong, "Left in the Dark: Inside the Buildings of Chinatown after Hurricane Sandy," The Margins, November 27, 2012, https://aaww.org.
3. Historically, public historians have grappled with the concerns of sharing authority, and in many instances, re-created the very power dynamics between the historian and subject. Aware of this past, we use the "public historian" moniker to gesture toward emergent scholarship and praxis that prioritizes and honors the work of multiple publics. In this instance, we are embedded in the organization as public historians, rather than public historians approaching a community-based organization, in order to conduct research. This distinction is central to our articulation of self-determinative archiving.
4. Tanay Warerkar, "New York's 10 Biggest Property Owners," *Curbed: New York*, September 14, 2018, https://ny.curbed.com.
5. For a primary source on the Asian American movement, see the Gidra Collection, *Densho Digital Repository*, 1969–2001, https://ddr.densho.org. For a historiographical essay on the Asian American movement, see Diane C. Fujino, "Who Studies the Asian American Movement?: A Historiographical Analysis," *Journal of Asian American Studies* 11, no. 2 (June 2008): 127–169.
6. Andrew Flinn, "Community Histories, Community Archives: Some Opportunities and Challenges," *Journal of the Society of Archivists* 28, no. 2 (October 2007): 153.
7. Vivian Wong, Tom Ikeda, Ellen-Rae Cachola, and Florante Peter Ibanez, "Archives (Re)Imagined Elsewhere: Asian American Community-Based Archival Organizations," in *Through the Archival Looking Glass: A Reader on Diversity and Inclusion*, eds. Mary A. Caldera and Kathryn M. Neal (Chicago: Society for American Archivists, 2014), 122.

8 Michelle Caswell, "Seeing Yourself in History: Community Archives and the Fight against Symbolic Annihilation," *Public Historian* 36, no. 4 (November 2014): 27.
9 Dorothy Fujita-Rony, "Illuminating Militarized Rupture: Four Asian American Community-Based Archives," *Journal of Asian American Studies* 23, no. 1 (February 2020): 2.
10 Michelle Caswell, *Urgent Archives: Enacting Liberatory Memory Work* (New York: Routledge, 2021), 8.
11 Ibid., 43.
12 Yuji Ichioka, "A Historian by Happenstance," *Amerasia Journal* 26, no. 1 (2000): 32–53.
13 Amy Tachiki, Eddie Wong, Franklin Odo, and Buck Wong, eds., *Roots: An Asian American Reader* (Los Angeles: UCLA Asian American Studies Center Press, 1971); Emma Gee, Bruce Iwasaki, Mike Murase, Megumi Dick Osumi, Jesse Quinsaat, and June Okida Kuramoto, eds., *Counterpoint: Perspectives on Asian America* (Los Angeles: UCLA Asian American Studies Center Press, 1976).
14 Asian Americans for Action, Newsletter, June 1969, Box 3, Folder 29, Kishi and Sun Collection, Fales Library, New York University.
15 See Daryl J. Maeda, *Chains of Babylon: The Rise of Asian America* (Minneapolis: University of Minnesota Press, 2009); Gary Y. Okihiro, *Third World Studies: Theorizing Liberation* (Durham, NC: Duke University Press, 2016).
16 See Minju Bae and Mark Tseng-Putterman, "Reviving the History of Radical Black-Asian Internationalism," *Roar Magazine*, July 21, 2020, for a discussion of the recent turn to unsettle "Asian America" as a political ideal.
17 Reflecting the transition from case-by-case advocacy to community organizing, the organization changed its name to CAAAV: Organizing Asian Communities in 1998 and later dropped the colon in the mid-2000s.
18 Monona Yin, interview with Emily Li, Kyla Cheung, and Vivian Truong, July 10, 2016, Brooklyn, NY.
19 Many others were involved in the process of launching the archive project and sustaining it since then. At the beginning of the project, the Asian/Pacific/American Institute at New York University directed Vivian to archivist Maggie Schreiner, who volunteered to assess the materials in the organization's back closet. After responding to the call for volunteers, Minju met with the then executive director Cathy Dang and scanned multiple newsletters, and then tagged each newsletter with key terms and themes. Managing a spreadsheet of metadata and information, Minju worked with web developer Manu Mei-Singh to load the digitized files onto the organizational website. By January 2015, web users could download the PDF files of the newsletters and view the reading guide (co-authored with Alison Roh Park) that outlined some of the newsletters' content and themes.
20 Maria Cotera, "'Invisibility Is an Unnatural Disaster': Feminist Archival Praxis after the Digital Turn," *South Atlantic Quarterly* 114, no. 4 (October 1, 2015): 781.
21 Wen Liu, "Complicity and Resistance: Asian American Body Politics in Black Lives Matter," *Journal of Asian American Studies* 21, no. 3 (October 2018): 421–451.

22 Qinglan Huang, "Opinion: Akai Gurley's Family Deserves Justice," MSNBC, April 12, 2016, www.msnbc.com.
23 For more, see May Fu, Simmy Makhijani, Anh-Thu Pham, Meejin Richart, Joanne Tien, and Diane Wong, "#Asians4BlackLives: Notes from the Ground," *Amerasia Journal* 45, no. 2 (2019): 253–270; Vivian Truong, "From State-Sanctioned Removal to the Right to the City: The Policing of Asian Immigrants in Southern Brooklyn 1987–1995," *Journal of Asian American Studies* 23, no. 1 (February 2020): 61–92.
24 For more on the youth programs at CAAAV, see Eric Tang, *Unsettled: Cambodian Refugees in the New York City Hyperghetto* (Philadelphia: Temple University Press, 2015).
25 Corey Kilgannon, "Amazon's New Neighbor: The Nation's Largest Housing Project," *New York Times*, November 12, 2018; Daniel A. Medina, "The Grassroots Coalition That Took On Amazon . . . and Won," *The Guardian*, March 24, 2019; J. David Goodman, "Amazon Went to City Hall. Things Got Loud, Quickly," *New York Times*, December 12, 2018. For a timeline of the struggle between New York City and Amazon, see Amy Plitt, "Amazon HQ2 and NYC: A Timeline of the Botched Deal," *Curbed: New York*, February 18, 2019, https://ny.curbed.com.
26 Mini Liu, email message to Vivian Truong, January 8, 2018.
27 We ask this question provocatively, recognizing the complexities of archival processes for Asian communities in New York. Another community-based instance of archiving was with the founding of the New York Chinatown History Project in 1976, which is now the Museum of Chinese in America (MOCA). Much of MOCA's archives were stored in a repurposed school (P.S. 23) at 70 Mulberry Street, but the museum's decisions to warehouse and exhibit materials in Manhattan's Chinatown represented permanence and defiance in the face of displacement, rejection, and crisis. The New York Chinatown History Project had been a grassroots reclamation of a neighborhood and its past, and its founders began this history project from the bottom up. The founders realized the necessity to remember, restore, and reconstruct the long-neglected histories of Chinese in New York. But MOCA has transformed significantly since its founding. Following up on a plan to close Rikers Island jail complex, $8.7 billion was allocated to build four borough-based jails, and one is slated for construction at 125 White Street in Manhattan's Chinatown. As part of the city's "community give-back" program to invest in the affected neighborhoods, MOCA will receive $35 million in funding. Activists have demanded that the museum divest from incarcerating the poor. While MOCA has roots in reclaiming historical pasts, recent events indicate that self-determinative archiving does not govern the museum's archiving practice. For more on the fire that set 70 Mulberry Street ablaze, see Sophia Chang and Sydney Pereira, "Museum of Chinese in America President Fears Damage to Archives from Chinatown Fire, Including "Priceless" Historical Items," *The Gothamist*, January 24, 2020, https://gothamist.com/; Ryan Lee Wong, "The Stories Lost in the Museum of Chinese in America Fire," *Frieze*, February 7, 2020, https://frieze.com.

14

Movement Joy, Seriously

Learning from AIDS Activism

ERIC C. WAT

In 2017 I embarked on an oral history project about Asian American AIDS activism in Los Angeles. I began that journey at the ONE National Gay & Lesbian Archives. Before I interviewed the thirty-five AIDS activists in the next two years, I pored over boxes of archival materials—mostly meeting minutes, official correspondence, funding proposals, research reports, and newspaper clippings. The documents refreshed my lapsed memories about the epidemic. AIDS activism was a constant backdrop in the formation of my racial, sexual, and political identities. I was barely a teenager coming to terms with my sexual desire at its advent in the early 1980s. A decade later, before new medications offered some glimpses of hope for people living with HIV in the mid-1990s, I became an outreach volunteer for the Asian Pacific AIDS Intervention Team (APAIT), the AIDS service organization that is so central to this oral history.

This oral history was eventually published as *Love Your Asian Body: AIDS Activism in Los Angeles* (University of Washington Press, 2022). During the book's production, my editors asked for my input about the cover art. I scoured the internet for images for other books about AIDS. At the bottom of that rabbit hole, I found a lot of images that reinforced those memories unearthed by my archival research: photos of angry (mostly white) protesters at demonstrations, images of emaciated figures (again, mostly white) with a hint of youth behind their hollow eyes, and plenty of bright red graphics (a bloody handprint, a syringe dripping with a drop of blood, and the ubiquitous red ribbon).

Asian American AIDS activists that I talked to are no strangers to these narratives of anger, grief, and horror. Yet, there is something incomplete about these memories of the AIDS movement that don't do justice to their memories and the stories that they shared with me. In my archival research, I also remembered coming across flyers, materials, and even comics that were fun and sex-positive, and these were produced by grassroots organizations, including APAIT. The contrast was so stark between these visual materials from the community and the more institutional documents that they struck me like a splash of color in a black-and-white film. Amid all the rage the epidemic brought—or maybe because of it—I knew that the community's resistance was generative and even joyous.

This chapter delves into how joy is uniquely central to the memory of the Asian American AIDS activists' experience, especially in the early 1990s. If joy is not part of the dominant narratives about the AIDS movement or in its archives, how do I, as an oral historian, fill the gaps in these institutional memories? Finally, I explore what joy means to a new generation of queer activists of color, and lessons learned on how we can better preserve these memories.

What Is Movement Joy?

Movement joy is not a new idea. To concretize what I mean by joy, I turn to the lesbian writers of color whose writing taught me everything I know about intersectionality. In a speech Audre Lorde gave in 1978, she described the "erotic" as "those physical, emotional, and psychic expressions of what is deepest and strongest and richest within each of us, being shared: the passions of love, in its deepest meanings."[1] She elaborated, "When I speak of the erotic, then, I speak . . . of that creative energy empowered, the knowledge and use of which we are now reclaiming in our language, our history, our dancing, our loving, our work, our lives." She went on to discuss how the erotic functions best communally: "The sharing of joy, whether physical, emotional, psychic, or intellectual, forms a bridge between the sharers which can be the basis of understanding much of what is not shared between them, and lessens the threat of their difference." Moreover, once we experience this sharing, it opens our "capacity for joy" and allows us to recognize its power so that "in honor and self-respect we can require no less of ourselves."[2] Lorde's definition of joy requires sharing. Storytelling is one vehicle for this joy. When we share our stories of joy, it allows people, especially those who have been disenfranchised, to find connections with others; to understand that their trauma does not result from personal deficits, but systematic ones; and in so doing, to find a path to healing together. We are seen as our full selves, not just the victimized parts.

I had not expected to find much joy in documenting the Asian American AIDS movement in Los Angeles, even though I had been a direct participant in it. This is a testament to the power of mainstream narratives about AIDS that are now inscribed in our collective memory, obscuring other equally important narratives that seemingly contradict it. Finding those joyous artifacts of the Asian American AIDS movement at the ONE Archives, even as they were buried among so many more official documents about AIDS, disrupted this memory. Discussing the limitations of traditional archives in her research about Black women at the turn of the twentieth century, historian Saidiya Hartman wrote, "The textual archive proved comparably distorted. From the 1890s through the 1920s, ordinary black women only seemed to make it into print when marked as a social problem: morally lax, suspected of prostitution, averse to work, indifferent to authority, and a threat and a lure to white lovers, audiences, and voyeurs." In her 2008 essay "Venus in Two Acts," Hartman lays out an innovative approach to writing this history that filled in the gaps between "the archive's scraps and shards" to tell more nuanced stories of Black women that were full of joy, experimentation, pleasures, and agency. She calls this approach "critical fabulation": using narrative techniques "both to tell an impossible story and to amplify the impossibility of its telling."[3]

While Hartman had no access to the Black women she was writing about, I was fortunate to be able to conduct oral history interviews with a community of AIDS activists and survivors. To preserve their voices in all their splendid selves, with all their humor, sex, and joy, I approached the writing of this history not as a scientific observer as a distance, but as a storyteller who uses a similar tone and narrative technique as those who shared their stories with me. I didn't shy away from any mention of fuck, dicks, and dildoes. I saw myself as a weaver of the stories, and not a theorizer of them. Once I made the decision to tell their stories this way, joy became a theme that made this Asian American AIDS narrative so unique, and still resonating today.

The Cultural Conventions of AIDS

To understand why joy was a unique response from the Asian American AIDS activists to the epidemic, it's important to understand how AIDS was imagined in the United States and how that imagination was passed down generations through what was written in the mainstream about the epidemic. The Centers for Disease Control and Prevention documented the first cases of AIDS in 1981. The year is significant in understanding why and how AIDS became a specter for more than just a medical problem.

First, gay men had spent just over a decade, since the Stonewall Rebellion in 1969, building a community based on a sexual liberation that flouted heteronormativity. That defiance was not only about having sexual and romantic relationships with someone of the same sex, but also about how many men they had these relationships with (i.e., non-monogamy). And once reproductive sex was no longer part of the equation, many men also explored sex that would be deemed "deviant" by mainstream society. The collective identity became the basis for social and political institutions in the fledgling gay community, and AIDS put many of these behaviors at risk.

Second, 1981 was the beginning of the Reagan administration. As part of his "traditional family values" agenda, the neoconservative president used the AIDS epidemic to demonize gay men as morally perverse, since they, especially white gay men, were who the virus seemed to affect primarily.[4] This fueled the general public's fear and paranoia not only of the AIDS epidemic but also of gay men, who were rendered "contemptible and suspect" by association.

This ideological assault split the gay community. Some gay men sought respect and legitimacy by blaming gay culture and urged the mimicry of heteronormative relationships, while others considered this approach a one-way ticket back to the Dark Ages. The battle lines became clear when even gay strongholds like New York and San Francisco closed down bathhouses, spaces that had been a symbol of sexual liberation for the community and a safe space for homoeroticism even before Stonewall. When the federal government started to invest in HIV education and prevention, the contents of these materials were so divorced from the reality of the kind of sex that people were having that put them at risk, that two activists I interviewed said it was as if the government didn't care if sex was not pleasurable for gay men.

In a 1987 essay, "How to Have Promiscuity in an Epidemic," art historian and AIDS activist Douglas Crimp found it "curious" that, charged with the responsibility of AIDS education with a lot of public funding, the advertising industry "that has used sexual desire to sell everything from cars to detergents suddenly finds itself at a loss for how to sell a condom."[5] In the same essay, Crimp took gay leaders, like Larry Kramer (playwright and co-founder of the Gay Men's Health Crisis in New York, the first AIDS service organization in the United States) and Randy Shilts (a journalist, he wrote the first book about the AIDS crisis, the bestseller *And the Band Played On*), to task for putting the blame of the epidemic on unconventional gay sexuality.[6] He offered a vehement defense of gay promiscuity:

> We were able to invent safe sex because we have always known that sex is not, in an epidemic or not, limited to penetrative sex. Our promiscuity taught us many things, not only about the pleasure of sex, but about the great multiplicity of those pleasures. It is that psychic preparation, that experimentation, that conscious work on our own sexualities that has allowed many of us to change our sexual behaviors.... Gay male promiscuity should be seen instead as a positive model of how sexual pleasures might be pursued by and granted to everyone if those pleasures were not confined within the narrow limits of institutionalized sexuality.[7]

This subversive social construction of AIDS—casting promiscuity or pleasure as the solution, and not a problem—is not the dominant narrative in our collective memory of the epidemic, but it is much closer to what the Asian American AIDS activists in Los Angeles had in mind in the early 1990s.

Love Your Asian Body and Queer Asian Activism

The Asian American AIDS activists' response to the epidemic was complicated by their racial formation. Just as the "gay" identity was relatively new before the AIDS crisis, the notion of a pan-ethnic "Asian American" identity was also rooted in late 1960s and the Third World ethnic studies strikes in San Francisco. Most gay Asian men in the following decade had to explore their racial and sexual identities in a bifurcated manner, with the two seldom intersecting. In many cases, they had to forgo their racial identity in order to claim a space in the gay community, or vice versa. The number of gay Asian men markedly increased in the 1970s, with the 1965 passage of immigration reform and the defeat of the United States in its war in Southeast Asia a decade later. The ensuing ethnic and linguistic complexity made it challenging to build a coherent gay Asian American identity. Even in coastal cities where there was a sizable Asian population, social organizations that were run by and for Asian gay men (and in some cases, lesbians) didn't come together until just before the AIDS crisis. Asian/Pacific Lesbians and Gays (A/PLG) was the first such organization in Los Angeles, and that group was founded in 1980.

For the first time, A/PLG provided the community network and leadership development for gay Asian men that became the bedrock for the local AIDS infrastructure in that community. However, the buy-in for collective action was not a slam dunk for many of its members. Because of the low incidence rate among the Asian population, many of A/PLG's Asian and white members thought AIDS education interfered with the social functions and "cruising" in the organization.[8] In its early years, because there had not been a documented case of an Asian American with AIDS, some even thought they were immune to the virus. In spite of this indifference, a small group of members within A/PLG started a working committee in 1987 when they found out a member had died, alone, of AIDS complications.

A few years later, a younger generation of queer Asians invigorated this committee and took a decided break from the apathy of most A/PLG members. I use the word "queer" deliberately here to signal a significant ideological shift in this group of younger activists. Many of them were radicalized by ACT-UP and Queer Nation.[9] With this new energy, the committee became more public-facing, acquiring both government and philanthropic funding to conduct outreach and education beyond A/PLG members. The committee eventually split off from its parent organization by late 1991 and became what is now the Asian Pacific AIDS Intervention Team (APAIT).

The queer Asian activists' more explicit political analysis was forged by a handful of other events in California, including the veto of Assembly Bill 101 by then Republican governor Pete Wilson, which would have outlawed discrimination against LGBT people in 1991; the acquittal of four Los Angeles Police Department police officers who beat Black motorist Rodney King almost to death, setting off a weeklong uprising in 1992 in Los Angeles; and the passage of Proposition 187 in 1994, a precursor to a new wave of federal anti-immigrant attacks under Democratic president Bill Clinton. Even amid these relentless conservative assaults, wave after white-capped wave, each crashing onto shore with the one before it barely receding, AIDS was not a distraction to these young activists. In fact, clamoring for a reckoning, this new generation of queer Asian activists found AIDS to be the nexus through which they enacted their visions of racial, gender, sexual, and political justice. And they knew they had to broaden their circle and recruit other young queer Asians like me. The Asian American AIDS activists had their share of agitational tactics, but they also built up a utopian community that centered joy and pleasure, even at the height of the epidemic.

HIV prevention was how these activists evangelized this new "Queer Asian" identity, and knowing one's status was a major part of HIV prevention. By the end of the first decade of the AIDS epidemic, traditional safer sex education was getting stale. Neither drilling into people's head about the different ways HIV could be transmitted nor demonstrating how to put a condom over a banana—the kind of knowledge outcomes funders often looked for—was adequate to change people's behavior, especially when people had epidemic-fatigue from hearing the same prohibitive and alarming messages over and over. Ric Parish and Joël Barraquiel Tan, two Filipino American activists who became APAIT's first outreach workers, had a different idea.

Early in the agency's life, Ric was tasked with developing APAIT's first social marketing campaign to encourage HIV testing among gay Asian men in Los Angeles. He drew his inspiration from an outreach encounter at a coffeehouse in West Hollywood in 1991. In an essay collaboration with Joël and others, Ric wrote:

> I overhear one of the younger Pilipino kids sitting at the table say "I wish my nose wasn't so flat . . . maybe if I got a nose job I could score better in

West Hollywood." I then hear "Sista . . . LOVE YO' ASIAN BODY!" I look up and of course it is my best "girlfriend" Joël Tan giving the naïve youth a retort and commentary on the importance of developing self-esteem and self-nurturing. "Besides, little sista, why do you want to spend so much time and money trying to impress white boys, when their dicks look like raw turkey necks anyway? You need to find you a good brown husband who will love you for the beautiful island girl you are, Missy!"

Shortly after, "Love Your Asian Body" became the tagline of this testing campaign and a rallying cry for a new generation of queer Asian Americans in Los Angeles. The campaign featured multiple photos of intimacy between Asian men and, in one instance, between two Asian women. In various stages of undress, the models touched, straddled, and embraced each other. They had clear, smiling faces, and often the models gazed longingly into one another's eyes. The models were APAIT staff and volunteers, mostly young queer Asian friends of Ric and Joël. In an interview with me, Ric reflected, "It was the first images we saw of Asian gay men together, making love. We never saw those images [before then]. There was always, you know, a white guy involved. It was new, and it got a lot of attention."

Eric Reyes, one of the models for the photo shoot, remarked on how these images broke from the traditional visual narratives about HIV prevention. He said, "I used to have a folder of all these old API [Asian/Pacific Islander] HIV/AIDS educational materials. You can see how Love Your Asian Body was so radical. [The old brochures] had these silhouette facials of an Asian person. It was horrible. They looked like things you see at a dentist's office. They had bamboo or Chinese lanterns, some API signifiers in a subtle way that said this is for APIs. They were so embarrassingly bad." Intentionally or not, the ambiguity and anonymity of these outreach materials reinforced AIDS stigma and shame.

HIV outreach workers often stationed outside of gay bars, catching patrons coming in and out and hoping to hold their attention long enough to talk about protecting themselves from the virus. A gay Asian man would just as likely turn away before an outreach worker could utter a first word. These sexy and joyous images on postcards upped the curiosity factor to draw in the target population long enough to start a conversation.

The words and images in the campaign worked together on different levels. They exhorted gay Asian men to love their bodies enough to protect them, through safer sex and regular HIV testing. At the same time, the campaign conveyed that sex could be fun, even when the epidemic continued to loom large in the early 1990s. In an era where sex—especially non-heteronormative and deviant sex—was equated as the grim harbinger of grisly death, Love Your Asian Body brought sexy back defiantly.

For me and my peers, newly adults looking for not only a community that embraced both our racial and sexual identities, but also a political vehicle to enact our newfound sense of social justice, this campaign captured our imagination at a whole other level. "Love Your Asian Body" meant loving each other and seeing each other as sexual beings with autonomy without the white gaze.

To understand this, it is important to appreciate the larger shift in consciousness among queer men of color in the 1990s as a result of AIDS activism. In our interview, Joël said, "So much of early [AIDS] activism was about art and cultural production. I saw 'Love Your Asian Body' in conversation with Gran Fury's 'Silence = Death' or 'Read My Lips.' At the time, it was pre-Facebook, pre-internet. It was about the power of the image." Gran Fury's "Read My Lips" graphic plastered the famous sloganeering of then President George H. W. Bush (as in "Read my lips: no new taxes") against two men locking lips, in military uniforms no less. The shock came from the unexpected juxtaposition of two things that didn't seem to come together at first.

Joël continued, "These artists I saw who were part of ACT-UP influenced what I was thinking about HIV/AIDS and what we need to do about it. Consequently, the movement in gay communities of color followed suit with similar aesthetics. . . . All of a sudden, a lot of these prevention campaigns were about Black on Black love, Latinos with Latinos. So we followed suit, and we had cause to, with all the rice queen syndrome."

This confluence of intra-racial sexual expressions was reflected in the magazine *Lavender Godzilla* by the Gay Asian Pacific Alliance (GAPA) in San Francisco. The magazine published a "smut" issue in fall 1992. Unabashedly pornographic, the forty-eight-page issue featured stories, comics, interviews, pictures of hard abs and harder dicks, and a poem. One of the images from the Love Your Asian Body campaign graced its early pages. The Asian-on-Asian erotic was so inspired that it united two often rivaling queer Asian metropoles. Joël called it a "utopia."

The sexual explicitness of Love Your Asian Body and *Lavender Godzilla* challenged the prevalent racial hierarchy that confined gay Asian men in either an invisible or subservient role. It was a frontrunner of an aesthetic tradition that would, a mere few years later, give rise to an emerging generation of young queer Asian visual artists. In his book *A View from the Bottom: Asian American Masculinity and Sexual Representation*, Nguyen Tan Hoang traces the unapologetically graphic works of gay Asian filmmakers in the mid-1990s, like Ming-Yuen S. Ma and Nguyen himself, to "a new queer Asian visibility in the 1990s as a result of political organizing around gay, Asian identity issues as well as HIV/AIDS activism, education, and prevention." Specifically, he cites "the frank discussions of gay sex practices and the various risks for HIV and other sexually transmitted infections in safer-sex pamphlets, along with multimedia campaigns such as flyers, posters, stickers, buttons, T-shirts and advertising at bus shelters, in subways, and on billboards. . . . [They] utilized the codes and conventions of explicit, hard-core gay male pornography to eroticize safe sex in the service of the reeducation of desire." Nguyen concludes, "A central component of reeducation of desire for these films' intended gay Asian male audience is with a supposedly more empowering desire for other Asian men—that is, the conversion of 'potato queens' into 'sticky rice.' To paraphrase Marlon Riggs's famous dictum concerning gay black male identity, the politics of gay Asian sticky rice desire can be summed up thus: 'Asian men loving Asian men is the revolutionary act.'"[10]

It didn't speak to only men in the queer Asian community. Diep Tran, an undergrad at the time of the Love Your Asian Body campaign, was drawn to the radical joy in these images so much that she joined APAIT staff in 1994, shortly after her college graduation. She said, "These ads were really fantastic. They were just really sex-positive and graphic ads [that said], If you're a freak, a queer, you still deserve to live. It was very strong to me."

Joy as a Communal Act of Reclamation

Asian American AIDS activists embraced a cultural organizing strategy to offer hope and possibilities to a queer Asian audience. A counternarrative to the stigma and shame in a world where the notion of "home" was rife with ambivalence, this strategy was front and center in HIV education.

APAIT's emphasis on cultural organizing as a community building strategy was not surprising, considering how many early staff were artists and writers. Joël, for instance, was a poet and a performance artist. So was Napoleon Lustre, who performed one of the most shocking monologues at an APAIT fundraiser in the late 1990s when the agency was broadening its appeal to the mainstream Hollywood crowd. Diep was a poet. Authors Noel Alumit (*Letter to Montgomery Clift*) and Ghalib Shiraz Dhalla (*Ode to Lata*) started their debut novels while working at APAIT. Karen Kimura, who managed APAIT's later social marketing campaigns after Ric, had a graduate degree in art from the State University of New York. Later she met her husband J. J. Joo at the agency; he had run a teen theater program for Asian American youths running productions on community issues like teen pregnancy, drug abuse, and HIV/AIDS.

It was no accident that the AIDS movement was an artist-driven one. AIDS decimated the arts community traumatically. Noel talked about losing a generation of gay writers who could have been a mentor to him. At the same time, these early staff at APAIT offered more than just pairs of hands when few people were interested in organizing around AIDS. They offered their creativity. As adrienne marie brown wrote, "I believe that all organizing is science fiction—that we are shaping the future we long for and have not yet experienced. . . . Our radical imagination is a tool for decolonization, for reclaiming our right to shape our lived reality."[11] The Love Your Asian Body campaign was an example of this. By visualizing the Asian-Asian intimacy, the campaign challenged a dominant narrative that fetishized our existence and offered an empowering and forward-looking alternative for a collective identity that made room for a more radical politics.

In addition to the social marketing campaigns, these artists, in the name of HIV prevention, created positive community spaces, like dances, readings, and even slumber parties where young queer Asians used storytelling to cultivate a sense of collective identity. In the late 1990s, my friends and I would use this as a template for a writers' group—calling ourselves SNAZZY—that at one time received public funding for our readings and workshops under the fiscal sponsorship of APAIT.

In the 1990s, no one was more consistent and strategic in cultivating an inclusive Asian American literary scene in Los Angeles than Irene Soriano Saxon. I first met Irene in 1993 through PEN Center USA West, indirectly. She started working at the writers' organization the week after I completed my summer internship there, but we were soon connected by Nana-Ama Danquah, another PEN staffer. In 1995, Nana-Ama, who was curating a literary series at the Los Angeles County Museum of Arts (LACMA), encouraged Irene, an aspiring poet, to carve out a similar niche for herself in the local Asian American community. Irene recalled, "She said there are so many writers out there, and the only way to make your mark, to stand apart from the crowd, is not only to submit and read [your work], but you also need to put events together, which is what she was doing at LACMA."

Nana-Ama also told Irene a principle of cultural organizing that Irene practices to this day: "You need to get writers paid. More importantly, you need to get yourself paid [for your organizing]." She helped Irene write her first grant proposal. At the time, the preeminent arts institution, the LACMA of the Asian American community, was the Japanese American National Museum (JANM). In 1995 Irene made a pitch to JANM staff about how several Asian American writers were finally knocking down the gates of mainstream publishing and how the museum could be at the forefront of this vanguard. She also was passionate about the need to nurture younger and emerging local Asian American writers like herself, who were thousands of miles away from the East Coast–based publishing industry. The pitch must have resonated with the JANM staff. Not only did they agree to give Irene's writing series—which she christened "Wrestling Tigers"—a try for a few months, but they also dedicated part of their program budget to pay for both Irene and the writers she would bring to the series. Just like that, Irene's long history of cultural organizing began.

Around the same time, Irene met Joël at his reading at UCLA. She thought his work was amazing and went up to him after the event to introduce herself as a fellow poet. Joël had a knack for "bringing people into the fold," said Irene. Later, when a treatment advocate position opened up at APAIT, Joel recruited Irene, and she ended up working at APAIT with him and other creative queer people in the agency. In 1995, when Irene was organizing her debut Wrestling Tigers event, she paired Joël up with established writer Karen Tei Yamashita.

The pairing was strategic. Irene was intent on bringing queer voices to JANM's hallowed hall and put these writers on equal footing with venerable trailblazers like Yamashita. Irene's idea was that a lot more people would come to hear Yamashita and then be introduced to Joël's work. Through his connection at APAIT, Joël brought a new audience to the JANM, a large queer crowd that made the event standing-room-only. Irene explained the event's success in this way: "We had local publications for API writers in *dIS.orient Journal*, and writers were publishing their chapbooks, but aside from that, there was no place for people to go and talk about Asian American literature. People were hungry for spaces like [Wrestling Tigers] in the community." Irene remembered that a lot of those in attendance were young college students who were so hungry for this space that they would venture off their respective campuses and pay the admission cost to JANM to be there. The success of the first reading locked in JANM as a home for the series. The museum successfully garnered a grant from the Lannan Foundation in its second year, and Wrestling Tigers would become JANM's quarterly literary event for the next four years.

Even though Wrestling Tigers was not explicitly queer, Irene had always conceived if it as a queer home. Over the course of its life—especially those early years when the series overlapped her time at APAIT—Irene featured every writer at APAIT at the time, as well as those in the broader queer Asian community, like me, whose lives the agency had touched in one way or another. "I got everybody in," she laughed—not only because of the lack of platforms for our work in those days. AIDS loomed heavily in why she felt compelled to create this space. "What brought us all together," she explained, "was the awareness that HIV/AIDS was knocking on all our doors. People like Joël and James Sakakura [another APAIT staff member, who died of AIDS in 1996] definitely read poems about HIV/AIDS. They talked about sex . . . not even sex, fucking. When James read, he was talking about open relationships."

As a treatment advocate at APAIT, Irene sometimes brought HIV-positive clients to the readings. She had fond memories of one Vietnamese client named Johnny: "Johnny was always in drag, always out with their makeup and the clothes. He might even have considered himself 'trans' [in today's environment]. Johnny commanded attention, especially before all this discourse about nonbinary identities. His presence just queered the space." (After my interview with her for this chapter, Irene wrote a poem about Johnny that ends in this image that navigates between grief and joy so emblematic of the movement: "Life for femme boys from faraway countries is hard / but all that was dim could never touch you / oh Johnny building galaxies on your face, bursting suns for eyes peeling off colors through clothes at the disco every Saturday night.")

More than just exposure for the general public, the reading series also built community for queer Asian folks. Irene reflected, "JANM's crowd was pretty conservative, and for a lot of college students that were there, this was probably the first time they were in a queer space. We couldn't pass out condoms, but there were flyers. That was one way to get it out to the community and to have people exposed to this thing that nobody wanted to talk about or didn't think mattered to them. And being in a cultural space . . . I think art just taps into people's humanity and makes them more open." Cultural organizing is more than event planning. Irene recalled people hanging out after the reading and her making introductions between new writers or between those new to the space and others who were steeped in AIDS or queer Asian community organizing. "What people don't realize is that [cultural organizers] don't disappear after an event. Everybody hung out after. It was the best part," she said. "It was like a cultural sex club! [Laughs] Because everybody was happy . . . and hungry."

Irene's cultural organizing strategy fit right into the political culture at APAIT that valued artistic expression as a basis for consciousness raising and community building. The genius of this strategy was not only in the joyful way queer writers shared their stories, but in filling a mainstream space with unapologetic queer bodies, a mainstream space that could have easily ignored the AIDS crisis. When a queer or questioning young person came into this space and saw sex-positive and gender-affirming people like Joël, James, and Johnny, they might encounter a sense of belonging and recognition that was lacking everywhere else in their lives.

The Queerness of Joy

I've conceived my oral history project on Asian American AIDS organizing in Los Angeles as a tool for intergenerational dialogue. A heteronormative society severs queer people from our past and leaves us without any tradition, isolated and ahistorical. I intend for the stories of this oral history to buttress current activists' break from a movement culture that devalues joy.

"White supremacy culture" pervades progressive movements past and current. Tema Okun and her colleagues' analysis exposes the characteristics of this culture, such as fear, perfectionism, binary thinking, progress as more, and urgency. These characteristics are often reinforced by our nonprofit-philanthropic complex that operates primarily on demonstrated harms and needs. It encourages competition and values productivity—the counting of widgets—over relationships. We miss the forest that is our social movements for the trees in our logic models. And it's reflected in how we approach our work. This is serious work. Not only is there no room for joy, but admitting the experience of joy also signals you're not working hard enough (or you don't really need that funding).

Because of Okun's work, many young activists are questioning and "divorcing" white supremacy culture, and their antidote of these bad habits is often joy. In my movement work today, young progressive activists, especially queer people of color, are telling me that joy is a key ingredient to their sustainability, to their healing. But more than a salve to stop the bleeding, joy is an effective political tactic that is especially subversive against white supremacists' hatred of the Other. Against blatant voter suppression and intimidation and in the middle of a pandemic, "Joy to the Polls" (which counted many queer people and people of color in its ranks and leadership) used music to attract so many voters of color to polling places in different states, including Georgia, where the hard-fought Democratic victories in the double run-offs in January 2021 wrested control of the U.S. Senate away from the Republican Party. That this Southern state sent not one but both Democratic senators to Washington, DC, was unprecedented. Organizers believed that the focus on joy gave people the motivation to exercise their right to vote, essentially putting their faith in a system that had disenfranchised them more often than not.[12]

In my work documenting progressive movements, I've encountered more and more examples of innovative mobilization strategies that utilize both joyful celebration and angry confrontations. Joy can catch our enemies off guard. Imagine you're in a huge argument with your partner, and in the middle of your impassioned speech, they couldn't stop smirking at you. Piss you off even more, right? It could unsettle you so much that you might even lose your game. Two days after the 2020 election, election protectors were actually dancing in the street of Philadelphia to the music of, among others, Beyoncé to make sure every vote was counted. Their noise drowned out the press conference across the street by Trump surrogates who cast aspersions on the integrity of the democratic process.[13] For an evaluation project on progressive narrative change, I interviewed Imara Jones, a Black trans activist and founder of TransLash. Imara believes that joy has to coexist with anger. "We have to be able to hold contradictions," she said. "We can't get trapped in binary thinking." In reflecting on the street protests in Philadelphia after the election, she said, "One of the most important things is how they [the protesters] just made the other side look like a fool. It was totally disarming. There is something that is actually more powerful about celebration than anger."

The more grief and trauma a movement holds—and the AIDS movement had both in spades—the more essential joy is to its organizing. Despite the mainstream media's often portrayals of trans people as tragic victims of discrimination and violence (which are real), Imara believes that joy is not a "manufactured" experience for trans communities of color, but a "reality." "We know there is intense suffering," she said, "but there's always something that is a spark within the darkness. I'm always blown away by the person who finds hope and joy. That's what infuses my work. That's the story I want to tell." In fact, joy in social protests, according to Imara, is very queer: "In queer protests you can be talking about something very heavy, very triggering, but at some point, people will start drumming or playing music, and it turns into a celebration. I think it is really powerful that people are giving you a glimpse into the world that they're actually trying to create! All of that is highly relevant in this moment; joy and celebration is required now more than ever."

Imara's words remind me of those by Audre Lorde, decades ago, about how the "erotic" is "creative energy empowered, the knowledge and use of which we are now reclaiming in our language, our history, our dancing, our loving, our work, our lives." The AIDS movement in the Asian American community illustrates the power of joy as a dynamic lens to reexamine our movement history, and it can also offer inspiration and affirmation for activists today, as we confront the racist and fascist assaults that try to chip away the gains we have made in the past decades.

Notes

1. Audre Lorde, "Uses of the Erotic: The Erotic as Power," in *Sister Outsider* (Freedom, CA: Crossing Press, 1996), 56.
2. Ibid., 54–56.
3. Saidiya Hartman, "Venus in Two Acts," *Small Axe* 12:2 (2008): 1–14.
4. While the overwhelming majority of the early documented AIDS cases were among gay white men, the trajectory of the global epidemic was decidedly different in that more transmissions occurred through unprotected heterosexual contact. Even then, many U.S. AIDS activists argued that the AIDS epidemic probably started in broader communities of color much earlier than epidemiological data suggested. Activists of color believe that the incidence rate in communities of color were obscured because of their lack of access to health care: so many were infected and died without being diagnosed.
5. Douglas Crimp, "How to Have Promiscuity in an Epidemic," *October* 43, AIDS: Cultural Analysis/Cultural Activism (Winter 1987): 266.
6. In this book, Shilts famously reinforced the "Patient Zero" myth about a gay white flight attendant named Gaëtan Dugas—a narrative device that made it seem like Dugas was recklessly transmitting HIV to thousands of men through sexual encounters. Researchers later dismissed this myth.
7. Crimp, "How to Have Promiscuity in an Epidemic," 253.
8. Cruising originated as a gay slang "code word" for those seeking casual sex through public or digital spaces.
9. ACT-UP was founded in 1987, and Queer Nation in 1990. Both activist organizations were known for their agitational and creative direct actions, their radical and decentralized democracy, and their embrace of differences and deviance, as a resistance against the gay community's move toward mainstream conformity.
10. Nguyen Tan Hoang, *A View from the Bottom: Asian American Masculinity and Sexual Representation* (Durham, NC: Duke University Press, 2014).
11. adrienne marie brown, *Pleasure Activism: The Politics of Feeling Good* (Chico, CA: AK Press, 2019).
12. Poppy Noor, "Joy to the Polls: The Group Performing for Americans as They Line Up to Vote," *The Guardian*, October 26, 2020, www.theguardian.com.
13. Amber Jamieson and Julia Reinstein, "Biden Supporters Played Beyoncé to Drown Out Trump Campaign Officials in Philly," *Buzzfeed*, November 5, 2020, www.buzzfeednews.com.

15

An Insurgent Manual on Organizing for Asian American Studies

AMBER LEE, LINDA LUU, KEVIN PARK, MIMI KHÚC,
AND LAWRENCE-MINH BÙI DAVIS

Editors' note: The academic field of Asian American studies was born in 1969, when student organizing at San Francisco State University and University of California, Berkeley led to the forming of the first Asian American studies programs. As of 2023 the Association of Asian American Studies (AAAS) lists seventy-one Asian American studies programs and centers at colleges and universities across the country. Yet the growth of Asian American studies has been uneven, and student-led campaigns continue to call on higher education institutions to commit to the field in the form of majors, minors, and tenure-track faculty lines. As this critical reflection crafted by past and present student organizers and contingent faculty in 2021 vividly shows, these campaigns must contend with the gaps between the radical commitments of organizers for Asian American studies and the field's conscription into the logics of the neoliberal university.

Welcome to our guide on organizing for Asian American studies. We come together as both current and expired student organizers and contingent faculty to document our journeys and provide insights for other Asian American studies dreamers. May this meandering road map help you navigate the many obstacles you will surely face. May it also remind you what you are fighting for. This is what they won't tell you.

The interwoven structure of voices is a form we co-created to reflect our collaborative process while preserving our distinct experiences and the lessons to be gleaned from their particularities. Consolidating the range of our experiences into one collective document results in a piece that shifts and builds upon itself, much like we have for each other and for other organizers of Asian American studies outside of these pages.

Linda Luu and Kevin Park organized at Hunter College as part of the Coalition for the Revitalization of Asian American studies at Hunter (CRAASH) from 2014 to 2017. In 2018 Amber Lee co-created an oral history project at Williams College that connected her with Kevin and Linda. Mimi Khúc and Lawrence-Minh Bùi Davis taught as adjuncts in the Asian American Studies Program at the University of Maryland in 2009–2017 and 2006–2017 respectively, working closely with students to organize for student needs. Organizing for Asian American studies across regions and histories brought this group together.

1. Be Ready to Continually Articulate, and Question, Why Asian American Studies Matters

The value of Asian American studies is not self-evident. You will find yourself explaining over and over why Asian American studies is important. Refine your talking points, then question them, then refine them again. Resist the impulse to say what you think is most palatable or logical to your audience, for example, "Our university is the top liberal arts program in the nation" or "Our student body is x percent Asian/Asian American." Don't forget that Asian American studies is part of the genealogy of critical ethnic studies; its commitments are not simply to the study of Asian Americans but to a global struggle for liberation. Think creatively about how to meet these commitments.

> KEVIN: You're an undergraduate student. You've found this lovely home called Asian American studies, filled with wonderful courses, faculty, and fellow students, passionate about Asian American identity, history, and experiences. You feel like it's the best thing you've ever found, if not the best thing in a while, a thing that has allowed you to breathe in a different way than you've been able to before.
>
>   You decide you want more Asian American studies, that everyone should take Asian American studies! But alas, there are only a few courses available and even fewer faculty to teach it. You ask yourself: why don't we have more?
>
> LINDA: During my time organizing at Hunter College, it was difficult to mobilize people to fight for Asian American studies. I often chalked this up to the fact that Hunter is a public university that serves

predominantly working-class students, the majority of whom work on top of going to school, or perhaps more accurately, school on top of going to work. I understood why people might not have time to care about an issue that does not seem to affect their immediate lives, but I also felt frustrated about a general political apathy. Why didn't people care about Asian American studies? These laments were surely fueled by the overall lack of campus activism, due to suppression by the Hunter and CUNY administrations. But I did not ask myself enough why I wanted people to care about Asian American studies. Why and how did I come to care about it? What was it that I thought Asian American studies could do for people, and why did I assume it was a given?

In making the case for why we needed Asian American studies, I had come to assume that caring about Asian American livelihoods meant caring about Asian American studies. "Hunter College is 30 percent Asian/Asian American; therefore we need Asian American studies," we argued. But what logic links these two statements? Why does the former presume the latter? It is easy to get swept up in the logics of the university, to start speaking in their tongue before you have found your own grounding. Most of us happen on Asian American studies, stumble into it through an affecting class, professor, friend, or experience. We want to preserve the spaces that transformed us and make more of them available for other people. We learn about the history of student movements for ethnic studies and want to carry on in that tradition. We want the university to make good on its promises and to change the histories that are taught and rehearsed and, in turn, the kind of education we receive. But the fight for Asian American studies is a fight for an institutional formation, and that is dangerous territory. You are now in the realm of institutional politics, money, and academia's systems of valuation. You are maneuvering in that space of constraint that shapes what you are fighting for each time you rearticulate it on their terms.

2. The Institution Has No Moral Compass/You Gotta Steal from the University

No ethnic studies program has ever come out of good will. Students may think the institution has a moral compass, but there is nothing structural that holds institutions accountable to the students or community. Do not be seduced by the institution's performance of care or its politics of respectability. Resist its siren call of conditional inclusion, its promise that if you just follow its rules you will be rewarded. That if you just better articulate your value to the university, it will believe you and give you what you deserve. Instead, recognize that the institution is a colonial resource extractor—and that the only ethical relationship is one in which we take the resources back.[1]

> AMBER: In 2018 I joined a three-decades-long organizing effort for Asian American studies at Williams College. Soon after, I began to collaborate with three other students on an independent study researching movements for Asian American studies at various universities and colleges across the United States. Over a semester, we conducted oral history interviews with seventeen students and recent alumni whom we had met through Facebook groups, mutual friends, and word of mouth. Today, a fifteen-page report, video recordings, and transcriptions of those conversations are held in the college's archives.
>
> Our conversations underscored the common logics used to delegitimize the urgency of Asian American studies organizing that we had heard time and time again from our own college administrators: there was limited funding already being directed at other "diversity-serving" programs; we already had an Asian studies department; we should just "trust the process." Under the guise of rationality and limited resources, these claims often diverted the attention of critical ethnic studies organizing away from the visions students held for their education and toward what would become the title of our study's report: "The Dangers of Bureaucratic Death." Conversely, we often heard student campaigns appealing to institutions' moral compasses and public image. Our interviewees at "peer" wealthy, private institutions, in an effort to turn the words of their school's mission statements back at those in power, commonly argued that top colleges and universities *should* model cutting-edge curriculum.
>
> Tethered as we were to the politics of bureaucracy that seemed to govern student organizing across the nation, we were acutely aware of our own project's relationship (and responsibility) to Williams College because so much of our project was resourced by the college.

Ironically, with funding from the Asian studies department, we hired four other students to transcribe our interviews. We also gained access to the college's archival procedures and presented our findings on campus and nationwide. As we authored a project that was in many ways about the allocation of funding and power, the privilege of our endeavor was not lost on us. We joked soberly that this was essentially what higher education is all about: learning how to squeeze the institution's pockets and funneling capital to the spaces of our choosing. At the same time, we asked how we could remain faithful to an ethic of stealing without forgetting the power of storytelling and the possibility of creating something meaningful.

MIMI & LAWRENCE:

From: <NewDirectorAAST@umd.edu>
To: <Contingent1AAST@umd.edu>,<Contingent2AAST@umd.edu>, . . .

Dear all,
I hope your semester is going well. I am writing to confirm that according to your current appointment agreements, your Fall semester part-time employment will end on January 7, 2018 and that your contracts will not be renewed for the Spring semester. As mentioned, when the contract was offered, updated university policy requires that I notify you of this. For reference, please refer to paragraph three of your signed appointment agreement that states *"This appointment creates no right, preference, entitlement or expectancy on behalf of the Appointee to be employed by the University for any other term or purpose."*
If you have any questions, please feel free to contact me. Many thanks for teaching and I wish you a continued successful Fall semester.

Best,
[The New Director]

This is how the adjuncts in UMD's Asian American Studies Program (AAST) were notified by the New Director in fall 2017 that we were all fired. We had no right to assume any further employment, any further inclusion in the program, any treatment as community members and stakeholders and collaborators—we were just contract-based employees who deserved only basic notification of policies. The New Director, despite being a relative stranger to the unit over the prior nine years, with minimal to no involvement in its program building, curriculum development, mentoring, work with student groups, community engagement, public programs, or fundraising, had, as tenured (i.e., permanent) faculty, the right to do whatever the fuck she wanted. No moral authority; absolute institutional authority.[2]

Here's the backstory to the email. The spring before, the New Director had already decided not to renew Mimi's annual contract, hiring someone new in her place. When we'd asked our dear friend, the Former Director, to demand Mimi's retention, she exclaimed, aghast, "I have to work with her!"—meaning the New Director. The Former Director didn't *have to* work with Mimi. Here were two Asian Americanists, naturalizing both their institutional power and our institutional disposability. The only relationships worth preserving are the ones structurally enabled. The Former Director is a tenured full professor. The New Director is a tenured associate professor. We're just adjuncts. We were already gone. We were gone before this even happened. We were never there at all.

We'd been with AAST for eleven and five years respectively, teaching and program building for it. Lawrence had taught more classes for the program than anyone in its history, under five different directors. But no one "has to" work with us. The lessons here: institutions are relationship- and trust-based up until they aren't. Institutional managers ultimately need to carry out the interests of the institution. The university's coloniality is—voice of Thanos—*inevitable*. Don't trust the institution's on-paper policies or its off-paper goodwill. Don't trust its tenured faculty, its staff, or its administrators.

That year, tenured faculty, staff, and administrators closed ranks on us, as we and students organized to ask for accountability, transparency, and community governance. It was a lesson in the inherent violence of institutions and those empowered within them, no matter how "good" those people are. A lesson that good people can do bad things; that they can start and stop being good at will. That institutions do not care, and even caring people learn to not care, because caring puts them in danger. Magistrates cannot care for the people they administer if it means undermining the systems upholding them as magistrates. That is, they can't if they are cowards.

Note: We thought carefully about whether or not to name names. Throughout any organizing work, you are continually asked to be reasonable and measured—if institutions don't invoke "civility" directly. Shame is among institutions' chief affective weaponry, their means of naturalizing certain modes of discourse and silencing dissent. Naming names is unseemly. It also potentially harms us, and our student collaborators, and the collection's editors, because of backlash. But doesn't anonymizing the account protect the perpetrator?

We think so. But we're choosing not to name names to hopefully mitigate blowback, with an understanding that our nameless accounts may bring harm to our collaborators and editors anyway. This kind of note feels necessary as part of an insurgent how-to: as an organizer, you have to continually endure institutional pressures that gaslight you into blaming yourself for triggering the damages that result from inherently violent structural dynamics, rather than the people who create, uphold, and benefit from them.

3. Study History/Build Institutional Memory/Be Part of Larger Movements

The university will wait you out. Waiting is its easiest and most effective tactic. Students graduate. Organizing work and relationships disappear, and are disappeared, all the time. Understanding movement history will help guide you and fortify you against the university's tactics of delay. Know that the fight for Asian American studies is an intergenerational struggle within larger movements. Study past movements, the histories of organizing at your school and other universities, the history of ethnic studies. Explore a variety of organizing tactics. Learn what's been done so that you don't get stuck reinventing the wheel. Feel connected to something larger than yourself. Build cross-university coalitions to grow your strength but also your institutional knowledge.

>KEVIN: At Hunter, in the absence of active student organizers, the former Asian American studies director became the bridge that connected CRAASH to invaluable institutional knowledge, which

she had gathered in the decade she had been a part of the Asian American Studies Program (AASP), as well as the network of CRAASH alumni who had laid the foundation of student organizing. We met CRAASH founder Olivia Lin, who shared an entire Google Drive of photos, letters, campaign graphics, and meeting notes from the original 2006 CRAASH campaign to revitalize the AASP. (Re)building upon that history allowed the new CRAASH generation to avoid the pitfalls the former members had experienced and mimic the strategies that led to their successes. Connecting with alumni provided a sense of clarity that kept us from feeling isolated in the midst of the uncertainty of our campaign and the hostility we faced. The alumni had our backs.

LINDA: Much has happened since the Third World Liberation Front that birthed Asian American studies, and the terrain of our struggle has vastly shifted. The university is an interlocutor with the state and capital in managing minority difference, precisely through programs and departments of race, ethnic, gender, and sexuality studies.[3] The institutionalization of ethnic studies programs marked the beginning of their detachment from radical movements on the ground and the disarticulation of minority representation from material redistribution. What should and can we demand of Asian American studies given our current landscape of liberal multiculturalism, that postwar brand of antiracism that stifles movements against settler colonial racial capitalism?[4] How does this context demand new articulations of what it is we are asking for and new tactics for organizing? Put differently, there are many ways one can teach "Introduction to Asian American studies," and I am not fighting for all of them.

AMBER: From the beginning, our independent study was an opportunistic endeavor. Our objective was to learn and build our own institutional knowledge—to gather data and then present that data to our own college—in order to strengthen our case for the development of an Asian American studies program at Williams. In the process, we could also gain academic credit.

But alliances and allyship would become central to this project. Our campus had recently designated a working group to assess the need for a potential Asian American studies program. Within this working group, student organizers had to continually justify the difference between Asian and Asian American studies—which is not only geographical but political and personal—to our peers, faculty members, and administrators. Unexpectedly, we were able to rely on the allyship of our independent study adviser, Professor Li Yu, a professor of Asian studies, because of her own personal commitments as an immigrant mother of an Asian American child.

In our interviews, we learned how student-led movements would unfold and how Asian American studies would gain recognition across campuses. Facebook groups and spiderwebs of relationships allowed us to speak with peers across both coasts, private and public universities, small and large schools, current and former students. Again and again, we heard that recognition from administration often manifested as public statements of support, perhaps the creation of an Asian American cultural center, perhaps even hiring teaching faculty for an academic program or department. These were the things we could ask for. These were the things we might be limited to.

We took our research to the Association for Asian American Studies (AAAS) conference in Madison, Wisconsin, where we connected with other student organizers across the country invested in leveraging institutional resources for the issues our institutions had chosen to neglect. I also befriended people with whom I would later organize at future AAAS conferences and even write this chapter.

4. Learn to Power-Map

People in the university are located and structurally empowered differently. This means people have different reasons for keeping things the way they are. Create a power map of your institution: learn the hierarchies, who is in charge of what, who is beholden to whom. Learn who your allies and co-conspirators are. To differing degrees, and not always, they will likely be other students, alumni, and contingent faculty. Certain academic units may also be strategic allies. Be careful of tenured faculty. Their loyalties are entangled with the university's in ways that complicate their ability (and willingness) to ally themselves with you. Learn your different targets: deans, deanlets, senior faculty, provosts, board members. Look for allies outside of your institution, too.

KEVIN: Now that you've committed to the fight for Asian American studies, how will you do it? Power mapping. Start by making a list: Who are the decision makers at your university? Who are the influencers? Who else has a stake in the fight for ethnic studies? Who do you define as an ally, and what kinds of resources do they have access to? What resources do you have access to?

Then think beyond the campus. What about community organizations that understand what's at stake if we lose ethnic studies? Which local elected officials would have an interest in Asian American studies? Think beyond your local geography and how to leverage online connections. How about other universities in other cities or states? What sorts of struggles are shared across all of these different groups?

MIMI: "I have to work with her!" my Former Director and former friend had said. She then lamented how hard this situation was for her, how she has to work with the New Director and the Dean, how she was mad at Lawrence for being angry and yelling at her, how she still had feeling in her heart for me because I hadn't yelled at her, how this situation was just so tough, so tough, for her. She was upset that we'd complained publicly that I was being pushed out. I listened to this absurd indulgence in shocked silence, my face forming a mask of polite understanding as I suddenly realized I needed to be careful here. Proceed with caution, like one does with white people up in their feelings. Handle with care; do not provoke their fragility and defensiveness; allow them to see themselves as allies; appeal to their desire to be a "good guy"; stroke their ego, make them feel safe, ask nicely, and smile, *so that they won't harm you.* There is nothing more dangerous than a white woman who feels under attack—but I began to understand that tenured faculty, even when Asian American, occupy a strangely analogous structural position. In a university, there is nothing more dangerous to folks at the bottom of the academic hierarchy—adjuncts and students—than tenured faculty who feel attacked. Tenured privilege is a helluva drug. Tenured fragility will be the death of us all.

I met with the dean of my college that summer after my contract was not renewed. I cringe now at my own naiveté: that I thought I could convince a dean of my worth, that I thought this was even the point of the meeting. He listened with polite interest, nodding, taking "notes." Near the end, when I asked directly whether he would agree to retain me in the program, he said, with the polite firmness and self-assuredness only mediocre white men in positions of power can express, "There's no programmatic need for you anymore." He, a white man who was relatively new to the deanship and barely knew anything about this ethnic studies program that students had fought for, that had blossomed despite terrible mismanagement over the years, that adjuncts had worked so damn hard for. I asked him if I would be fairly considered for an administrative position now available in the program. His answer: well, he and both the Former Director and the New Director had felt attacked. By the student organizing. By letters of support for me. By calls for transparency. Tenured fragility, so dangerous. He told me I needed to go meet with the New Director and apologize and make her feel better, since anyone who got the administrative position would be working directly with her. I should go apologize to the colleague who had now essentially fired me without any explanation other than Policies and Procedures. In the hopes it would allow me fair consideration for a job working directly under her. Tenured privilege, a grotesquery.

So I met with her. I had no intention of apologizing for anything—I hadn't done anything to her!—but I was willing to try to smooth things over for the sake of moving forward. I sat through an hour of her crying, actually crying, about how hard these last months had been for her, the hardest time she had ever experienced at UMD. A White Woman Deanlet, tasked to observe and "mediate"—that is, cover the university's ass—listened and murmured empathetic noises, validating her. My mask slid into place again. There was no goodwill here, only a pair of fragile administrators totally unwilling to resist the siren call of institutional power. Like white tears, tenured tears filled the room, ate the air, left no space for anything that might be called justice or collaboration or restoration or even just plain old communication. So I swallowed my pride again. I simply told her I recognize it'd been hard for her, I would like to move past this, would like to remain part of the program, will work with her in good faith for the benefit of the program. I let her cry some more.

Two months later she sent that email to all the adjuncts. I guess I didn't let her cry enough.

5. Build Relationships and Pipelines

Without relationships, there is no movement. Connect with others with the same commitments, the same longings. Figure out what meaningful relationships look like for you, and map out how to do meaningful work in these relationships. Build trust. Explore what co-governance looks and feels like. Do the hard work of accountability. Think intergenerationally: make the organizing space one that new and older folks will want to join. Build in structures to pass on institutional knowledge. Make friends. Invest in each other's humanity; invest in your own. Take, and give, care.

> KEVIN: What does it mean to build relationships by way of the fight for ethnic studies? Think about the different kinds of relationships that are possible between faculty, students, alumni. What about incoming freshmen and prospective students? How can they be plugged in earlier so that they don't end up with the same story of stumbling upon Asian American studies in the second semester of junior year? What about relationships after you graduate? What kinds of relationships last beyond the boundaries of an institution or the time frame of a degree?
>
> During the years I was active with CRAASH, informal networks and relationships were at the core of what sustained our organizing. After witnessing the Coalition for Critical Asian American Studies (CCAAS) at the University of California, San Diego (UCSD) put forth a list of demands to the UCSD administration in response to the hate crimes that took place on campus in 2014, we reached out to CCAAS through student organizers I had met at the Asian Americans Advancing Justice Conference in 2013.[5] The overlap between the Asian American organizer and Asian American studies community was and is unsurprisingly huge. Through this introduction, CRAASH and CCAAS members were able to connect and share knowledge on our respective struggles and campaigns. We would end up collaborating on what would become an annual series of undergraduate panels on Asian American studies organizing at the Association for Asian American Studies (AAAS) conference, starting in 2015.

At the first AAAS roundtable, which included organizers from UCSD, Oberlin College, DePauw University, and Northwestern University, we discussed what organizing looked like for our respective campuses and how to build a wider network that cut across campuses. This was the first time these students, let alone these campuses, were able to convene, strategize, vent, imagine, and come up with actionable ways to support each other's campaigns. In the subsequent 2016–2019 conferences, even more campuses, ranging in size, region, racial demographics, and public versus private, would participate in these roundtables, including University of Massachusetts Lowell, Cornell University, Dartmouth College, and Williams College. These roundtables served as a critical space for building relationships and sharing knowledge, as well as a springboard for joint actions for campaigns—collaborative virtual political education events, Facebook groups and group chats, the founding of the Undergraduate Section at AAAS, knowledge and resource sharing, and meaningful friendships.[6]

One of the student leaders at Northwestern behind the successful campaign for an Asian American studies major later told me that the AAAS roundtable that he participated in had inspired him to start that campaign. The fact that a singular moment like the roundtable had even a fraction to do with their win for an AAS major only underscores the importance of building these spaces that allow for students to connect with each other. Where there is connection and community, there is endless possibility.

AAAS was also where I first met my contingent faculty coauthors. From the beginning, Mimi and Lawrence would make sure to attend as many of the undergraduate sessions as possible, recruit other faculty to come to the student sessions, affirm student voices during and after the sessions, introduce students to key figures at AAAS, hold other faculty accountable to follow through on supporting students, and funnel material resources to students (e.g., secure funding for travel and channel institutional support and resources for student campaigns). We didn't have to go the extra mile to make them understand our struggles and what we were doing; they just got it.

In work that often can feel isolating for students, witnessing the unwavering solidarity of contingent faculty like Mimi and Lawrence helped me understand how showing up builds trust and sustains movements. Whether with students at their former university or at AAAS, as faculty they never backed down from putting student voices and needs first. It is through these acts of care that I intimately understood how relationships between contingent faculty and students embody what solidarity could (should) look like. What does it mean to show up for each other? At the end of the day, students, faculty, administrations, and institutions come and go, but what sustains a movement and the people in it?

AMBER: Using this independent study as an excuse to find more friends and role models felt like a special gift. That year, my peers became my teachers. Helen from Duke University, for example, taught me that the motives for ethnic studies constantly oscillate between the personal and the political and that university organizing needs to be in conversation with labor rights and prison abolition. Jeremiah from Cornell University challenged me to think about the meaning of Asian American studies beyond the localized issues at any one school to the broader meaning of an Asian American studies orientation for the realm of liberation. I am grateful to have connected with the kind and curious Professor Yu, who despite our disciplinary differences encouraged us to think critically about strategy and personal stakes in the movement. It was a wonder to center these relationships in an academic context (for credit!)—relationships that hold the same aliveness today, years after former student organizers have left their respective institutions.

LAWRENCE: Somewhere in the middle of my and Mimi's saga of contingent ruin (a redundant expression, apologies!), I started to figure out that not trusting an institution has everything to do with relationship building.

I mean, adjuncts everywhere work closely with students and student groups. But that's not the same thing as divesting trust from departmental agendas ("Up class enrollments!"), professionalizing agendas ("Don't focus on teaching or mentoring; focus on your own writing!"), university-wide agendas ("Diverse Tech, Inclusive Futures!"), and even field-wide agendas ("Global Borderlands + Trans/National Imaginaries!").

For me and Mimi, reorienting trust from institutions to students has meant changing how we teach, fumbling toward what have come to look like standard disability justice teaching practices during the COVID-19 pandemic: greater flexibility on attendance and sick leave policies. Considering student capacity, factoring basic things like housing, access to Wi-Fi, and health, especially mental health. Considering mental health in terms of the campus's racist (and queer and transphobic, classist, misogynist, and ableist) climate. Shifting assignments in relation to student need, from tests and papers to projects and discussions—often ones that have less to do with course readings, and more with on-the-ground urgencies. Deemphasizing grading. Giving over space to care and reciprocity. Building shared understandings of differential but interlinked struggles.

Dear student, you want a university that values the safety of queer and trans people of color. I want that too; that's why I'm at this student-run workshop. Meanwhile, I want to not be so fungible, a less polite word for contingent that actually more accurately expresses what it means. Meaning I might not be able to be here for your workshop next semester. I'm late to class today because I have kids but no childcare. You're late because you're depressed (because of course you are, you're an Asian American student). I'll show up to your post-Ferguson student demands session to help you strategize because I believe in the need for those demands, and want you to know I believe in them, and you. I thank you for seeing that I'm deeply exploited by the university, and therefore exhausted and soulsick. You're allowed to want your grade changed, but argh. I'll be honest with you about why I need to cancel class today. I don't expect you to be honest with me about missing class all last week—not until you decide I've earned the trust to make it safe for you to share.

(This was Mimi's breakthrough, realizing student "excuses"/"lies" are actually faculty failures to ensure safety.)

Stealing from the university isn't just sticky tabs from storage. It's stealing loyalties—back. I tell myself, stop thinking I need to [grade/research/poop] this way because my dean, my chair, my colleagues, my field say so. I have to remember that our existing systems are a colonial architecture predicated upon the exploitation and erasure of BIPOC students, staff, faculty, and local community. I need to remember what la paperson points out, that within every colonizing university are "decolonizing dreamers who are subversively part of the machinery and part machines themselves. These subversive beings wreck, scavenge, retool, and reassemble the colonizing university into decolonizing contraptions. They are scyborgs with a decolonizing desire. You might choose to be one of them."[7]

I choose to be. I learn how to learn from other "scyborgs," mostly students. I learn how to say what matters to me, and care what matters to others. I see fulfilling those needs as important, and tied up together. Be generous. Show up. This is relationship work. I'm not a lone cat burglar—I'm stealing from the university in a team.

Mimi and I have collaborated with our coauthor Kevin since at least 2016. I'm remembering a panel we co-organized on student organizing fifty years after the TWLF strikes [the 1968 Third World Liberation Front student protests], with undergrad organizers from five different campuses, for an AAAS conference—part of Kevin's extensive work advocating for undergrad inclusion in AAAS, and bringing some flicker of awareness across the field to the state of ongoing student organizing nationally. There, and for every other project, Kevin has wanted to find consensus, even when it was uncomfortable or ultimately the opposite of what he himself first proposed. So now we trust implicitly that he will not go forward in a way that serves him but not others. We trust his heart because he fought for our dear friend Jen Hayashida, former director of Asian American studies at Hunter, even when fighting for her put him in harm's way. He knows people matter. We want to honor his commitments, and return them, even when it puts us in harm's way. That's a relationship.

6. Beware Burnout/Beware Guilt

Burnout is real and must be planned for. This work comes with losses and grief. Figure out the care you need individually and collectively to carry you through the work. And remember that the actions of the institution and its shortcomings are never your fault as an individual. You are doing *extra work* for an institution that is failing you. It is not your burden to bear when it fucks you over (cuz it was always gonna). Know that there are affective structures generated by the institution and by organizing culture that will compel you to do more, give more, and push past your limits. Everything will tell you that you're not doing enough. You're doing more than enough. You're probably doing too much.

> KEVIN: Sometimes campaigns work![8] Sometimes they don't. Sometimes a lot of things are under your control or influence. Sometimes they're not. This was something I wish I had learned from the beginning, when it felt like we, as the students, had to figure out how to fix everything.
>
> Someone needs to organize a campaign for an Asian American studies department? Sure, we'll do it! Someone needs to speak out against the administration for their lack of investment in the program? We'll do it! Someone needs to organize the other Asian American student groups? You got it! The list goes on.
>
> Understandably, many student organizers end up burning out from this work. The amount of emotional labor and cost from both the wins and the losses make it incredibly difficult not to burn out. It didn't help that I thought that our status as students made us more protected from the wrath of the administration, since we were not employees of the institutions, so I felt like we could handle whatever came our way.
>
> That proved to be false when we witnessed ten years of dedication to the Asian American Studies Program (AASP) at Hunter College end at the whim of one person. After CRAASH presented our demands for an Asian American studies department in front of students, administration, and staff (with a slide that read, "Why Haven't We Seen More Support from the Hunter Administration?"), the administration informed the AASP director of ten years that week that they were not renewing her contract for the subsequent year.[9] She was essentially fired. All of the countless hours of labor and love put into building a program from nothing into one that offered the highest number of Asian American studies courses in New York City—now erased.
>
> It was hard to walk back into the empty AASP office and see her empty chair. It felt like we had lost, that we had failed her and the

program, even if the overall campaign was still far from finished. It was hard to feel like things mattered again after that.

In these moments, I wish I had reminded myself that *organizing is not a personality or a whole identity*. It was too easy for organizing to start consuming my life. The amount of hours spent trying to keep our campaign and programming afloat and the extra time spent strategizing against the administration's counterinsurgency tactics felt all-consuming. And yet, the guilt and the feeling that we had to win because of the losses we had endured during this process made the burnout feel "necessary." After all, the organizers at Northwestern University were able to secure a major, and the students and faculty at the College of William and Mary were able to establish a new program, so we should be able to win our campaigns! If we didn't, then we must have done something wrong. And when things did go wrong, like when we lost the AASP director or when I lost my job, it felt like we *had* to win. Otherwise, it was all for naught. And when things continued to fall apart, other thoughts kept swirling in my head: was this our fault for asking too much? Was this because we didn't do this right or failed to be smart or strategic enough? What was ever going to be enough?

LAWRENCE: Rather than offer my own reflections on burnout, I want to devote space here to an additional voice, a current student organizer from Davidson College I've had the privilege of working with recently who, on top of their organizing, has been doing theoretical and reflective work on activist burnout. Sanzari Aranyak's work builds out our manual through a much-needed disability studies and disability justice framework:

"While I was trying to figure out what my place as an Indian American, queer/trans student organizer was in the middle of the mass uprising of 2020, I started making graphics to help fundraise for Black, trans, houseless women I knew through friends and organizers in Charlotte, North Carolina. Eventually this work became the Davidson Community Fund, which was labor that my friends and I did on top of organizing for Asian American studies through the Asian American Initiative I co-founded at Davidson College. Burning out seemed like the inevitable end point of this work. The reality was that I had been burnt out for several years.

Burnout isn't some dystopic state of being, it's an embodied experience that I, and everyone I know, is dealing with *all the time*.

Centering disability justice frameworks in how we talk about burnout is really the only way to do the work of dreaming revolution. These frameworks insist "that we organize from our sick, disabled, 'brokenbeautiful' bodies' wisdom, need, and desire."[10] This looks like missing deadlines, grappling with panic attacks at inconvenient times, and sometimes having three half-hour meetings on Zoom instead of one long meeting because people just can't sit for that long. This means that in order to get anything done, we are going to have to embrace the slow, and the dirty, and the working from bed.[11] If we understand that existence in a body is and always will be fragile and vulnerable, then prioritizing care for each other in real and concrete ways is the most basic form of resistance. Our work will become even messier, our timelines slower, but we will enact this decolonial politics of care to build a world in which liberation is not dependent on our capacity for work."[12]

7. Be Careful What You Ask For/The Container Is Not the Dream

Just because an Asian American studies program exists doesn't mean it's the one we want or need. Just because you fight for and get a tenure line doesn't mean that tenure line will be filled by someone who will fight for you. Don't get attached to particular shapes for building Asian American studies at your institution. Departments are just containers for the relationships we want to build and the communal governance of education we deserve. Continually find better containers. What students build can have a life beyond that of the bodies that fill seats or faculty offices. Dreams are bigger than the institutional things we create to house them.

> LINDA: What does it mean to organize for Asian American studies? And might that not (only) look like organizing for a department? What does it mean to *do* Asian American studies, to enact its politics and ethics, which would actually orient us away from institutionality and toward each other?[13] I think there are steps in between getting activated around Asian American studies and becoming invested in a campaign to establish a department, and thinking

through those steps might lead us elsewhere. Departmental status and institutionalization may very well be the only path toward stability and a future for what might otherwise remain a set of precarious relationships and shitty working conditions that hold on year after year until an opportune moment arises for the administration to excise them. Securing a hire or hires may be the minimal first step toward doing the kind of relationship building we have written about here. And these are real and urgent concerns to be weighed and pursued. Certainly they were for us. But I also imagine all the things that could have happened in the space of fighting the administration with that one end in sight. I believe there is no demand that is too "pie in the sky," but I also do not think academic departments are or should be the horizon of possibilities.

In an effort to appease and stifle us, in September 2016, six months after the launch of our campaign for an Asian American studies department alongside other demands, the president of Hunter College, Jennifer Raab, announced that an Asian American studies Center would be built. This news was sprung on us before our presentation to the governing body of the college, as a way of undermining our claims about the school's lack of institutional support for Asian American studies. The announcement was meant to be proof of their support and dedication to Asian American studies in contrast to the reality we were painting that they had structurally abandoned the existing Asian American studies Program. Looking back, this moment marked the beginning of what I understand to be a counterinsurgency strategy aimed at weeding out student dissent.

The details surrounding the creation of this new center are important. The existing AASP would be moved out of the School of Arts and Sciences and into the Office of the Provost, and a new "Asian American studies Center" would be created. This decision was made without any notice or consultation with current AASP faculty or students. It was not clear who would be involved or charged with heading this new center along with the responsibilities of the academic program. Furthermore, two days following this announcement, the director of the AASP received a notice of non-reappointment without any explanation—one day after securing a $1.7 million Department of Education grant for high-need Asian

Pacific American students. At a later "Asian American studies breakfast" hosted by the president—to which no current AASP faculty, students, or the director were invited—the center was discussed as a public-facing research hub, which would highlight and connect faculty at Hunter who do Asian American studies, understood to be anything vaguely "Asian," from nutrition in Asian/American communities, to Asian/American theater, to Asian languages. Furthermore, the only two programs at the time housed in the Provost's Office offered certificate degrees geared toward professionalization—and programs in the Provost's Office have no recourse to faculty governance laws and are therefore more susceptible to the whims of administrative decision making.

The president had once told us explicitly she did not know what Asian American studies was. Yet she was empowered to make decisions like this one. While we might understand Asian American studies to be a political project, we must also recognize what it represents to administrators and presidents of colleges and its status in the neoliberal university today. Two faculty members who had been at the breakfast meeting shared with us President Raab's plans for the center: "The administration has no idea what they're doing. They know they want to do something with Asian Americans. They recognize they're in a good position as a school with 30–40 percent Asian students to do something. They want to do something to advance the name of the school/prestige. It sounds like they just want to hire a prestigious person to run the center and have them figure it out." There it was, the numbers we had cited and brought to the table. Effectively, we had made a pitch to Raab (who had climbed the ladder in New York City politics before being appointed Hunter's president by Mayor Rudolph Giuliani), and she merely did her job of identifying a new area of investment.

Ultimately, CRAASH fought successfully for the AASP to remain in the School of Arts and Sciences by calling attention to the fact that the move would violate CUNY bylaws and that the administration was engaging in unilateral decision making, with total disregard for the academic integrity of Asian American studies. But this "win" was coupled with the firing of our director. A new director was eventually hired—one who was willing to play the games of the institution.

This was made clear to me when she colluded with the administration in the surveillance and attempted censorship of an archiving project I had undertaken to preserve the history of the program. Many of us who were active in those years graduated, and those of us who did not voluntarily leave on our own were fired and kicked out. Sometimes, it feels as though the administration won, that they got what they wanted and weeded us out. But I know people are always whispering, plotting, and scheming. That is the nature of insurgency. People—maybe you—will pick up where we left off.

I tell this story because programs, centers, and departments are just containers for the relationships we want to build. One day, they are staffed by people you love deeply, who are your lifeline and intellectual community, and the next, by model minority prestige-chasing researchers trying to distance themselves from any semblance of student activism, proclaiming to do the very same thing: Asian American studies.

KEVIN: After the devastating removal of our former Asian American studies Program director, the Hunter College administration began the search to find a new director. This time, this role would be filled by a tenure-track faculty for Asian American studies. Finally! One of our demands had been met! But at what cost?

We had been demanding tenure-track faculty positions for years, but it felt so bittersweet that it came at the cost of the former director, who had been the pillar of the program for a decade. The job candidates could never fill her shoes, and yet, we had to make sure that the role was filled anyway. The structural stability we had fought for for years *needed to* amount to something. And it did amount to something: a tenure-track professor who did not end up being the advocate we wanted and did not share the radical vision for Asian American studies that CRAASH stood for; a tenure-track professor who instead ignored the reasons that CRAASH had laid out in protest of the new "Asian American Center" in the first place and accepted the new role as its director. Thank goodness we asked for that tenure-track line!

MIMI & LAWRENCE: The moment an Asian American studies program tells students that they need to follow the rules, that its authority supersedes theirs, that they shouldn't ask for more transparency, that they need to stop saying what they need—that they should put their heads down and do their work and be grateful for what they have—it is telling them to be model minorities, and it is officially part of the problem.

To our loving, generous, full-hearted students at UMD, we are writing you from the underworld of institutional exile. Thank you for fighting for us for as long and as much as you could. You were fighting for yourselves too, and for a program that you felt was yours. But that program failed you. You did not fail it, nor did you fail us. You fought for us because we fought for you, and that is the true spirit and hallmark of an Asian American studies program, whether or not we succeeded in making any structural change. That is the thing institutional containers cannot hold.

All of you have graduated by now; there are whole crops of minors now who never knew us, never even heard of us (and the program has done a very thorough job of scrubbing our existences from its spaces and memories). The program may no longer feel like it's ours or yours—but it is both. You are the heart of AAST. Administrators come and go. And students come and go, which is what administrators bank on. But what students build can have a life beyond that of the bodies that fill seats or faculty offices. Dreams are bigger than the institutional things we create to house them. They can adapt and morph and grow. They can be renewed.

AMBER: In some ways, our oral history project attempted to document what this chapter is about: histories and troubles of Asian American studies activism. We hoped that by exposing the ways in which student activism was typically ignited, sustained, and even contested, we would fortify our own movement in the eyes of Williams's administration. Certainly, the project facilitated our relationships with faculty allies and student groups from other schools. Ironically, in pursuit of tips and tricks that we assumed would help us finally gain recognition from the college, I found thinking partners with whom I could imagine a more radical version of Asian American studies beyond the parameters of what an institutionalized department or program could offer us. While initially our independent study group held some bitterness (and suspicion) toward the students at Cornell or large schools on the West Coast that could "afford" to be rejecting a formalized structure around Asian American studies because those structures had already been established for years, these are concerns that I think all students in the fight for ethnic studies should be considering. I can't speak to the difference it would have made to have program-specific directors and professors hired to support our education, but I do know the autonomy and mobility we held precisely because our research was responsible primarily to ourselves and those who come after us.

At Williams, we also inspired students to build upon our project. The following semester, two other students pursued a "part two" of the study, turning inward to interview student activists from Williams. Now, even older alumni come to us requesting to read our reports and asking us how the Asian American alumni network can mobilize its power as donors and Williams degree-carriers in support of ongoing Asian American studies organizing. Perhaps others in the years to come, no matter the "status" of Asian American studies at Williams, might return to our report, share our curiosities, and even challenge our conclusions. Perhaps from there, they will be able to dream bigger.

This Manual Will Self-Destruct

If this is a manual, it falls apart. We cannot give universal instructions because the conditions within which each of us struggle—region, institutional size, public/private designation, demographic makeup, historical relationship to ethnic studies—differ so drastically, and often shift over time. Any principles we outline must be adapted to the contexts of particular institutions, and entire worlds exist in the adaptation labors. Why are the stories we tell mainly stories of failure? Because for Asian American studies there is mainly failure, or fleeting possibility. If a manual is supposed to help build something, this is a manual for juggling and dropping the pieces of containers that will always be falling apart. We are unconvinced Asian American studies can exist in stable forms inside the institution, not in the forms we dream and need, with community governance, accountability, radical mutability, and insistence upon shared liberation. These approaches and values are antithetical to the university as it exists today; the university must destroy them, or sanitize them to the point of meaninglessness. This is true too of Asian American studies as an association and Asian American studies as a field, larger pan-institutional containers that are always under siege (including from inside the house!) and that can only hold Asian American studies provisionally. Maybe the only way Asian American studies can exist anywhere is provisionally.

Embrace failure as the starting point of insurgency. We are reminded by the process of thinking and writing together here that Asian American studies can exist most fully, most lastingly, as it began: in protest, across organizing bodies, across relationships and coalitional networks. First and foremost, in the imaginations of those demanding our education be commensurate with, and answerable to, community needs: student organizers. May we remain lifelong students and organizers.

Notes

1 As famously articulated in Fred Moten and Stefano Harney, *The Undercommons: Fugitive Planning & Black Study* (New York: Autonomedia, 2013).
2 A quick primer on tenure: a limited number of faculty are hired into tenure-track lines, meaning full-time employment positions that begin on a seven-year probationary period in which new professors work to prove they deserve to be granted permanent employment, usually through meeting threshold amounts of published scholarship. Once they earn tenure, faculty are essentially unfireable. The majority of university courses, however, are taught not by tenured faculty but by adjuncts—faculty hired on contingent semesterly or annual contracts, who are often hired and fired at will, *by tenured faculty* who are in charge of running departments. Adjuncts teach the classes and support the students; tenured faculty teach but also do their own research and administer their departments, and the wider university—and get paid up to fifty times more than their adjunct counterparts. Adjuncts form an underclass labor force whose exploitation tenured faculty depend upon for their own job security.
3 Roderick A. Ferguson, *The Reorder of Things: The University and Its Pedagogies of Minority Difference* (Minneapolis: University of Minnesota Press, 2012).
4 Jodi Melamed, *Represent and Destroy: Rationalizing Violence in the New Racial Capitalism* (Minneapolis: University of Minnesota Press, 2011).
5 "Open Letter," February 26, 2014, https://apimeda.ucsd.edu.
6 "Where Are We Now in the #Fight4AAS?," May 9, 2016, https://www.youtube.com.
7 la paperson, *A Third University Is Possible* (Minneapolis: University of Minnesota Press, 2017), xiii.
8 Fathma Rahman, "Major Approved: Asian-American Studies Major Approved after Faculty Passes Proposal," *Daily Northwestern*, February 25, 2016, https://issuu.com.

9 We had five demands: the implementation of an Asian American Studies Department and major; the creation of hiring lines for five full-time Asian American studies faculty; increased funding for the newly created Asian American Studies Department; disaggregation of data on Asian/Asian American students to properly assess needs; and the creation of financial scholarships for Asian/Asian American students in critical needs, especially undocumented, low-income, and LGBTQIA students.
10 Leah Lakshmi Piepzna-Samarasinha, "Preface: Writing (with) a Movement from Bed," in *Care Work* (Vancouver: Arsenal Pulp Press, 2018), 12.
11 L. H. Stallings, *A Dirty South Manifesto: Sexual Resistance and Imagination in the New South* (Oakland: University of California Press, 2020).
12 Johanna Hevda, "Sick Woman Theory," *Mask Magazine*, January 19, 2016, www.maskmagazine.com.
13 Jennifer Hayashida, "Removal, Refusal, Rehearsal: 15 Fridays," *Women & Performance*, September 4, 2020, www.womenandperformance.org.

ACKNOWLEDGMENTS

This book is dedicated to our students, past and future. For everything they have taught us about the world we live in. For asking necessary questions of liberation that have been grounded in courageous hope, radical imagination, and dreams of a better world. And to our teachers (who are so often also students) who have reached us in classrooms, in movements, and in archives to open our minds to the histories and practices of resistance that inform this book.

We are eternally grateful to the activists, organizations, and movements that have inspired and informed this work, and for the relationships that give this book meaning and keep us rooted in the communities we write in solidarity alongside. In particular, we want to thank our friends at 18 Million Rising—Taz Ahmed, Pakou Her, Cayden Mak, and Oanh-Nhi Nguyen—for providing a digital container in which to meet and plant the first seeds of this project.

We are so lucky to have worked with Sonia Tsuroka as our editor at NYU Press. It was a gift to collaborate with an editor who always understood and affirmed the significance of this work, who supported our early visions for this project and trusted us to push the boundaries of what an academic text can do.

We are thankful for interdisciplinary convenings like the 2022 Association of Asian American studies Conference in Long Beach, California, which brought some of us together in person for the first time. We are grateful for those who participated in our roundtable—Loan Thi Dao, Diane Fujino, Rachel Kuo, Amber Lee, Candace Fujikane, Vichet Chhuon, and Ched Nin—for joining us in conversation and karaoke.

Most of all, we want to thank the many contributing authors who have given their time and their brilliance to this book. Our contributors have generously and patiently walked with us through the process of co-creating this book while balancing the demands of leading national and local organizations, rapid-response campaigns, and navigating academic precarity—all during a period of compounding crises. We always envisioned this book as an exercise in decentering the university as a site of knowledge production about social movements—a task that has required sustained collaboration across structural positions in and beyond our academic institutions. We are deeply grateful to the many contributors embedded in movements who have trusted us in that vision and offered grace as we navigated the particularities of these kinds of collaborations.

Last, we would like to thank our friends, families, furry companions, and partners who have offered us support, encouragement, respite, and welcome distractions in the work that we do. Our deepest hope is that this book can be a small but useful offering to the movements that have incubated and inspired our work.

ABOUT THE CONTRIBUTORS

Minju Bae is a historian of Asian America and assistant professor at the Gallatin School of Individualized Study at New York University. Her current research investigates how Asian/Americans navigated the politics of work, racial difference, and the radical restructuring of the urban-based global economy in the late twentieth century. Alongside Vivian Truong, she has been working to preserve, digitize, and engage the archives of CAAAV Organizing Asian Communities (formerly the Committee Against Anti-Asian Violence).

Salonee Bhaman is a scholar of history, gender, sexuality, and race. She is a co-leader of the Asian American Feminist Collective. Her forthcoming book project explores the social and economic history of the first decades of the HIV/AIDS epidemic in New York City by centering the experiences of women, people of color, and care workers. She is currently the Mellon Foundation Postdoctoral Fellow in Women's and Public History at the New-York Historical Society.

Ja Bulsombut is a former program coordinator at the W.O.W. Project and is currently a PhD student in the Sociology Department at the University of California, Santa Cruz. Her research interests are in Asian/American conservatisms and the racial politics of grievance.

Kristin Chang is a former program manager at the W.O.W. Project and currently lives in California, where she works as a freelance writer. She is a Kundiman Fellow and a Lambda Literary Award finalist for her gay and angsty little chapbook, *Past lives, future bodies*. She is the author of the *New York Times* Editors' Choice novel *Bestiary*, which was longlisted for the Center for Fiction First Novel Prize and the PEN/Faulkner Award. Her short story collection, *Resident Aliens*, is forthcoming from One World.

SALLY CHEN is an organizer and advocate based in San Francisco who is dedicated to building the capacity of working-class communities of color to feel safety, joy, and a sense of autonomy in their own neighborhoods. She is currently the education equity policy manager at Chinese for Affirmative Action, where she advocates for universal, no-cost, and racially diverse K-16 education for all students. As a first-generation college graduate from a working-class immigrant family, she is a proud alumna of Harvard College, where she organized for racial justice issues, including ethnic studies and race-conscious admissions. In 2018 she was one of the eight students and alumni who testified in favor of affirmative action in the Supreme Court case *Students for Fair Admissions v. Harvard*. Her testimony, writing, and analysis on the importance of affirmative action are featured in the *Los Angeles Times*, *Bustle Magazine*, and *CalMatters*.

VICHET CHHUON is associate professor of education and Asian American studies at the University of Minnesota. His work has appeared in leading publications including *American Educational Research Journal*, *The Urban Review*, and *Youth & Society*. His writings have also appeared in the *Star Tribune*, *MinnPost*, and *Angry Asian Man*. In 2015 he received the Presidential Research Award from the National Association for Multicultural Education.

KIM COMPOC is assistant professor of history at University of Hawai'i at West Oahu. She was born in California to a Kahuku-born father and an Alabama-born mother who met in the Marshall Islands via the U.S. military. Before entering graduate school at UH Mānoa, Kim spent fifteen years outside academia as a health educator, theater artist, and mediator in San Francisco and Maui. Her research focuses on U.S. empire in the Philippines and Hawai'i, Asian American studies, and diasporic Filipinx studies with an emphasis on Indigenous, feminist, and queer critique. In her activism, teaching, and scholarship, she is interested in how the story of empire becomes more evident through continued engagement with each other's stories of resistance.

LOAN THI DAO is professor and director of ethnic studies at St. Mary's College of California. She specializes in Southeast Asian refugee migration and community development, immigrant and refugee youth, social movements, and community-based participatory research (CBPR). Dao has published on topics related to memory and war in cultural productions, Vietnamese American female leadership, undocumented AAPI activists, transnational activism, oral history, and Southeast Asian American deportation. She is author of *Generation Rising: A New Politics of Southeast Asian American Activism*. She teaches interdisciplinary ethnic studies courses, and her service has included leadership positions in student groups, film productions, diversity and inclusion initiatives and training, immigrant rights and policy advocacy, and on boards of Southeast Asian American community organizations.

LAWRENCE-MINH BÙI DAVIS is a mixed Viet diasporic editor, writer, and troublemaker. He passes by day as a mild-mannered curator for the Smithsonian Asian Pacific American Center, based on the ancestral lands of the Piscataway Nation, sometimes also known as Washington, DC. He has supported student organizing for Asian American studies as an adjunct at the University of Maryland from 2005 to 2017. By night and on alternating weekends, he is active with (and a co-founder of) the pop-up Center for Refugee Poetics and a contributing janitor for the arts antiprofit *Asian American Literary Review*. Sometimes you can see new things by the light of his ADD.

CANDACE FUJIKANE was born in Honolulu and grew up in Pukalani, Maui, on the slopes of Haleakalā. She has stood for lands and waters in Hawai'i for the past twenty years. An English professor at the University of Hawai'i, she teaches classes on the stand that aloha 'āina are taking to protect lands, waters, and skies in Hawai'i. She is author of *Mapping Abundance for a Planetary Future: Kanaka Maoli and Critical Settler Cartographies in Hawai'i* and coeditor of *Asian Settler Colonialism: From Local Governance to the Habits of Everyday Life in Hawai'i*.

DIANE C. FUJINO is a professor (and former chair) of Asian American studies at the University of California, Santa Barbara and immediate past coeditor in chief of the *Journal of Asian American studies*. Her writings on Asian American activism include *Heartbeat of Struggle: The Revolutionary Life of Yuri Kochiyama*; *Contemporary Asian American*

Activism: Building Movements for Liberation; *Nisei Radicals: The Feminist Poetics and Transformative Ministry of Mitsuye Yamada and Michael Yasutake*; *Samurai among Panthers: Richard Aoki on Race, Resistance, and a Paradoxical Life*; *Wicked Theory, Naked Practice: A Fred Ho Reader*; and a special issue of *Amerasia Journal* on Asian American activism studies. Her commentary and research have been featured in media outlets, including the *New York Times*, NBC, CBS, NPR, *Democracy Now!*, *Rafu Shimpo*, and *Discover Nikkei*. She is co-PI on the Organizing Knowledge Project, a member of Ethnic Studies Now! Santa Barbara, and a contributor to an Asian American studies high school textbook project.

FRANCES HUYNH is a writer who covers topics on community health, Asian American studies, storytelling, foodways, and Los Angeles Chinatown.

MIMI KHÚC supported student organizing for Asian American studies as an adjunct at the University of Maryland from 2013 to 2017. She is a writer, scholar, and teacher of things unwell, and the creator of mental health projects Open in Emergency and the Asian American Tarot. Her book *dear elia: Letters from the Asian American Abyss* is a deep dive into the depths of Asian American unwellness at the intersections of ableism, model minoritization, and the university, and an exploration of new approaches to building collective care. She is a Scorpio through and through.

JULIE AE KIM is a writer and organizer from Queens, New York. She is a co-founder of the Asian American Feminist Collective. Currently, she is an MFA candidate in creative nonfiction at the Ohio State University, where she serves as the Associate Creative Nonfiction editor of *The Journal*. She has received support from Kundiman and the Mendocino Coast Writer's Conference. Previously she has worked in New York City local politics.

RACHEL KUO is assistant professor at the University of Wisconsin-Madison, where she studies race, social movements, media, and technology. She is a co-founder of the Asian American Feminist Collective and founding affiliate of the Center for Critical Race and Digital Studies.

AMBER LEE is an aspiring arts disorganizer currently based on the ancestral lands of the Ohlone people, also known as Berkeley, California. Previously, she organized with the Asian American studies Movement as an undergraduate student at Williams College, where she began mapping out archives of Asian American feelings through oral history, food, and media.

DOUGLAS H. LEE has been working in higher education and social justice issues for the Asian American community over the past fifteen years in a variety of roles. His career is centered on understanding and meeting the needs of communities, especially to underserved Asian American groups. Previously, he was the assistant director of the Asian American Center at Northeastern University and first associate director of student leadership and programming at the University of Utah Asia Campus.

JACQUELINE LEUNG is the executive director of the nonprofit Micronesian Islander Community (MIC) and is an assistant professor at Linfield University. Her background is in public health advocacy, policy, and research. She works in perinatal health care, Medicaid, early childhood education, health care access, chronic diseases, COVID-19 wrap-around services, and leadership pathways for community health workers. She also serves in several leadership positions, including co-chairing the Commission on Asian and Pacific Islander Affairs, and is a traditional health worker representative on the Oregon Maternal Mortality & Morbidity Committee. She enjoys spending time with her family and long scenic drives along the coast and through the agricultural landscapes that make Oregon the beauty it is today.

SHAUN X. LIN is pursuing a PhD in geography at the CUNY Graduate Center, where his research interests include immigrant communities, food and foodways, and abolition geography. He is an adjunct lecturer in Urban Studies at Queens College. Originally from Los Angeles, he is a longtime resident of Sunset Park, Brooklyn, where he organizes against gentrification, displacement, policing, and prisons with Sunset Park for a Liberated Future, Sunset Park Popular Assembly, and No New Jails NYC.

LINDA LUU is a graduate of Hunter College, where they organized with the Coalition for the Revitalization of Asian American studies at Hunter.

They are currently a PhD candidate in American Studies at NYU, studying war, race, and the psyche in the context of the Vietnam War.

REKHA MALHOTRA (also known as DJ Rekha) has developed an artistic oeuvre anchored in their practice as a deejay and cultural instigator. Their work is centered in providing spaces for people craving environments to move freely to familiar and energizing sounds sans xenophobic gaze. They founded the iconic Basement Bhangra (1997–2017), one of New York City's longest-running night clubs anchored in resilience and resistance. Their dynamic deejay sets incorporate South Asian diasporic dance music rooted in dub and hip-hop with ears to a global sound that builds inclusive environments of joy. Their commissioned work has appeared in radio with NPR, *Drama Desk,* and Obie-nominated theater productions, film, TV in *Taste the Nation*, and remixes. As a curator, their work includes presenting at Celebrate Brooklyn, Summer Stage in Central Park, Flushing Meadow Corona Park, Lincoln Center, and others. They live in Jackson Heights, Queens, and will gladly give the willing a food tour of their neighborhood.

YVES TONG NGUYEN is a Vietnamese queer disabled abolitionist organizer and cultural worker currently organizing with Red Canary Song and Survived & Punished NY, and formerly with Free Them All 4 Public Health and others. They are personally concerned with supporting survivors of all forms of violence through organizing and informal community support. They have experience supporting sex workers, migrant workers, and survivors of gender-based violence, particularly criminalized survivors of abuse.

CHED NIN was born in the jungles of Prachinburi, Thailand, before arriving at the Khao-I-Dang refugee camp. He came to the United States at the age of six as a refugee with his family after escaping the Khmer Rouge genocide. He gained visibility as a part of the #ReleaseMN8 campaign, responding to the detention of eight Cambodian Minnesotans by Immigration, Customs and Enforcement (ICE) in 2016. After over six months in ICE custody, he won his immigration case and returned home to his family. He now advocates for Southeast Asian families and individuals experiencing criminalization and deportation. When he is not volunteering and advocating, he is a commercial carpenter for the local 322 carpenters union in Saint Paul, Minnesota. He enjoys fishing and spending time with his family, including his wife, Jenny Srey, and six children.

Born and raised in New York City, KEVIN PARK was an undergraduate student at Hunter College majoring in Asian American studies and Critical Ethnic Studies through the CUNY BA Program. As a member of the Coalition for the Revitalization of Asian American studies at Hunter (CRAASH), he campaigned for an Asian American studies department and helped start the Undergraduate Section at the annual Association for Asian American studies conference, connecting undergraduates who are organizing for Asian American studies across the United States.

OIYAN A. POON is a longtime researcher and leader for intersectional racial equity in education. She is the author of *Asian American Is Not a Color: Conversations on Race, Affirmative Action, and Family*, which explores how Asian Americans are shaping the future of race relations through debates over education policies like affirmative action, using personal narrative and interviews of Asian Americans across the country. In *Rethinking College Admissions: Research-Based Practice and Policy*, she and her co-editor, Mike Bastedo, and colleagues examine and offer new ideas to transform the unequal structures and systemic norms of college-going in the United States. An award-winning scholar, her commentary and research have been featured in media outlets such as the *New York Times*, *The New Yorker*, *The Atlantic*, the *Washington Post*, and NPR.

VIVIAN SHAW is the Mellon Assistant Professor in Asian American studies at Vanderbilt University, where she was the inaugural hire for the Asian American & Asian Diaspora Studies program. She earned her PhD in sociology from the University of Texas at Austin with graduate portfolios in Asian American studies and Women's and Gender Studies. She previously held appointments at Harvard University, first as a postdoctoral fellow at the Weatherhead Center for International Relations and later as a college fellow in the Department of Sociology. In collaboration with Harvard Sociology, she is the lead researcher and co-PI of the AAPI COVID-19 Project, a multi-method investigation into the impacts of the pandemic on the lives of Asian American, Native

Hawaiian, and Pacific Islander communities. Her research has received grants and awards from the National Science Foundation, the Social Science Research Council, and the Natural Hazards Center.

SENTI SOJWAL is an India-born, New York City–bred writer, digital strategist, and reproductive justice advocate based in Brooklyn. She is communications director at Planned Parenthood of Greater New York and co-founder of the Asian American Feminist Collective. Her writing on reproductive health and feminist issues has been featured in the *Huffington Post, Rewire, Mic,* and elsewhere. She currently serves as co-editor of the Black/Asian Feminist Solidarities project at the Asian American Writers' Workshop. She holds a BA from Hampshire College in Gender Studies and Politics and an MPH from NYU.

JENNY SREY faced the harsh realities of the U.S. immigration system when Immigration Customs and Enforcement (ICE) detained her husband in August 2016. This experience propelled her into direct action and started #ReleaseMN8, a grassroots campaign she and affected family members formed in response to the abrupt separation of eight Cambodian Minnesotans from their families. Having successfully reunited with her husband, she remains deeply affected by the ongoing separation of families. Committed to dismantling harmful systems, she co-founded ReleaseMN8, an organization and ever-growing movement that serves the crucial purpose of safeguarding the community from detrimental deportation policies. She attended the University of Minnesota, is a Humphrey Policy Fellow, and loves spending quality time with her family.

LAKSHMI SRIDARAN was co-director of South Asian Americans Leading Together (SAALT), a national South Asian movement strategy and advocacy organization that experimented with a shared leadership model and anti-caste political education after operating as a traditional nonprofit since 2004. Her social justice approach is grounded in her experiences organizing in the South. Before moving to Washington, DC, she lived in New Orleans, where she worked in Black-led organizations immediately following Hurricane Katrina. She worked on improving federal contracting opportunities for Black- and women-owned businesses; instituting participatory budgeting to expose inequitable distribution of federal recovery dollars; and preserving public schools and infrastructure from rapid privatization. In her early organizing days, she supported labor organizing campaigns for campus workers and land retention efforts for Black farmers in her home state of Georgia.

JULIE SZE is professor of American Studies and the founding director of the Environmental Justice Project at UC Davis. She has authored three books: *Noxious New York: The Racial Politics of Urban Health and Environmental Justice*, *Fantasy Islands: Chinese Dreams and Ecological Fears in an Age of Climate Crisis*, and most recently in 2020, *Environmental Justice in a Moment of Danger*. She edited *Sustainability: Approaches to Environmental Justice and Social Power* (2018) and has written over sixty-five articles and book chapters. She actively works in interdisciplinary collaborations and with community-based organizers in California and New York.

VIVIAN TRUONG is assistant professor of history at Swarthmore College. She is a community-engaged scholar whose research and teaching focuses on Asian American, urban, and social movement history. Her current work examines Asian American and multiracial movements against police violence in late twentieth century New York City. As a public historian, she co-coordinates a project engaging the archives of the grassroots organization CAAAV Organizing Asian Communities (formerly the Committee Against Anti-Asian Violence), where she formerly worked as a youth organizer and currently serves as co-chair of the board of directors.

TIFFANY DIANE TSO is a writer/editor, producer, and cultural organizer based in New York City. Her work focuses on Asian American issues and identity, Black and Asian solidarities, labor, advocacy, and art, and has been published in *HuffPost*, *Allure*, *Refinery29*, *Rewire News Group*, and elsewhere.

ERIC C. WAT is author of *Love Your Asian Body: AIDS Activism in Los Angeles*, which won the book award in Outstanding Achievement in History from the Association of Asian American studies. His *Los Angeles Times*-best-selling novel, *SWIM*, is about a gay Asian man dealing with drug addiction and caregiving for his immigrant family. His early social justice work in the 1990s centered on AIDS activism and immigrant workers' rights, which continue to inform both his creative writing and community work. He lives and writes in Los Angeles.

JANELLE WONG is the former and current director of the Asian American studies program (AAST) at the University of Maryland, College Park. The AAST program marked significant growth after 2017 and now enrolls eighty to one hundred minors each year. She is also a professor of American Studies and government and politics. She is coauthor of three amicus briefs submitted in the *SFFA v. Harvard* case and three other legal briefs submitted in educational equity and voting rights cases. She has authored or coauthored four books and numerous articles on Asian American politics and other topics. A senior researcher at AAPI Data, she works regularly with APIAVote, Asian Americans Advancing Justice, Hamkae Center, AALEAD, Montgomery County Black and Brown Coalition for Educational Equity, and Montgomery County NAACP Parent Council. Her writing has appeared in a range of nonacademic outlets, including the *Los Angeles Times* and *Washington Post*.

ABOUT THE EDITORS

Diane Wong is an artist and educator from Queens, New York City. She is assistant professor of political science at Rutgers University, Newark, where she teaches Asian American politics, colonial racial capitalism, urban social movements, and abolition feminisms.

Mark Tseng-Putterman is a writer, educator, and historian based in New York City. His work focuses on the intersections of empire, Asian American community politics, and grassroots diplomacy during the Cold War.

INDEX

AAPI COVID-19 Project, 243
abolition, 3, 4, 16, 22, 32n11, 76, 78, 107–108, 153–154, 158, 169–170, 194, 268; "anti-Asian hate" and, 166–169; caste and, 64; co-optation of, 163–166; militarism and, 136–138, 139, 143–145, 147, 149–150; settler colonialism and, 112–116; sex workers and, 161–163
Abrons Art Center, 256
ACT-UP, 327, 330
Advocate Visitors for Immigrants in Detention (AVID), 74, 76
affirmative action: Asian American support for, 210–211, 220–225; Chinese American opposition to, 208–209, 212–216; student testimony and, 216–219. *See also* Students for Fair Admissions
Ahuja, Neel, 245, 246, 247
AIDS crisis, 30, 299; Asian American activism during, 322–338; cultural organizing in, 331–335; education, 327–331; sexuality during, 326–328, 330, 331
aloha 'āina, 113, 120–126, 128
Alumit, Noel, 332
Amazon, plans for a second headquarters in Queens, NY, 1, 3, 314–316
anti-Asian violence, 10, 11, 20, 21, 63–69, 73, 107, 112, 153, 160, 167, 187, 202, 236, 238
Anzaldúa, Gloria, 248
Arbery, Ahmaud, 7
Archives: AIDS activism and, 322–323, 324; climate crisis and, 301–303, 318; community-based, 302–306, 308–16;
feminist, 178, 180, 184, 185, 193; universities and, 303, 342, 343
Arrests: Mauna Kea and, 113, 116, 122, 124, 127, 129, 130; Wilcox insurrection and, 113, 123, 128
Asian American AIDS activism in Los Angeles, 322, 324, 326
Asian American Coalition for Education (AACE), 212–216, 220
Asian American Feminist Collective (AAFC), 175–194
Asian American Legal Foundation (AALF), 212, 214
Asian American movement, 2, 4–6, 10–12, 42; characteristics of, 12–27; legacy of, 28–31; role of archives in, 304, 306–308, 318–319; women in, 13–19
Asian American Political Alliance (AAPA), 14, 17, 18, 33n13, 307
Asian Americans Advancing Justice, 44, 216, 220, 224, 350
Asian Americans for Action (AAA), 14, 18, 30, 307
Asian American studies, 2–3, 6, 11, 30, 41, 90, 218; institutionalization of, 299, 339–363; Native Hawaiian and Pacific Islander erasure within, 234, 237, 240
Asian Americans United (AAU), 46
Asian American Women's Association (AAWA), 217
Asian American Writers' Workshop, 185
Asian Immigrant Women Advocates (AIWA), 19, 26, 33n21
Asian Law Caucus, 26

379

Asian Pacific AIDS Intervention Team (APAIT), 322, 323, 327, 328, 329, 331–335
Asian Pacific Environmental Network (APEN), 23, 30, 35n35, 235
Asian Pacific Islander Coalition for Action and Diversity (APICAD), 264, 265
Asian Pacific Islander Legal Outreach, 26
Asian/Pacific Lesbians and Gays (A/PLG), 327
#Asians4BlackLives, 7, 22, 34n31
Asian Youth in Action, 313, 314
Association of Asian American Studies (AAAS), 347, 350, 351, 352, 354
Astoria, Queens, 2, 301
Atlanta spa shootings, 8, 10, 11, 15, 21, 160, 166, 192, 243

Bandung conference, 14, 20
Barraquiel Tan, Joël, 328, 329, 330, 332, 333, 334, 335
Basement Bhangra, 196–294
Bhattacharya, Joy, 200
Biden, Joseph, 67, 107
Black Panther Party (BPP), 14, 18, 21, 23
Black Women Radicals, 185, 188, 189
Blossom Plaza Apartments, 279, 291
Blum, Ed, 212, 220, 224
Board of Land and Natural Resources (BLNR), 109, 118
Borough-Based Jail Plan (BBJP), 7, 155–159, 163–164, 168–170
Bowman, Isa Ua Ceallaigh, 237
Bridge magazine, 6
Bronx, New York, 156, 157, 237, 310
Browder, Kalief, 153–155, 163, 165

CAAAV Organizing Asian Communities, 1, 22, 30, 46, 178, 299; founding of, 307–308; organizational archives of, 302–306, 308–319
Call Her Ganda, 144
Cambodian Americans: detention of, 39–41, 44–46, 87–91; migration and resettlement of, 84–86, 237; repatriation, 86; youth, 49, 85, 86, 95. *See also* Khmer Americans, deportation of
caste, 64, 68–72, 76–81, 82n19
Caswell, Michelle, 305, 306
Center for Autonomous Social Action (CASA), 18
Chan, Angela, 264
Chen, Bonnie, 264
Chen, Sally, 205, 219, 225
Chhaya CDC, 1
Chin, Vincent, 308
Chinatown, Los Angeles, 232, 272; Business Improvement District, 277–278, 279; commercial development, 278–281; gardening and, 281–295; Union Station and destruction of, 273, 275
Chinatown, Manhattan: environmental justice and, 266–268, 270; jail construction in, 156, 167, 168–169, 257; natural disasters in, 301–303, 318; tenant organizing in, 301, 314–315; women's leadership in, 256–257, 261, 281; youths, 232, 255, 258, 270
Chinatown, San Francisco, 21, 30
Chinatown Art Brigade, 156, 257, 314
Chinatown Business Improvement District, 277, 278
Chinatown Community for Equitable Development (CCED), 280, 281, 294
Chinatown Youth Council (CYC), 284
Chinese Americans: conservatism of, 2–3, 22, 208–209; exclusion of, 37, 186, 274–275; housing discrimination towards, 274–275; opposition to affirmative action, 212–216; support for affirmative action, 220–221, 223
Chinese Exclusion Act, 37, 186, 274
Chiu, Phyllis, 284
Chun, Danny, 7
climate change, 231, 234, 236, 302, 318; colonialism and, 245–246, 268;

Indigenous politics and, 112, 113, 116, 127; Pacific Islanders and, 245–247
Clinton, Bill, 45, 328
Coalition for Critical Asian American Studies (CCAAS), 350
Coalition for the Revitalization of Asian American Studies at Hunter (CRAASH), 340, 345, 346, 350, 355, 359, 360, 372
Combahee River Collective, 177, 179, 183
Community Transformational Organizing Strategy (CTOS), 19
Compact of Free Association (COFA) citizens, 239, 240, 241, 242, 244
counterterrorism, 65–67
COVID-19 pandemic, 7, 8, 147, 175, 190, 240; anti-Asian violence during, 10, 11, 21, 107, 112, 153, 160, 167, 187, 236, 238; disproportionate impact of, 24, 67, 231, 233, 237, 243–245, 250; environmental justice perspectives on, 234–235, 270; mutual aid during, 159, 162, 169, 193; teaching practices during, 353
Crimp, Douglas, 326
CUNY, 164, 178, 341, 359, 360

Dalits, 64, 68, 77, 79
Danquah, Nana-Ama, 333
data disaggregation, 220, 248–249, 250, 364n9
Decolonial Pin@ys, 139, 145
Defend Boyle Heights, 280
Delano grape strike, 22
Densho Digital Repository, 305
Department of Homeland Security (DHS), 44, 66, 73, 83, 87, 94, 102. *See also* Immigration and Customs Enforcement
Deportation: campaigns against, 43–46, 52–53, 83–104; of Khmer Americans, 37, 39, 83–104; of Laotian Americans, 44
Desis Rising Up and Moving (DRUM), 1, 48, 65, 72, 156

Detained Migrant Solidarity Committee (DMSC), 74, 76
Diaz, Vicente, 239
Diep, Thang, 217
Domestic Workers United, 308
Dotbusters, 202
Duterte, Rodrigo, 141, 144

East Wind (Los Angeles organization), 17
East Wind magazine, 6
Echo-Hawk, Abigail, 248
18 Million Rising (18MR), 7, 22, 98
Enomoto, Joy Lehuanani, 131, 132
environmental justice, 30, 231, 233–236, 243, 266; gentrification and, 255, 270; jail construction and, 157; militarism and, 237
ethnic studies, 120, 218, 219, 241, 339, 340, 342, 346, 348, 349, 350, 252

Fantanos, Naomi, 140–141
feminism, 16–19; media-making, 177–189; militarism and, 139, 142; Third World movement and, 22, 29, 307. *See also* Asian American Feminist Collective
Filipinos, 1, 17, 22; AIDS activism, 328; militarism, 137, 140, 141, 144, 145, 149; nursing, 237, 250
Flinn, Andrew, 305
Floyd, George, 7, 29, 77
Freedom, Inc., 22
Fujiyoshi, Ron, 111, 113, 128

Garner, Eric, 312
Gentrification: and archives, 302–304, 306, 308, 310, 314–318; and the Asian American Movement, 28, 30; in Los Angeles Chinatown, 273–281, 282–284; in Manhattan Chinatown, 257, 265–268; real estate speculation, 273, 278, 283; rent gap and, 283
Gidra magazine, 6, 14, 23, 319n5
Giuliani, Rudy, 312, 359

GoFundMe, 92
Goodyear-Kaʻōpua, Noelani, 124
Gran Fury, 330
Grassroots Asians Rising (GAR), 27, 35n40
Guaåhan (Guam), 15, 142, 143, 237, 244
Gurley, Akai, 7, 22, 215, 312

Hartman, Saidiya, 324
Harvard Ethnic Studies Coalition (HESC), 218
Harvard University, affirmative action and, 205, 207, 208, 209, 212, 216–219, 221
hate crimes legislation, 4, 63, 66, 107, 166, 171n1
hate violence, 63–69, 73, 310
Hawaiʻi for Black Lives, 132
Hawaiʻi Peace and Justice, 145
Hawaiʻi Supreme Court, 109, 118, 119, 120, 134
Henderson, Ash-Lee, 233
Highlander Research and Education Center, 233
Hindman, Tamae, 143
Hindu nationalism, 68, 69, 70, 74
Hmong, 85
homophobia, 183, 309. *See also* queer politics
Huang, Qing Lan, 312
Huang, Yong Xin, 312
HULI, 109
human rights, refugees and, 41, 43, 48–53, 57–60
Hunter College, 340, 341, 345, 346, 354, 355, 358, 359, 360
Hurricane Katrina, 24, 47, 237
Hurricane Sandy, 301–302

Ichioka, Yuji, 307
Ige, David, 109
Iijima, Chris, 173
Iijima, Kazu, 16, 307
Illegal Immigration Reform and Immigrant Responsibility Act of 1996, 45, 50, 86
Immigration and Customs Enforcement (ICE), 44, 72–76, 83, 87–94, 99, 102

Immigration and Nationality Act of 1965, 70–72, 274
Incarcerated Workers Organizing Committee (IWOC), 156
Inouye, Daniel, 121
International Hotel, 28
International Women's Network Against Militarism (IWNAM), 142, 143, 146
Islamophobia, 65–66, 67, 68, 69, 197
I Wor Kuen, 14, 15, 17, 18

Japanese American National Museum (JANM), 333, 334, 335
Jones, Imara, 337
Junoon, 200
Just Leadership USA (JLUSA), 163

Kaba, Mariame, 139
Kalama, Camille, 110
Kānaka Maoli, 109–113, 118, 120–126, 128, 130–133
Katipunan ng mga Demokratikong Pilipino (KDP), 17, 18, 29
Kekoʻolani, Terry, 139
Khmer Americans: deportation of, 37, 39, 83–104; transnational organizing of, 40, 47, 53–56. *See also* 1Love Cambodia
Khmer Rouge government, 84–85, 95, 99, 187
Kim, Gwen, 110–113, 120, 134
Kimura, Karen, 332
King, Rodney, 313, 328
King, Tiffany Lethabo, 113
Kitchen Table Press, 183
Klobuchar, Amy, 91, 94
Koa Futures, 145
Kramer, Larry, 326
Kundiman, 191

LANDBACK movement, 113, 120, 130
Laotian Americans: deportation of, 44; environmental racism and, 24, 236, 243; resettlement and, 45, 235
Laotian Organizing Project (LOP), 24, 235

Laude, Jennifer, 107, 137, 139, 140, 141, 144, 146
Lavender Godzilla magazine, 330, 331
Lee, Pam Tau, 243
Liang, Peter, 7, 22, 168, 215, 311–313
Lim, Genny, 182
Lim, Yee, 292
Lin Olivia, 346
Liu, Mini, 302, 307, 308, 316, 318
Lorde, Audre, 323, 337
Los Angeles County Museum of Arts (LACMA), 333
Los Angeles Rent Stabilization Ordinance, 281
Los Angeles Tenants Union, 280
Lum, Gary, 258
Lum, Mei, 256, 258
Lustre, Napoleon, 332

Make the Road New York, 163
Mao Zedong, influence of, 13, 15, 18, 21, 23
Marshallese, 239, 241, 242, 250
Marshall Islands, 138, 241, 242, 244
Marxism-Leninism-Maoism, 13, 15, 18
Mauna Kea, 30, 109–119, 121, 127–133, 148–149
McIntyre, "Gino" D'Angelo, 112
Mekong NYC, 48, 308
Micronesian Islander Community (MIC), 239–240, 242, 243, 245
Mijente, 94
militarism, 21, 52, 130, 142, 151; Asian American movement and, 11, 12, 14, 15; in Hawaiʻi, 121, 136, 138–139, 146
Minnesota Immigration Rights Action Committee (MIRAC), 94
Modi, Narendra, 68, 73
Moskowitz, Peter, 275
Movement for Black Lives, 29, 97, 100, 113, 120, 147, 149, 150, 247, 312; in Hawaiʻi, 131–132; Movement Generation, 247
Muslim Ban, 67, 69

NAACP, 216, 224
National Asian Pacific American Women's Forum (NAPAWF), 178, 180
National Lawyers Guild, 100
National Network for Immigrant and Refugee Rights (NNIRR), 48
National Security Entry Exit Registration System (NSEERS), 65–66
Native Americans, 136, 233; affirmative action and, 220; Asian American movement and, 22; ethnic studies, 218; Los Angeles and, 273, 295n3
Navigate MN, 83, 94
NDN Collective, 113, 130
Neighbors United Below Canal, 156
New York Civil Liberties Union (NYCLU), 163
New York Taxi Workers Alliance (NYTWA), 24, 202, 308
Nieto, Alex, 7
Nikkei for Civil Rights and Redress, 26
9/11, 46, 51, 63, 65, 79, 196
No New Jails, 154, 156–159, 163, 169–170; protests and, 257, 258, 268

Obama, Barack, 37, 40, 66, 143
Okinawa, 15, 21, 141–143, 146
Okinawa Women Act against Military Violence, 21, 142
Okun, Tema, 336
Omar, Ilhan, 98
1Love Cambodia, 46–48, 53–55
ONE National Gay & Lesbian Archives, 322, 324
Organization of Asian Women (OAW), 307

Pacific Islanders, 233; Asian American solidarity with, 234, 237, 239; data disaggregation, 248–249; migration of, 241–243
Palestine, 8, 112, 145
Pang, Baak, 290
Parish, Ric, 328, 329, 332

384 | INDEX

Parveen, Abidha, 200
Patel, Sureshbhai, 63
Perez, Andre, 109, 122, 130, 132
Philippines, 138, 140, 144, 145
Philips, Juliet, 256
police violence, 3, 7, 22, 27, 29, 112, 146, 147, 148, 165, 173, 177, 219, 241, 308, 311; against Asian Americans, 49, 63–64, 159, 162, 312; support for victims of, 3, 312–313, 314
political prisoners, 16, 32n11, 66; in Hawai'i, 120–128
Price, Sheka Torrey, 112, 130, 131
prison industrial complex, 65, 98, 136, 138, 147, 153, 160, 162, 165, 168, 170
Progressive Asian Network for Action in Los Angeles, 26
Protect Mauna Kea, 109, 111, 114, 122, 127
Punjabi Americans: detention of, 72–74; early migration of, 70; music and, 198–199
Pu'uhuluhulu, 110, 113, 132, 133

Queen Lili'uokalani, 113, 121, 123, 142
Queens, New York, 1, 2, 156, 159, 160, 171n8, 187, 198, 301, 304, 314, 315
Queens Neighborhoods United, 1
queer politics, 27, 29–30, 180, 182, 202; AIDS crisis and, 326–331; cultural organizing and, 331–335; and mutual aid, 162; joy and, 335–338; state violence and, 136, 141
Q-Wave, 256

Reagan, Ronald, 299, 325
Red Canary Song (RCS), 154, 159–163, 169–170
Red Guard Party, 14, 18, 20, 21, 30
Refugees: anti-deportation organizing and, 43–46, 52–53, 83–104; climate and, 245–247; human rights and, 41, 43, 48–53, 57–60; transnational organizing of, 40, 47, 53–56; United Nations commission on, 48, 51

ReleaseMN8 campaign, 38, 83–104
Resistencia, 74, 76
Resist Recycle Regenerate (RRR), 255; fellows, 256, 260
Returnee Assistance Program (RAP), 39, 40
Returnee Integration Support Centre (RISC), 40
#Right2Return campaign, 37, 41, 43, 46–59. *See also* Southeast Asian Freedom Network (SEAFN)
Rikers Island, campaign to close, 154–159, 163, 164, 169, 321n27
Rim of the Pacific exercises (RIMPAC), 145, 149

Sagoo, Bally, 199, 202
Sakakura, James, 334
Sakhi for South Asian Women, 202
Sand Island, 124, 141
Sarah Lawrence College, 264
Saran, Kaushal, 202
Say Her Name, 146
SCA-5, 208, 215
Schlund-Vials, Cathy, 236
SEARAC, 44, 46, 91, 98, 100
Sentenced Home, 91
settler colonialism, 30, 120, 124–127, 136, 180, 273
sexual violence: policing and, 159, 161–162; militarism and, 137, 140, 142, 143, 146
Shimabukuro, Rina, 107, 137, 139, 141–142, 145
Shomof, Izek, 278
Sikh Americans, 66–67, 70, 77, 197
Singh, Malkit, 198, 199
Sodhi, Balbir, 197
Solano Canyon Community Garden, 291, 292
Solidarity "AAPI" umbrella and, 238–241, 250; : abolition and, 170; affirmative action and, 205, 209, 211, 216–219; cross-racial, 19–23, 27, 136, 313; feminist, 180, 182, 188, 189–190; with Kānaka

Maoli, 125, 131, 132, 139; transnational, 13–15, 42, 47, 142, 145–148
Sonoda Pale, Healani, 125, 126
Soriano, Irene Saxon, 333, 334
Sounds of Brazil (SOB's), 196, 197, 201, 202, 204
South Asian American Digital Archive (SAADA), 305
South Asian Americans Leading Together (SAALT), 63–80
South Asian popular culture, 197–199, 201, 202, 204
Southeast Asian Freedom Network (SEAFN), 27, 37, 40–50; #RightToReturn campaign of, 46–59
Standing Rock Indian Reservation, 110, 133n9
Status of Forces Agreements (SOFA), 137, 143, 148
Stonewall Rebellion, 325
Stop Asian Hate, 8, 120, 153, 154, 167–168
Stringer, Scott, 163
Student Non-Violent Coordinating Committee (SNCC), 16
Students for a Democratic Society, 16
Students for Fair Admissions (SFFA), 205, 207, 209, 212, 216, 220, 221, 224
Suarez, Virginia, 144
Sunset Park for a Liberated Future (SPLF), 156
Survived and Punished (S&P), 156
Swift, Jaimee, 188

Táíwò, Olúfemi, 245, 246
Tajima-Peña, Renee, 205
Take Back the Bronx, 156
Tam Gong Gong, 281–284, 287, 288, 293
Tang, Eric, 237
Task Force for Asian American Progressive Advocacy and Studies (TAPAS), 219

Taylor, Breonna, 7
Temporary Protected Status (TPS), 72, 221
tenants unions, 280, 314, 315
Third Worldism, 4, 12, 14, 19, 20, 43, 307; and feminism, 22, 29, 307
Third World Liberation Front, 21, 42, 327, 346, 354
Third World Women's Alliance, 179
Thirty Meter Telescope (TMT), 109, 114, 115, 117–119, 120, 134
Tourmaline, 189
Tran, Diep, 331, 332
transformative justice, 104, 137, 145
Trask, Haunani-Kay, 30, 113, 124, 139
Trice, Madison, 217
Trump, Donald, 7, 337; anti-Asian racism and, 236; Asian American support for, 214; election of, 57, 80, 178; feminist organizing under, 176, 179; immigration policy under, 40, 44, 70, 74, 75; Muslim ban under, 67, 69
Tsui, Kitty, 182

Unbound Feet Collective, 30, 182
undocumented youth, 37, 70, 72
Urban Indian Health Institute, 248
Urban Justice Center, 163

Vaid-Menon, Alok, 182
Veterans for Peace, 145
Vietnamese: community post-Katrina, 47; youth in Oakland, 39
Vietnamese American Youth of Louisiana (VAYLA), 46
Vietnam War, opposition to, 12, 14, 15, 42; refugees from, 40, 43, 49
VOCAL New York, 163

Walters, Karina, 241
Welfare Reform Act of 1996, 45
White, Monica, 285
White House Initiative for Asian Americans and Pacific Islanders, 98

Williams College, 340, 342
Wilson, Pete, 328
Wing On Wo, 258, 270
Women's Voices, Women Speak (WVWS), 139, 142, 145
Wong, Nellie, 182
Woods, Mario, 7
W.O.W. Project, 255–271
Wurdeman, Richard Naiwieha, 109

Yaar, 202
Yamada, Mitsuye, 182
Yamashita, Karen Tei, 24, 333, 334
Yang Song, 153, 159–160, 163, 164, 165
Yellow Pearl, 173
Yellow Seeds newsletter, 6
Yin, Monona, 307, 308, 309
Young, Kalaniopua, 136
Yu, George, 279
Yu Sook, 292

www.ingramcontent.com/pod-product-compliance
Lightning Source LLC
Chambersburg PA
CBHW020349080526
44584CB00014B/955